THIRD EDITION

Mining the Social Web

Matthew A. Russell and Mikhail Klassen

Beijing · Boston · Farnham · Sebastopol · Tokyo

Mining the Social Web

by Matthew A. Russell and Mikhail Klassen

Copyright © 2019 Matthew Russell, Mikhail Klassen. All rights reserved.

Printed in Canada.

Published by O'Reilly Media, Inc., 1005 Gravenstein Highway North, Sebastopol, CA 95472.

O'Reilly books may be purchased for educational, business, or sales promotional use. Online editions are also available for most titles (*http://oreilly.com/safari*). For more information, contact our corporate/institutional sales department: 800-998-9938 or *corporate@oreilly.com*.

Acquistions Editor: Mary Treseler
Development Editor: Alicia Young
Production Editor: Nan Barber
Copyeditor: Rachel Head
Proofreader: Kim Cofer

Indexer: WordCo Indexing Services, Inc.
Interior Designer: David Futato
Cover Designer: Karen Montgomery
Illustrator: Rebecca Demarest

December 2018:   Third Edition

Revision History for the Third Edition
2018-11-29:   First Release

See *http://oreilly.com/catalog/errata.csp?isbn=9781491985045* for release details.

The O'Reilly logo is a registered trademark of O'Reilly Media, Inc. *Mining the Social Web*, the cover image, and related trade dress are trademarks of O'Reilly Media, Inc.

The views expressed in this work are those of the authors, and do not represent the publisher's views. While the publisher and the authors have used good faith efforts to ensure that the information and instructions contained in this work are accurate, the publisher and the authors disclaim all responsibility for errors or omissions, including without limitation responsibility for damages resulting from the use of or reliance on this work. Use of the information and instructions contained in this work is at your own risk. If any code samples or other technology this work contains or describes is subject to open source licenses or the intellectual property rights of others, it is your responsibility to ensure that your use thereof complies with such licenses and/or rights.

978-1-491-98504-5

[MBP]

If the ax is dull and its edge unsharpened, more strength is needed, but skill will bring success.

    —Ecclesiastes 10:10

Table of Contents

Part III. Appendixes

Preface

The Web is more a social creation than a technical one.

I designed it for a social effect—to help people work together—and not as a technical toy. The ultimate goal of the Web is to support and improve our weblike existence in the world. We clump into families, associations, and companies. We develop trust across the miles and distrust around the corner.

> —Tim Berners-Lee, *Weaving the Web* (Harper)

A Note from Matthew Russell

It's been more than five years since I put the final finishing touches on the manuscript for *Mining the Social Web*, 2nd Edition, and a lot has changed since then. I have lived and learned a lot of new things, technology has continued to evolve at a blistering pace, and the social web itself has matured to such an extent that governments are now formulating legal policy around how data can be collected, shared, and used.

Knowing that my own schedule could not possibly allow for the immense commitment needed to produce a new edition to freshen up and expand on the content, but believing wholeheartedly that there has never been a better moment for the message this book delivers, I knew that it was time to find a coauthor to help deliver it to the next wave of entrepreneurs, technologists, and hackers who are curious about mining the social web. It took well over a year for me to find a coauthor who shared the same passion for the subject and possessed the skill and determination that's required to write a book.

I can't even begin to tell you how grateful I am for Mikhail Klassen and his incredible contributions in keeping this labor of love alive for many more years to come. In the pages ahead, you'll see that he's done a tremendous job of modernizing the code, improving the accessibility of its runtime environment, and expanding the content with a substantial new chapter—all in addition to editing and freshening up the overall manuscript itself and enthusiastically carrying the mantle forward for the next wave of entrepreneurs, technologists, and hackers who are curious about mining the social web.

README.1st

This book has been carefully designed to provide an incredible learning experience for a particular target audience, and in order to avoid any unnecessary confusion about its scope or purpose by way of disgruntled emails, bad book reviews, or other misunderstandings that can come up, the remainder of this preface tries to help you determine whether you are part of that target audience. As busy professionals, we consider our time our most valuable asset, and we want you to know right from the beginning that we believe that the same is true of you. Although we often fail, we really do try to honor our neighbors above ourselves as we walk out this life, and this preface is our attempt to honor you, the reader, by making it clear whether or not this book can meet your expectations.

Managing Your Expectations

Some of the most basic assumptions this book makes about you as a reader are that you want to learn how to mine data from popular social web properties, avoid technology hassles when running sample code, and have *lots* of fun along the way. Although you could read this book solely for the purpose of learning what is possible, you should know up front that it has been written in such a way that you really could follow along with the many exercises and become a data miner once you've completed the few simple steps to set up a development environment. If you've done some programming before, you should find that it's relatively painless to get up and running with the code examples. Even if you've never programmed before, if you consider yourself the least bit tech-savvy I daresay that you could use this book as a starting point to a remarkable journey that will stretch your mind in ways that you probably haven't even imagined yet.

To fully enjoy this book and all that it has to offer, you need to be interested in the vast possibilities for mining the rich data tucked away in popular social websites such as Twitter, Facebook, LinkedIn, and Instagram, and you need to be motivated enough to install Docker, use it to run this book's virtual machine experience, and follow along with the book's example code in the Jupyter Notebook, a fantastic web-based tool that features all of the examples for every chapter. Executing the examples is usually as easy as pressing a few keys, since all of the code is presented to you in a friendly user interface.

This book will teach you a few things that you'll be thankful to learn and will add a few indispensable tools to your toolbox, but perhaps even more importantly, it will tell you a story and entertain you along the way. It's a story about data science involving social websites, the data that's tucked away inside of them, and some of the intriguing possibilities of what you (or anyone else) could do with this data.

If you were to read this book from cover to cover, you'd notice that this story unfolds on a chapter-by-chapter basis. While each chapter roughly follows a predictable template that introduces a social website, teaches you how to use its API to fetch data, and presents some techniques for data analysis, the broader story the book tells crescendos in complexity. Earlier chapters in the book take a little more time to introduce fundamental concepts, while later chapters systematically build upon the foundation from earlier chapters and gradually introduce a broad array of tools and techniques for mining the social web that you can take with you into other aspects of your life as a data scientist, analyst, visionary thinker, or curious reader.

Some of the most popular social websites have transitioned from fad to mainstream to household names over recent years, changing the way we live our lives on and off the web and enabling technology to bring out the best (and sometimes the worst) in us. Generally speaking, each chapter of this book interlaces slivers of the social web along with data mining, analysis, and visualization techniques to explore data and answer the following representative questions:

- Who knows whom, and which people are common to their social networks?
- How frequently are particular people communicating with one another?
- Which social network connections generate the most value for a particular niche?
- How does geography affect your social connections in an online world?
- Who are the most influential/popular people in a social network?
- What are people chatting about (and is it valuable)?
- What are people interested in based upon the human language that they use in a digital world?

The answers to these basic kinds of questions often yield valuable insights and present (sometimes lucrative) opportunities for entrepreneurs, social scientists, and other curious practitioners who are trying to understand a problem space and find solutions. Activities such as building a turnkey killer app from scratch to answer these questions, venturing far beyond the typical usage of visualization libraries, and constructing just about anything state-of-the-art are not within the scope of this book. You'll be really disappointed if you purchase this book because you want to do one of those things. However, the book does provide the fundamental building blocks to answer these questions and provide a springboard that might be exactly what you need to build that killer app or conduct that research study. Skim a few chapters and see for yourself. This book covers a lot of ground.

One important thing to note is that APIs are constantly changing. Social media hasn't been around all that long, and even the platforms that appear the most established today are still adapting to how people use them and confronting new threats to security and privacy. As such, the interfaces between our code and their platforms (the APIs) are liable to change too, which means that the code examples provided in this book may not work as intended in the future. We've tried to create realistic examples that are useful for general purposes and app developers, and therefore some of them will require submitting an application for review and approval. We'll do our best to flag those with notes, but be advised API terms of service can change at any time. Nevertheless, as long as your app abides by the terms of service, it will likely get approved, so it's worth the effort.

Python-Centric Technology

This book intentionally takes advantage of the Python programming language for all of its example code. Python's intuitive syntax, amazing ecosystem of packages that trivialize API access and data manipulation, and core data structures that are practically JSON (*http://bit.ly/1a1kFaF*) make it an excellent teaching tool that's powerful yet also very easy to get up and running. As if that weren't enough to make Python both a great pedagogical choice and a very pragmatic choice for mining the social web, there's the Jupyter Notebook (*http://bit.ly/2LOhGvt*), a powerful, interactive code interpreter that provides a notebook-like user experience from within your web browser and combines code execution, code output, text, mathematical typesetting, plots, and more. It's difficult to imagine a better user experience for a learning environment, because it trivializes the problem of delivering sample code that you as the reader can follow along with and execute with no hassles. Figure P-1 provides an illustration of the Jupyter Notebook experience, demonstrating the dashboard of notebooks for each chapter of the book. Figure P-2 shows a view of one notebook.

Figure P-1. Overview of the Jupyter Notebook; a dashboard of notebooks

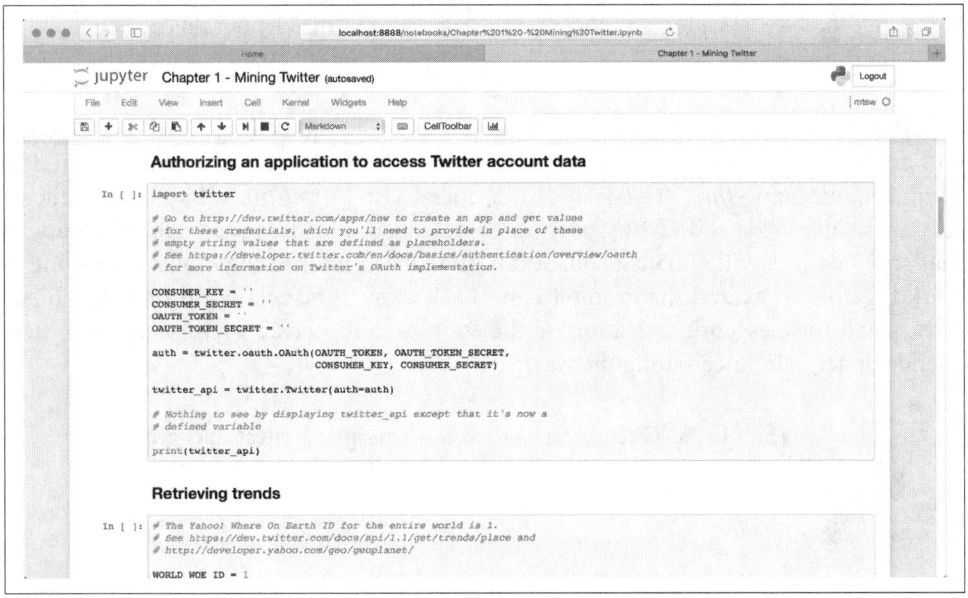

Figure P-2. The "Chapter 1 - Mining Twitter" notebook

Every chapter in this book has a corresponding Jupyter Notebook with example code that makes it a pleasure to study the code, tinker around with it, and customize it for your own purposes. If you've done some programming but have never seen Python syntax, skimming ahead a few pages should hopefully be all the confirmation that you need. Excellent documentation is available online, and the official Python tutorial (*http://bit.ly/1a1kDj8*) is a good place to start if you're looking for a solid introduction to Python as a programming language. This book's Python source code has been overhauled for the third edition to be written in Python 3.6.

The Jupyter Notebook is great, but if you're new to the Python programming world, advising you to just follow the instructions online to configure your development environment would be a bit counterproductive (and possibly even rude). To make your experience with this book as enjoyable as possible, a turnkey virtual machine is available that has the Jupyter Notebook and all of the other dependencies that you'll need to follow along with the examples from this book preinstalled and ready to go. All that you have to do is follow a few simple steps, and in about 15 minutes, you'll be off to the races. If you have a programming background, you'll be able to configure your own development environment, but our hope is that we'll convince you that the virtual machine experience is a better starting point.

 See Appendix A for more detailed information on the virtual machine experience for this book. Appendix C is also worth your attention: it presents some Jupyter Notebook tips and common Python programming idioms that are used throughout this book's source code.

Whether you're a Python novice or a guru, the book's latest bug-fixed source code and accompanying scripts for building the virtual machine are available on GitHub (*http://bit.ly/Mining-the-Social-Web-3E*), a social Git (*http://bit.ly/16mhOep*) repository that will always reflect the most up-to-date example code available. The hope is that social coding will enhance collaboration between like-minded folks who want to work together to extend the examples and hack away at fascinating problems. Hopefully, you'll fork, extend, and improve the source—and maybe even make some new friends or acquaintances along the way.

 The official GitHub repository containing the latest and greatest bug-fixed source code for this book is available at *http://bit.ly/ Mining-the-Social-Web-3E*.

Improvements to the Third Edition

As mentioned earlier in this preface, the third edition of this book has brought on Mikhail Klassen as a coauthor.

Technology changes fast, and social media platforms along with it. When we began revising the second edition, it became clear that the book would benefit from an update to reflect all the changes that were taking place. The first and most obvious change was to update the code from Python 2.7 to a more recent version of Python 3.0+. While there are still diehard users of Python 2.7, moving to Python 3 has a lot of advantages, not the least of which is better support for Unicode. When dealing with social media data, which often includes emojis and text from other alphabets, having good support for Unicode is critical.

In a climate of increasing concerns over user privacy, social media platforms are changing their APIs to better safeguard user information by limiting the extent to which third-party applications can access their platforms—even applications that have been vetted and approved.

Some of the code examples in earlier editions of this book simply didn't work anymore because data access restrictions had changed. In these cases, we created new examples within those constraints, but that nevertheless illustrated something interesting.

At other times, social media platforms changed their APIs in ways that broke the code examples in this book, but the same data was still accessible, just in a different way. By spending time reading the developer documentation of each platform, the code examples from the second edition were recreated using the new API calls.

Perhaps the largest change made to the third edition was the addition of the chapter on mining Instagram (Chapter 3). Instagram is a hugely popular platform that we felt couldn't be left out of the text. This also gave us an opportunity to showcase some technologies useful in performing data mining on image data, specifically the application of deep learning. That subject can quickly get extremely technical, but we introduce the basics in an accessible way, and then apply a powerful computer vision API to do the heavy lifting for us. The end result is that in a few lines of Python, you have a system that can look at photos posted to Instagram and tell you about what's in them.

Another substantial change was that Chapter 5 was heavily edited and reframed as a chapter on mining text files as opposed to being rooted in the context of Google+. The fundamentals for this chapter are unchanged, and the content is more explicitly generalizable to any API response that returns human language data.

A few other technology decisions were made along the way that some readers may disagree with. In the chapter on mining mailboxes (Chapter 7), the second edition presented the use of MongoDB, a type of database, for storing and querying email data. This type of system makes a lot of sense, but unless you are running the code for this book inside a Docker container, installing a database system creates some extra overhead. Also, we wanted to show more examples of how to use the *pandas* library, introduced in Chapter 2. This library has quickly become one of the most important in the data scientist's toolbox because of how easy it makes the manipulation of tabular data. Leaving it out of a book on data mining seemed wrong. Nevertheless, we kept the MongoDB examples that are part of Chapter 9, and if you are using the Docker container for this book, it should be breeze anyway.

Finally, we removed what was previously Chapter 9 (Mining the Semantic Web). This chapter was originally drafted as part of the first edition in 2010, and the overall utility of it, given the direction that the social web has generally taken, seemed questionable nearly a decade later.

 Constructive feedback is always welcome, and we'd enjoy hearing from you by way of a book review, tweet to @SocialWebMining (*http://bit.ly/1a1kHzq*), or comment on *Mining the Social Web*'s Facebook wall (*http://on.fb.me/1a1kHPQ*). The book's official website and the blog that extends the book with longer-form content are at *http://MiningTheSocialWeb.com*.

The Ethical Use of Data Mining

At the time of this writing, the provisions of the General Data Protection Regulation (GDPR) have just come into full effect in the European Union (EU). The regulation stipulates how companies must protect the privacy of the citizens and residents of the EU, giving users more control over their data. Because companies all around the world do business in Europe, virtually all of them have been forced to make changes to their terms of use and privacy policies, or else face penalties. The GDPR sets a new global baseline for privacy; one that will hopefully be a positive influence on companies everywhere, even if they conduct no business in Europe.

The third edition of *Mining the Social Web* comes amidst a climate of greater concern over the ethical use of data and user privacy. Around the world, data brokers are collecting, collating, and reselling data about internet users: their consumer behavior, preferences, political leanings, postal codes, income brackets, ages, etc. Sometimes, within certain jurisdictions, this activity is entirely legal. Given enough of this type of data, it becomes possible to manipulate behavior by exploiting human psychology through highly targeted messaging, interface design, or misleading information.

As the authors of a book about how to mine data from social media and the web, and have fun doing it, we are fully aware of the irony. We are also aware that what is legal is not, by necessity, therefore ethical. Data mining, by itself, is a collection of practices using particular technologies that are, by themselves, morally neutral. Data mining can be used in a lot of tremendously helpful ways. An example that I (Mikhail Klassen) often turn to is the work of the UN Global Pulse, an initiative by the United Nations to use big data for global good. For example, by using social media data, it is possible to measure sentiment toward development initiatives (such as a vaccination campaign) or toward a country's political process. By analyzing Twitter data, it may be possible to respond faster to an emerging crisis, such as an epidemic or natural disaster.

The examples need not be humanitarian. Data mining is being used in exciting ways to develop personalized learning technologies for education and training, and some commercial efforts by startups. In other domains, data mining is used to predict pandemics, discover new drugs, or determine which genes may be responsible for particular diseases or when to perform preventative maintenance on an engine. By responsibly using data and respecting user privacy, it is possible to use data mining ethically, while still turning a profit and achieving amazing things.

A relatively small number of technology companies currently have an incredible amount of data about people's lives. They are under increasing societal pressure and government regulation to use this data responsibly. To their credit, many are updating their policies as well as their APIs. By reading this book, you will gain a better understanding of just what kind of data a third-party developer (such as yourself) can obtain from these platforms, and you will learn about many tools used to turn data into knowledge. You will also, we hope, gain a greater appreciation for how technologies may be abused. Then, as an informed citizen, you can advocate for sensible laws to protect everyone's privacy.

Conventions Used in This Book

This book is *extensively* hyperlinked, which makes it ideal to read in an electronic format such as a DRM-free PDF that can be purchased directly from O'Reilly as an ebook. Purchasing it as an ebook through O'Reilly also guarantees that you will get automatic updates for the book as they become available. The links have been shortened using the *bit.ly* service for the benefit of customers with the printed version of the book. All hyperlinks have been vetted.

The following typographical conventions are used in this book:

Italic
Indicates new terms, URLs, email addresses, filenames, and file extensions.

`Constant width`
Indicates program listings, and is used within paragraphs to refer to program elements such as variable or function names, databases, data types, environment variables, statements, and keywords.

`Constant width bold`
Shows commands or other text that should be typed literally by the user. Also occasionally used for emphasis in code listings.

Constant width italic

> Shows text that should be replaced with user-supplied values or values determined by context.

This icon signifies a general note.

This icon signifies a tip or suggestion.

This icon indicates a warning or caution.

Using Code Examples

The latest sample code for this book is maintained on GitHub at *http://bit.ly/Mining-the-Social-Web-3E*, the official code repository for the book. You are encouraged to monitor this repository for the latest bug-fixed code as well as extended examples by the author and the rest of the social coding community. If you are reading a paper copy of this book, there is a possibility that the code examples in print may not be up to date, but so long as you are working from the book's GitHub repository, you will always have the latest bug-fixed example code. If you are taking advantage of this book's virtual machine experience, you'll already have the latest source code, but if you are opting to work in your own development environment, be sure to take advantage of the ability to download a source code archive directly from the GitHub repository.

Please log issues involving example code to the GitHub repository's issue tracker as opposed to the O'Reilly catalog's errata tracker. As issues are resolved in the source code on GitHub, updates are published back to the book's manuscript, which is then periodically provided to readers as an ebook update.

In general, you may use the code in this book in your programs and documentation. You do not need to contact us for permission unless you're reproducing a significant portion of the code. For example, writing a program that uses several chunks of code from this book does not require permission. Selling or distributing a CD-ROM of examples from O'Reilly books does require permission. Answering a question by citing this book and quoting example code does not require permission. Incorporating a significant amount of example code from this book into your product's documentation does require permission.

We require attribution according to the OSS license under which the code is released. An attribution usually includes the title, author, publisher, and ISBN. For example: "*Mining the Social Web, 3rd Edition*, by Matthew A. Russell and Mikhail Klassen. Copyright 2018 Matthew A. Russell and Mikhail Klassen, 978-1-491-98504-5."

If you feel your use of code examples falls outside fair use or the permission given above, feel free to contact us at *permissions@oreilly.com*.

O'Reilly Safari

Safari (formerly Safari Books Online) is a membership-based training and reference platform for enterprise, government, educators, and individuals.

Members have access to thousands of books, training videos, Learning Paths, interactive tutorials, and curated playlists from over 250 publishers, including O'Reilly Media, Harvard Business Review, Prentice Hall Professional, Addison-Wesley Professional, Microsoft Press, Sams, Que, Peachpit Press, Adobe, Focal Press, Cisco Press, John Wiley & Sons, Syngress, Morgan Kaufmann, IBM Redbooks, Packt, Adobe Press, FT Press, Apress, Manning, New Riders, McGraw-Hill, Jones & Bartlett, and Course Technology, among others.

For more information, please visit *http://oreilly.com/safari*.

How to Contact Us

Please address comments and questions concerning this book to the publisher:

O'Reilly Media, Inc.
1005 Gravenstein Highway North
Sebastopol, CA 95472
800-998-9938 (in the United States or Canada)
707-829-0515 (international or local)
707-829-0104 (fax)

We have a web page for this book, where we list *non-code-related errata* and additional information. You can access this page at *http://bit.ly/mining-social-web-3e*.

Any errata related to the sample code should be submitted as a ticket through GitHub's issue tracker at *http://github.com/ptwobrussell/Mining-the-Social-Web/issues*.

To comment or ask technical questions about this book, send email to *bookquestions@oreilly.com*.

For more information about our books, courses, conferences, and news, see our website at *http://www.oreilly.com*.

Find us on Facebook: *http://facebook.com/oreilly*

Follow us on Twitter: *http://twitter.com/oreillymedia*

Watch us on YouTube: *http://www.youtube.com/oreillymedia*

Acknowledgments for the Third Edition

I (Mikhail Klassen) would not have been involved in this book if not for a chance meeting with Susan Conant from O'Reilly Media. She saw the potential for the collaboration with Matthew Russell on the third edition of this book, and it has been great to work on this project. The editorial team at O'Reilly has been great to work with, and I'd like to thank Tim McGovern, Ally MacDonald, and Alicia Young. Connected with this book project is a series of video lectures produced by O'Reilly, and I'd also like to thank the team that worked with me on these: David Cates, Peter Ong, Adam Ritz, and Amanda Porter.

Being only able to work on the project evenings and weekends means time taken away from family, so thank you to my wife, Sheila, for understanding.

Acknowledgments for the Second Edition

I (Matthew Russell) will reiterate from my acknowledgments for the first edition that writing a book is a tremendous sacrifice. The time that you spend away from friends and family (which happens mostly during an extended period on nights and weekends) is quite costly and can't be recovered, and you really do need a certain amount of moral support to make it through to the other side with relationships intact. Thanks again to my very patient friends and family, who really shouldn't have tolerated me writing another book and probably think that I have some kind of chronic disorder that involves a strange addiction to working nights and weekends. If you can find a rehab clinic for people who are addicted to writing books, I promise I'll go and check myself in.

Every project needs a great project manager, and my incredible editor Mary Treseler and her amazing production staff were a pleasure to work with on this book (as always). Writing a technical book is a long and stressful endeavor, to say the least, and it's a remarkable experience to work with professionals who are able to help you make it through that exhausting journey and deliver a beautifully polished product that you can be proud to share with the world. Kristen Brown, Rachel Monaghan, and Rachel Head truly made all the difference in taking my best efforts to an entirely new level of professionalism.

The detailed feedback that I received from my very capable editorial staff and technical reviewers was also nothing short of amazing. Ranging from very technically oriented recommendations to software-engineering-oriented best practices with Python to perspectives on how to best reach the target audience as a mock reader, the feedback was beyond anything I could have ever expected. The book you are about to read would not be anywhere near the quality that it is without the thoughtful peer review feedback that I received. Thanks especially to Abe Music, Nicholas Mayne, Robert P.J. Day, Ram Narasimhan, Jason Yee, and Kevin Makice for your *very* detailed reviews of the manuscript. It made a tremendous difference in the quality of this book, and my only regret is that we did not have the opportunity to work together more closely during this process. Thanks also to Tate Eskew for introducing me to Vagrant, a tool that has made all the difference in establishing an easy-to-use and easy-to-maintain virtual machine experience for this book.

I also would like to thank my many wonderful colleagues at Digital Reasoning for the enlightening conversations that we've had over the years about data mining and topics in computer science, and other constructive dialogues that have helped shape my professional thinking. It's a blessing to be part of a team that's so talented and capable. Thanks especially to Tim Estes and Rob Metcalf, who have been supportive of my work on time-consuming projects (outside of my professional responsibilities to Digital Reasoning) like writing books.

Finally, thanks to every single reader or adopter of this book's source code who provided constructive feedback over the lifetime of the first edition. Although there are far too many of you to name, your feedback has shaped this second edition in immeasurable ways. I hope that this second edition meets your expectations and finds itself among your list of useful books that you'd recommend to a friend or colleague.

Acknowledgments from the First Edition

To say the least, writing a technical book takes a *ridiculous* amount of sacrifice. On the home front, I gave up more time with my wife, Baseeret, and daughter, Lindsay Belle, than I'm proud to admit. Thanks most of all to both of you for loving me in spite of my ambitions to somehow take over the world one day. (It's just a phase, and I'm really trying to grow out of it—honest.)

I sincerely believe that the sum of your decisions gets you to where you are in life (especially professional life), but nobody could ever complete the journey alone, and it's an honor to give credit where credit is due. I am truly blessed to have been in the company of some of the brightest people in the world while working on this book, including a technical editor as smart as Mike Loukides, a production staff as talented as the folks at O'Reilly, and an overwhelming battery of eager reviewers as amazing as everyone who helped me to complete this book. I especially want to thank Abe Music, Pete Warden, Tantek Celik, J. Chris Anderson, Salvatore Sanfilippo, Robert Newson, DJ Patil, Chimezie Ogbuji, Tim Golden, Brian Curtin, Raffi Krikorian, Jeff Hammerbacher, Nick Ducoff, and Cameron Marlowe for reviewing material or making particularly helpful comments that absolutely shaped its outcome for the best. I'd also like to thank Tim O'Reilly for graciously allowing me to put some of his Twitter and Google+ data under the microscope; it definitely made those chapters much more interesting to read than they otherwise would have been. It would be impossible to recount all of the other folks who have directly or indirectly shaped my life or the outcome of this book.

Finally, thanks to you for giving this book a chance. If you're reading this, you're at least thinking about picking up a copy. If you do, you're probably going to find something wrong with it despite my best efforts; however, I really do believe that, in spite of the few inevitable glitches, you'll find it an enjoyable way to spend a few evenings/weekends and you'll manage to learn a few things somewhere along the line.

A Guided Tour of the Social Web

Part I of this book is called "a guided tour of the social web" because it presents some practical skills for getting immediate value from some of the most popular social websites. You'll learn how to access APIs to analyze social data from Twitter, Facebook, LinkedIn, Instagram, web pages, blogs and feeds, emails, and GitHub accounts. In general, each chapter stands alone and tells its own story, but the flow of chapters throughout Part I is designed to also tell a broader story. There is a gradual crescendo in terms of complexity, with some techniques or technologies introduced in early chapters seeing reuse in a later chapter.

Because of this gradual increase in complexity, you are encouraged to read each chapter in turn, but you also should be able to cherry-pick chapters and follow along with the examples should you choose to do so. Each chapter's sample code is consolidated into a single Jupyter Notebook that is named according to the number of the chapter in this book.

> The source code for this book is available on GitHub (*http://bit.ly/ Mining-the-Social-Web-3E*). You are highly encouraged to take advantage of Docker to build a self-contained virtual machine experience. This will allow you to work through the sample code in a preconfigured development environment that "just works."

Prelude

Although it's been mentioned in the preface and will continue to be casually reiterated in every chapter at some point, this isn't your typical tech book with an archive of sample code that accompanies the text. It's a book that attempts to rock the status quo and define a new standard for tech books in which the code is managed as a first-class, open source software project, with the book being a form of "premium" support for that code base.

To address that objective, serious thought has been put into synthesizing the discussion in the book with the code examples into as seamless a learning experience as possible. After much discussion with readers of the first edition and reflection on lessons learned, it became apparent that an interactive user interface backed by a server running on a virtual machine and rooted in solid configuration management was the best path forward. There is not a simpler and better way to give you total control of the code while also ensuring that the code will "just work"—regardless of whether you use macOS, Windows, or Linux; whether you have a 32-bit or 64-bit machine; and whether third-party software dependencies change APIs and break.

For the book's third edition, the power of Docker was leveraged for the virtual machine experience. Docker is a technology that can be installed on the most common computer operating systems and is used to create and manage "containers." Docker containers act much like virtual machines, creating self-contained environments that have all of the necessary source code, executables, and dependencies needed to run a given piece of software. Containerized versions of many pieces of complex software exist, making the installation of these a breeze on any system running Docker.

The GitHub repository (*http://bit.ly/Mining-the-Social-Web-3E*) for this book now includes a *Dockerfile*. Dockerfiles act like recipes that tell Docker how to "build" the containerized software. Instructions on how to get up and running quickly can be found in Appendix A.

Take advantage of this powerful tool for interactive learning.

Read "Reflections on Authoring a Minimum Viable Book" (*http://bit.ly/1a1kPyJ*) for more reflections on the process of developing a virtual machine for the second edition.

Although Chapter 1 is the most logical place to turn next, you should take a moment to familiarize yourself with Appendixes A and C when you are ready to start running the code examples. Appendix A points to an online document and accompanying screencasts that walk you through a quick and easy setup process for using Docker to build this book's virtual experience. Appendix C points to an online document that provides some background information you may find helpful in getting the most value out of the interactive virtual machine experience.

Even if you are a seasoned developer who is capable of doing all of this work yourself, give the Docker experience a try the first time through the book so that you don't get derailed with the inevitable software installation hiccups.

## CHAPTER 1

Mining Twitter: Exploring Trending Topics, Discovering What People Are Talking About, and More

Since this is the first chapter, we'll take our time acclimating to our journey in social web mining. However, given that Twitter data is so accessible and open to public scrutiny, Chapter 9 further elaborates on the broad number of data mining possibilities by providing a terse collection of recipes in a convenient problem/solution format that can be easily manipulated and readily applied to a wide range of problems. You'll also be able to apply concepts from future chapters to Twitter data.

 Always get the latest bug-fixed source code for this chapter (and every other chapter) on GitHub (*http://bit.ly/Mining-the-Social-Web-3E*). Be sure to also take advantage of this book's virtual machine experience, as described in Appendix A, to maximize your enjoyment of the sample code.

1.1 Overview

In this chapter, we'll ease into the process of getting situated with a minimal (but effective) development environment with Python, survey Twitter's API, and distill some analytical insights from tweets using frequency analysis. Topics that you'll learn about in this chapter include:

- Twitter's developer platform and how to make API requests
- Tweet metadata and how to use it
- Extracting entities such as user mentions, hashtags, and URLs from tweets

- Techniques for performing frequency analysis with Python
- Plotting histograms of Twitter data with the Jupyter Notebook

1.2 Why Is Twitter All the Rage?

Most chapters won't open with a reflective discussion, but since this is the first chapter of the book and introduces a social website that is often misunderstood, it seems appropriate to take a moment to examine Twitter at a fundamental level.

How would you define Twitter?

There are many ways to answer this question, but let's consider it from an overarching angle that addresses some fundamental aspects of our shared humanity that any technology needs to account for in order to be useful and successful. After all, the purpose of technology is to enhance our human experience.

As humans, what are some things that we want that technology might help us to get?

- We want to be heard.
- We want to satisfy our curiosity.
- We want it easy.
- We want it now.

In the context of the current discussion, these are just a few observations that are generally true of humanity. We have a deeply rooted need to share our ideas and experiences, which gives us the ability to connect with other people, to be heard, and to feel a sense of worth and importance. We are curious about the world around us and how to organize and manipulate it, and we use communication to share our observations, ask questions, and engage with other people in meaningful dialogues about our quandaries.

The last two bullet points highlight our inherent intolerance to friction. Ideally, we don't want to have to work any harder than is absolutely necessary to satisfy our curiosity or get any particular job done; we'd rather be doing "something else" or moving on to the next thing because our time on this planet is so precious and short. Along similar lines, we want things *now* and tend to be impatient when actual progress doesn't happen at the speed of our own thought.

One way to describe Twitter is as a microblogging service that allows people to communicate with short messages that roughly correspond to thoughts or ideas. Historically, these tweets were limited to 140 characters in length, although this limit has been expanded and is liable to change again in the future. In that regard, you could think of Twitter as being akin to a free, high-speed, global text-messaging service. In other words, it's a piece of valuable infrastructure that enables rapid and easy communication. However, that's not all of the story. Humans are hungry for connection and want to be heard, and Twitter has 335 million monthly active users worldwide (*http://bit.ly/2p2GSV0*) expressing ideas, communicating directly with each other, and satisfying their curiosity.

Besides the macro-level possibilities for marketing and advertising—which are always lucrative with a user base of that size—it's the underlying network dynamics that created the gravity for such a user base to emerge that are truly interesting, and that's why Twitter is all the rage. While the communication bus that enables users to share short quips at the speed of thought may be a *necessary* condition for viral adoption and sustained engagement on the Twitter platform, it's not a *sufficient* condition. The extra ingredient that makes it sufficient is that Twitter's asymmetric following model satisfies our curiosity. It is the asymmetric following model that casts Twitter as more of an interest graph than a social network, and the APIs that provide just enough of a framework for structure and self-organizing behavior to emerge from the chaos.

In other words, whereas some social websites like Facebook and LinkedIn require the mutual acceptance of a connection between users (which usually implies a real-world connection of some kind), Twitter's relationship model allows you to keep up with the latest happenings of *any* other user, even though that other user may not choose to follow you back or even know that you exist. Twitter's *following* model is simple but exploits a fundamental aspect of what makes us human: our curiosity. Whether it be an infatuation with celebrity gossip, an urge to keep up with a favorite sports team, a keen interest in a particular political topic, or a desire to connect with someone new, Twitter provides you with boundless opportunities to satisfy your curiosity.

 Although I've been careful in the preceding paragraph to introduce Twitter in terms of "following" relationships, the act of *following* someone is sometimes described as "friending" (albeit it's a strange kind of one-way friendship). While you'll even run across the "friend" nomenclature in the official Twitter API documentation (*http://bit.ly/2QskIYD*), it's probably best to think of Twitter in terms of the following relationships I've described.

Think of an *interest graph* as a way of modeling connections between people and their arbitrary interests. Interest graphs provide a profound number of possibilities in the data mining realm that primarily involve measuring correlations between things for the objective of making intelligent recommendations and other applications in machine learning. For example, you could use an interest graph to measure correlations and make recommendations ranging from whom to follow on Twitter to what to purchase online to whom you should date. To illustrate the notion of Twitter as an interest graph, consider that a Twitter user need not be a real person; it very well could be a person, but it could also be an inanimate object, a company, a musical group, an imaginary persona, an impersonation of someone (living or dead), or just about anything else.

For example, the @HomerJSimpson (*http://bit.ly/1a1kQD1*) account is the official account for Homer Simpson, a popular character from *The Simpsons* television show. Although Homer Simpson isn't a real person, he's a well-known personality throughout the world, and the @HomerJSimpson Twitter persona acts as a conduit for him (or his creators, actually) to engage his fans. Likewise, although this book will probably never reach the popularity of Homer Simpson, @SocialWebMining (*http://bit.ly/1a1kHzq*) is its official Twitter account and provides a means for a community that's interested in its content to connect and engage on various levels. When you realize that Twitter enables you to create, connect with, and explore a community of interest for an arbitrary topic of interest, the power of Twitter and the insights you can gain from mining its data become much more obvious.

There is very little governance of what a Twitter account can be aside from the badges on some accounts that identify celebrities and public figures as "verified accounts" and basic restrictions in Twitter's Terms of Service agreement (*http://bit.ly/1a1kRXl*), which is required for using the service. It may seem subtle, but it's an important distinction from some social websites in which accounts must correspond to real, living people, businesses, or entities of a similar nature that fit into a particular taxonomy. Twitter places no particular restrictions on the persona of an account and relies on self-organizing behavior such as following relationships and folksonomies that emerge from the use of hashtags to create a certain kind of order within the system.

Taxonomies and Folksonomies

A fundamental aspect of human intelligence is the desire to classify things and derive a hierarchy in which each element "belongs to" or is a "child" of a parent element one level higher in the hierarchy. Leaving aside some of the finer distinctions between a taxonomy and an ontology (*http://bit.ly/1a1kRXy*), think of a *taxonomy* as a hierarchical structure like a tree that classifies elements into particular parent/child relationships, whereas a *folksonomy* (*http://bit.ly/1a1kU5C*) (a term coined around 2004) describes the universe of collaborative tagging and social indexing efforts that emerge in various ecosystems of the web. It's a play on words in the sense that it blends *folk* and *taxonomy*. So, in essence, a folksonomy is just a fancy way of describing the decentralized universe of tags that emerges as a mechanism of *collective intelligence* when you allow people to classify content with labels. One of the things that's so compelling about the use of hashtags on Twitter is that the folksonomies that organically emerge act as points of aggregation for common interests and provide a focused way to explore while still leaving open the possibility for nearly unbounded serendipity.

1.3 Exploring Twitter's API

Having a proper frame of reference for Twitter, let us now transition our attention to the problem of acquiring and analyzing Twitter data.

1.3.1 Fundamental Twitter Terminology

Twitter might be described as a real-time, highly social microblogging service that allows users to post short status updates, called *tweets*, that appear on timelines. Tweets may include one or more entities in their (currently) 280 characters of content and reference one or more places that map to locations in the real world. An understanding of users, tweets, and timelines is particularly essential to effective use of Twitter's API (*http://bit.ly/1a1kSKQ*), so a brief introduction to these fundamental concepts is in order before we interact with the API to fetch some data. We've largely discussed Twitter users and Twitter's asymmetric following model for relationships thus far, so this section briefly introduces tweets and timelines in order to round out a general understanding of the Twitter platform.

Tweets are the essence of Twitter, and while they are notionally thought of as short strings of text content associated with a user's status update, there's really quite a bit more metadata there than meets the eye. In addition to the textual content of a tweet itself, tweets come bundled with two additional pieces of metadata that are of particular note: *entities* and *places*. Tweet entities are essentially the user mentions, hashtags, URLs, and media that may be associated with a tweet, and places are locations in the real world that may be attached to a tweet. Note that a place may be the actual location in which a tweet was authored, but it might also be a reference to the place described in a tweet.

To make it all a bit more concrete, let's consider a sample tweet with the following text:

> @ptwobrussell is writing @SocialWebMining, 2nd Ed. from his home office in Franklin, TN. Be #social: *http://on.fb.me/16WJAf9*

The tweet is 124 characters long and contains 4 tweet entities: the user mentions @ptwobrussell and @SocialWebMining, the hashtag #social, and the URL *http://on.fb.me/16WJAf9*. Although there is a place called Franklin, Tennessee, that's explicitly mentioned in the tweet, the *places* metadata associated with the tweet might include the location in which the tweet was authored, which may or may not be Franklin, Tennessee. That's a lot of metadata that's packed into fewer than 140 characters and illustrates just how potent a short quip can be: it can unambiguously refer to multiple other Twitter users, link to web pages, and cross-reference topics with hashtags that act as points of aggregation and horizontally slice through the entire Twitterverse in an easily searchable fashion.

Finally, *timelines* are chronologically sorted collections of tweets. Abstractly, you might say that a timeline is any particular collection of tweets displayed in chronological order; however, you'll commonly see a couple of timelines that are particularly noteworthy. From the perspective of an arbitrary Twitter user, the *home timeline* is the view that you see when you log into your account and look at all of the tweets from users that you are following, whereas a particular *user timeline* is a collection of tweets only from a certain user.

For example, when you log into your Twitter account, your home timeline is located at *https://twitter.com*. The URL for any particular user timeline, however, must be suffixed with a context that identifies the user, such as *https://twitter.com/SocialWebMin ing*. If you're interested in seeing who a particular user is following, you can access a list of users with the additional *following* suffix appended to the URL. For example, what Tim O'Reilly sees on his home timeline when he logs into Twitter is accessible at *https://twitter.com/timoreilly/following*.

An application like TweetDeck provides several customizable views into the tumultuous landscape of tweets, as shown in Figure 1-1, and is worth trying out if you haven't journeyed far beyond the Twitter.com user interface.

Whereas timelines are collections of tweets with relatively low velocity, *streams* are samples of public tweets flowing through Twitter in real time. The *public firehose* of all tweets has been known to peak at hundreds of thousands of tweets per minute (*http://bit.ly/2xenpnR*) during events with particularly wide interest, such as presidential debates or major sporting events. Twitter's public firehose emits far too much data to consider for the scope of this book and presents interesting engineering challenges, which is at least one of the reasons that various third-party commercial vendors have partnered with Twitter to bring the firehose to the masses in a more consumable fashion. That said, a small random sample of the public timeline (*http://bit.ly/2p7G8hf7*) is available that provides filterable access to enough public data for API developers to develop powerful applications.

Figure 1-1. TweetDeck provides a highly customizable user interface that can be helpful for analyzing what is happening on Twitter and demonstrates the kind of data that you have access to through the Twitter API

The remainder of this chapter and Part II of this book assume that you have a Twitter account, which is required for API access. If you don't have an account already, take a moment to create one and then review Twitter's liberal terms of service (*http://bit.ly/ 2e63DvY*), API documentation (*http://bit.ly/1a1kSKQ*), and Developer Rules of the Road (*http://bit.ly/2MsrryS*). The sample code for this chapter and Part II of the book generally doesn't require you to have any friends or followers of your own, but some of the examples in Part II will be a lot more interesting and fun if you have an active account with a handful of friends and followers that you can use as a basis for social web mining. If you don't have an active account, now would be a good time to get plugged in and start priming your account for the data mining fun to come.

1.3.2 Creating a Twitter API Connection

Twitter has taken great care to craft an elegantly simple RESTful (*http://bit.ly/ 1a1kVX5*) API that is intuitive and easy to use. Even so, there are great libraries available to further mitigate the work involved in making API requests. A particularly beautiful Python package that wraps the Twitter API and mimics the public API semantics almost one-to-one is `twitter`. Like most other Python packages, you can install it with `pip` by typing **pip install twitter** in a terminal. If you don't happen to like the `twitter` Python library, there are many others to choose from. One popular alternative is `tweepy` (*http://bit.ly/2M41GbY*).

See Appendix C for instructions on how to install `pip`.

Python Tip: Harnessing pydoc for Effective Help During Development

We'll work though some examples that illustrate the use of the `twitter` package, but just in case you're ever in a situation where you need some help (and you will be), it's worth remembering that you can always skim the documentation for a package (its pydoc (*http://bit.ly/1a1kVXg*)) in a few different ways. Outside of a Python shell, running pydoc in your terminal on a package in your PYTHONPATH is a nice option. For example, on a Linux or macOS system, you can simply type **pydoc twitter** in a terminal to get the package-level documentation, whereas **pydoc twitter.Twitter** provides documentation on the `Twitter` class included with that package. On Windows systems, you can get the same information, albeit in a slightly different way, by executing pydoc as a package. Typing **python -mpydoc twitter.Twitter**, for example, would provide information on the `twitter.Twitter` class. If you find yourself reviewing the documentation for certain modules often, you can elect to pass the `-w` option to pydoc and write out an HTML page that you can save and bookmark in your browser.

However, more than likely you'll be in the middle of a working session when you need some help. The built-in `help` function accepts a package or class name and is useful for an ordinary Python shell, whereas IPython (*http://bit.ly/2oiWhSw*) users can suffix a package or class name with a question mark to view inline help. For example, you could type **help(twitter)** or **help(twitter.Twitter)** in a regular Python interpreter, while you can use the shortcut **twitter?** or **twitter.Twitter?** in IPython or the Jupyter Notebook.

It is highly recommended that you adopt IPython as your standard Python shell when working outside of the Jupyter Notebook because of the various convenience functions, such as tab completion, session history, and "magic functions" (*http://bit.ly/2nII3ce*) that it offers. Recall that Appendix A provides minimal details on getting oriented with recommended developer tools such as IPython.

We'll opt to make programmatic API requests with Python, because the `twitter` package so elegantly mimics the RESTful API. If you're interested in seeing the raw requests that you could make with HTTP or exploring the API in a more interactive manner, however, check out the developer docs (*http://bit.ly/2OpiF6c*) on how to use a tool like Twurl to explore the Twitter API.

Before you can make any API requests to Twitter, you'll need to create an application at *https://dev.twitter.com/apps*. Creating an application is the standard way for developers to gain API access and for Twitter to monitor and interact with third-party platform developers as needed. In light of recent abuse of social media platforms, you must apply for a Twitter developer account (*http://bit.ly/2AHBWO3*) and be approved in order to create new apps. Creating an app will also create a set of authentication tokens that will let you programmatically access the Twitter platform.

In the present context, *you* are creating an app that you are going to authorize to access *your* account data, so this might seem a bit roundabout; why not just plug in your username and password to access the API? While that approach might work fine for you, a third party such as a friend or colleague probably wouldn't feel comfortable forking over a username/password combination in order to enjoy the same insights from your app. Giving up credentials is never a sound practice. Fortunately, some smart people recognized this problem years ago, and now there's a standardized protocol called OAuth (*http://bit.ly/1a1kZWN*) (short for Open Authorization) that works for these kinds of situations in a generalized way for the broader social web. The protocol is a social web standard at this point.

If you remember nothing else from this tangent, just remember that OAuth is a way to let users authorize third-party applications to access their account data without needing to share sensitive information like a password. Appendix B provides a slightly broader overview of how OAuth works if you're interested, and Twitter's OAuth documentation (*http://bit.ly/2NawA3v*) offers specific details about its particular implementation.[1]

For simplicity of development, the key pieces of information that you'll need to take away from your newly created application's settings are its consumer key, consumer secret, access token, and access token secret. In tandem, these four credentials provide everything that an application would ultimately be getting to authorize itself through a series of redirects involving the user granting authorization, so treat them with the same sensitivity that you would a password.

 See Appendix B for details on implementing an OAuth 2.0 flow, which you will need to build an application that requires an arbitrary user to authorize it to access account data.

Figure 1-2 shows the context of retrieving these credentials.

---

[1] Although it's an implementation detail, it may be worth noting that Twitter's v1.1 API still implements OAuth 1.0a, whereas many other social web properties have since upgraded to OAuth 2.0.

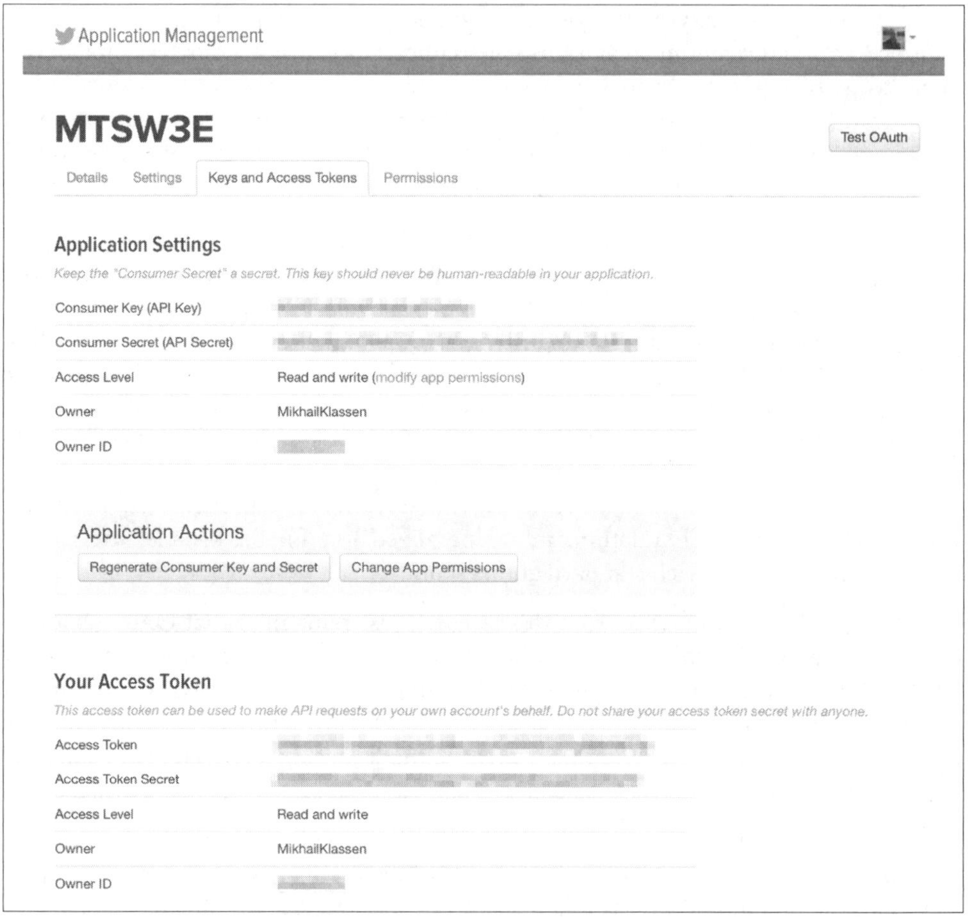

Figure 1-2. Create a new Twitter application to get OAuth credentials and API access at https://dev.twitter.com/apps; the four (blurred) OAuth fields are what you'll use to make API calls to Twitter's API

Without further ado, let's create an authenticated connection to Twitter's API and find out what people are talking about by inspecting the trends available to us through the GET trends/place resource (*http://bit.ly/2BGWJBU*). While you're at it, go ahead and bookmark the official API documentation (*http://bit.ly/1a1kSKQ*) as well as the API reference (*http://bit.ly/2Nb9CJS*), because you'll be referencing them regularly as you learn the ropes of the developer-facing side of the Twitterverse.

As of March 2017, Twitter's API operates at version 1.1 and is significantly different in a few areas from the previous v1 API that you may have encountered. Version 1 of the API passed through a deprecation cycle of approximately six months and is no longer operational. All sample code in this book presumes version 1.1 of the API.

Let's fire up the Jupyter Notebook and initiate a search. Follow along with Example 1-1 by substituting your own account credentials into the variables at the beginning of the code example and execute the call to create an instance of the Twitter API. The code works by using your OAuth credentials to create an object called auth that represents your OAuth authorization, which can then be passed to a class called `Twitter` that is capable of issuing queries to Twitter's API.

Example 1-1. Authorizing an application to access Twitter account data

```
import twitter

# Go to http://dev.twitter.com/apps/new to create an app and get values
# for these credentials, which you'll need to provide in place of these
# empty string values that are defined as placeholders.
# See https://developer.twitter.com/en/docs/basics/authentication/overview/oauth
# for more information on Twitter's OAuth implementation.

CONSUMER_KEY = ''
CONSUMER_SECRET = ''
OAUTH_TOKEN = ''
OAUTH_TOKEN_SECRET = ''

auth = twitter.oauth.OAuth(OAUTH_TOKEN, OAUTH_TOKEN_SECRET,
                           CONSUMER_KEY, CONSUMER_SECRET)

twitter_api = twitter.Twitter(auth=auth)

# Nothing to see by displaying twitter_api except that it's now a
# defined variable

print(twitter_api)
```

The results of this example should simply display an unambiguous representation of the `twitter_api` object that you've constructed, such as:

```
<twitter.api.Twitter object at 0x39d9b50>
```

This indicates that you've successfully used OAuth credentials to gain authorization to query Twitter's API.

1.3.3 Exploring Trending Topics

With an authorized API connection in place, you can now issue a request. Example 1-2 demonstrates how to ask Twitter for the topics that are currently trending worldwide, but keep in mind that the API can easily be parameterized to constrain the topics to more specific locales if you feel inclined to try out some of the possibilities. The device for constraining queries is via Yahoo! GeoPlanet's Where On Earth (WOE) ID system (*http://bit.ly/2NHdAJB*), which is an API unto itself that aims to provide a way to map a unique identifier to any named place on Earth (or theoretically, even in a virtual world). If you haven't already, go ahead and try out the example, which collects a set of trends for both the entire world and just the United States.

Example 1-2. Retrieving trends

```
# The Yahoo! Where On Earth ID for the entire world is 1.
# See http://bit.ly/2BGWJBU and
# http://bit.ly/2MsvwCQ

WORLD_WOE_ID = 1
US_WOE_ID = 23424977

# Prefix ID with the underscore for query string parameterization.
# Without the underscore, the twitter package appends the ID value
# to the URL itself as a special case keyword argument.

world_trends = twitter_api.trends.place(_id=WORLD_WOE_ID)
us_trends = twitter_api.trends.place(_id=US_WOE_ID)

print(world_trends)
print()
print(us_trends)
```

You should see a semireadable response that is a list of Python dictionaries from the API (as opposed to any kind of error message), such as the following truncated results, before proceeding further (in just a moment, we'll reformat the response to be more easily readable):

```
[{u'created_at': u'2013-03-27T11:50:40Z', u'trends': [{u'url':
        u'http://twitter.com/search?q=%23MentionSomeoneImportantForYou'...
```

Notice that the sample result contains a URL for a trend represented as a search query that corresponds to the hashtag #MentionSomeoneImportantForYou, where %23 is the URL encoding for the hashtag symbol. We'll use this rather benign hashtag throughout the remainder of the chapter as a unifying theme for the examples that follow. Although a sample data file containing tweets for this hashtag is available with the book's source code, you'll have much more fun exploring a topic that's trending at the time you read this as opposed to following along with a canned topic that is no longer trending.

The pattern for using the `twitter` module is simple and predictable: instantiate the `Twitter` class with an object chain corresponding to a base URL and then invoke methods on the object that correspond to URL contexts. For example, `twit ter_api.trends.place(_id=WORLD_WOE_ID)` initiates an HTTP call to GET `https:// api.twitter.com/1.1/trends/place.json?id=1`. Note the URL mapping to the object chain that's constructed with the `twitter` package to make the request and how query string parameters are passed in as keyword arguments. To use the `twitter` package for arbitrary API requests, you generally construct the request in that kind of straightforward manner, with just a couple of minor caveats that we'll encounter soon enough.

Twitter imposes *rate limits* on how many requests an application can make to any given API resource within a given time window. Twitter's rate limits (*http://bit.ly/ 2x8c6yq*) are well documented, and each individual API resource also states its particular limits for your convenience (see Figure 1-3). For example, the API request that we just issued for trends limits applications to 75 requests per 15-minute window. For more nuanced information on how Twitter's rate limits work, consult the documentation (*http://bit.ly/2MsLpcH*). For the purposes of following along in this chapter, it's highly unlikely that you'll get rate-limited. (Example 9-17 will introduce some techniques demonstrating best practices while working with rate limits.)

 The developer documentation states that the results of a Trends API query are updated only once every five minutes, so it's not a judicious use of your efforts or API requests to ask for results more often than that.

Although it hasn't explicitly been stated yet, the semireadable output from Example 1-2 is printed out as native Python data structures. While an IPython interpreter will "pretty print" the output for you automatically, the Jupyter Notebook and a standard Python interpreter will not. If you find yourself in these circumstances, you may find it handy to use the built-in `json` package to force a nicer display, as illustrated in Example 1-3.

Twitter Developer Documentation

Docs / REST APIs / Rate Limits: Chart

Products & Services

Best practices
API overview
Websites
Cards
OAuth
REST APIs
API Rate Limits
Rate Limits: Chart
The Search API
The Search API: Tweets by Place
Working with Timelines
Collections

Rate Limits: Chart

Rate limits per window

The API rate limits described in this table refer to read-only / GET endpoints. Note that endpoints / resources not listed in the chart default to 15 requests per allotted user. All request windows are 15 minutes in length.

For POST operations, refer to Twitter's Account Limits support page in order to understand the daily limits that apply on a per-user basis.

Endpoint	Resource family	Requests / window (user auth)	Requests / window (app auth)
GET account/verify_credentials	application	75	0
GET application/rate_limit_status	application	180	180
GET favorites/list	favorites	75	75
GET followers/ids	followers	15	15
GET followers/list	followers	15	15

Figure 1-3. Rate limits for Twitter API resources are identified in the online documentation for each API call; shown here is the top of the chart of API calls and their respective rate limits

 JSON (*http://bit.ly/1a1l2lJ*) is a data exchange format that you will encounter on a regular basis. In a nutshell, JSON provides a way to arbitrarily store maps, lists, primitives such as numbers and strings, and combinations thereof. In other words, you can theoretically model just about anything with JSON should you desire to do so.

Example 1-3. Displaying API responses as pretty-printed JSON

```
import json

print(json.dumps(world_trends, indent=1))
print()
print(json.dumps(us_trends, indent=1))
```

An abbreviated sample response from the Trends API produced with `json.dumps` would look like the following:

```
[
 {
  "created_at": "2013-03-27T11:50:40Z",
  "trends":
  [
   {
```

```
    "url": "http://twitter.com/search?q=%23MentionSomeoneImportantForYou",
    "query": "%23MentionSomeoneImportantForYou",
    "name": "#MentionSomeoneImportantForYou",
    "promoted_content": null,
    "events": null
  },
   ...
 ]
}
]
```

Although it's easy enough to skim the two sets of trends and look for commonality, let's use Python's set (*http://bit.ly/1a1l2Sw*) data structure to automatically compute this for us, because that's exactly the kind of thing that sets lend themselves to doing. In this instance, a *set* refers to the mathematical notion of a data structure that stores an unordered collection of unique items and can be computed upon with other sets of items and setwise operations. For example, a setwise intersection computes common items between sets, a setwise union combines all of the items from sets, and the setwise difference among sets acts sort of like a subtraction operation in which items from one set are removed from another.

Example 1-4 demonstrates how to use a Python list comprehension (*http://bit.ly/ 1a1l1hy*) to parse out the names of the trending topics from the results that were previously queried, cast those lists to sets, and compute the setwise intersection to reveal the common items between them. Keep in mind that there may or may not be significant overlap between any given sets of trends, all depending on what's actually happening when you query for the trends. In other words, the results of your analysis will be entirely dependent upon your query and the data that is returned from it.

 Recall that Appendix C provides a reference for some common Python idioms like list comprehensions that you may find useful to review.

Example 1-4. Computing the intersection of two sets of trends

```
world_trends_set = set([trend['name']
                       for trend in world_trends[0]['trends']])

us_trends_set = set([trend['name']
                    for trend in us_trends[0]['trends']])

common_trends = world_trends_set.intersection(us_trends_set)

print(common_trends)
```

You should complete Example 1-4 before moving on in this chapter to ensure that you are able to access and analyze Twitter data. Can you explain what, if any, correlation exists between trends in your country and the rest of the world?

Set Theory, Intuition, and Countable Infinity

Computing setwise operations may seem a rather primitive form of analysis, but the ramifications of set theory for general mathematics are considerably more profound since it provides the foundation for many mathematical principles.

Georg Cantor is generally credited with formalizing the mathematics behind set theory, and his paper "On a Characteristic Property of All Real Algebraic Numbers" (1874) described it as part of his work on answering questions related to the concept of infinity. To understand how it works, consider the following question: is the set of positive integers larger in cardinality than the set of both positive and negative integers?

Although common intuition may be that there are twice as many positive and negative integers as positive integers alone, Cantor's work showed that the cardinalities of the sets are actually equal! Mathematically, he showed that you can map both sets of numbers such that they form a sequence with a definite starting point that extends forever in *one* direction like this: *{1, –1, 2, –2, 3, –3, …}*.

Because the numbers can be clearly enumerated but there is never an ending point, the cardinalities of the sets are said to be *countably infinite*. In other words, there is a definite sequence that could be followed deterministically if you simply had enough time to count them.

1.3.4 Searching for Tweets

One of the common items between the sets of trending topics turns out to be the hashtag #MentionSomeoneImportantForYou, so let's use it as the basis of a search query to fetch some tweets for further analysis. Example 1-5 illustrates how to exercise the GET search/tweets resource (*http://bit.ly/2QtIeF0*) for a particular query of interest, including the ability to use a special field that's included in the metadata for the search results to easily make additional requests for more search results. Coverage of Twitter's Streaming API (*http://bit.ly/2p7G8hf*) resources is out of scope for this chapter but it's introduced in Example 9-9 and may be more appropriate for many situations in which you want to maintain a constantly updated view of tweets.

The use of *args and **kwargs as illustrated in Example 1-5 as parameters to a function is a Python idiom for expressing arbitrary arguments and keyword arguments, respectively. See Appendix C for a brief overview of this idiom.

Example 1-5. Collecting search results

```python
# Set this variable to a trending topic, or anything else
# for that matter. The example query below was a
# trending topic when this content was being developed
# and is used throughout the remainder of this chapter.

q = '#MentionSomeoneImportantForYou'

count = 100

# Import unquote to prevent URL encoding errors in next_results
from urllib.parse import unquote

# See https://dev.twitter.com/rest/reference/get/search/tweets

search_results = twitter_api.search.tweets(q=q, count=count)

statuses = search_results['statuses']


# Iterate through 5 more batches of results by following the cursor
for _ in range(5):
    print('Length of statuses', len(statuses))
    try:
        next_results = search_results['search_metadata']['next_results']
    except KeyError as e: # No more results when next_results doesn't exist
        break

    # Create a dictionary from next_results, which has the following form:
    # ?max_id=847960489447628799&q=%23RIPSelena&count=100&include_entities=1
    kwargs = dict([ kv.split('=') for kv in unquote(next_results[1:]).split("&") ])

    search_results = twitter_api.search.tweets(**kwargs)
    statuses += search_results['statuses']

# Show one sample search result by slicing the list...
print(json.dumps(statuses[0], indent=1))
```

Although we're just passing in a hashtag to the Search API at this point, it's well worth noting that it contains a number of powerful operators (*http://bit.ly/2CTxv3O*) that allow you to filter queries according to the existence or nonexistence of various keywords, originator of the tweet, location associated with the tweet, etc.

In essence, all the code does is repeatedly make requests to the Search API. One thing that might initially catch you off guard if you've worked with other web APIs (including version 1 of Twitter's API) is that there's no explicit concept of *pagination* in the Search API itself. Reviewing the API documentation reveals that this is an intentional decision, and there are some good reasons for taking a *cursoring* approach instead, given the highly dynamic state of Twitter resources. The best practices for cursoring vary a bit throughout the Twitter developer platform, with the Search API providing a slightly simpler way of navigating search results than other resources such as timelines.

Search results contain a special `search_metadata` node that embeds a `next_results` field with a query string that provides the basis of a subsequent query. If we weren't using a library like `twitter` to make the HTTP requests for us, this preconstructed query string would just be appended to the Search API URL, and we'd update it with additional parameters for handling OAuth. However, since we are not making our HTTP requests directly, we must parse the query string into its constituent key/value pairs and provide them as keyword arguments.

In Python parlance, we are *unpacking* the values in a dictionary into keyword arguments that the function receives. In other words, the function call inside of the `for` loop in Example 1-5 ultimately invokes a function like

```
twitter_api.search.tweets(q='%23MentionSomeoneImportantForYou',
    include_entities=1, max_id=313519052523986943)
```

even though it appears in the source code as `twitter_api.search.tweets(**kwargs)`, with `kwargs` being a dictionary of key/value pairs.

 The `search_metadata` field also contains a `refresh_url` value that can be used if you'd like to maintain and periodically update your collection of results with new information that's become available since the previous query.

The next sample tweet shows the search results for a query for #MentionSomeoneImportantForYou. Take a moment to peruse (all of) it. As I mentioned earlier, there's a lot more to a tweet than meets the eye. The particular tweet that follows is fairly representative and contains in excess of 5 KB of total content when represented in uncompressed JSON. That's more than 40 times the amount of data that makes up the 140 characters of text (the limit at the time) that's normally thought of as a tweet!

```
[
  {
    "contributors": null,
    "truncated": false,
    "text": "RT @hassanmusician: #MentionSomeoneImportantForYou God.",
```

```
"in_reply_to_status_id": null,
"id": 316948241264549888,
"favorite_count": 0,
"source": "Twitter for Android",
"retweeted": false,
"coordinates": null,
"entities": {
 "user_mentions": [
  {
    "id": 56259379,
    "indices": [
     3,
     18
    ],
    "id_str": "56259379",
    "screen_name": "hassanmusician",
    "name": "Download the NEW LP!"
  }
 ],
 "hashtags": [
  {
    "indices": [
     20,
     50
    ],
    "text": "MentionSomeoneImportantForYou"
  }
 ],
 "urls": []
},
"in_reply_to_screen_name": null,
"in_reply_to_user_id": null,
"retweet_count": 23,
"id_str": "316948241264549888",
"favorited": false,
"retweeted_status": {
 "contributors": null,
 "truncated": false,
 "text": "#MentionSomeoneImportantForYou God.",
 "in_reply_to_status_id": null,
 "id": 316944833233186816,
 "favorite_count": 0,
 "source": "web",
 "retweeted": false,
 "coordinates": null,
 "entities": {
  "user_mentions": [],
  "hashtags": [
   {
     "indices": [
      0,
      30
```

```
      ],
      "text": "MentionSomeoneImportantForYou"
    }
  ],
  "urls": []
},
"in_reply_to_screen_name": null,
"in_reply_to_user_id": null,
"retweet_count": 23,
"id_str": "316944833233186816",
"favorited": false,
"user": {
 "follow_request_sent": null,
 "profile_use_background_image": true,
 "default_profile_image": false,
 "id": 56259379,
 "verified": false,
 "profile_text_color": "3C3940",
 "profile_image_url_https": "https://si0.twimg.com/profile_images/...",
 "profile_sidebar_fill_color": "95E8EC",
 "entities": {
  "url": {
   "urls": [
    {
     "url": "http://t.co/yRX89YM4J0",
     "indices": [
      0,
      22
     ],
     "expanded_url": "http://www.datpiff.com/mixtapes-detail.php?id=470069",
     "display_url": "datpiff.com/mixtapes-detai\u2026"
    }
   ]
  },
  "description": {
   "urls": []
  }
 },
 "followers_count": 105041,
 "profile_sidebar_border_color": "000000",
 "id_str": "56259379",
 "profile_background_color": "000000",
 "listed_count": 64,
 "profile_background_image_url_https": "https://si0.twimg.com/profile...",
 "utc_offset": -18000,
 "statuses_count": 16691,
 "description": "#TheseAreTheWordsISaid LP",
 "friends_count": 59615,
 "location": "",
 "profile_link_color": "91785A",
 "profile_image_url": "http://a0.twimg.com/profile_images/...",
 "following": null,
```

```json
    "geo_enabled": true,
    "profile_banner_url": "https://si0.twimg.com/profile_banners/...",
    "profile_background_image_url": "http://a0.twimg.com/profile_...",
    "screen_name": "hassanmusician",
    "lang": "en",
    "profile_background_tile": false,
    "favourites_count": 6142,
    "name": "Download the NEW LP!",
    "notifications": null,
    "url": "http://t.co/yRX89YM4J0",
    "created_at": "Mon Jul 13 02:18:25 +0000 2009",
    "contributors_enabled": false,
    "time_zone": "Eastern Time (US & Canada)",
    "protected": false,
    "default_profile": false,
    "is_translator": false
  },
  "geo": null,
  "in_reply_to_user_id_str": null,
  "lang": "en",
  "created_at": "Wed Mar 27 16:08:31 +0000 2013",
  "in_reply_to_status_id_str": null,
  "place": null,
  "metadata": {
   "iso_language_code": "en",
   "result_type": "recent"
  }
 },
 "user": {
 "follow_request_sent": null,
 "profile_use_background_image": true,
 "default_profile_image": false,
 "id": 549413966,
 "verified": false,
 "profile_text_color": "3D1957",
 "profile_image_url_https": "https://si0.twimg.com/profile_images/...",
 "profile_sidebar_fill_color": "7AC3EE",
 "entities": {
  "description": {
   "urls": []
  }
 },
 "followers_count": 110,
 "profile_sidebar_border_color": "FFFFFF",
 "id_str": "549413966",
 "profile_background_color": "642D8B",
 "listed_count": 1,
 "profile_background_image_url_https": "https://si0.twimg.com/profile_...",
 "utc_offset": 0,
 "statuses_count": 1294,
 "description": "i BELIEVE do you? I admire n adore @justinbieber ",
 "friends_count": 346,
```

```
     "location": "All Around The World ",
     "profile_link_color": "FF0000",
     "profile_image_url": "http://a0.twimg.com/profile_images/3434...",
     "following": null,
     "geo_enabled": true,
     "profile_banner_url": "https://si0.twimg.com/profile_banners/...",
     "profile_background_image_url": "http://a0.twimg.com/profile_...",
     "screen_name": "LilSalima",
     "lang": "en",
     "profile_background_tile": true,
     "favourites_count": 229,
     "name": "KoKo :D",
     "notifications": null,
     "url": null,
     "created_at": "Mon Apr 09 17:51:36 +0000 2012",
     "contributors_enabled": false,
     "time_zone": "London",
     "protected": false,
     "default_profile": false,
     "is_translator": false
    },
    "geo": null,
    "in_reply_to_user_id_str": null,
    "lang": "en",
    "created_at": "Wed Mar 27 16:22:03 +0000 2013",
    "in_reply_to_status_id_str": null,
    "place": null,
    "metadata": {
     "iso_language_code": "en",
     "result_type": "recent"
    }
   },
   ...
]
```

Tweets are imbued with some of the richest metadata that you'll find on the social web, and Chapter 9 elaborates on some of the many possibilities.

1.4 Analyzing the 140 (or More) Characters

The online documentation is always the definitive source for Twitter platform objects, and it's worthwhile to bookmark the Tweet objects (*http://bit.ly/2OhPimp*) page, because it's one that you'll refer to quite frequently as you get familiarized with the basic anatomy of a tweet. No attempt is made here or elsewhere in the book to regurgitate online documentation, but a few notes are of interest given that you might still be a bit overwhelmed by the 5 KB of information that a tweet comprises. For simplicity of nomenclature, let's assume that we've extracted a single tweet from the search results and stored it in a variable named t. For example, t.keys() returns the top-level fields for the tweet and t['id'] accesses the identifier of the tweet.

If you're following along with the Jupyter Notebook for this chapter, the exact tweet that's under scrutiny is stored in a variable named t so that you can interactively access its fields and explore more easily. The current discussion assumes the same nomenclature, so values should correspond one-for-one.

Here are a few points of interest:

- The human-readable text of a tweet is available through t['text']:

```
RT @hassanmusician: #MentionSomeoneImportantForYou God.
```

- The entities in the text of a tweet are conveniently processed for you and available through t['entities']:

```
{
  "user_mentions": [
    {
      "indices": [
        3,
        18
      ],
      "screen_name": "hassanmusician",
      "id": 56259379,
      "name": "Download the NEW LP!",
      "id_str": "56259379"
    }
  ],
  "hashtags": [
    {
      "indices": [
        20,
        50
      ],
      "text": "MentionSomeoneImportantForYou"
    }
  ],
  "urls": []
}
```

- Clues to the "interestingness" of a tweet are available through t['favorite_count'] and t['retweet_count'], which return the number of times it's been bookmarked or retweeted, respectively.

- If a tweet has been retweeted, the t['retweeted_status'] field provides significant detail about the original tweet itself and its author. Keep in mind that sometimes the text of a tweet changes as it is retweeted, as users add reactions or otherwise manipulate the content.

- The t['retweeted'] field denotes whether or not the authenticated user (via an authorized application) has retweeted this particular tweet. Fields whose values vary depending upon the point of view of the particular user are denoted in Twitter's developer documentation as *perspectival*.

- Additionally, note that only original tweets are retweeted from the standpoint of the API and information management. Thus, the retweet_count reflects the total number of times that the original tweet has been retweeted and should reflect the same value in both the original tweet and all subsequent retweets. In other words, retweets aren't retweeted. It may be a bit counterintuitive at first, but if you think you're retweeting a retweet, you're actually just retweeting the original tweet that you were exposed to through a proxy. See "Examining Patterns in Retweets" on page 35 later in this chapter for a more nuanced discussion about the difference between retweeting versus quoting a tweet.

A common mistake is to check the value of the retweeted field to determine whether or not a tweet has ever been retweeted by anyone. To check whether a tweet has ever been retweeted, you should instead see whether a retweeted_status node wrapper exists in the tweet.

You should tinker around with the sample tweet and consult the documentation to clarify any lingering questions you might have before moving forward. A good working knowledge of a tweet's anatomy is critical to effectively mining Twitter data.

1.4.1 Extracting Tweet Entities

Next, let's distill the entities and the text of some tweets into a convenient data structure for further examination. Example 1-6 extracts the text, screen names, and hashtags from the tweets that are collected and introduces a Python idiom called a *double* (or *nested*) *list comprehension*. If you understand a (single) list comprehension, the code formatting should illustrate the double list comprehension as simply a collection of values that are derived from a nested loop as opposed to the results of a single loop. List comprehensions are particularly powerful because they usually yield substantial performance gains over nested lists and provide an intuitive (once you're familiar with them) yet terse syntax.

List comprehensions are used frequently throughout this book, and it's worth consulting Appendix C or the official Python tutorial (*http://bit.ly/2otMTZc*) for more details if you'd like additional context.

Example 1-6. Extracting text, screen names, and hashtags from tweets

```
status_texts = [ status['text']
                 for status in statuses ]

screen_names = [ user_mention['screen_name']
                 for status in statuses
                     for user_mention in status['entities']['user_mentions'] ]

hashtags = [ hashtag['text']
             for status in statuses
                 for hashtag in status['entities']['hashtags'] ]

# Compute a collection of all words from all tweets
words = [ w
          for t in status_texts
              for w in t.split() ]

# Explore the first 5 items for each...

print(json.dumps(status_texts[0:5], indent=1))
print(json.dumps(screen_names[0:5], indent=1))
print(json.dumps(hashtags[0:5], indent=1))
print(json.dumps(words[0:5], indent=1))
```

In Python, syntax in which square brackets appear after a list or string value, such as `status_texts[0:5]`, is indicative of *slicing*, whereby you can easily extract items from lists or substrings from strings. In this particular case, `[0:5]` indicates that you'd like the first five items in the list `status_texts` (corresponding to items at indices 0 through 4). See Appendix C for a more extended description of slicing in Python.

Sample output follows—it displays five status texts, screen names, and hashtags to provide a feel for what's in the data:

```
[
 "\u201c@KathleenMariee_: #MentionSomeOneImportantForYou @AhhlicksCruise...,
 "#MentionSomeoneImportantForYou My bf @Linkin_Sunrise.",
 "RT @hassanmusician: #MentionSomeoneImportantForYou God.",
 "#MentionSomeoneImportantForYou @Louis_Tomlinson",
 "#MentionSomeoneImportantForYou @Delta_Universe"
]
[
 "KathleenMariee_",
 "AhhlicksCruise",
 "itsravennn_cx",
 "kandykisses_13",
 "BMOLOGY"
]
```

```
[
  "MentionSomeOneImportantForYou",
  "MentionSomeoneImportantForYou",
  "MentionSomeoneImportantForYou",
  "MentionSomeoneImportantForYou",
  "MentionSomeoneImportantForYou"
]
[
  "\u201c@KathleenMariee_:",
  "#MentionSomeOneImportantForYou",
  "@AhhlicksCruise",
  ",",
  "@itsravennn_cx"
]
```

As expected, #MentionSomeoneImportantForYou dominates the hashtag output. The output also provides a few commonly occurring screen names that are worth investigating.

1.4.2 Analyzing Tweets and Tweet Entities with Frequency Analysis

Virtually all analysis boils down to the simple exercise of counting things on some level, and much of what we'll be doing in this book is manipulating data so that it can be counted and further manipulated in meaningful ways.

From an empirical standpoint, counting observable things is the starting point for just about everything, and thus the starting point for any kind of statistical filtering or manipulation that strives to find what may be a faint signal in noisy data. Whereas we just extracted the first 5 items of each unranked list to get a feel for the data, let's now take a closer look at what's in the data by computing a frequency distribution and looking at the top 10 items in each list.

As of Python 2.4, a collections (*http://bit.ly/2nIrA6n*) module is available that provides a counter that makes computing a frequency distribution rather trivial. Example 1-7 demonstrates how to use a Counter to compute frequency distributions as ranked lists of terms. Among the more compelling reasons for mining Twitter data is to try to answer the question of what people are talking about *right now*. One of the simplest techniques you could apply to answer this question is basic frequency analysis, just as we are performing here.

Example 1-7. Creating a basic frequency distribution from the words in tweets

```
from collections import Counter

for item in [words, screen_names, hashtags]:
    c = Counter(item)
    print(c.most_common()[:10]) # top 10
    print()
```

Here are some sample results from frequency analysis of tweets:

```
[(u'#MentionSomeoneImportantForYou', 92), (u'RT', 34), (u'my', 10),
(u',', 6), (u'@justinbieber', 6), (u'<3', 6), (u'My', 5), (u'and', 4),
(u'I', 4), (u'te', 3)]

[(u'justinbieber', 6), (u'Kid_Charliej', 2), (u'Cavillafuerte', 2),
(u'touchmestyles_', 1), (u'aliceorr96', 1), (u'gymleeam', 1), (u'fienas', 1),
(u'nayely_1D', 1), (u'angelchute', 1)]

[(u'MentionSomeoneImportantForYou', 94), (u'mentionsomeoneimportantforyou', 3),
(u'Love', 1), (u'MentionSomeOneImportantForYou', 1),
(u'MyHeart', 1),  (u'bebesito', 1)]
```

The result of the frequency distribution is a map of key/value pairs corresponding to terms and their frequencies, so let's make reviewing the results a little easier on the eyes by emitting a tabular format. You can install a package called `prettytable` by typing **pip install prettytable** in a terminal; this package provides a convenient way to emit a fixed-width tabular format that can be easily copied and pasted.

Example 1-8 shows how to use it to display the same results.

Example 1-8. Using prettytable to display tuples in a nice tabular format

```
from prettytable import PrettyTable

for label, data in (('Word', words),
                    ('Screen Name', screen_names),
                    ('Hashtag', hashtags)):
    pt = PrettyTable(field_names=[label, 'Count'])
    c = Counter(data)
    [ pt.add_row(kv) for kv in c.most_common()[:10] ]
    pt.align[label], pt.align['Count'] = 'l', 'r' # Set column alignment
    print(pt)
```

The results from Example 1-8 are displayed as a series of nicely formatted text-based tables that are easy to skim, as the following output demonstrates:

```
+----------------------------------+-------+
| Word                             | Count |
+----------------------------------+-------+
| #MentionSomeoneImportantForYou   |    92 |
| RT                               |    34 |
| my                               |    10 |
| ,                                |     6 |
| @justinbieber                    |     6 |
| &lt;3                            |     6 |
| My                               |     5 |
| and                              |     4 |
| I                                |     4 |
| te                               |     3 |
```

```
+----------------------------------+------+
+----------------+------+
| Screen Name    | Count |
+----------------+------+
| justinbieber   |    6 |
| Kid_Charliej   |    2 |
| Cavillafuerte  |    2 |
| touchmestyles_ |    1 |
| aliceorr96     |    1 |
| gymleeam       |    1 |
| fienas         |    1 |
| nayely_1D      |    1 |
| angelchute     |    1 |
+----------------+------+
+---------------------------------+------+
| Hashtag                         | Count |
+---------------------------------+------+
| MentionSomeoneImportantForYou   |   94 |
| mentionsomeoneimportantforyou   |    3 |
| NoHomo                          |    1 |
| Love                            |    1 |
| MentionSomeOneImportantForYou   |    1 |
| MyHeart                         |    1 |
| bebesito                        |    1 |
+---------------------------------+------+
```

A quick skim of the results reveals at least one marginally surprising thing: Justin Bieber is high on the list of entities for this small sample of data, and given his popularity with tweens on Twitter he may very well have been the "most important someone" for this trending topic, though the results here are inconclusive. The appearance of <3 is also interesting because it is an escaped form of <3, which represents a heart shape (that's rotated 90 degrees, like other emoticons and smileys) and is a common abbreviation for "loves." Given the nature of the query, it's not surprising to see a value like <3, although it may initially seem like junk or noise.

Although the entities with a frequency greater than two are interesting, the broader results are also revealing in other ways. For example, "RT" was a very common token, implying that there were a significant number of retweets (we'll investigate this observation further in "Examining Patterns in Retweets" on page 35). Finally, as might be expected, the #MentionSomeoneImportantForYou hashtag and a couple of case-sensitive variations dominated the hashtags; a data-processing takeaway is that it would be worthwhile to normalize each word, screen name, and hashtag to lowercase when tabulating frequencies since there will inevitably be variation in tweets.

1.4.3 Computing the Lexical Diversity of Tweets

A slightly more advanced measurement that involves calculating simple frequencies and can be applied to unstructured text is a metric called *lexical diversity*. Mathematically, this is an expression of the number of *unique* tokens in the text divided by the *total* number of tokens in the text, which are both elementary yet important metrics in and of themselves. Lexical diversity is an interesting concept in the area of interpersonal communications because it provides a quantitative measure for the diversity of an individual's or group's vocabulary. For example, suppose you are listening to someone who repeatedly says "and stuff" to broadly generalize information as opposed to providing specific examples to reinforce points with more detail or clarity. Now, contrast that speaker to someone else who seldom uses the word "stuff" to generalize and instead reinforces points with concrete examples. The speaker who repeatedly says "and stuff" would have a lower lexical diversity than the speaker who uses a more diverse vocabulary, and chances are reasonably good that you'd walk away from the conversation feeling as though the speaker with the higher lexical diversity understands the subject matter better.

As applied to tweets or similar online communications, lexical diversity can be worth considering as a primitive statistic for answering a number of questions, such as how broad or narrow the subject matter is that an individual or group discusses. Although an overall assessment could be interesting, breaking down the analysis to specific time periods could yield additional insight, as could comparing different groups or individuals. For example, it would be interesting to measure whether or not there is a significant difference between the lexical diversity of two soft drink companies such as Coca-Cola (*http://bit.ly/1a1l5xR*) and Pepsi (*http://bit.ly/1a1l7pt*) as an entry point for exploration if you were comparing the effectiveness of their social media marketing campaigns on Twitter.

With a basic understanding of how to use a statistic like lexical diversity to analyze textual content such as tweets, let's now compute the lexical diversity for statuses, screen names, and hashtags for our working data set, as shown in Example 1-9.

Example 1-9. Calculating lexical diversity for tweets

```
# A function for computing lexical diversity
def lexical_diversity(tokens):
    return len(set(tokens))/len(tokens)

# A function for computing the average number of words per tweet
def average_words(statuses):
    total_words = sum([ len(s.split()) for s in statuses ])
    return total_words/len(statuses)

print(lexical_diversity(words))
```

```
print(lexical_diversity(screen_names))
print(lexical_diversity(hashtags))
print(average_words(status_texts))
```

 Prior to Python 3.0, the division operator (/) applies the floor function and returns an integer value (unless one of the operands is a floating-point value). If we were using Python 2.x, we would have had to multiply either the numerator or the denominator by 1.0 to avoid truncation errors.

The results of Example 1-9 follow:

```
0.67610619469
0.955414012739
0.0686274509804
5.76530612245
```

There are a few observations worth considering in the results:

- The lexical diversity of the words in the text of the tweets is around 0.67. One way to interpret that figure would be to say that about two out of every three words is unique, or you might say that each status update carries around 67% unique information. Given that the average number of words in each tweet is around six, that translates to about four unique words per tweet. Intuition aligns with the data in that the nature of a #MentionSomeoneImportantForYou trending hashtag is to solicit a response that will probably be a few words long. In any event, a value of 0.67 is on the high side for lexical diversity of ordinary human communication, but given the nature of the data, it seems reasonable.

- The lexical diversity of the screen names, however, is even higher, with a value of 0.95, which means that about 19 out of 20 screen names mentioned are unique. This observation also makes sense given that many answers to the question will be a screen name, and that most people won't be providing the same responses for the solicitous hashtag.

- The lexical diversity of the hashtags is extremely low, with a value of around 0.068, implying that very few values other than the #MentionSomeoneImportant-ForYou hashtag appear multiple times in the results. Again, this makes good sense given that most responses are short and that hashtags really wouldn't make much sense to introduce as a response to the prompt of mentioning someone important for you.

- The average number of words per tweet is very low at a value of just under 6, which makes sense given the nature of the hashtag, which is designed to solicit short responses consisting of just a few words.

What would be interesting at this point would be to zoom in on some of the data and see if there were any common responses or other insights that could come from a more qualitative analysis. Given an average number of words per tweet as low as 6, it's unlikely that users applied any abbreviations to stay within the character limit, so the amount of noise for the data should be remarkably low, and additional frequency analysis may reveal some fascinating things.

1.4.4 Examining Patterns in Retweets

Even though the user interface and many Twitter clients have long since adopted the native Retweet API used to populate status values such as `retweet_count` and `retwee ted_status`, some Twitter users may prefer to retweet with comment (*http://bit.ly/ 1a1l7FZ*), which entails a workflow involving copying and pasting the text and prepending "RT @*username*" or suffixing "/via @*username*" to provide attribution.

 When mining Twitter data, you'll probably want to both account for the tweet metadata and use heuristics to analyze the character strings for conventions such as "RT @*username*" or "/via @*user-name*" when considering retweets, in order to maximize the efficacy of your analysis. See "Finding Users Who Have Retweeted a Status" for a more detailed discussion on retweeting with Twitter's native Retweet API versus "quoting" tweets and using conventions to apply attribution.

A good exercise at this point would be to further analyze the data to determine if there was a particular tweet that was highly retweeted or if there were just lots of "one-off" retweets. The approach we'll take to find the most popular retweets is to simply iterate over each status update and store out the retweet count, originator of the retweet, and text of the retweet if the status update is a retweet. Example 1-10 demonstrates how to capture these values with a list comprehension and sort by the retweet count to display the top few results.

Example 1-10. Finding the most popular retweets

```
retweets = [
            # Store out a tuple of these three values...
            (status['retweet_count'],
             status['retweeted_status']['user']['screen_name'],
             status['text'])

            # ... for each status...
            for status in statuses

            # ... so long as the status meets this condition
                if 'retweeted_status' in status.keys()
```

```
                    ]

# Slice off the first 5 from the sorted results and display each item in the tuple

pt = PrettyTable(field_names=['Count', 'Screen Name', 'Text'])
[ pt.add_row(row) for row in sorted(retweets, reverse=True)[:5] ]
pt.max_width['Text'] = 50
pt.align= 'l'
print(pt)
```

Results from Example 1-10 are interesting:

```
+-------+-----------------+----------------------------------------------------+
| Count | Screen Name     | Text                                               |
+-------+-----------------+----------------------------------------------------+
| 23    | hassanmusician  | RT @hassanmusician: #MentionSomeoneImportantForYou |
|       |                 | God.                                               |
| 21    | HSweethearts    | RT @HSweethearts: #MentionSomeoneImportantForYou   |
|       |                 | my high school sweetheart ❤                        |
| 15    | LosAlejandro_   | RT @LosAlejandro_: ¿Nadie te menciono en           |
|       |                 | "#MentionSomeoneImportantForYou"? JAJAJAJAJAJAJAJA  |
|       |                 | JAJAJAJAJAJAJAJAJAJAJAJAJAJAJAJAJAJAJAJA Ven, ...   |
| 9     | SCOTTSUMME      | RT @SCOTTSUMME: #MentionSomeoneImportantForYou My   |
|       |                 | Mum. Shes loving, caring, strong, all in one. I    |
|       |                 | love her so much ❤❤❤❤                              |
| 7     | degrassihaha    | RT @degrassihaha: #MentionSomeoneImportantForYou I  |
|       |                 | can't put every Degrassi cast member, crew member, |
|       |                 | and writer in just one tweet....                   |
+-------+-----------------+----------------------------------------------------+
```

"God" tops the list, followed closely by "my high school sweetheart," and coming in at number four on the list is "My Mum." None of the top five items in the list correspond to Twitter user accounts, although we might have suspected this (with the exception of @justinbieber) from the previous analysis. Inspection of results further down the list does reveal particular user mentions, but the sample we have drawn from for this query is so small that no trends emerge. Searching for a larger sample of results would likely yield some user mentions with a frequency greater than one, which would be interesting to further analyze. The possibilities for further analysis are pretty open-ended, and by now, hopefully, you're itching to try out some custom queries of your own.

 Suggested exercises are at the end of this chapter. Be sure to also check out Chapter 9 as a source of inspiration: it includes more than two dozen recipes presented in a cookbook-style format.

Before we move on, a subtlety worth noting is that it's quite possible (and probable, given the relatively low frequencies of the retweets observed in this section) that the original tweets that were retweeted may not exist in our sample search results set. For example, the most popular retweet in the sample results originated from a user with a screen name of @hassanmusician and was retweeted 23 times. However, closer inspection of the data reveals that we collected only 1 of the 23 retweets in our search results. Neither the original tweet nor any of the other 22 retweets appears in the data set. This doesn't pose any particular problems, although it might beg the question of who the other 22 retweeters for this status were.

The answer to this kind of question is a valuable one because it allows us to take content that represents a concept, such as "God" in this case, and discover a group of other users who apparently share the same sentiment or common interest. As previously mentioned, a handy way to model data involving people and the things that they're interested in is called an *interest graph*; this is the primary data structure that supports analysis in Chapter 8. Interpretative speculation about these users could suggest that they are spiritual or religious individuals, and further analysis of their particular tweets might corroborate that inference. Example 1-11 shows how to find individuals with the GET statuses/retweets/:id API (*http://bit.ly/2BHBEaq*).

Example 1-11. Looking up users who have retweeted a status

```
# Get the original tweet id for a tweet from its retweeted_status node
# and insert it here in place of the sample value that is provided
# from the text of the book

_retweets = twitter_api.statuses.retweets(id=317127304981667841)
print([r['user']['screen_name'] for r in _retweets])
```

Further analysis of the users who retweeted this particular status for any particular religious or spiritual affiliation is left as an independent exercise.

1.4.5 Visualizing Frequency Data with Histograms

A nice feature of the Jupyter Notebook is its ability to generate and insert high-quality and customizable plots of data as part of an interactive workflow. In particular, the matplotlib (*http://bit.ly/1a1l7Wv*) package and other scientific computing tools that are available for the Jupyter Notebook are quite powerful and capable of generating complex figures with very little effort once you understand the basic workflows.

To illustrate the use of matplotlib's plotting capabilities, let's plot some data for display. To get warmed up, we'll consider a plot that displays the results from the words variable as defined in Example 1-9. With the help of a Counter, it's easy to generate a sorted list of tuples where each tuple is a (word, frequency) pair; the x-axis value will correspond to the index of the tuple, and the y-axis will correspond to the frequency for the word in that tuple. It would generally be impractical to try to plot each word as a value on the x-axis, although that's what the x-axis is representing. Figure 1-4 displays a plot for the same words data that we previously rendered as a table in Example 1-8. The y-axis values on the plot correspond to the number of times a word appeared. Although labels for each word are not provided, x-axis values have been sorted so that the relationship between word frequencies is more apparent. Each axis has been adjusted to a logarithmic scale to "squash" the curve being displayed. The plot can be generated directly in the Jupyter Notebook with the code shown in Example 1-12.

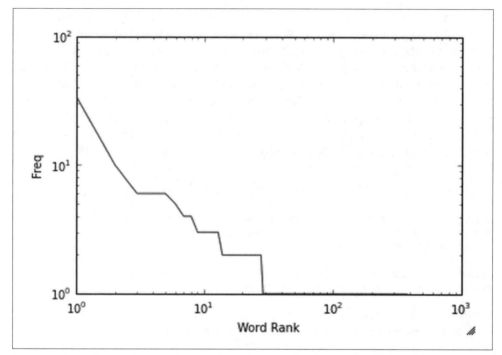

Figure 1-4. A plot displaying the sorted frequencies for the words computed by Example 1-8

In 2014, the use of the `--pylab` flag when launching the IPython/ Jupyter Notebook was deprecated. The same year, Fernando Pérez launched Project Jupyter. In order to enable inline plots within the Jupyter Notebook, include the `%matplotlib` magics (*http://bit.ly/ 2nrbbkQ*) within a code cell:

```
%matplotlib inline
```

Example 1-12. Plotting frequencies of words

```python
import matplotlib.pyplot as plt
%matplotlib inline

word_counts = sorted(Counter(words).values(), reverse=True)

plt.loglog(word_counts)
plt.ylabel("Freq")
plt.xlabel("Word Rank")
```

A plot of frequency values is intuitive and convenient, but it can also be useful to group together data values into bins that correspond to a range of frequencies. For example, how many words have a frequency between 1 and 5, between 5 and 10, between 10 and 15, and so forth? A *histogram (http://bit.ly/1a1l6Sk)* is designed for precisely this purpose and provides a convenient visualization for displaying tabulated frequencies as adjacent rectangles, where the area of each rectangle is a measure of the data values that fall within that particular range of values. Figures 1-5 and 1-6 show histograms of the tabular data generated from Examples 1-8 and 1-10, respectively. Although the histograms don't have x-axis labels that show us which words have which frequencies, that's not really their purpose. A histogram gives us insight into the underlying frequency distribution, with the x-axis corresponding to a range for words that each have a frequency within that range and the y-axis corresponding to the total frequency of all words that appear within that range.

When interpreting Figure 1-5, look back to the corresponding tabular data and consider that there are a large number of words, screen names, or hashtags that have low frequency and appear few times in the text; however, when we combine all of these low-frequency terms and bin them together into a range of "all words with frequency between 1 and 10," we see that the total number of these low-frequency words accounts for most of the text. More concretely, we see that there are approximately 10 words that account for almost all of the frequencies as rendered by the area of the large blue rectangle, while there are just a couple of words with much higher frequencies: "#MentionSomeoneImportantForYou" and "RT," with respective frequencies of 34 and 92 as given by our tabulated data.

Likewise, when interpreting Figure 1-6, we see that there are a select few tweets that are retweeted with a much higher frequencies than the bulk of the tweets, which are retweeted only once and account for the majority of the volume given by the largest blue rectangle on the left side of the histogram.

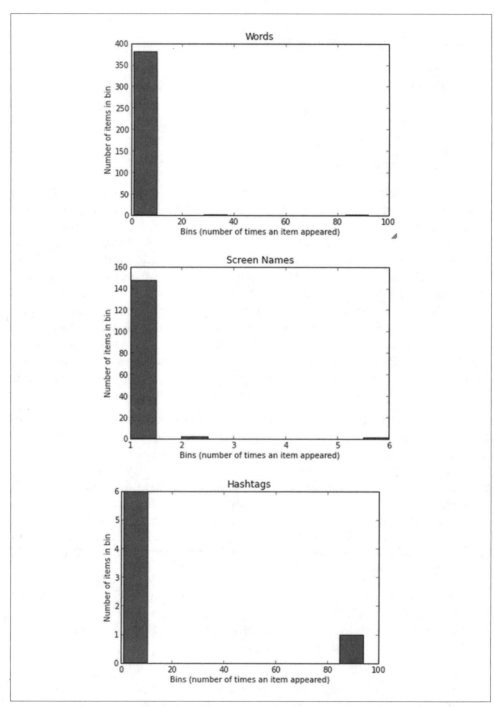

Figure 1-5. Histograms of tabulated frequency data for words, screen names, and hash-tags, each displaying a particular kind of data that is grouped by frequency

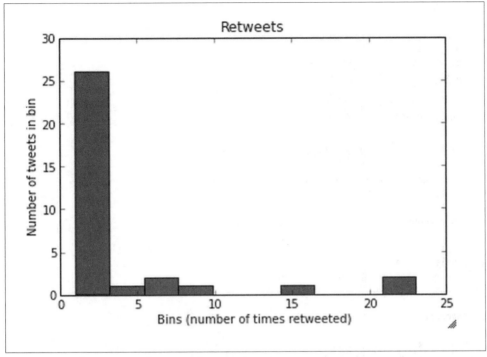

Figure 1-6. A histogram of retweet frequencies

The code for generating these histograms directly in the Jupyter Notebook is given in Examples 1-13 and 1-14. Taking some time to explore the capabilities of `matplotlib` and other scientific computing tools is a worthwhile investment.

 Installation of scientific computing tools such as `matplotlib` can potentially be a frustrating experience because of certain dynamically loaded libraries in their dependency chains, and the pain involved can vary from version to version and operating system to operating system. It is highly recommended that you take advantage of the virtual machine experience for this book, as outlined in Appendix A, if you don't already have these tools installed.

Example 1-13. Generating histograms of words, screen names, and hashtags

```
for label, data in (('Words', words),
                    ('Screen Names', screen_names),
                    ('Hashtags', hashtags)):

    # Build a frequency map for each set of data
    # and plot the values
    c = Counter(data)
```

```
plt.hist(c.values())

# Add a title and y-label...
plt.title(label)
plt.ylabel("Number of items in bin")
plt.xlabel("Bins (number of times an item appeared)")

# ... and display as a new figure
plt.figure()
```

Example 1-14. Generating a histogram of retweet counts

```
# Using underscores while unpacking values in
# a tuple is idiomatic for discarding them

counts = [count for count, _, _ in retweets]

plt.hist(counts)
plt.title("Retweets")
plt.xlabel('Bins (number of times retweeted)')
plt.ylabel('Number of tweets in bin')

print(counts)
```

1.5 Closing Remarks

This chapter introduced Twitter as a successful technology platform that has grown virally and become "all the rage," given its ability to satisfy some fundamental human desires relating to communication, curiosity, and the self-organizing behavior that has emerged from its chaotic network dynamics. The example code in this chapter got you up and running with Twitter's API, illustrated how easy (and fun) it is to use Python to interactively explore and analyze Twitter data, and provided some starting templates that you can use for mining tweets. We started out the chapter by learning how to create an authenticated connection and then progressed through a series of examples that illustrated how to discover trending topics for particular locales, how to search for tweets that might be interesting, and how to analyze those tweets using some elementary but effective techniques based on frequency analysis and simple statistics. Even what seemed like a somewhat arbitrary trending topic turned out to lead us down worthwhile paths with lots of possibilities for additional analysis.

 Chapter 9 contains a number of Twitter recipes covering a broad array of topics that range from tweet harvesting and analysis to the effective use of storage for archiving tweets to techniques for analyzing followers for insights.

One of the primary takeaways from this chapter from an analytical standpoint is that counting is generally the first step to any kind of meaningful quantitative analysis. Although basic frequency analysis is simple, it is a powerful tool for your repertoire that shouldn't be overlooked just because it's so obvious; besides, many other advanced statistics depend on it. On the contrary, frequency analysis and measures such as lexical diversity should be employed early and often, for precisely the reason that doing so is so obvious and simple. Oftentimes, but not always, the results from the simplest techniques can rival the quality of those from more sophisticated analytics. With respect to data in the Twitterverse, these modest techniques can usually get you quite a long way toward answering the question, "What are people talking about right now?" Now that's something we'd all like to know, isn't it?

 The source code outlined for this chapter and all other chapters is available on GitHub (*http://bit.ly/Mining-the-Social-Web-3E*) in a convenient Jupyter Notebook format that you're highly encouraged to try out from the comfort of your own web browser.

1.6 Recommended Exercises

- Bookmark and spend some time reviewing the API reference index (*http://bit.ly/2Nb9CJS*). In particular, spend some time browsing the information on the REST API (*http://bit.ly/2nTNndF*) and API objects (*http://bit.ly/2oL2EdC*).

- If you haven't already, get comfortable working in IPython (*http://bit.ly/1a1laRY*) and the Jupyter Notebook (*http://bit.ly/2omIqdG*) as more productive alternatives to the traditional Python interpreter. Over the course of your social web mining career, the saved time and increased productivity will really start to add up.

- If you have a Twitter account with a nontrivial number of tweets, request your historical tweet archive from your account settings (*http://bit.ly/1a1lb8D*) and analyze it. The export of your account data includes files organized by time period in a convenient JSON format. See the *README.txt* file included in the downloaded archive for more details. What are the most common terms that appear in your tweets? Who do you retweet the most often? How many of your tweets are retweeted (and why do you think this is the case)?

- Take some time to explore Twitter's REST API using the command-line tool Twurl (*http://bit.ly/2NlQlte*). Although we opted to dive in with the `twitter` Python package in a programmatic fashion in this chapter, the console can be useful for exploring the API, the effects of parameters, and more.

- Complete the exercise of determining whether there seems to be a spiritual or religious affiliation for the users who retweeted the status citing "God" as someone important to them, or follow the workflow in this chapter for a trending topic or arbitrary search query of your own choosing. Explore some of the advanced search features (*http://bit.ly/2xlEHzB*) that are available for more precise querying.

- Explore Yahoo! GeoPlanet's Where On Earth ID API (*http://bit.ly/2MsvwCQ*) so that you can compare and contrast trends from different locales.

- Take a closer look at `matplotlib` (*http://bit.ly/1a1l7Wv*) and learn how to create beautiful plots of 2D and 3D data with the Jupyter Notebook (*http://bit.ly/1a1lccP*).

- Explore and apply some of the exercises from Chapter 9.

1.7 Online Resources

The following list of links from this chapter may be useful for review:

- Beautiful plots of 2D and 3D data with the Jupyter Notebook (*http://bit.ly/1a1lccP*)
- IPython "magic functions" (*http://bit.ly/2nII3ce*)
- json.org (*http://bit.ly/1a1l2lJ*)
- Python list comprehensions (*http://bit.ly/2otMTZc*)
- The official Python tutorial (*http://bit.ly/2oLozBz*)
- OAuth (*http://bit.ly/1a1kZWN*)
- Twitter API documentation (*http://bit.ly/1a1kSKQ*)
- Twitter API Rate Limiting in v1.1 (*http://bit.ly/2MsLpcH*)
- Twitter Developer Agreement & Policy (*http://bit.ly/2MSrryS*)
- Twitter's OAuth documentation (*http://bit.ly/2NawA3v*)
- Twitter Search API operators (*http://bit.ly/2xkjW7D*)
- Twitter Streaming API (*http://bit.ly/2Qzcdvd*)
- Twitter Terms of Service (*http://bit.ly/1a1kWKB*)
- Twurl (*http://bit.ly/1a1kZq1*)
- Yahoo! GeoPlanet's Where On Earth ID (*http://bit.ly/2NHdAJB*)

## CHAPTER 2

Mining Facebook: Analyzing Fan Pages, Examining Friendships, and More

In this chapter, we'll tap into the Facebook platform through its (Social) Graph API and explore some of the vast possibilities. Facebook is arguably the heart of the social web and is somewhat of an all-in-one wonder, given that more than half of its 2 billion users[1] are active each day updating statuses, posting photos, exchanging messages, chatting in real time, checking in to physical locales, playing games, shopping, and just about anything else you can imagine. From a social web mining standpoint, the wealth of data that Facebook stores about individuals, groups, and products is quite exciting, because Facebook's clean API presents incredible opportunities to synthesize it into information (the world's most precious commodity) and glean valuable insights. On the other hand, this great power brings great responsibility and Facebook has instrumented the most sophisticated set of online privacy controls (*http://on.fb.me/1a1llg9*) that the world has ever seen in order to help protect its users from exploit.

It's worth noting that although Facebook is self-proclaimed as a social graph, it's been steadily transforming into a valuable interest graph as well, because it maintains relationships between people and the things that they're interested in through its Facebook pages and the ability to indicate reactions (e.g., by clicking "Like"). In this regard, you may increasingly hear it framed as a "social interest graph." For the most part, you can make a case that interest graphs implicitly exist and can be bootstrapped from most sources of social data. As an example, Chapter 1 made the case that Twitter is actually an interest graph because of its asymmetric "following" (or, to say it

---

1 Internet usage statistics (*http://bit.ly/1a1ljF8*)show that the world's population in 2017 was estimated to be approximately 7.5 billion, with the estimated number of internet users being almost 3.9 billion.

another way, "interested in") relationships between people and other people, places, or things. The notion of Facebook as an interest graph will come up throughout this chapter, and we'll return to the idea of explicitly bootstrapping an interest graph from social data in Chapter 8.

The remainder of this chapter assumes that you have an active Facebook account (*http://on.fb.me/1a1lkcd*), which is required to gain access to the Facebook APIs. In 2015, Facebook made changes to its API (*http://tcrn.ch/2zFetfo*) that limited the kind of data that was available to third parties. For instance, you could no longer access your friend's status updates or interests over the API. This change was prompted by privacy concerns. Because of these changes, this chapter will focus more on how the Facebook API can be used to measure user engagement on public pages, such as those created by product companies or celebrities. Even this data is becoming increasingly privileged, and you may have to request approval from the Facebook developer platform to gain access to some of these features.

 Always get the latest bug-fixed source code for this chapter (and every other chapter) online at *http://bit.ly/Mining-the-Social-Web-3E*. Be sure to also take advantage of this book's virtual machine experience, as described in Appendix A, to maximize your enjoyment of the sample code.

2.1 Overview

As this is the second chapter in the book, the concepts we'll cover are a bit more complex than those in Chapter 1, but they should still be highly accessible to a broad audience. In this chapter you'll learn about:

- Facebook's Graph API and how to make API requests
- The Open Graph protocol and its relationship to Facebook's social graph
- Programmatically accessing the feeds of public pages, such as those of major brands and celebrities
- Extracting key social metrics, such as the number of likes, comments, and shares, as a measure of audience engagement
- Manipulating data using `pandas DataFrames`, then visualizing the results

2.2 Exploring Facebook's Graph API

The Facebook platform is a mature, robust, and well-documented gateway into what may be the most comprehensive and well-organized information store ever amassed, both in terms of breadth and depth. It's broad in that its user base represents about one-quarter of the entire world population, and it's deep with respect to the amount of information that's known about any one of its particular users. Whereas Twitter features an asymmetric friendship model that is open and predicated on following other users without any particular consent, Facebook's friendship model is symmetric and requires a mutual agreement between users to gain visibility into one another's interactions and activities.

Furthermore, whereas virtually all interactions except for private messages between users on Twitter are public statuses, Facebook allows for much more finely grained privacy controls in which friendships can be organized and maintained as lists with varying levels of visibility available to a friend on any particular activity. For example, you might choose to share a link or photo only with a particular list of friends as opposed to your entire social network.

As a social web miner, the only way that you can extract data from Facebook is by registering an application and using that application as the entry point into the Facebook developer platform. Moreover, the only data that's available to an application is whatever the user has explicitly authorized it to access. For example, as a developer writing a Facebook application, you'll be the user who's logging into the application, and the application will be able to access any data that you explicitly authorize it to access. In that regard, as a Facebook user you might think of an application a bit like any of your Facebook friends, in that you're ultimately in control of what the application can access and you can revoke access at any time. The Facebook Platform Policy document (*http://bit.ly/1a1lm3C*) is a must-read for any Facebook developer, as it provides the comprehensive set of rights and responsibilities for all Facebook users as well as the spirit and letter of the law for Facebook developers. If you haven't already, it's worth taking a moment to review Facebook's developer policies and to bookmark the Facebook Developers home page (*http://bit.ly/1a1lm3Q*), since it is the definitive entry point into the Facebook platform and its documentation. Also keep in mind that APIs can change. Concerns over security and privacy mean that the privileges available to you as you experiment with the Facebook platform will be limited. To access some features and API endpoints, you may have to submit your application (*http://bit.ly/2vDb2B1*) for review and be approved. As long as your application abides by the terms of service (*http://on.fb.me/1a1lMXM*), you should be fine.

 As a developer mining your own account, you may not have a problem allowing your application to access all of your account data. Beware, however, of aspiring to develop a successful *hosted* application that requests access to more than the minimum amount of data necessary to complete its task, because it's quite likely that a user will not trust your application to command that level of privilege (and rightly so).

Although we'll programmatically access the Facebook platform later in this chapter, Facebook provides a number of useful developer tools (*http://bit.ly/1a1lnVf*), including a Graph API Explorer app (*http://bit.ly/2jd5Xdq*)that we'll be using for initial familiarization with the social graph. The app provides an intuitive and turnkey way of querying the social graph, and once you're comfortable with how the social graph works, translating queries into Python code for automation and further processing comes quite naturally. Although we'll work through the Graph API as part of the discussion, you may benefit from an initial review of the well-written Graph API Overview (*http://bit.ly/1a1lobU*) as a comprehensive preamble.

 Please note that Facebook has ended support for its Facebook Query Language (FQL) (*http://bit.ly/1a1lmRd*). As of August 8, 2016, FQL can no longer be queried. Developers are required to make Graph API calls instead. If you have previously developed an app making use of FQL, Facebook has created an API Upgrade Tool (*http://bit.ly/2MGU7Z9*) that you can use to update it.

2.2.1 Understanding the Graph API

As its name implies, Facebook's social graph is a massive graph (*http://bit.ly/1a1loIX*) data structure representing social interactions and consisting of nodes and connections between the nodes. The Graph API provides the primary means of interacting with the social graph, and the best way to get acquainted with the API is to spend a few minutes tinkering around with the Graph API Explorer (*http://bit.ly/2jd5Xdq*).

It is important to note that the Graph API Explorer is not a particularly special tool of any kind. Aside from being able to prepopulate and debug your access token, it is an ordinary Facebook app that uses the same developer APIs that any other developer application would use. In fact, the Graph API Explorer is handy when you have a particular OAuth token that's associated with a specific set of authorizations for an application that you are developing and you want to run some queries as part of an exploratory development effort or debug cycle. We'll revisit this general idea shortly as we programmatically access the Graph API. Figures 2-1 through 2-3 illustrate a progressive series of Graph API queries that result from clicking the plus (+) symbol and adding connections and fields. There are a few items to note in these figures:

Access token

The access token that appears in the application is an OAuth (*http://bit.ly/ 1a1kZWN*) token that is provided as a courtesy for the logged-in user; it is the same OAuth token that your application would need to access the data in question. We'll opt to use this access token throughout this chapter, but you can consult Appendix B for a brief overview of OAuth, including details on implementing an OAuth flow for Facebook in order to retrieve an access token. As mentioned in Chapter 1, if this is your first encounter with OAuth, it's probably sufficient at this point to know that the protocol is a social web standard that stands for Open Authorization. In short, OAuth is a means of allowing users to authorize third-party applications to access their account data without needing to share sensitive information like a password.

 See Appendix B for details on implementing an OAuth 2.0 flow, which you will need to build an application that requires an arbitrary user to authorize it to access account data.

Node IDs

The basis of the query is a node with an ID (identifier) of "644382747," corresponding to a person named "Matthew A. Russell," who is preloaded as the currently logged-in user for the Graph Explorer. The "id" and "name" values for the node are called *fields*. The basis of the query could just as easily have been any other node, and as we'll soon see, it's very natural to "walk" or traverse the graph and query other nodes (which may be people or things, like books or TV shows).

Connection constraints

You can modify the original query with a "friends" connection, as shown in Figure 2-2, by clicking the + and then scrolling to "friends" in the "connections" pop-up menu. The "friends" connections that appear in the console represent nodes that are connected to the original query node. At this point, you could click any of the blue "id" fields in these nodes and initiate a query with that particular node as the basis. In network science terminology, you now have what is called an *ego graph*, because it has an actor (or *ego*) as its focal point or logical center, which is connected to other nodes around it. An ego graph would resemble a hub and spokes if you were to draw it.

Likes constraints

A further modification to the original query is to add "likes" connections for each of your friends, as shown in Figure 2-3. However, this data is now restricted and apps can no longer gain access to your friends' likes. Facebook has made changes to its API limiting the kinds of information apps have access to.

Debugging

The Debug button can be useful for troubleshooting queries that you think should be returning data but aren't doing so based on the authorizations associated with the access token.

JSON response format

The results of a Graph API query are returned in a convenient JSON format that can be easily manipulated and processed.

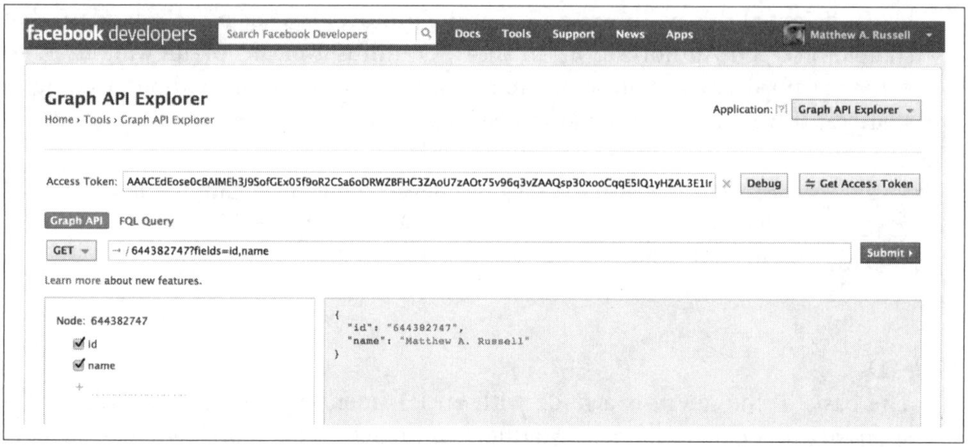

Figure 2-1. Using the Graph API Explorer application to query for a node in the social graph

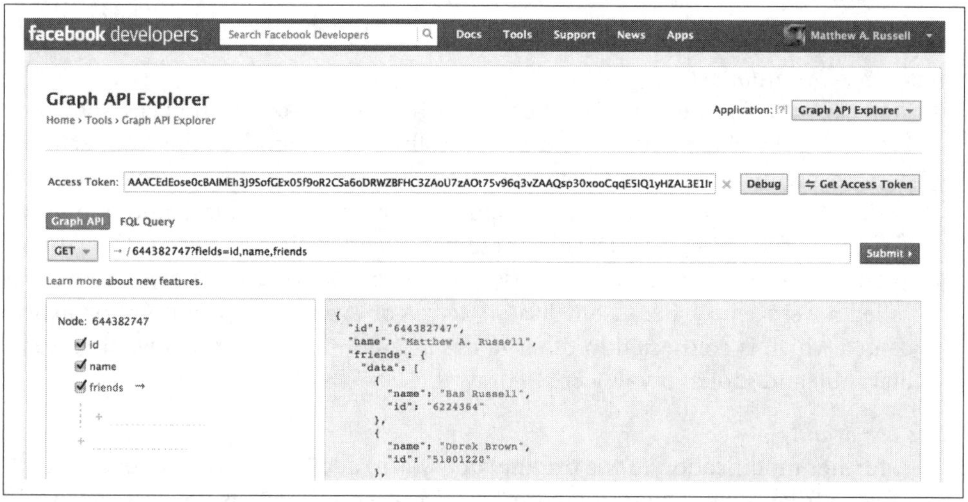

Figure 2-2. Using the Graph API Explorer application to progressively build up a query for a node and connections to friends. Keep in mind that certain data may require privileged access, and sandboxed applications have access to only very limited data. Facebook has made many changes to its data policies over the years.

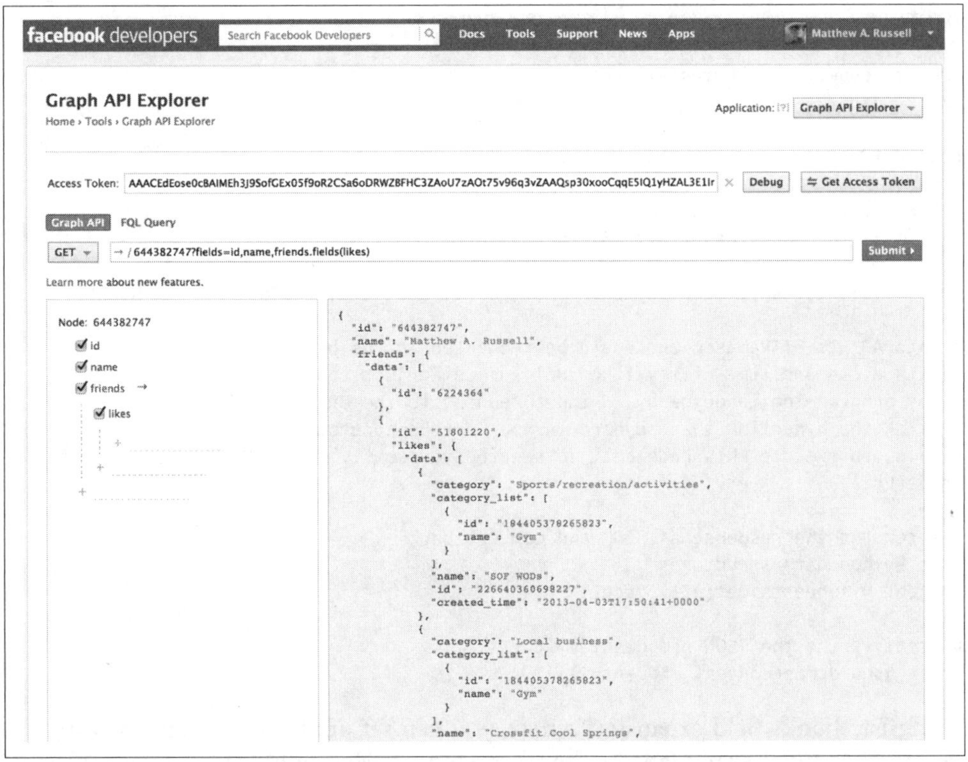

Figure 2-3. Using the Graph API Explorer application to progressively build up a query for friends' interests: a query for a node, connections to friends, and likes for those friends. This example is meant to be illustrative; Facebook's changing data policies have become stricter, with a greater emphasis on user privacy.

Although we'll programmatically explore the Graph API with a Python package later in this chapter, you could opt to make Graph API queries more directly over HTTP yourself by mimicking the request that you see in the Graph API Explorer. For example, Example 2-1 uses the `requests` (*http://bit.ly/1a1lrEt*) package to simplify the process of making an HTTP request (as opposed to using a much more cumbersome package from Python's standard library, such as `urllib`) for fetching your friends and their likes. You can install this package in a terminal with the predictable **pip install requests** command. The query is driven by the values in the `fields` parameter and is the same as what would be built up interactively in the Graph API Explorer. Of particular interest is that the `likes.limit(10){about}` syntax uses a feature of the Graph API called field expansion (*http://bit.ly/1a1lsIE*) that allows you to make nested graph queries in a single API call.

Example 2-1. Making Graph API requests over HTTP

```
import requests # pip install requests
import json

base_url = 'https://graph.facebook.com/me'

# Specify which fields to retrieve
fields = 'id,name,likes.limit(10){about}'

url = '{0}?fields={1}&access_token={2}'.format(base_url, fields, ACCESS_TOKEN)

# This API is HTTP-based and could be requested in the browser,
# with a command line utlity like curl, or using just about
# any programming language by making a request to the URL.
# Click the hyperlink that appears in your notebook output
# when you execute this code cell to see for yourself...
print(url)

# Interpret the response as JSON and convert back
# to Python data structures
content = requests.get(url).json()

# Pretty-print the JSON and display it
print(json.dumps(content, indent=1))
```

Using Facebook's field expansion syntax, you can set limits and offsets on your API query. This initial example is just to illustrate that Facebook's API is built on top of HTTP. A couple of field limit/offset examples that illustrate the possibilities with field selectors follow:

```
# Get 10 of my likes
fields = 'id,name,likes.limit(10)'

# Get the next 10 of my likes
fields = 'id,name,likes.offset(10).limit(10)'
```

Facebook's API automatically paginates the results it returns, meaning that if your query has a ton of results, the API will not pass them all back to you at once. Instead, it will break them up into chunks (*pages*) and give you a *cursor* that points to the next page of results. For more information about how to *paginate* through your results, consult the pagination documentation (*http://bit.ly/1a1ltMP*).

2.2.2 Understanding the Open Graph Protocol

In addition to sporting a powerful Graph API that allows you to traverse the social graph and query familiar Facebook objects, you should also know that Facebook unveiled something called the Open Graph protocol (*http://bit.ly/1a1lu3m*) (OGP) back in April 2010, at the same F8 conference at which it introduced the social graph. In short, OGP is a mechanism that enables developers to make any web page an object in Facebook's social graph by injecting some RDFa metadata (*http://bit.ly/1a1lujR*) into the page. Thus, in addition to being able to access from within Facebook's "walled garden" the dozens of objects that are described in the Graph API reference (*http://bit.ly/1a1lvEr*) (users, pictures, videos, check-ins, links, status messages, etc.), you might also encounter pages from the web that represent meaningful concepts that have been grafted into the social graph. In other words, OGP is a means of "opening up" the social graph, and you'll see these concepts described in Facebook's developer documentation as its "Open Graph."[2]

There are practically limitless options for leveraging OGP to graft web pages into the social graph in valuable ways, and the chances are good that you've already encountered many of them and not even realized it. For example, consider Figure 2-4, which illustrates a page for the movie *The Rock* from IMDb.com (*http://imdb.com*). In the sidebar to the right, you see a rather familiar-looking Like button with the message "19,319 people like this. Be the first of your friends." IMDb enables this functionality by implementing OGP for each of its URLs that correspond to objects that would be relevant for inclusion in the social graph. With the right RDFa metadata in the page, Facebook is then able to unambiguously enable *connections* to these objects and incorporate them into activity streams and other key elements of the Facebook user experience.

Figure 2-4. An IMDb page featuring an implementation of OGP for The Rock

Implementation of OGP manifesting as Like buttons on web pages may seem a bit obvious if you've gotten used to seeing them over the past few years, but the fact that Facebook has been fairly successful at opening up its development platform in a way

---

2 Throughout this section describing the implementation of OGP, the term *social graph* is generically used to refer to both the social graph and Open Graph, unless explicitly emphasized otherwise.

that allows for arbitrary inclusion of objects on the web is rather profound and has some potentially significant consequences.

Back in 2013, Facebook implemented a semantic search engine called Facebook Graph Search. It was a way for users to make natural language queries directly from the search bar. For example, you could write "My friends who live in London and like cats" into the search bar and it would find you the intersection of your friends living in London who were also cat-lovers. But this new way of querying Facebook would not last long. At the end of 2014, Facebook dropped this semantic search feature in favor of a keyword-based approach. Nevertheless, the graph connecting objects on Facebook to other artifacts remains in place. In November 2017, Facebook launched a standalone mobile app called Facebook Local centered around connecting physical places and events, and making it social. For instance, the app will tell you which restaurants are popular with your friends on Facebook. The technology powering this app is almost certainly Facebook's social graph.

Let's briefly take a look at the gist of implementing OGP before moving on to Graph API queries. The canonical example from the OGP documentation that demonstrates how to turn IMDb's page on *The Rock* into an object in the Open Graph protocol as part of an XHTML document that uses namespaces looks something like this:

```
<html xmlns:og="http://ogp.me/ns#">
<head>
<title>The Rock (1996)</title>
<meta property="og:title" content="The Rock" />
<meta property="og:type" content="movie" />
<meta property="og:url" content="http://www.imdb.com/title/tt0117500/" />
<meta property="og:image" content="http://ia.media-imdb.com/images/rock.jpg" />
...
</head>
...
</html>
```

These bits of metadata have great potential once realized at a massive scale, because they enable a URI like *http://www.imdb.com/title/tt0117500* to unambiguously represent any web page—whether it's for a person, company, product, etc.—in a machine-readable way and further the vision for a semantic web. In addition to being able to "like" *The Rock*, users could potentially interact with this object in other ways through custom actions. For example, users might be able to indicate that they have watched *The Rock* (*http://bit.ly/2Qx0Kfo*), since it is a movie. OGP allows for a wide and flexible set of actions between users and objects as part of the social graph.

 If you haven't already, go ahead and view the source HTML for *http://www.imdb.com/title/tt0117500* and see for yourself what the RDFa looks like out in the wild.

At its core, querying the Graph API for Open Graph objects is incredibly simple: append a web page URL or an object's ID to *http(s)://graph.facebook.com/* to fetch details about the object. For example, fetching the URL *http://graph.facebook.com/ http://www.imdb.com/title/tt0117500* in your web browser would return this response:

```json
{
    "share": {
        "comment_count": 0,
        "share_count": 1779
    },
    "og_object": {
        "id": "10150461355237868",
        "description": "Directed by Michael Bay.  With Sean Connery, ...",
        "title": "The Rock (1996)",
        "type": "video.movie",
        "updated_time": "2018-09-18T08:39:39+0000"
    },
    "metadata": {
        "fields": [
            {
                "name": "id",
                "description": "The URL being queried",
                "type": "string"
            },
            {
                "name": "app_links",
                "description": "AppLinks data associated with the URL",
                "type": "applinks"
            },
            {
                "name": "development_instant_article",
                "description": "Instant Article object for the URL, in developmen...",
                "type": "instantarticle"
            },
            {
                "name": "instant_article",
                "description": "Instant Article object for the URL",
                "type": "instantarticle"
            },
            {
                "name": "og_object",
                "description": "Open Graph Object for the URL",
                "type": "opengraphobject:generic"
            },
            {
                "name": "ownership_permissions",
                "description": "Permissions based on ownership of the URL",
                "type": "urlownershippermissions"
            }
        ],
        "type": "url"
    },
```

```
    "id": "http://www.imdb.com/title/tt0117500"
}
```

If you inspect the source for the URL *http://www.imdb.com/title/tt0117500*, you'll find that fields in the response correspond to the data in the meta tags of the page, and this is no coincidence. The delivery of rich metadata in response to a simple query is the whole idea behind the way OGP is designed to work. Using the Graph API Explorer, it's possible to access even more metadata around objects in the graph. Try pasting 380728101301?metadata=1 into the Graph API Explorer, where we have used the ID for *The Rock* and requested additional metadata. Here is a sample response:

```
{
  "created_time": "2007-11-18T20:32:10+0000",
  "title": "The Rock (1996)",
  "type": "video.movie",
  "metadata": {
    "fields": [
      {
        "name": "id",
        "description": "The Open Graph object ID",
        "type": "numeric string"
      },
      {
        "name": "admins",
        "description": "A list of admins",
        "type": "list<opengraphobjectprofile>"
      },
      {
        "name": "application",
        "description": "The application that created this object",
        "type": "opengraphobjectprofile"
      },
      {
        "name": "audio",
        "description": "A list of audio URLs",
        "type": "list<opengraphobjectaudio>"
      },
      {
        "name": "context",
        "description": "Context",
        "type": "opengraphcontext"
      },
      {
        "name": "created_time",
        "description": "The time the object was created",
        "type": "datetime"
      },
      {
        "name": "data",
        "description": "Custom properties of the object",
        "type": "opengraphstruct:video.movie"
```

```
  },
  {
    "name": "description",
    "description": "A short description of the object",
    "type": "string"
  },
  {
    "name": "determiner",
    "description": "The word that appears before the object's title",
    "type": "string"
  },
  {
    "name": "engagement",
    "description": "The social sentence and like count for this object and
    its associated share. This is the same info used for the like button",
    "type": "engagement"
  },
  {
    "name": "image",
    "description": "A list of image URLs",
    "type": "list<opengraphobjectimagevideo>"
  },
  {
    "name": "is_scraped",
    "description": "Whether the object has been scraped",
    "type": "bool"
  },
  {
    "name": "locale",
    "description": "The locale the object is in",
    "type": "opengraphobjectlocale"
  },
  {
    "name": "location",
    "description": "The location inherited from Place",
    "type": "location"
  },
  {
    "name": "post_action_id",
    "description": "The action ID that created this object",
    "type": "id"
  },
  {
    "name": "profile_id",
    "description": "The Facebook ID of a user that can be followed",
    "type": "opengraphobjectprofile"
  },
  {
    "name": "restrictions",
    "description": "Any restrictions that are placed on this object",
    "type": "opengraphobjectrestrictions"
  },
```

```
    {
      "name": "see_also",
      "description": "An array of URLs of related resources",
      "type": "list<string>"
    },
    {
      "name": "site_name",
      "description": "The name of the web site upon which the object resides",
      "type": "string"
    },
    {
      "name": "title",
      "description": "The title of the object as it should appear in the graph",
      "type": "string"
    },
    {
      "name": "type",
      "description": "The type of the object",
      "type": "string"
    },
    {
      "name": "updated_time",
      "description": "The last time the object was updated",
      "type": "datetime"
    },
    {
      "name": "video",
      "description": "A list of video URLs",
      "type": "list<opengraphobjectimagevideo>"
    }
  ],
  "type": "opengraphobject:video.movie",
  "connections": {
    "comments": "https://graph.facebook.com/v3.1/380728101301/comments?access
    _token=EAAYvPRk4YUEBAHvVKqnhZBxMDAwBKEpWrsM6J8ZCxHkLu...&pretty=0",
    "likes": "https://graph.facebook.com/v3.1/380728101301...&pretty=0",
    "picture": "https://graph.facebook.com/v3.1/380728101...&pretty=0",
    "reactions": "https://graph.facebook.com/v3.1/38072810...reactions?
    access_token=EAAYvPRk4YUEBAHvVKqnhZBxMDAwBKEpWrsM6J8ZC...&pretty=0"
  }
},
"id": "380728101301"
}
```

The items in `metadata.connections` are pointers to other nodes in the graph that you can crawl to get to other intriguing bits of data, although what you find might be heavily limited by Facebook's privacy settings.

Try using the Facebook ID "MiningTheSocialWeb" to retrieve details about the official Facebook fan page for this book (*http://on.fb.me/1a1lAI8*) with the Graph API Explorer. You could also modify Example 2-1 to programmatically query for *https://graph.facebook.com/MiningTheSocialWeb* to retrieve basic page information, including content posted to the page. For example, appending a query string with a qualifier such as "?fields=posts" to that URL would return a listing of its posted content.

As a final note of advice before moving on to programmatically accessing the Graph API, when considering the possibilities with OGP, be forward-thinking and creative, but bear in mind that it's still evolving. As it relates to the semantic web and web standards in general, the use of "open" (*http://tcrn.ch/1a1lAYF*) has understandably generated some consternation. Various kinks in the spec have been worked out along the way (*http://bit.ly/1a1lAbd*), and some are still probably being worked out. You could also make the case that OGP is essentially a single-vendor effort, and it's little more than on par with the capabilities of `meta` elements (*http://bit.ly/1a1lBMa*) from the much earlier days of the web, although the social effects appear to be driving a very different outcome.

Although whether OGP or some successor to Graph Search will one day dominate the web is a highly contentious topic, the potential is certainly there; the indicators for success are trending in a positive direction, and many exciting things may happen as the future unfolds and innovation continues to take place. Now that you have an appreciation for the fuller context of the social graph, let's turn back and hone in on how to access the Graph API.

2.3 Analyzing Social Graph Connections

The official Python SDK for the Graph API (*http://bit.ly/2kpej52*) is a community fork of that repository previously maintained by Facebook and can be installed per the standard protocol with `pip` via **pip install facebook-sdk**. This package contains a few useful convenience methods that allow you to interact with Facebook in a number of ways. However, there are really just a few key methods from the `GraphAPI` class (defined in the *facebook.py* source file) that you need to know about in order to use the Graph API to fetch data, so you could just as easily opt to query over HTTP directly with `requests` (as was illustrated in Example 2-1) if you prefer. The methods are:

```
get_object(self, id, **args)
    Example usage: get_object("me", metadata=1)

get_objects(self, id, **args)
    Example usage: get_objects(["me", "some_other_id"], metadata=1)
```

```
get_connections(self, id, connection_name, **args)
    Example usage: get_connections("me", "friends", metadata=1)

request(self, path, args=None, post_args=None)
    Example usage: request("search", {"q" : "social web", "type" :
    "page"})
```

 While Facebook does apply rate limiting (*http://bit.ly/2iXSeKs*) to its API, the limits are on a per-user basis. The more users your app has, the higher your rate limit. Nevertheless, you should still carefully design your application to use the APIs as little as possible and handle any and all error conditions as a recommended best practice.

The most common (and often, the only) keyword argument you'll probably use is metadata=1, in order to get back the connections associated with an object in addition to just the object details themselves. Take a look at Example 2-2, which introduces the GraphAPI class and uses its methods to query for information about you, your connections, or a search term such as *social web*. This example also introduces a helper function called pp that is used throughout the remainder of this chapter for pretty-printing results as nicely formatted JSON to save some typing.

 Facebook's API has undergone some changes, and the necessary privileges to programmatically retrieve public content from Facebook pages require submitting an app (*http://bit.ly/2vDb2B1*) for review and approval.

Example 2-2. Querying the Graph API with Python

```python
import facebook # pip install facebook-sdk
import json

# A helper function to pretty-print Python objects as JSON
def pp(o):
    print(json.dumps(o, indent=1))

# Create a connection to the Graph API with your access token
g = facebook.GraphAPI(ACCESS_TOKEN, version='2.7')

# Execute a few example queries:

# Get my ID
pp(g.get_object('me'))

# Get the connections to an ID
# Example connection names: 'feed', 'likes', 'groups', 'posts'
```

```
pp(g.get_connections(id='me', connection_name='likes'))

# Search for a location, may require approved app
pp(g.request("search", {'type': 'place', 'center': '40.749444, -73.968056',
                        'fields': 'name, location'}))
```

The query involving a location search is interesting because it will return items from the graph that correspond to places geographically close to the latitude and longitude provided. Some sample results from this query are shown here:

```
{
  "data": [
    {
      "name": "United Nations",
      "location": {
       "city": "New York",
       "country": "United States",
       "latitude": 40.748801288774,
       "longitude": -73.968307971954,
       "state": "NY",
       "street": "United Nations Headquarters",
       "zip": "10017"
      },
      "id": "54779960819"
    },
    {
      "name": "United Nations Security Council",
      "location": {
       "city": "New York",
       "country": "United States",
       "latitude": 40.749283619093,
       "longitude": -73.968088677538,
       "state": "NY",
       "street": "760 United Nations Plaza",
       "zip": "10017"
      },
      "id": "113874638768433"
    },
    {
      "name": "New-York, Time Square",
      "location": {
       "city": "New York",
       "country": "United States",
       "latitude": 40.7515,
       "longitude": -73.97076,
       "state": "NY"
      },
      "id": "1900405660240200"
    },
    {
      "name": "Penn Station, Manhattan, New York",
      "location": {
```

```
    "city": "New York",
    "country": "United States",
    "latitude": 40.7499131,
    "longitude": -73.9719497,
    "state": "NY",
    "zip": "10017"
   },
   "id": "1189802214427559"
  },
  {
   "name": "Central Park Manhatan",
   "location": {
    "city": "New York",
    "country": "United States",
    "latitude": 40.7660016,
    "longitude": -73.9765709,
    "state": "NY",
    "zip": "10021"
   },
   "id": "328974237465693"
  },
  {
   "name": "Delegates Lounge, United Nations",
   "location": {
    "city": "New York",
    "country": "United States",
    "latitude": 40.749433,
    "longitude": -73.966938,
    "state": "NY",
    "street": "UN Headquarters, 10017",
    "zip": "10017"
   },
   "id": "198970573596872"
  },
  ...
 ],
 "paging": {
  "cursors": {
   "after": "MjQZD"
  },
  "next": "https://graph.facebook.com/v2.5/search?access_token=..."
 }
}
```

 If you were using the Graph API Explorer, the results would be identical. During development, it can often be very handy to use the Graph API Explorer and a Jupyter Notebook in tandem, depending on your specific objective. The advantage of the Graph API Explorer is the ease with which you can click ID values and spawn new queries during exploratory efforts.

At this point, you have the power of both the Graph API Explorer and the Python console—and all that they have to offer—at your fingertips. Now that we've scaled the walled garden, let's turn our attention to analyzing some of its data.

2.3.1 Analyzing Facebook Pages

Although Facebook started out as more of a pure social networking site without a social graph or a good way for businesses and other entities to have a presence, it quickly adapted to take advantage of the market needs. Now, businesses, clubs, books, and many other kinds of nonperson entities have Facebook pages (*http://on.fb.me/1a1lCzQ*) with fan bases. Facebook pages are a powerful tool for businesses to engage their customers, and Facebook has gone to some lengths to enable Facebook page administrators to understand their fans with a small toolbox that is appropriately called Insights (*http://2Ox6W7j*).

If you're already a Facebook user, the chances are pretty good that you've already liked one or more Facebook pages that represent something that you approve of or think is interesting, and in this regard, Facebook pages significantly broaden the possibilities for the social graph as a platform. The explicit accommodation of nonperson user entities through Facebook pages, the Like button, and the social graph fabric collectively provide a powerful arsenal for an interest graph platform, which carries with it a profundity of possibilities. (Refer back to "Why Is Twitter All the Rage?" for a discussion of why interest graphs are so abundant with useful possibilities.)

Analyzing this book's Facebook page

Given that this book has a corresponding Facebook page that happened to turn up as the top result in a search for "social web," it seems natural enough to use it as an illustrative starting point for some instructive analysis here in this chapter.[3]

Here are just a few questions that might be worth considering with regard to this book's Facebook page, or just about any other Facebook page:

- How popular is the page?
- How engaged are the page's fans?
- Are any of the fans for the page particularly outspoken and participatory?
- What are the most common topics being talked about on the page?

---

3 Throughout this section, keep in mind that Facebook limits public content access for apps that have not been submitted and approved by the company. The code in this section, and its output, is provided for illustration purposes. Please review the developer documentation link:https://developers.facebook.com/docs/apps/review).

Your imagination is the only limitation to what you can ask of the Graph API when mining a Facebook page's content for insights, and these questions should get you headed in the right direction. Along the way, we'll also use these questions as the basis for some comparisons among other pages.

Recall that the starting point for our journey might have been a search for "social web" that revealed a book entitled *Mining the Social Web* per the following search result item:

```
{
 "data": [
  {
   "name": "Mining the Social Web",
   "id": "146803958708175"
  },
  {
   "name": "R: Mining spatial, text, web, and social media",
   "id": "321086594970335"
  }
 ],
 "paging": {
  "cursors": {
   "before": "MAZDZD",
   "after": "MQZDZD"
  }
 }
}
```

For any of the items in the search results, we could use the ID as the basis of a graph query through `get_object` with an instance of `facebook.GraphAPI`. If you don't have a numeric string ID handy, you could perform a search request on the name and see what turns up. Using the `get_object` method, we can then retrieve more information, such as the number of fans the Facebook page has, as shown in Example 2-3.

Example 2-3. Querying the Graph API for Mining the Social Web and counting fans

```
# Search for a page's ID by name
pp(g.request("search", {'q': 'Mining the Social Web', 'type': 'page'}))

# Grab the ID for the book and check the number of fans
mtsw_id = '146803958708175'
pp(g.get_object(id=mtsw_id, fields=['fan_count']))
```

The output of this code looks like:

```
{
 "data": [
  {
   "name": "Mining the Social Web",
   "id": "146803958708175"
```

```
    },
    {
     "name": "R: Mining spatial, text, web, and social media",
     "id": "321086594970335"
    }
   ],
   "paging": {
    "cursors": {
     "before": "MAZDZD",
     "after": "MQZDZD"
    }
   }
  }
 }
 {
  "fan_count": 2563,
  "id": "146803958708175"
 }
```

Counting the number of fans that a page has and comparing it to other pages in a similar category is a way of measuring the strength of a "brand" on Facebook. *Mining the Social Web* is a fairly niche technical book, so it might make sense to compare it against other books published by O'Reilly Media that have Facebook pages.

For any kind of popularity analysis, comparables are essential for understanding the broader context. There are a lot of ways to draw comparisons, but a couple of striking data points are that the book's publisher, O'Reilly Media (*http://on.fb.me/1a1lD6F*), has around 126,000 likes, and the Python programming language (*http://on.fb.me/1a1lD6V*) has around 121,000 likes at the time of this writing. Thus, the popularity of *Mining the Social Web* is around 2% of the publisher's entire fan base and of the programming language's fan base. Clearly, there is a lot of room for this book's popularity to grow, even though it's a niche topic.

Although a better comparison might have been to a niche book similar to *Mining the Social Web*, it isn't easy to find any good apples-to-apples comparisons by reviewing Facebook page data. For example, you can't search for pages and limit the result set to books in order to find a good comparable; instead, you'd have to search for pages and then filter the result set by category to retrieve only the books. Still, there are a couple of options to consider.

One option is to search for a similar O'Reilly title. For example, at the time of writing the second edition of this book, Graph API search results for a query of *Programming Collective Intelligence* (a similar kind of niche book from O'Reilly) turned up a community page with around 925 likes.

Another option to consider is taking advantage of concepts from Facebook's Open Graph protocol in order to draw a comparison. For example, the O'Reilly online catalog used to implement OGP for all of its titles, and there were Like buttons for both *Mining the Social Web*, 2nd Edition (*http://oreil.ly/1cMLoug*), and *Programming Col-*

lective Intelligence (http://oreil.ly/1a1lGzw). We can easily make requests to the Graph API to see what data is available by simply querying for these URLs in the browser as follows:

Graph API query for Mining the Social Web
    https://graph.facebook.com/http://shop.oreilly.com/product/0636920030195.do

Graph API query for Programming Collective Intelligence
    https://graph.facebook.com/http://shop.oreilly.com/product/9780596529321.do

In terms of a programmatic query with Python, the URLs are the objects that we are querying (just like the URL for the IMDb entry for *The Rock* was what we were querying earlier), so in code, we can query these objects as shown in Example 2-4.

Example 2-4. Querying the Graph API for Open Graph objects by their URLs

```
# MTSW catalog link
pp(g.get_object('http://shop.oreilly.com/product/0636920030195.do'))

# PCI catalog link
pp(g.get_object('http://shop.oreilly.com/product/9780596529321.do'))
```

As a subtle but very important distinction, keep in mind that even though both the O'Reilly catalog page and the Facebook fan page for *Mining the Social Web* logically represent the same book, the nodes (and accompanying metadata, such as the number of likes) that correspond to the Facebook page versus the O'Reilly catalog page are completely independent. It just so happens that each represents the same real-world concept.

> An entirely separate kind of analysis known as *entity resolution* (or *entity disambiguation*, depending on how you frame the problem) is the process of aggregating mentions of things into a single Platonic concept. For example, in this case, an entity resolution process could observe that there are multiple nodes in the Open Graph that actually refer to the same Platonic idea of *Mining the Social Web* and create connections between them indicating that they are in fact equivalent as an entity in the real world. Entity resolution is an exciting field of research that will continue to have profound effects on how we use data as the future unfolds.

Figure 2-5 demonstrates an exploration of the Graph API with the Jupyter Notebook.

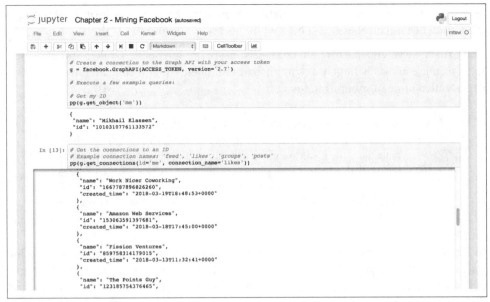

Figure 2-5. Exploring the Graph API is a breeze with the help of an interactive programming environment like the Jupyter Notebook

Although it's often not the case that you'll be able to make an apples-to-apples comparison that provides an authoritative result when data mining, there's still a lot to be learned. Exploring a data set long enough to accumulate strong intuitions about the data often provides all the insight that you'll initially need when encountering a problem space for the first time.

Engaging fans and measuring the strength of a social media brand

While some celebrities are very active on social media, others leave the task of engaging an online audience to a dedicated social media marketing or public relations team. Facebook pages are a great way to engage with fans, and that's true whether you're a major celebrity, a minor YouTube star, or simply run the Facebook page for a nonprofit at which you volunteer.

In this section, we'll explore how to mine the Facebook pages of three extremely popular musicians for information about how strongly their Facebook audiences react to the things they post on their own pages. You can understand why these artists (and their publicity managers) might care about this information. Keeping fans engaged and connected is vital to successful product launches, selling tickets to an event, or mobilizing fans for a cause.

Communicating effectively with your audience therefore matters a lot, and if you get your messaging wrong, you could turn away some of your most loyal fans. For that reason, an artist or a publicist might want to get some hard numbers on how engaged their audience on Facebook is. That's what this section is about.

The artists we've chosen for our comparison are Taylor Swift, Drake, and Beyoncé. Each of these artists is hugely accomplished and talented, and they all have Facebook pages with a large number of followers.

 You can use the search tools we covered earlier to find the page IDs for each artist. Of course, while the examples here use Facebook page data, the ideas are more general. You could try to retrieve similar statistics from other platforms such as Twitter. You could also write some code that crawls news portals looking for mentions of a particular celebrity or brand you wish to follow. If you've ever used Google Alerts, you have an idea of what this could look like.

In Example 2-5, we identify each artist by their page ID, which can be retrieved using a search as in Example 2-3. We then define a helper function for retrieving the number of page fans as an integer. We save these numbers to three different variables and then print the results.

 At the time of writing, in order to retrieve public page content from Facebook, the developer's app must be submitted for review (*http:// bit.ly/2vDb2B1*) via the developer platform and be approved. This is in response to Facebook's efforts at making its platform more secure and preventing abuse.

Example 2-5. Counting total number of page fans

```
# The following code may require the developer's app to be submitted for review and
# approved. See https://developers.facebook.com/docs/apps/review.

# Take, for example, three popular musicians and their page IDs
taylor_swift_id = '19614945368'
drake_id = '83711079303'
beyonce_id = '28940545600'

# Declare a helper function for retrieving the total number of fans ('likes')
# a page has
def get_total_fans(page_id):
    return int(g.get_object(id=page_id, fields=['fan_count'])['fan_count'])

tswift_fans = get_total_fans(taylor_swift_id)
drake_fans = get_total_fans(drake_id)
beyonce_fans = get_total_fans(beyonce_id)

print('Taylor Swift: {0} fans on Facebook'.format(tswift_fans))
```

```
print('Drake:        {0} fans on Facebook'.format(drake_fans))
print('Beyoncé:      {0} fans on Facebook'.format(beyonce_fans))
```

The result of running this code looks something like:

```
Taylor Swift: 73896104 fans on Facebook
Drake:        35821534 fans on Facebook
Beyoncé:      63974894 fans on Facebook
```

The total number of fans on Facebook is the first and most basic metric of a page's popularity. However, we know nothing about how active these fans are, how likely they are to react to a post, or whether they will engage with it by commenting or sharing. These different ways of engaging with a post are important to the page owner, because each of those fans likely has many friends on Facebook and the Facebook news feed algorithm will often surface one's activities to one's friends. This means that active fans will result in posts being seen by more people—and more publicity translates into more attention, more fans, more clicks, more sales, or more of whatever other metric you are trying to drive.

To begin the process of measuring engagement, you need to retrieve a page's feed. This involves connecting to the Graph API via the page's ID and selecting the posts. Each post will be returned as a JSON object with lots of rich metadata. Python treats JSON as a dictionary with keys and values.

In Example 2-6, we first define a function that retrieves a page's feed and concatenates all of the feed's data into a list, returning a specified number of posts. Since the API automatically paginates the results, the function will continue paging until the specified number of posts has been reached and then return that number. Now that we can build a list of post data from a page's feed, we want to be able to extract information from those posts. We might be interested in the content of the post—e.g., a message to fans—so the next helper function extracts and returns the post's message.

Example 2-6. Retrieving a page's feed

```
# Declare a helper function for retrieving the official feed from a given page
def retrieve_page_feed(page_id, n_posts):
    """Retrieve the first n_posts from a page's feed in reverse
    chronological order."""
    feed = g.get_connections(page_id, 'posts')
    posts = []
    posts.extend(feed['data'])

    while len(posts) < n_posts:
        try:
            feed = requests.get(feed['paging']['next']).json()
            posts.extend(feed['data'])
        except KeyError:
            # When there are no more posts in the feed, break
```

```python
            print('Reached end of feed.')
            break

    if len(posts) > n_posts:
        posts = posts[:n_posts]

    print('{} items retrieved from feed'.format(len(posts)))
    return posts

# Declare a helper function for returning the message content of a post
def get_post_message(post):
    try:
        message = post['story']
    except KeyError:
        # Post may have 'message' instead of 'story'
        pass
    try:
        message = post['message']
    except KeyError:
        # Post has neither
        message = ''
    return message.replace('\n', ' ')

# Retrieve the last 5 items from the feeds
for artist in [taylor_swift_id, drake_id, beyonce_id]:
    print()
    feed = retrieve_page_feed(artist, 5)
    for i, post in enumerate(feed):
        message = get_post_message(post)[:50]
        print('{0} - {1}...'.format(i+1, message))
```

In the final block of code, we loop over the three artists in our example and retrieve the most recent 5 posts on their feeds, printing just the first 50 characters of each to the screen. The resulting output is:

```
5 items retrieved from feed
1 - Check out a key moment in Taylor writing "This Is ...
2 - ...
3 - ...
4 - The Swift Life is available for free worldwide in ...
5 - #TheSwiftLife App is available NOW for free in the...

5 items retrieved from feed
1 - ...
2 - http://www.hollywoodreporter.com/features/drakes-h...
3 - ...
4 - Tickets On Sale Friday, September 15....
5 - https://www.youcaring.com/jjwatt...

5 items retrieved from feed
1 - ...
2 - ...
```

```
3 - ...
4 - New Shop Beyoncé 2017 Holiday Capsule: shop.beyonc...
5 - Happy Thiccsgiving. www.beyonce.com...
```

Items marked with only an ellipsis (…) contained no text (recall that Facebook lets you post videos and photos to the feed as well).

Facebook allows its users many different ways of engaging with a post. The Like button first appeared in 2009, and it has been transformative for all of social media. Because Facebook and many other social media platforms are used by advertisers, a Like button, or something similar, sends a strong signal that a message is resonating with its intended audience. It has also had some undoubtedly unintended consequences, with many people increasingly tailoring what they post so as to generate the most "likes."

In 2016, Facebook extended what sorts of reactions were possible, adding "Love," "Haha," "Wow," "Sad," and "Angry." As of May 2017, users could also signal similar reactions to comments.

Besides responding emotively, users can engage with posts by commenting or sharing. Any one of these activities increases the likelihood of the original post surfacing on the news feeds of other users. We would like to have the tools needed to measure how many users are responding to a page's posts in any one of these ways. For the sake of simplicity, we've limited the emotive responses to just the Like button, although the code can be modified to explore these responses with more granularity.

The number of responses a post generates will be roughly proportional to the post's audience size. The number of fans that a page has is one rough measure of a post's audience size, although not all fans will necessarily see each post. Who sees what is determined by Facebook's proprietary news feed algorithm, and post authors can also "boost" a post's visibility by paying Facebook an advertising fee.

Let's assume for the sake of argument that in our example each artist's entire fan base always sees each post. We'd like to measure what fraction of the artist's fan base engages with the post in some way, either by liking, commenting on, or sharing the post. This allows us to better compare the fan bases of each artist: Who has the most active fans? Who shares the most?

If you are a publicist for one of these artists, trying to maximize engagement on each of the posts, you might be interested in seeing which posts do best. Do your client's fans react more to video content, relative to photos or text? Are the fans more active on certain days of the week, or at certain times of the day? The last question about post timing does not matter quite so much for Facebook, since the news feed algorithm controls who sees what, but it is nevertheless something you may wish to study.

In Example 2-7, we bring the different pieces together. A helper function, meas ure_response, is used to count the number of likes, shares, and comments on each post. A different helper function called measure_engagement compares these numbers to the page's total number of fans.

Example 2-7. Measuring engagement

```
# Measure the response to a post in terms of likes, shares, and comments
def measure_response(post_id):
    """Returns the number of likes, shares, and comments on a
    given post as a measure of user engagement."""
    likes = g.get_object(id=post_id,
                         fields=['likes.limit(0).summary(true)'])\
                         ['likes']['summary']['total_count']
    shares = g.get_object(id=post_id,
                         fields=['shares.limit(0).summary(true)'])\
                         ['shares']['count']
    comments = g.get_object(id=post_id,
                         fields=['comments.limit(0).summary(true)'])\
                         ['comments']['summary']['total_count']
    return likes, shares, comments

# Measure the relative share of a page's fans engaging with a post
def measure_engagement(post_id, total_fans):
    """Returns the number of likes, shares, and comments on a
    given post as a measure of user engagement."""
    likes = g.get_object(id=post_id,
                         fields=['likes.limit(0).summary(true)'])\
                         ['likes']['summary']['total_count']
    shares = g.get_object(id=post_id,
                         fields=['shares.limit(0).summary(true)'])\
                         ['shares']['count']
    comments = g.get_object(id=post_id,
                         fields=['comments.limit(0).summary(true)'])\
                         ['comments']['summary']['total_count']
    likes_pct = likes / total_fans * 100.0
    shares_pct = shares / total_fans * 100.0
    comments_pct = comments / total_fans * 100.0
    return likes_pct, shares_pct, comments_pct

# Retrieve the last 5 items from the artists' feeds, and print the
# reaction and the degree of engagement
artist_dict = {'Taylor Swift': taylor_swift_id,
               'Drake': drake_id,
               'Beyoncé': beyonce_id}
for name, page_id in artist_dict.items():
    print()
    print(name)
    print('------------')
    feed = retrieve_page_feed(page_id, 5)
    total_fans = get_total_fans(page_id)
```

```
for i, post in enumerate(feed):
    message = get_post_message(post)[:30]
    post_id = post['id']
    likes, shares, comments = measure_response(post_id)
    likes_pct, shares_pct, comments_pct = measure_engagement(post_id, total_fans)
    print('{0} - {1}...'.format(i+1, message))
    print('    Likes {0} ({1:7.5f}%)'.format(likes, likes_pct))
    print('    Shares {0} ({1:7.5f}%)'.format(shares, shares_pct))
    print('    Comments {0} ({1:7.5f}%)'.format(comments, comments_pct))
```

Looping over each of the three artists in our example and measuring fan engagement gives the following output:

```
Taylor Swift
------------
5 items retrieved from feed
1 - Check out a key moment in Tayl...
    Likes 33134 (0.04486%)
    Shares 1993 (0.00270%)
    Comments 1373 (0.00186%)
2 - ...
    Likes 8282 (0.01121%)
    Shares 19 (0.00003%)
    Comments 353 (0.00048%)
3 - ...
    Likes 11083 (0.01500%)
    Shares 8 (0.00001%)
    Comments 383 (0.00052%)
4 - The Swift Life is available fo...
    Likes 39237 (0.05312%)
    Shares 926 (0.00125%)
    Comments 1012 (0.00137%)
5 - #TheSwiftLife App is available...
    Likes 60721 (0.08221%)
    Shares 1895 (0.00257%)
    Comments 2105 (0.00285%)

Drake
------------
5 items retrieved from feed
1 - ...
    Likes 23938 (0.06685%)
    Shares 2907 (0.00812%)
    Comments 3785 (0.01057%)
2 - http://www.hollywoodreporter.c...
    Likes 4474 (0.01250%)
    Shares 166 (0.00046%)
    Comments 310 (0.00087%)
3 - ...
    Likes 44887 (0.12536%)
    Shares 8 (0.00002%)
```

```
        Comments 1895 (0.00529%)
   4 - Tickets On Sale Friday, Septem...
        Likes 19003 (0.05307%)
        Shares 1343 (0.00375%)
        Comments 6459 (0.01804%)
   5 - https://www.youcaring.com/jjwa...
        Likes 17109 (0.04778%)
        Shares 1777 (0.00496%)
        Comments 859 (0.00240%)

Beyoncé
-----------
5 items retrieved from feed
1 - ...
        Likes 8328 (0.01303%)
        Shares 134 (0.00021%)
        Comments 296 (0.00046%)
2 - ...
        Likes 18545 (0.02901%)
        Shares 250 (0.00039%)
        Comments 819 (0.00128%)
3 - ...
        Likes 21589 (0.03377%)
        Shares 460 (0.00072%)
        Comments 453 (0.00071%)
4 - New Shop Beyoncé 2017 Holiday ...
        Likes 10717 (0.01676%)
        Shares 246 (0.00038%)
        Comments 376 (0.00059%)
5 - Happy Thiccsgiving. www.beyonc...
        Likes 25497 (0.03988%)
        Shares 653 (0.00102%)
        Comments 610 (0.00095%)
```

It may seem like engaging only 0.04% of your fan base on a post is small, but remember that most people do not respond in any way to most posts they see. And when you have tens of millions of fans, mobilizing even a small fraction can have a big impact.

2.3.2 Manipulating Data Using pandas

The pandas Python library has become an essential tool in every data scientist's toolkit, and we'll be using it in various parts of this book. It provides high-performance data structures for holding tabular data and powerful data analysis tools written in Python, with some of the most computationally intensive parts optimized using C or Cython. The project was started in 2008 by Wes McKinney for analyzing financial data.

One of the central new data structures that `pandas` supplies is the `DataFrame`, which is essentially like a database or table. It has labeled columns and an index. It gracefully handles missing data, supports time series data and time indices, allows easy merging and slices of data, and has many handy tools for reading and writing data.

To learn more, check out the `pandas` GitHub repository (*http://bit.ly/2C2k4gt*) and the official documentation (*http://bit.ly/2BRE3vC*). For a quick introduction, check out the tutorial called 10 Minutes to pandas (*http://bit.ly/2Dyd20w*).

Visualizing audience engagement using matplotlib

Now we have the tools needed to measure engagement on a Facebook page's posts, but we want to be able to compare different pages to each other easily (instead of musicians, you might be looking at how well your company's page engages its followers, and you'll want to compare that to competitors in your industry).

We need some way of easily aggregating data from multiple sources into a single table so that we can manipulate it easily and maybe generate some quick charts from that data. This is where the `pandas` library for Python really shines. It is a library that provides a set of powerful data structures and analysis tools that will make your life as a data scientist or analyst much easier.

In the following example, we're going to aggregate data from the pages of the same three musicians we've been using as an example in this part of the chapter, and we're going to store all of this in a `pandas` `DataFrame`, a tabular data structure supplied by the library.

`pandas` is as easy to install as typing **`pip install -U pandas`** into the command line. The `-U` flag will ensure that you have the latest version installed.

We can start as in Example 2-8 by defining the columns of an empty `DataFrame` that will hold our data.

Example 2-8. Defining an empty pandas DataFrame

```
import pandas as pd  # pip install pandas

# Create a pandas DataFrame to contain artist page
# feed information
columns = ['Name',
           'Total Fans',
           'Post Number',
           'Post Date',
           'Headline',
           'Likes',
           'Shares',
           'Comments',
           'Rel. Likes',
```

```
        'Rel. Shares',
        'Rel. Comments']
musicians = pd.DataFrame(columns=columns)
```

Here we've outlined the columns of interest to us. As we loop over the posts in each musician's feed, we'll get a measure of each post's likes, shares, and comments, as well as the relative measures of each (i.e., the fraction of the artist's total number of fans that reacted). How to do this is shown in Example 2-9.

Example 2-9. Storing data in a pandas DataFrame

```
# Build the DataFrame by adding the last 10 posts and their audience
# reaction measures for each of the artists
for page_id in [taylor_swift_id, drake_id, beyonce_id]:
    name = g.get_object(id=page_id)['name']
    fans = get_total_fans(page_id)
    feed = retrieve_page_feed(page_id, 10)
    for i, post in enumerate(feed):
        likes, shares, comments = measure_response(post['id'])
        likes_pct, shares_pct, comments_pct = measure_engagement(post['id'], fans)
        musicians = musicians.append({'Name': name,
                                      'Total Fans': fans,
                                      'Post Number': i+1,
                                      'Post Date': post['created_time'],
                                      'Headline': get_post_message(post),
                                      'Likes': likes,
                                      'Shares': shares,
                                      'Comments': comments,
                                      'Rel. Likes': likes_pct,
                                      'Rel. Shares': shares_pct,
                                      'Rel. Comments': comments_pct,
                                    }, ignore_index=True)
# Fix the dtype of a few columns
for col in ['Post Number', 'Total Fans', 'Likes', 'Shares', 'Comments']:
    musicians[col] = musicians[col].astype(int)
```

We loop over each artist's page by page ID, retrieving the name, number of fans, and the latest 10 posts from the page feed. Then an inner for loop iterates through each of the 10 posts in the feed and gets things like the total number of likes, shares, and comments, as well as calculating what percentage of the total fan base these numbers represent. All this information is written as a row in the DataFrame. By setting the ignore_index keyword to True, we indicate that each row doesn't have a predetermined index and pandas will enumerate the rows as they are added.

The very last loop in the example modifies the data type (dtype) of a few columns of numerical data so that pandas knows that those are intended to be integers, not floating-point numbers or otherwise.

Running this code may take some time, as the data is aggregated from Facebook over the API, but in the end we'll have a nice table to work with. `pandas DataFrames` have a convenient method defined on them called `.head()`, which allows you to preview the first five rows of the table (see Figure 2-6). We strongly recommend performing any exploratory data analysis in a Jupyter Notebook (*http://bit.ly/2omIqdG*), such as in those supplied in the accompanying GitHub repository for this book (*http://bit.ly/Mining-the-Social-Web-3E*).

	Name	Total Fans	Post Number	Post Date	Headline	Likes	Shares	Comments	Rel. Likes	Rel. Shares	Rel. Comments
0	Taylor Swift	73862332	1	2017-12-19T17:07:33+0000	Check out a key moment in Taylor writing "This...	33134	1994	1373	0.044859	0.002700	0.001859
1	Taylor Swift	73862332	2	2017-12-17T16:42:38+0000		8282	19	353	0.011213	0.000026	0.000478
2	Taylor Swift	73862332	3	2017-12-17T03:51:04+0000		11083	8	383	0.015004	0.000011	0.000519
3	Taylor Swift	73862332	4	2017-12-16T20:19:52+0000	The Swift Life is available for free worldwide...	39237	925	1012	0.053122	0.001252	0.001370
4	Taylor Swift	73862332	5	2017-12-15T13:18:45+0000	#TheSwiftLife App is available NOW for free in...	60721	1895	2105	0.082210	0.002566	0.002850

Figure 2-6. The first five rows of the "musicians" pandas DataFrame

`pandas DataFrames` have some plotting functions defined on them that make it easy to quickly visualize your data. These functions call `matplotlib` on the backend, so make sure you have this library installed as well.

Example 2-10 shows one of the nice indexing features that `pandas` has. We are taking the `musicians DataFrame`, and indexing on a selection of rows where the `Name` column matches `Drake`. This allows us to perform further operations on just the data related to Drake, and not on those rows corresponding to Taylor Swift or Beyoncé.

Example 2-10. Plotting a bar chart from a pandas DataFrame

```
import matplotlib # pip install matplotlib

musicians[musicians['Name'] == 'Drake'].plot(x='Post Number', y='Likes', kind='bar')
musicians[musicians['Name'] == 'Drake'].plot(x='Post Number', y='Shares', kind='bar')
musicians[musicians['Name'] == 'Drake'].plot(x='Post Number',
                                             y='Comments', kind='bar')
```

This code generates a bar chart (see Figure 2-7) of the number of likes generated by the last 10 posts on Drake's Facebook page.

We immediately see in Figure 2-7 that post #8 performed extremely well, which may be of interest to us. Just as easily, we can see what proportion of the total number of fans these posts engaged in Figure 2-8.

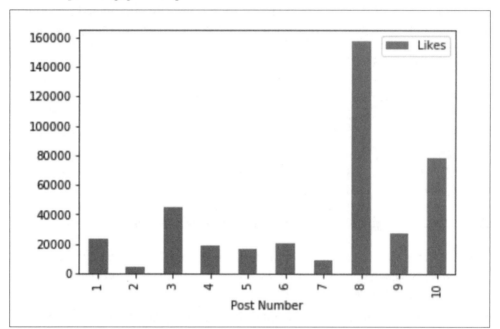

Figure 2-7. A bar chart of the number of likes received on the last 10 posts

Post #8 engaged 0.4% of the total audience, which is probably a relatively large amount.

Suppose now that you want to compare the three artists to each other. Currently the DataFrame's index is just a boring row number, but we can change it to something more meaningful that will help us better manipulate the data—we're going to modify our DataFrame slightly by setting a *multi-index*.

A multi-index is a hierarchical index. The top level for us is going to be the artist's name: Taylor Swift, Drake, or Beyoncé. The next level down is going to the post number (1 through 10). Specifying the artist and post number together uniquely indicates a row in our DataFrame.

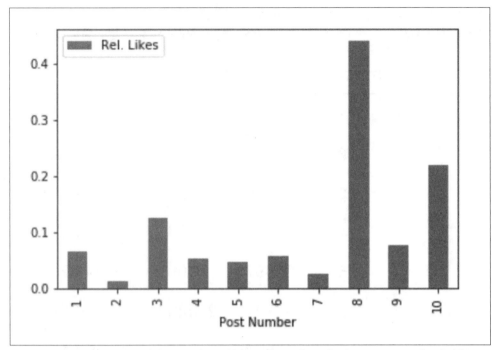

Figure 2-8. A bar chart of the number of likes received on the last 10 posts, divided by the number of page followers (fans)

Setting the multi-index is achieved with the code in Example 2-11.

Example 2-11. Setting a multi-index on a DataFrame

```
# Reset the index to a multi-index
musicians = musicians.set_index(['Name','Post Number'])
```

Once the multi-index has been set, we can also perform powerful pivoting operations on the data using the `unstack` method, as shown in Example 2-12. Figure 2-9 shows the initial rows of the `DataFrame` after we've applied the unstack operation.

Example 2-12. Using the unstack method to pivot a DataFrame

```
# The unstack method pivots the index labels
# and lets you get data columns grouped by artist
musicians.unstack(level=0)['Likes']
```

Name	Beyoncé	Drake	Taylor Swift
Post Number			
1	8328	23938	33134
2	18545	4474	8282
3	21589	44887	11083
4	10717	19003	39237
5	25497	17109	60721
6	17744	20328	41359
7	8934	9178	54012
8	10605	157515	29189
9	72254	27186	38439
10	10889	78674	33159

Figure 2-9. The DataFrame resulting from Example 2-12

Of course, this kind of information is better understood visually, so we use built-in plotting operations to produce another bar chart, as in Example 2-13.

Example 2-13. Generating a bar chart of total likes per post and per artist for the last 10 posts

```
# Plot the comparative reactions to each artist's last 10 Facebook posts
plot = musicians.unstack(level=0)['Likes'].plot(kind='bar', subplots=False,
                                        figsize=(10,5), width=0.8)
plot.set_xlabel('10 Latest Posts')
plot.set_ylabel('Number of Likes Received')
```

This results in the plot shown in Figure 2-10.

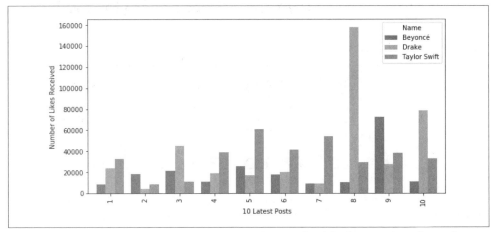

Figure 2-10. The total numbers of likes received on each of the last 10 posts for each artist

This is a really handy way of comparing different data sets to each other. Next, since each artist has a different-sized fan base, let's normalize the like counts by the total number of fans (page followers) for each artist, as shown in Example 2-14.

Example 2-14. Generating a bar chart of the relative number of likes per post and per artist for the last 10 posts

```
# Plot the engagement of each artist's Facebook fan base with the last 10 posts
plot = musicians.unstack(level=0)['Rel. Likes'].plot(kind='bar', subplots=False,
                                                    figsize=(10,5), width=0.8)
plot.set_xlabel('10 Latest Posts')
plot.set_ylabel('Likes / Total Fans (%)')
```

The resulting bar chart is shown in Figure 2-11.

We notice from this that although Drake has considerably fewer followers on Facebook relative to either Beyoncé or Taylor Swift, many of the posts on his Facebook page manage to garner likes from a larger share of his fan base. Although not conclusive, this could suggest that Drake's fans, while fewer in number, are more ardently loyal and active on Facebook. Alternatively, it could mean that Drake (or his social media manager) is very good at posting highly engaging content on Facebook.

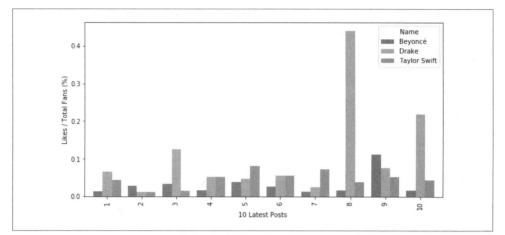

Figure 2-11. The relative numbers of likes received on each of the last 10 posts for each artist

A deeper analysis might consider the content of each post, the content type (text, image, or video), the language used in comments, and what other reactions (besides likes) are being expressed.

Calculating mean engagement

Another useful feature of multi-index `DataFrames` is the ability to compute statistics by index. We've looked at the performance of the last 10 posts for each of three musicians. We can calculate the mean relative number of likes, shares, or comments that each artist receives using the code in Example 2-15.

Example 2-15. Calculating the mean level of engagement across the last 10 posts

```
print('Average Likes / Total Fans')
print(musicians.unstack(level=0)['Rel. Likes'].mean())

print('\nAverage Shares / Total Fans')
print(musicians.unstack(level=0)['Rel. Shares'].mean())

print('\nAverage Comments / Total Fans')
print(musicians.unstack(level=0)['Rel. Comments'].mean())
```

We make use again of the `unstack` method to pivot the table so that each of the original columns ("Likes," "Shares," "Rel. Comments," etc.) are subindexed by the artists' names. The only rows in the `DataFrame` are now the individual posts, sorted by post number.

Example 2-15 shows how we can select one of the variables of interest, such as "Rel. Likes," and compute the mean on this column.

The output of Example 2-15 is:

```
Average Likes / Total Fans
Name
Beyoncé        0.032084
Drake          0.112352
Taylor Swift   0.047198
dtype: float64

Average Shares / Total Fans
Name
Beyoncé        0.000945
Drake          0.017613
Taylor Swift   0.001962
dtype: float64

Average Comments / Total Fans
Name
Beyoncé        0.001024
Drake          0.016322
Taylor Swift   0.002238
dtype: float64
```

2.4 Closing Remarks

The goal of this chapter was to teach you about the Graph API, how the Open Graph protocol can create connections between arbitrary web pages and Facebook's social graph, and how to programmatically query the social graph to gain insight into Facebook pages and your own social network. If you've worked through the examples in this chapter, you should have little to no trouble probing the social graph for answers to questions that may prove valuable. Keep in mind that when you explore a data set as enormous and interesting as Facebook's social graph, you really just need a good starting point. As you investigate answers to an initial query, you'll likely follow a natural course of exploration that will successively refine your understanding of the data and get you closer to the answers that you are looking for.

The possibilities for mining data on Facebook are immense, but be respectful of privacy, and always comply with Facebook's terms of service (*http://on.fb.me/1a1lMXM*) to the best of your ability. Unlike data from Twitter and some other sources that are inherently more open in nature, Facebook data can be quite sensitive, especially if you are analyzing your own social network. Hopefully, this chapter has made it apparent that there are many exciting possibilities for what can be done with social data, and that there's enormous value tucked away on Facebook.

The source code outlined for this chapter and all other chapters is available on GitHub (*http://bit.ly/1a1kNqy*) in a convenient Jupyter Notebook format that you're highly encouraged to try out from the comfort of your own web browser.

2.5 Recommended Exercises

- Retrieve data from the fan page for something you're interested in on Facebook and attempt to analyze the natural language in the comments stream to gain insights. What are the most common topics being discussed? Can you tell if fans are particularly happy or upset about anything?

- Select two different fan pages that are similar in nature and compare/contrast them. For example, what similarities and differences can you identify between fans of Chipotle Mexican Grill and Taco Bell? Can you find anything surprising?

- Pick a celebrity or brand that is very active on social media. Download a large number of their public posts and look at how strongly fans engage with the content. Are there any patterns? Which posts do really well in terms of likes, comments, or shares? Do the top-performing posts have anything in common with each other? What about those posts with poorer engagement levels?

- The number of Facebook objects available to the Graph API is enormous. Can you examine objects such as photos or check-ins to discover insights about anyone in your network? For example, who posts the most pictures, and can you tell what they are about based on the comments stream? Where do your friends check in most often?

- Use histograms (introduced in "Visualizing Frequency Data with Histograms" on page 37) to further slice and dice the Facebook page data. Create a histogram of the number of posts by time of day. Do the posts show up at all hours of the day and night? Or is there a preferred time of day to post?

- Further to this, try measuring the number of likes that posts get as a function of the time of day when they were posted. Social media marketers care a lot about maximizing the impact of a post, and timing plays a role here, although with Facebook's algorithmic news feed it's hard to say when exactly your audience is going to be exposed to your posts.

2.6 Online Resources

The following list of links from this chapter may be useful for review:

- Facebook Developers (*http://bit.ly/1a1lm3Q*)
- Facebook Developers pagination documentation (*http://bit.ly/1a1ltMP*)
- Facebook Platform Policy (*http://bit.ly/1a1lm3C*)
- Graph API Explorer (*http://bit.ly/2jd5Xdq*)
- Graph API Overview (*http://bit.ly/1a1lobU*)
- Graph API Reference (*http://bit.ly/1a1lvEr*)
- HTML meta elements (*http://bit.ly/1a1lBMa*)
- OAuth (*http://bit.ly/1a1kZWN*)
- Open Graph protocol (*http://bit.ly/1a1lu3m*)
- Python requests library (*http://bit.ly/1a1lrEt*)
- RDFa (*http://bit.ly/1a1lujR*)

## CHAPTER 3

Mining Instagram: Computer Vision, Neural Networks, Object Recognition, and Face Detection

In previous chapters we have focused on how to analyze text-based data retrieved from social networks, the structure of the networks themselves, or how strongly people in your network are engaging with the content posted to the platform. Instagram, as a social network, is primarily an image and video-sharing app. It launched in 2010 and quickly gained popularity. The app made it very easy to edit photos and apply various filters. Since it was intended for use on smartphones, it became an easy way to share photos with the world.

Facebook acquired Instagram less than two years after its launch, and as of June 2018 the app had a staggering 1 billion monthly after users, making it one of the most popular social networks in the world.

As social networks have expanded, technology companies have sought new ways of extracting value from all the data being loaded onto their platforms. For example, companies like Facebook and Google have been aggressively hiring people with expertise in the field of machine learning—i.e., teaching computers to recognize patterns in data, to put it very broadly.

The applications of machine learning are myriad: predicting what content you'll enjoy viewing, which ads you'll most likely click on, how best to autocorrect the words you're clumsily typing with your thumbs, etc. As with most things, machine learning can be used nefariously, and so it is important to be aware of its applications and to advocate for better data ethics.

One exciting technological breakthrough of recent years is vastly improved computer vision algorithms. These latest algorithms are applying deep neural networks trained to recognize objects in images, which has huge relevance for things like self-driving vehicles. Artificial neural networks are biologically inspired machine learning algorithms that must be shown many examples, but can be trained to recognize all kinds of patterns in different types of data, including image data.

Since Instagram is a social network with an emphasis on sharing photos, one of the best ways of mining this data is applying these kinds of neural networks. The first question you try to answer is, "What is this a photo of?" Does it contain mountains? Lakes? People? Cars? Animals? These types of algorithms can also be used to filter out illegal or adult content posted to the web, which allows moderators to keep up with the flood of data.

In this chapter, we'll introduce how neural networks work. We'll build our own simple neural net to recognize handwritten digits. Python makes this fairly simple, thanks to some powerful machine learning libraries. We'll then use Google's Vision API to do some heavy lifting: recognizing objects and faces in the photos of Instagram feeds. Since we're just building a small test application to access Instagram's API, you'll only be able to use photos from your own feed, so in order to run the code examples you'll need an Instagram account and at least a few photos posted to the platform.

 Always get the latest bug-fixed source code for this chapter (and every other chapter) on GitHub (*http://bit.ly/Mining-the-Social-Web-3E*). Be sure to also take advantage of this book's virtual machine experience, as described in Appendix A, to maximize your enjoyment of the sample code.

3.1 Overview

This chapter introduces machine learning, a topic that has been getting a lot of attention recently because of its application in artificial intelligence. Thousands of startups have emerged applying machine learning to various problems. In this chapter, we'll look at how this technology can be applied to image data retrieved from a primarily image-focused social media platform. In particular, you'll learn about:

- Instagram's API and how to make API requests
- How data retrieved over Instagram's API is structured
- The basic ideas behind neural networks
- How neural networks can be used to "look" at images and recognize objects in them
- How to apply a powerful pretrained neural network to recognize objects and faces inside posts to your Instagram feed

3.2 Exploring the Instagram API

In order to access the Instagram API, you will need to create an app and register it. This can be done fairly easily on the Instagram Developer platform (*http://bit.ly/1rbjGmz*). From there, simply register a new client, give it a name and description (e.g. "my test application"), and set a redirect URL to a website (e.g., *www.google.com*). The reason for the redirect URL will become clear shortly.

Your newly created client exists in a *sandbox mode* (*http://bit.ly/2Ia88Nr*), which limits its capabilities. Apps in sandbox mode are restricted to a maximum of 10 users and can access only the 20 most recently posted media by each of those users. Stricter rate limits on the API are also imposed. These restrictions are so that you can test your app before submitting it for review. The Instagram staff can then vet your app. If it falls within the permitted use cases, it will be approved and those restrictions will be lifted. Since our focus is on learning about the API, all our examples assume an app in sandbox mode. This chapter is designed to give you the tools to continue learning on your own and build more sophisticated apps.

 At the time of the writing of this chapter, in early 2018, many social media platforms are coming under increasing public scrutiny for how they are handling their data, and how much access third-party apps can get to users' data. Despite the fact that much of the data posted to Instagram is public, Instagram is in the process of tightening access of its API and some features are being deprecated. Always check the developer documentation (*http://bit.ly/2Ibb4JL*) for the latest information.

3.2.1 Making Instagram API Requests

Figure 3-1 shows what a newly created client in sandbox mode looks like. Now that you've created yours, you're almost ready to begin making API requests. From the Manage Clients page (*http://bit.ly/2IayH4Z*) on the developer platform, click the button to manage your newly-created app, then find the client ID and client secret and copy them into the variable declarations in Example 3-1. Also, copy the website URL exactly as it is declared in your registered client and paste it into the REDIRECT_URI variable declaration of Example 3-1.

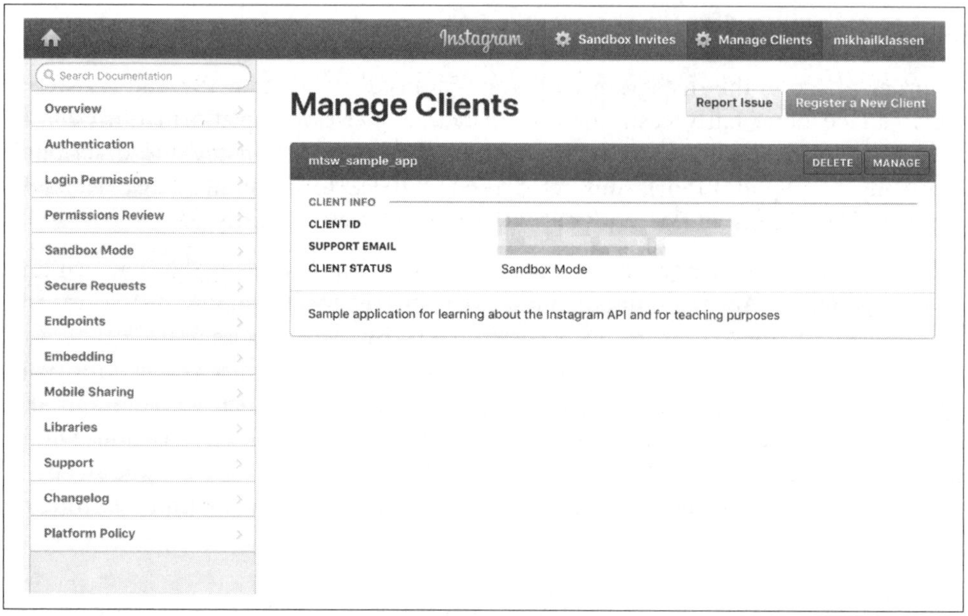

Figure 3-1. The client management page on the Instagram developer platform showing our app in sandbox mode

Example 3-1. Authenticating on the Instagram API

```
# Fill in your client ID, client secret, and redirect URL

CLIENT_ID = ''
CLIENT_SECRET = ''

REDIRECT_URI = ''

base_url = 'https://api.instagram.com/oauth/authorize/'

url='{}?client_id={}&redirect_uri={}&response_type=code&scope=public_content'\
    .format(base_url, CLIENT_ID, REDIRECT_URI)

print('Click the following URL, \
which will take you to the REDIRECT_URI \
you set in creating the APP.')
print('You may need to log into Instagram.')
print()
print(url)
```

Running this code will produce output that looks something like the following, but with unique `client_id` and `redirect_uri` parameters in the generated URL:

```
Click the following URL, which will take you to the REDIRECT_URI you set in
    creating the APP.
```

```
You may need to log into Instagram.
```

```
https://api.instagram.com/oauth/authorize/?client_id=...&redirect_uri=...
    &response_type=code&scope=public_content
```

The output contains a URL that you can copy and paste into the address bar of a web browser. If you follow that link, you'll be redirected to log into your Instagram account and finally redirected again to the website URL you declared when registering your client. The URL has a special token in the form of *?code=...* appended to it. Copy and paste this code into Example 3-2 to complete the authentication process and enable access to the Instagram API.

Example 3-2. Obtaining an access token

```python
import requests # pip install requests

CODE = ''

payload = dict(client_id=CLIENT_ID,
               client_secret=CLIENT_SECRET,
               grant_type='authorization_code',
               redirect_uri=REDIRECT_URI,
               code=CODE)

response = requests.post(
    'https://api.instagram.com/oauth/access_token',
    data = payload)

ACCESS_TOKEN = response.json()['access_token']
```

Executing the code in Example 3-2 will store a special access token into the ACCESS_TOKEN variable, and you will make use of this access token every time you make an API request.

Finally, test the app by retrieving the metadata of your own Instagram profile. Running the code in Example 3-3 should return a response structured as JSON that includes youruser name, the location of your profile picture, and your bio, as well as information about the number of posts you've made, number of people you follow, and number of followers you have.

Example 3-3. Confirming access to the platform using your access token, obtained in Example 3-2

```python
url = 'https://api.instagram.com/v1/users/self/?access_token='
response = requests.get(url+ACCESS_TOKEN)
print(response.text)
```

This looks something like:

```
{"data": {"id": "...", "username": "mikhailklassen", "profile_picture":
"https://scontent.cdninstagram.com/vp/bf2fed5bbce922f586e55db2944fdc9c/5B908514
/t51.2885-19/s150x150/22071355_923830121108291_7212344241492590592_n.jpg",
"full_name": "Mikhail Klassen", "bio": "Ex-astrophysicist, entrepreneur, traveler,
wine \u0026 spirits geek.\nPhotography: #travel #architecture #art #urban
#outdoors #wine #spirits", "website": "http://www.mikhailklassen.com/",
"is_business": false, "counts": {"media": 162, "follows": 450, "followed_by":
237}}, "meta": {"code": 200}}
```

3.2.2 Retrieving Your Own Instagram Feed

Unlike in many of the other chapters in this book, we're not making use of a special-purpose Python library for accessing the Instagram feed. At the time of this writing Instagram's API is in flux, and Instagram is rolling out its new Graph API (*http://bit.ly/2jTGHce*), likely borrowing heavily from the technology stack that its parent company Facebook created for its own Graph API (see Chapter 2). One of the official Python Instagram libraries has been mothballed.

Instead, we're making use of the requests (*http://bit.ly/1a1lrEt*) library in Python. It's one of the core libraries, and since Instagram has a RESTful API (*http://bit.ly/2rC8oJW*), we can make our API requests over HTTP using this core Python library. Another advantage of this is that the code we're writing is very transparent, not hidden behind a clever wrapper that abstracts away what's really going on under the hood. And as you will see, it does not take that many lines of code to access the Instagram API anyway.

In Example 3-4 you retrieve your own user feed with a single line of Python using the requests.get() method, touching an API endpoint that represents your feed and authenticating using the access token you created earlier. The rest of the example includes a function for displaying the image feed. This example is intended to be run inside a Jupyter Notebook and makes use of IPython widgets to display inline images.

Example 3-4. Display images and captions from your Instagram feed

```
from IPython.display import display, Image
url = 'https://api.instagram.com/v1/users/self/media/recent/?access_token='
response = requests.get(url+ACCESS_TOKEN)
recent_posts = response.json()

def display_image_feed(feed, include_captions=True):
    for post in feed['data']:
        display(Image(url=post['images']['low_resolution']['url']))
        print(post['images']['standard_resolution']['url'])
        if include_captions: print(post['caption']['text'])
        print()
```

```
display_image_feed(recent_posts, include_captions=True)
```

The JSON response retrieved from the Instagram API doesn't contain the image data itself, but rather a link to where the media can be found. For performance reasons, Facebook and Instagram host content on a delivery network (*http://bit.ly/2Gb0DzH*) of data centers geographically spread out around the world to ensure fast delivery.

The output of running the code in Example 3-4 looks like Figure 3-2, with an inline image displayed first, followed by its public URL and any figure caption.

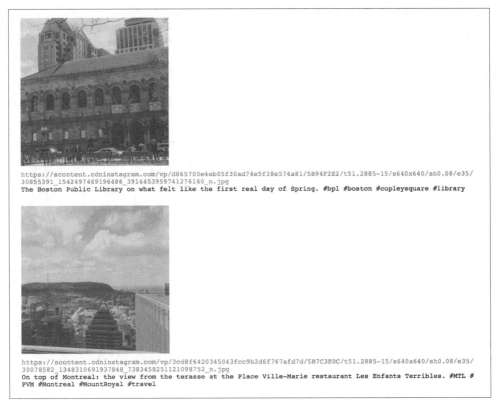

Figure 3-2. A sample of the output from Example 3-4 showing the last two posts in the retrieved Instagram feed, including the public URL of the image and its caption

3.2.3 Retrieving Media by Hashtag

In our earlier code examples, we were using the requests library to hit an API endpoint in the form of a URL (e.g., *https://api.instagram.com/v1/users/self/media/recent/?access_token=…*).

The structure of this URL tells the Instagram API what data to return and the access token achieves the required authentication. The developer documentation has complete descriptions of all the different endpoints (*http://bit.ly/2I9iAEF*) and the kinds of information you can retrieve from them.

Example 3-4 retrieved the 20 most recent posts in your personal Instagram feed (the maximum permitted by a sandboxed application). Of interest for data mining purposes might be to filter this feed by the user-submitted hashtags that are all over Instagram.

Hashtag use began around 2007 on Twitter as a means of grouping tweets, and in 2009 they were hyperlinked to enable searching for results containing the same hashtags. They're also used to measure trending topics and have proved very versatile. Hashtags are a way for users to add their own metadata, allowing them to contribute to particular conversations happening on the platform and to reach a wider audience.

Instagram adopted hashtags for its platform as well, and their use allows for posts to be discovered by people searching for particular hashtags.

To search Instagram by hashtag, we use a slightly different API endpoint and insert the hashtag into the structure of the URL, as shown in Example 3-5.

Example 3-5. Searching for media by hashtag

```
hashtag = 'travel'
response = requests.get('https://api.instagram.com/v1/tags/'
                        +hashtag+'/media/recent?access_token='
                        +ACCESS_TOKEN)

display_image_feed(response.json(), include_captions=True)
```

In this example, we search on the popular #travel hashtag, and we make use of the `display_image_feed` subroutine defined in Example 3-4. The output of this type of query looks similar to Figure 3-2, except filtered to only show posts containing the #travel hashtag. Recall that a sandboxed application will only return media from your own feed, and only from the most recent 20 posts.

3.3 Anatomy of an Instagram Post

Responses from the Instagram API are structured as JSON, which we've seen before. It's a way of transmitting human-readable structured data over APIs as a hierarchical collection of attribute/value pairs. Instagram's developer documentation (*http://bit.ly/2I9iAEF*) contains the latest specifications for how the data is structured, but we'll take a quick look here.

Using Python's `json` library, we'll dump the contents of the API's response to screen for examination. The code to accomplish this is shown in Example 3-6.

Example 3-6. Taking a closer look at the API's response by printing it and using Python's json library

```
import json

uri = ('https://api.instagram.com/v1/users/self/media/recent/?access_token='
    response = requests.get(uri+ACCESS TOKEN)

print(json.dumps(recent_posts, indent=1))
```

Here's some sample output:

```
{
 "pagination": {},
 "data": [
  {
   "id": "1762766336475047742_1170752127",
   "user": {
    "id": "1170752127",
    "full_name": "Mikhail Klassen",
    "profile_picture": "https://...",
    "username": "mikhailklassen"
   },
   "images": {
    "thumbnail": {
     "width": 150,
     "height": 150,
     "url": "https://...jpg"
    },
    "low_resolution": {
     "width": 320,
     "height": 320,
     "url": "https://...jpg"
    },
    "standard_resolution": {
     "width": 640,
     "height": 640,
     "url": "https://...jpg"
    }
   },
   "created_time": "1524358144",
   "caption": {
    "id": "17912334256150534",
    "text": "The Boston Public Library...#bpl #boston #copleysquare #library",
    "created_time": "1524358144",
    "from": {
     "id": "1170752127",
     "full_name": "Mikhail Klassen",
```

```
      "profile_picture": "https://...jpg",
      "username": "mikhailklassen"
     }
    },
    "user_has_liked": false,
    "likes": {
     "count": 15
    },
    "tags": [
     "bpl",
     "copleysquare",
     "library",
     "boston"
    ],
    "filter": "Reyes",
    "comments": {
     "count": 1
    },
    "type": "image",
    "link": "https://www.instagram.com/p/Bh2mqS7nKc-/",
    "location": {
     "latitude": 42.35,
     "longitude": -71.076,
     "name": "Copley Square",
     "id": 269985898
    },
    "attribution": null,
    "users_in_photo": []
   },
   {
    ...
   }
  ],
  "meta": {
   "code": 200
  }
 }
```

You may notice that the hierarchical structure looks a lot like a Python dictionary, and in fact, they're practically interchangeable.

The top-level attributes of the response (the "envelope") are meta, data, and pagina tion. meta contains information about the response itself. If everything goes well, you'll only see the code key, with a value of 200 ("OK"). However, if things go wrong, such as if you were to submit a bad access token, you'll get an exception with an accompanying error message.

The data key contains the real meat of the response. The value may be in the form of JSON, as shown in the sample output. The data returned from the query in Example 3-6 contains information about the user who posted the media (including username, full name, ID, and profile picture), the images (URLs pointing to the image locations) at different resolutions, and information about the post itself (such as when it was created, its caption, any hashtags, any applied filters, the number of likes, and possibly a geographic location).

In our case, the sandboxed application returned 20 images, and all the relevant information is contained in the `data` key/value pair. If we were running an approved app out of Instagram's sandbox, a query would very likely return more than 20 results. You wouldn't want all that information to be returned at once over the Instagram API, which is why the developers implemented pagination.

Pagination (*http://bit.ly/2Kio0K6*) means the data is partitioned into manageable chunks. The API response contains a `pagination` keyword. The value of this attribute will be a URL pointing to the next "page" of data. Calling the URL will return the next chunk of our query response, which will itself contain another pagination key pointing to the next chunk, and so on.

With the image URLs from the `data` key in our API response, we can now fetch the images themselves and apply data mining techniques to them. Instagram is a platform that encourages public sharing of media, much like Twitter. While it is possible to create private accounts and make your posts only visible to the individuals you approve, the vast majority of accounts on Instagram are public, meaning that (as you probably know already) the images are public.

3.4 Crash Course on Artificial Neural Networks

Image analysis has a long history, but teaching computers to look at images (*http://bit.ly/2IygU79*) and recognize things in them (like a dog or a car) is a more recent technological achievement.

Imagine if you had to describe to a robot what a dog looks like. You might describe the animal as having four legs, pointy ears, two eyes, large teeth, etc. The robot would faithfully apply these rules, but it would return thousands of false positives—other animals that also have four legs, pointy ears, etc. The robot might also fail to detect real dogs because instead of pointy ears, they had droopy ears.

If only there was a way for the robot to learn about dogs in the same way that humans learn about dogs—that is, by seeing many examples of dogs, starting from our earliest infant days when a parent might have pointed at one and said "dog."

Inside that infant's brain is a growing, evolving network of biological neurons (*http://bit.ly/2KWaOvR*), forming and severing connections. Feedback from the environment reinforces key connections, while others atrophy. With enough exposure to dogs, for instance, we have a pretty clear idea of what a dog is, even if we find it difficult to put this idea into words.

Artificial neural networks (*http://bit.ly/2IcVrkK*) are inspired by the biological neural networks that exist in the nervous systems of many organisms. A neural network can be understood as an information processing system with inputs and outputs. An artificial neural network usually consists of *layers* of *neurons*, such as the one depicted in Figure 3-3. Each neuron is defined by an *activation function* that takes multiple inputs, each weighted by some value, and maps them to an output, usually a value between 0 and 1.

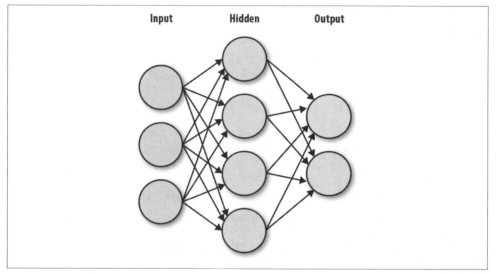

Figure 3-3. A schematic representation of an artificial neural network containing an input layer with three neurons, a single hidden layer with four neurons, and an output layer with two neurons (image by Glosser.ca, CC BY-SA 3.0, from Wikimedia Commons)

The outputs from one layer become the inputs for the next layer. A neural network will have an *input layer*, where each neuron in the input layer corresponds to a single feature of interest. These could be the pixel values in an image, for instance.

The *output layer* often consists of neurons with each representing a class. You could create a network with two output neurons, and the purpose of the network might be to determine whether a photo contains the image of a cat or not. This is a binary classifier. Or you could have many output neurons, with each output neuron representing a different object that could be present in the image.

Most neural networks also contain one or more *hidden layers* between the input and output layers. The presence of these makes the internal workings of the network more opaque to our understanding, but they are vital for detecting complex nonlinear structures that could be present in the input patterns.

A neural network must be "trained" in order for it to have any reasonable degree of accuracy. Training is the process by which the network is shown inputs and the predicted output is compared to some ground truth output. The difference between predicted output and true output represents an error (also called the *loss* (*http://bit.ly/2KdyVoo*)) to be minimized. Using an algorithm called backpropagation (*http://bit.ly/2jRgYRB*), these errors are used to update the weights on the inputs for each neuron throughout the network. Through successive iterations, the network can reduce its overall error and improve its accuracy.

There's a lot more nuance to it than is covered here, but there are many good resources online if you want to go further.

3.4.1 Training a Neural Network to "Look" at Pictures

One of the earliest practical applications of artificial neural networks was reading the zip codes on US postal mail. Envelopes need to be sorted efficiently for distribution, which necessitates reading the postal codes. These are often written by hand. In the United States, postal codes are represented by a five- or nine-digit *zip code* (*http://bit.ly/2IuPpvt*). The first five digits correspond to a geographic area, and the optional additional four digits correspond to a particular delivery route.

The US Post Office uses optical character recognition (OCR) (*http://bit.ly/2IjnqLX*) technology to rapidly read the zip codes for mail sorting. There are several computer vision approaches that can be taken to translate an image of a handwritten digit into a computer character. As it happens, artificial neural networks are particularly well suited to the task.

In fact, one of the first problems that students of machine learning and neural networks learn to solve is the problem of recognizing handwritten digits. A research data set called the MNIST database (*http://bit.ly/2IaAxmC*) has been created to assist with research efforts into neural networks and to benchmark various computer vision algorithms. A sample of the images in the database is shown in Figure 3-4.

Figure 3-4. A sample of images from the MNIST data set (image by Josef Steppan (https://bit.ly/2oblf3f), CC BY-SA 4.0 (https://bit.ly/1upaQv7), from Wikimedia Commons)

The MNIST database contains 60,000 training images and 10,000 test images. An extended version of the database, called EMNIST (*http://bit.ly/2rAZrS4*), also exists; it contains even more images, extending MNIST to handwritten letters.

Each image in the MNIST database consists of 28×28 grayscaled pixels. The values of these pixels, usually normalized to lie between 0 and 1, must be passed to an algorithm whose output is a single digit between 0 and 9.

What does it mean for the neural network to "look" at an image? If we have a single input neuron for each pixel, then we require 784 input neurons (28×28). Each image can represent only 1 of 10 possible digits, so the output layer has 10 neurons, the output value of each being the predicted likelihood of the image representing that digit. The digit with the highest predicted likelihood is returned as the neural network's best guess.

In between the input and output layers we can set "hidden" layers. These neurons are just like all the others, but take as input the output from the preceding layer.

Things quickly get technical from here, and our goal is to begin applying neural networks to image data. If this topic interests you, I recommend checking out a book, such as *Hands-On Machine Learning with Scikit-Learn and TensorFlow* by Aurélien Géron (*https://oreil.ly/2KVa4XS*) (O'Reilly), or Chapter 1 of Michael Nielsen's online book, *Neural Networks and Deep Learning* (*http://bit.ly/2IjE1Pm*).

3.4.2 Recognizing Handwritten Digits

In Example 3-7 we build our own multilayer neural network (*http://bit.ly/2Ie80ME*) to classify handwritten digits, making use of the `scikit-learn` Python library. Conveniently, handwritten digit data can be quickly loaded using a helper function. This data is lower-resolution than the MNIST database, with digits being encoded in 8×8 pixels. A total of 1,797 images are contained in the `scikit-learn` digit database.

> You can install `scikit-learn` from the command line by typing **`pip install scikit-learn`**, and install scipy (a dependency) using **`pip install scipy`**.

Example 3-7. Using the multilayer perceptron (MLP) classifier from the scikit-learn library to identify handwritten digits

```
# Install scikit-learn and scipy (a dependency) using the following commands:
# pip install scikit-learn
# pip install scipy
from sklearn import datasets, metrics
from sklearn.neural_network import MLPClassifier
from sklearn.model_selection import train_test_split

digits = datasets.load_digits()

# Rescale the data and split into training and test sets
X, y = digits.data / 255., digits.target
X_train, X_test, y_train, y_test = train_test_split(X, y, test_size=0.25,
                                                    random_state=42)


mlp = MLPClassifier(hidden_layer_sizes=(100,), max_iter=100, alpha=1e-4,
                    solver='adam', verbose=10, tol=1e-4, random_state=1,
                    learning_rate_init=.1)

mlp.fit(X_train, y_train)
print()
print("Training set score: {0}".format(mlp.score(X_train, y_train)))
print("Test set score: {0}".format(mlp.score(X_test, y_test)))
```

Sample output from this code follows:

```
    Iteration 1, loss = 2.08212650
    Iteration 2, loss = 1.03684958
    Iteration 3, loss = 0.46502758
    Iteration 4, loss = 0.29285682
    Iteration 5, loss = 0.22862621
    Iteration 6, loss = 0.18877491
    Iteration 7, loss = 0.15163667
```

```
Iteration 8, loss = 0.13317189
Iteration 9, loss = 0.11696284
Iteration 10, loss = 0.09268670
Iteration 11, loss = 0.08840361
Iteration 12, loss = 0.08064708
Iteration 13, loss = 0.06800582
Iteration 14, loss = 0.06649765
Iteration 15, loss = 0.05651331
Iteration 16, loss = 0.05649585
Iteration 17, loss = 0.06339016
Iteration 18, loss = 0.06884457
Training loss did not improve more than tol=0.000100 for two consecutive epochs.
Stopping.

Training set score: 0.9806978470675576
Test set score: 0.9577777777777777
```

One thing to pay attention to in Example 3-7 is how we split the data set into a "training" set and a "test" set using the train_test_split method. This function randomly shuffles the data into two sets, one for training and one for model testing, with the size of the test set specified. In our example it is 0.25; i.e., one-quarter of the data is set aside for testing.

It is very important to set aside some data at the beginning of any machine learning task to use for evaluating how well your machine learning algorithm is performing. This is to help avoid overfitting (*https://bit.ly/2mRDi0l*). The algorithm never sees the test data during training, so the accuracy measure you get when running it against the test data is the more honest evaluation of how good your model is.

We see from the output of our code that we achieved a test set accuracy of almost 96% —in other words, our error rate is about 4%. Not too bad! The best algorithms (*http://bit.ly/2G8eSpa*), however, manage to achieve an error rate of about 0.2% on the MNIST database using a special type of deep learning algorithm called a convolutional neural network (*http://bit.ly/2rDgnHD*).

Notice also how our training set score is higher than our test set score? We achieved a training set accuracy of just over 98%. It is typical for machine learning models to perform better on the training set than the test set. That is because the model is learning how to identify digits in the training set. It hasn't yet seen any of the images in the test set. A model that performs really well on the training data but poorly on the test data is said to be "overfit."

One criticism of neural networks (*http://bit.ly/2jSTlbr*) is that they are "black box" algorithms. We feed the network training data, optimize the weights, and run the model on the test data. If the test set results look good, it's tempting to move on without really questioning how the algorithm is arriving at its conclusions.

This might not seem like a big deal if your algorithm is just reading zip codes, but if it's making high-stakes decisions, understanding matters a great deal. You can imagine scenarios where neural networks are making determinations about how to trade on the stock market, who should be eligible for a bank loan, or how high an insurance premium to charge a client.

So, to catch a glimpse of what our algorithm might be "thinking" about, let's visualize the matrix of weights going into each neuron in the hidden layer. To do this, we run the code in Example 3-8. This code is intended to be run in a Jupyter Notebook environment and uses `matplotlib`, a data visualization library for Python that can be installed from the command line using **`pip install matplotlib`**. The Jupyter "magic" command `%matplotlib inline` tells Jupyter that you wish to show images inline with the code cells.

Example 3-8. Visualizing the hidden layer of our neural network

```
# pip install matplotlib
import matplotlib.pyplot as plt

# If using the Jupyter Notebook, for inline data visualizations
%matplotlib inline

fig, axes = plt.subplots(10,10)
fig.set_figwidth(20)
fig.set_figheight(20)

for coef, ax in zip(mlp.coefs_[0].T, axes.ravel()):
    ax.matshow(coef.reshape(8, 8), cmap=plt.cm.gray, interpolation='bicubic')
    ax.set_xticks(())
    ax.set_yticks(())

plt.show()
```

Our hidden layer contains 100 neurons responsible for some aspect of helping the network decide on a digit assignment. The input layer contains 64 neurons (because our digit images are 8×8 pixels) so each of the 100 hidden layer neurons receives 64 inputs. In Example 3-8, we visualize the weight matrix for each neuron by reshaping those 64 values to an 8×8 matrix and drawing a grayscaled image, shown in Figure 3-5. The images for the 100 neurons in the hidden layer of our neural network are shown as 10×10 grid.

Figure 3-5. A visualization of the weight matrix for each neuron in the hidden layer

While most of the images in Figure 3-5 don't look like much, some of them definitely resemble a number, and you get the sense that the network is thinking about how to consider different shapes and how to weight different pixel values when trying to assign a label.

Finally, we show in Example 3-9 how to use our trained neural network to recognize digits pulled from the test data set. You'll need the numpy library, which can be installed with the **pip install numpy** command.

Example 3-9. Using the trained neural network to classify a few of the images in the test set

```python
import numpy as np # pip install numpy
predicted = mlp.predict(X_test)

for i in range(5):
    image = np.reshape(X_test[i], (8,8))
    plt.imshow(image, cmap=plt.cm.gray_r, interpolation='nearest')
    plt.axis('off')
    plt.show()
    print('Ground Truth: {0}'.format(y_test[i]))
    print('Predicted: {0}'.format(predicted[i]))
```

Some sample output from running Example 3-9 is shown in Figure 3-6. Beneath each image is the ground truth label for the handwritten digit, followed by the number predicted by the neural network classifier. We can see that the network is classifying the images accurately.

Ground Truth: 6
Predicted: 6

Ground Truth: 9
Predicted: 9

Ground Truth: 3
Predicted: 3

Ground Truth: 7
Predicted: 7

Figure 3-6. Output of Example 3-9, which shows several images of handwritten digits from the test set, as well as the ground truth label and the prediction by the trained neural network.

3.4.3 Object Recognition Within Photos Using Pretrained Neural Networks

Neural networks—in particular "deep learning" systems, which are neural networks with many complex hidden layers—are transforming entire industries. What is commonly thought of as "artificial intelligence" today is largely (though not exclusively) the many applications of deep learning systems, which includes machine translation, computer vision, natural language understanding, natural language generation, and many others.

If you would like to take some next steps into understanding how artificial neural networks work, a good resource is Michael Nielsen's book *Neural Networks and Deep Learning* (*http://bit.ly/2IzOycW*), which is available online. Also check out *Machine Learning for Artists* (*http://bit.ly/2rChK9i*), especially the chapter titled "Looking Inside Neural Networks (*http://bit.ly/2Kimo3c*)."

Setting up and training an artificial neural network for object recognition is not a simple task. It requires selecting the right neural network architecture, curating a large collection of prelabeled images for training the network, selecting the right hyperparameters, and then training the network long enough for it to provide accurate results.

Luckily, this work has already been done and the technology has been sufficiently commodified that now anyone has access to near-cutting-edge computer vision APIs.

We are going to use the Google Cloud Vision API, a tool that allows developers to analyze images with Google's powerful pretrained neural networks. It is capable of detecting a broad range of objects within images, detecting faces, extracting text, and flagging explicit content, among other features.

Navigate to the Cloud Vision API (*http://bit.ly/2IEmOny*) page, and then scroll down to "Try the API." You will need to register an account on the Google Cloud Platform if you don't already have one. At the time of writing, Google is offering a Free Tier (*http://bit.ly/2wCXKbC*) with $300 in credits for 12 months. You will still need to add a credit card when you sign up, but it is only used for identification. If you do not have a credit card, you can add bank information instead.

Next you will need to create a project (*http://bit.ly/2rE0Zul*) on the Google Cloud Platform. Think of these projects like the client you had to create on the Instagram developer platform.

Projects can be created from the Cloud Resource Manager (*http://bit.ly/2wyV5zD*) page. Go ahead and create one, calling it whatever you wish (for example, "MTSW"). Attach it to your billing account. Even if you are not on Google's Free Tier, the first 1,000 Cloud Vision API calls are free.

Once you've created your project, visit the API Dashboard (*http://bit.ly/2rARWdU*). It looks something like Figure 3-7.

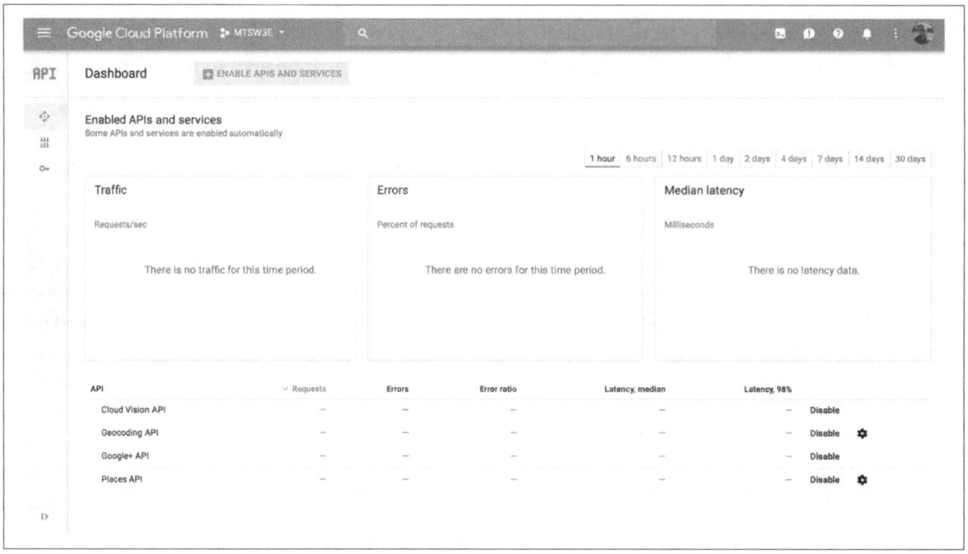

Figure 3-7. The Google Cloud Platform API Dashboard

You need to enable the Cloud Vision API, so click "Enable APIs and Services," then search for "Vision API." Enable the API for your project.

The last step is to get your API key. From the API Dashboard, navigate to the Credentials page (*http://bit.ly/2I9JT1H*). You should see the link in the navigation bar. From there, click "Create credentials" and choose "API key."

Congratulations! You now have all you need to access Google's Cloud Vision API. While that may have felt like a lot of steps, these are necessary in order for Google to secure its platform and to allow fair use of the technology it has created.

Copy the API key you just created and paste it into Example 3-10, storing it in the `GOOGLE_API_KEY` variable. The Google Cloud Platform comes with a Python library for accessing the platform programmatically. Install it using **pip install google-api-python-client**. We also make use of the `Pillow` Python library for image manipulation. Install `Pillow` using the command **pip install Pillow**.

Example 3-10. Leveraging the Google Cloud Vision API to perform label detection on images

```
import base64
import urllib
import io
import os
```

```
import PIL # pip install Pillow
from IPython.display import display, Image

GOOGLE_API_KEY = ''

# pip install google-api-python-client
from googleapiclient.discovery import build
service = build('vision', 'v1', developerKey=GOOGLE_API_KEY)

cat = 'resources/ch05-instagram/cat.jpg'

def label_image(path=None, URL=None, max_results=5):
    '''Read an image file (either locally or from the web) and pass the image data
    to Google's Cloud Vision API for labeling. Use the URL keyword to pass in the
    URL to an image on the web. Otherwise, pass in the path to a local image file.
    Use the max_results keyword to control the number of labels returned by
    the Cloud Vision API.
    '''

    if URL is not None:
        image_content = base64.b64encode(urllib.request.urlopen(URL).read())
    else:
        image_content = base64.b64encode(open(path, 'rb').read())
    service_request = service.images().annotate(body={
        'requests': [{
            'image': {
                'content': image_content.decode('UTF-8')
            },
            'features': [{
                'type': 'LABEL_DETECTION',
                'maxResults': max_results
            }]
        }]
    })
    labels = service_request.execute()['responses'][0]['labelAnnotations']
    if URL is not None:
        display(Image(url=URL))
    else:
        display(Image(path))
    for label in labels:
        print ('[{0:3.0f}%]: {1}'.format(label['score']*100, label['description']))

    return

# Finally, call the image labeling function on the image of a cat
label_image(cat)
```

Interacting with the Vision API can be a bit tricky, so the sample code in Example 3-10 contains all you need to perform object detection and labeling for an image that is either stored locally on your hard drive or accessible over the web.

Running the code in Example 3-10 opens an image file containing a photo of a cat (see Figure 3-8). The image file is read and the image data is passed over the API to Google. In the service_request variable, we have loaded a request to perform image labeling.

Figure 3-8. A photograph of a cat on snow (image by Von.grzanka (https://bit.ly/2obUbly), CC BY-SA 3.0 (https://bit.ly/1pawxfE) or GFDL (http://2wlkJoO), from Wikimedia Commons)

Here's the result of running our code:

```
[ 99%]: cat
[ 94%]: fauna
[ 93%]: mammal
[ 91%]: small to medium sized cats
[ 90%]: whiskers
```

The Cloud Vision API returns five labels for the photograph, with 99% confidence that this is a cat. The other labels ("fauna," "mammal," etc.) are also accurate and appropriate.

Feel free to experiment with this code, uploading other files from your computer, and see what labels it returns.

3.5 Applying Neural Networks to Instagram Posts

Now that you've learned the basics of how a neural network works and have the code for accessing powerful cloud-hosted neural networks behind an API, we'll put the final pieces together. This section covers object recognition and face detection and makes use of our Instagram feeds for some source images.

3.5.1 Tagging the Contents of an Image

The hardest part is over. We're now ready to feed the Cloud Vision API images from our Instagram feeds. These images are not hosted on our computer, but on Instagram's servers. No worry. The way we wrote our label_image function means we can pass in a URL, as we do in Example 3-11.

Example 3-11. Performing object detection and labeling on images in your Instagram feed

```
uri = ('https://api.instagram.com/v1/users/self/media/recent/?access_token='
response = requests.get(uri+ACCESS_TOKEN)
recent_posts = response.json()

for post in recent_posts['data']:
    url = post['images']['low_resolution']['url']
    label_image(URL=url)
```

Try this for yourself and see how accurate the labels are. Some sample output is shown in Figure 3-9.

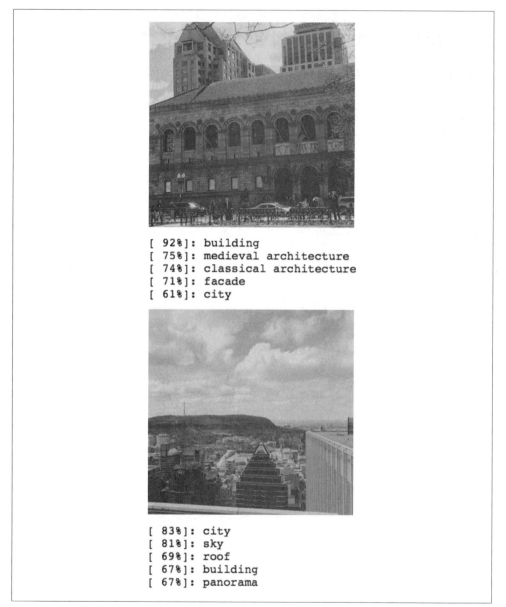

```
[ 92%]: building
[ 75%]: medieval architecture
[ 74%]: classical architecture
[ 71%]: facade
[ 61%]: city
```

```
[ 83%]: city
[ 81%]: sky
[ 69%]: roof
[ 67%]: building
[ 67%]: panorama
```

Figure 3-9. The results of running the code in Example 3-11 on images in the author's Instagram feed

3.5.2 Detecting Faces in Images

Facial recognition systems (*http://bit.ly/2KTvuEy*) are extremely useful. You've probably encountered them already if you've used a modern digital camera, such as those in smartphones. In photography they are used to identify the subject of a photo and focus the image on the subject.

Detecting faces requires that we change the service request to the API slightly. The modified code is given in Example 3-12.

Example 3-12. Sample code for a face detection function using Google's Cloud Vision API

```python
from PIL import Image as PImage
from PIL import ImageDraw

def detect_faces(path=None, URL=None):
    '''Read an image file (either locally or from the web) and pass the image data
    the URL to Google's Cloud Vision API for face detection. Use the URL keyword
    to pass in to an image on the web. Otherwise, pass in the path to a local image
    file. Use the max_results keyword to control the number of labels returned by
    Cloud Vision API.
    '''
    if URL is not None:
        image_content = base64.b64encode(urllib.request.urlopen(URL).read())
    else:
        image_content = base64.b64encode(open(path, 'rb').read())
    service_request = service.images().annotate(body={
        'requests': [{
            'image': {
                'content': image_content.decode('UTF-8')
            },
            'features': [{
                'type': 'FACE_DETECTION',
                'maxResults': 100
            }]
        }]
    })
    try:
        faces = service_request.execute()['responses'][0]['faceAnnotations']
    except:
        # No faces found...
        faces = None
    if URL is not None:
        im = PImage.open(urllib.request.urlopen(URL))
    else:
        im = PImage.open(path)
    draw = ImageDraw.Draw(im)

    if faces:
        for face in faces:
            box = [(v.get('x', 0.0), v.get('y', 0.0))
            for v in face['fdBoundingPoly']['vertices']]
            draw.line(box + [box[0]], width=5, fill='#ff8888')
```

```
    display(im)
    return
```

You can apply the face detection system to your Instagram feed in the same way as before, or to any single image. Here, we apply it to an image taken of the Beatles in 1967. As you can see in Figure 3-10, the algorithm correctly identifies all four faces.

Figure 3-10. The results of running the face detection code from Example 3-12 on a press photo of the Beatles from 1967 (original image by Parlophone Music Sweden, CC BY 3.0 (https://bit.ly/1b8Hyff), via Wikimedia Commons)

3.6 Closing Remarks

Instagram has created an enormously popular platform for sharing photographs used by hundreds of millions of people around the world. The type of data on the platform is different from the data we've analyzed in other chapters. Instagram content mostly consists of captioned images, and so it demands a different set of tools for analysis.

Some of the most advanced tools that exist today for teaching computers how to look at image data consist of artificial neural networks that have been trained to recognize things. "Training" means showing the neural network thousands of examples that have already been labeled by humans, and tuning the network to make the same associations.

These types of computer vision systems are being built into cameras, security systems, self-driving cars, and countless other products. In this chapter, we opened the door to building your own computer vision systems and showed you how to connect to some of the most powerful vision APIs.

Researchers developing these systems must often pay human assistants to go through large image databases and manually label each image. This is time-consuming and expensive. Social platforms like Facebook and Instagram, where people are uploading countless images every day and adding their own hashtags, are realizing how useful this information is. Facebook has begun using billions of hashtagged Instagram images to train its artificial intelligence systems (*http://bit.ly/2IzMPEs*) to look at photos the way humans do.

Helping machines understand the world visually opens up incredible possibilities. The best outcomes of this kind of research are technologies that help humans, such as autonomous vehicles that can safely navigate amidst pedestrians, cyclists, and other obstacles, or medical imaging technology that can accurately identify a tumor in its earliest stages. Of course, the same tools can also be used for oppression. Knowing how these technologies work is the first step to advocating for their appropriate use.

 The source code outlined for this chapter and all other chapters is available on GitHub (*http://bit.ly/Mining-the-Social-Web-3E*) in a convenient Jupyter Notebook format that you're highly encouraged to try out from the comfort of your own web browser.

3.7 Recommended Exercises

- Instagram stores uploaded photos at different resolutions, and you should be able to find their URLs by examining the post metadata returned by the API. Compare the accuracy of the image labeling or face detection system on the same image, at different resolutions.

- Try playing around with the neural network architecture we built to identify handwritten digits. In this chapter we used a single hidden layer with 100 neurons. How does the test set accuracy change when we reduce the number of neurons in the hidden layer to 50, 20, 10, or 5? What about changing the number of hidden layers? Take a look at the scikit-learn documentation for the MLP classifier (*http://bit.ly/2jQt90V*). MLP is short for multilayer perceptron (*http://bit.ly/2Ie80ME*), the type of neural network architecture that we are using.

- If you've uploaded photos to Instagram from your phone, it's very likely that geographic coordinates were associated with the images. Instagram uses your phone's GPS sensor (if you allow the app to access location services) to detect your location at the time you snap the photo and helps you tag the location or landmark when editing your post. See if you can find the geographic information in the post metadata. Loop over the posts in your feed and print all the latitudes and longitudes to screen.

- In Chapter 4, you'll learn to make use of another Google API—the one for geocoding to look up locations on Earth. After you've read that chapter, return to these Instagram examples, and try to extract geographic information contained in the metadata of an Instagram post, or an object mentioned in the image description. Try creating a KML file from this data and open it with Google Earth. This is a neat way to visualize on a map all the places you've taken a photo.

- If you use hashtags when posting photos to Instagram, compare how similar your hashtags are to the labels that the Google Cloud Vision API returned for your photos. How could you use a computer vision system such as the Cloud Vision API to build an automated hashtag recommendation system?

3.8 Online Resources

The following list of links from this chapter may be useful for review:

- Instagram's developer documentation (*http://bit.ly/2Ibb4JL*)
- Instagram's application sandbox mode (*http://bit.ly/2Ia88Nr*)
- Representational State Transfer (*http://bit.ly/2rC8oJW*)
- Instagram's Graph API (*http://bit.ly/2jTGHce*)
- Instagram's API endpoints (*http://bit.ly/2I9iAEF*)
- Content delivery network (*http://bit.ly/2Gb0DzH*)
- Biological neural network (*http://bit.ly/2KWaOvR*)
- Artificial neural network (*http://bit.ly/2IcVrkK*)
- Backpropagation algorithm (*http://bit.ly/2jRgYRB*)

- Loss function (*http://bit.ly/2KdyVoo*)
- Computer vision (*http://bit.ly/2IygU79*)
- Face detection (*http://bit.ly/2KTvuEy*)
- Optical character recognition (*http://bit.ly/2IjnqLX*)
- MNIST database (*http://bit.ly/2IaAxmC*)
- EMNIST (*http://bit.ly/2rAZrS4*)
- *Hands-On Machine Learning with Scikit-Learn and TensorFlow* (*https://oreil.ly/2KVa4XS*)
- *Neural Networks and Deep Learning*, Chapter 1 ("Using Neural Nets to Recognize Handwritten Digits") (*http://bit.ly/2IzOycW*)
- Multilayer perceptron (*http://bit.ly/2Ie80ME*)
- `scikit-learn`'s MLP classifier (*http://bit.ly/2jQt90V*)
- Convolutional neural network (*http://bit.ly/2rDgnHD*)
- Results of state-of-the-art computer vision algorithms on classification problems, including MNIST (*http://bit.ly/2G8eSpa*)
- "The Dark Secret at the Heart of AI" (*http://bit.ly/2jSTlbr*)
- Machine Learning for Artists (*http://bit.ly/2rChK9i*)
- "Looking inside neural nets" (part of Machine Learning for Artists) (*http://bit.ly/2Kimo3c*)
- Google Vision API (*http://bit.ly/2IEmOny*)
- Google Cloud Platform Console (*http://bit.ly/2Kin4FM*)
- Google Cloud Platform API Dashboard (*http://bit.ly/2rARWdU*)

## CHAPTER 4

Mining LinkedIn: Faceting Job Titles, Clustering Colleagues, and More

This chapter introduces techniques and considerations for mining the troves of data tucked away at LinkedIn, a social networking site focused on professional and business relationships. Although LinkedIn may initially seem like any other social network, the nature of its API data is inherently quite different. If you liken Twitter to a busy public forum like a town square and Facebook to a very large room filled with friends and family chatting about things that are (mostly) appropriate for dinner conversation, then you might liken LinkedIn to a private event with a semiformal dress code where everyone is on their best behavior and trying to convey the specific value and expertise that they can bring to the professional marketplace.

Given the somewhat sensitive nature of the data that's tucked away at LinkedIn, its API has its own nuances that make it a bit different from many of the others we look at in this book. People who join LinkedIn are principally interested in the business opportunities that it provides as opposed to arbitrary socializing and will necessarily be providing sensitive details about business relationships, job histories, and more. For example, while you can generally access all of the details about *your* LinkedIn connections, educational histories, and previous work positions, you cannot determine whether two arbitrary people are "mutually connected." The absence of such an API method is intentional. The API doesn't lend itself to being modeled as a social graph like Facebook or Twitter, therefore requiring that you ask different types of questions about the data that's available to you.

The remainder of this chapter gets you set up to access data with the LinkedIn API and introduces some fundamental data mining techniques that can help you cluster colleagues according to a similarity measurement in order to answer the following kinds of questions:

- Which of your connections are the most similar based upon a criterion like job title?
- Which of your connections have worked in companies you want to work for?
- Where do most of your connections reside geographically?

In all cases, the pattern for analysis with a clustering technique is essentially the same: extract some features from data in a connection's profile, define a similarity measurement to compare the features from each profile, and use a clustering technique to group together connections that are "similar enough." The approach works well for LinkedIn data, and you can apply these same techniques to just about any kind of other data that you'll ever encounter.

 Always get the latest bug-fixed source code for this chapter (and every other chapter) on GitHub (*http://bit.ly/Mining-the-Social-Web-3E*). Be sure to also take advantage of this book's virtual machine experience, as described in Appendix A, to maximize your enjoyment of the sample code.

4.1 Overview

This chapter introduces content that is foundational in machine learning and in general is a bit more advanced than the two chapters before it. It is recommended that you have a firm grasp on the previous two chapters before working through the material presented here. In this chapter, you'll learn about:

- LinkedIn's Developer Platform and making API requests
- Three common types of clustering, a fundamental machine-learning topic that applies to nearly any problem domain
- Data cleansing and normalization
- Geocoding, a means of arriving at a set of coordinates from a textual reference to a location
- Visualizing geographic data with Google Earth and with cartograms

4.2 Exploring the LinkedIn API

You'll need a LinkedIn account and a handful of connections in your professional network to follow along with this chapter's examples in a meaningful way. If you don't have a LinkedIn account, you can still apply the fundamental clustering techniques that you'll learn about to other domains, but this chapter won't be quite as engaging since you can't follow along with the examples without your own LinkedIn data. Start developing a LinkedIn network if you don't already have one as a worthwhile investment in your professional life.

Although most of the analysis in this chapter is performed against a comma-separated values (CSV) file of your LinkedIn connections that you can download, this section maintains continuity with other chapters in the book by providing an overview of the LinkedIn API. If you're not interested in learning about the LinkedIn API and would like to jump straight into the analysis, skip ahead to "Downloading LinkedIn Connections as a CSV File" on page 125 and come back to the details about making API requests at a later time.

4.2.1 Making LinkedIn API Requests

As is the case with other social web properties, such as Twitter and Facebook (discussed in the preceding chapters), the first step involved in gaining API access to LinkedIn is to create an application. You'll be able to create a sample application via the developer portal (*https://bit.ly/2swubEU*); you will want to take note of your application's client ID and client secret; these are your authentication credentials, which you'll use to programmatically access the API. Figure 4-1 illustrates the form that you'll see once you have created an application.

With the necessary OAuth credentials in hand, the process for obtaining API access to your own personal data involves providing these credentials to a library that will take care of the details involved in making API requests. If you're not taking advantage of the book's virtual machine experience, you'll need to install it by typing **pip install python3-linkedin** in a terminal.

 See Appendix B for details on implementing an OAuth 2.0 flow, which you will need to build an application that requires an arbitrary user to authorize it to access account data.

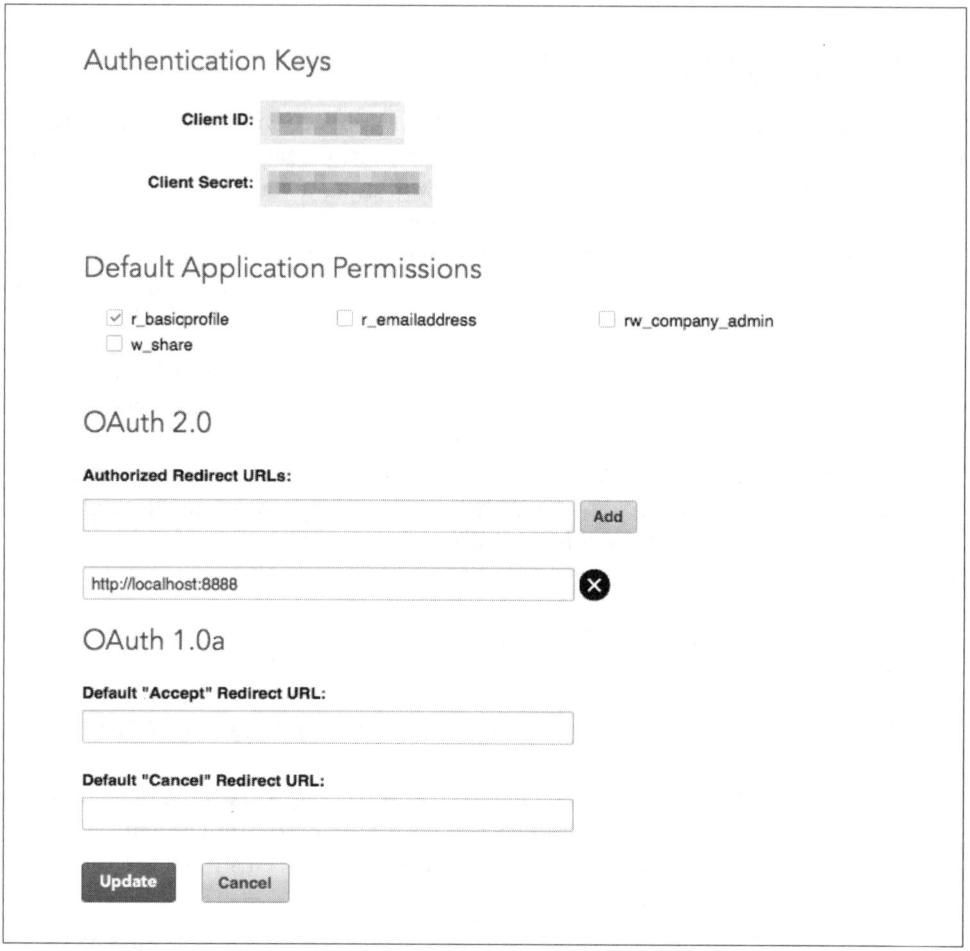

Figure 4-1. To access the LinkedIn API, create an application and take note of the client ID and secret (shown here as blurred values) that are available from the application details page

Example 4-1 illustrates a sample script that uses your LinkedIn credentials to ultimately create an instance of a `LinkedInApplication` class that can access your account data. Notice that the final line of the script retrieves your basic profile information, which includes your name and headline. Before going too much further, you should take a moment to read about what LinkedIn API operations are available to you as a developer by browsing the REST API documentation (*http://linkd.in/ 1a1lZuj*), which provides a broad overview of what you can do. Although we'll be accessing the API through a Python package that abstracts the HTTP requests that are involved, the core API documentation is always your definitive reference, and most good libraries mimic its style.

Example 4-1. Using LinkedIn OAuth credentials to receive an access token suitable for development and accessing your own data

```
from linkedin import linkedin # pip install python3-linkedin

APPLICATON_KEY    = ''
APPLICATON_SECRET = ''

# OAuth redirect URL, must match the URL specified in the app settings
RETURN_URL = 'http://localhost:8888'

authentication = linkedin.LinkedInAuthentication(
                    APPLICATON_KEY,
                    APPLICATON_SECRET,
                    RETURN_URL)

# Open this URL in the browser and copy the section after 'code='
print(authentication.authorization_url)

# Paste it here, careful not to include '&state=' and anything afterwards
authentication.authorization_code = ''

result = authentication.get_access_token()

print ("Access Token:", result.access_token)
print ("Expires in (seconds):", result.expires_in)

# Pass the access token to the application
app = linkedin.LinkedInApplication(token=result.access_token)

# Retrieve user profile
app.get_profile(selectors=['id', 'first-name', 'last-name',
                           'location', 'num-connections', 'headline'])
```

In short, the calls available to you through an instance of `LinkedInApplication` are the same as those available through the REST API, and the `python-linkedin` documentation (*http://bit.ly/1a1m2Gk*) on GitHub provides a number of queries to get you started. A couple of APIs of particular interest are the Connections API and the Search API. You'll recall from our introductory discussion that you cannot get "friends of friends" ("connections of connections," in LinkedIn parlance), but the Connections API returns a list of your connections, which provides a jumping-off point for obtaining profile information. The Search API provides a means of querying for people, companies, or jobs that are available on LinkedIn.

Additional APIs are available, and it's worth your while to take a moment and familiarize yourself with them. One thing to note, however, is that LinkedIn has made changes to its API over the years and become more restrictive in what information is freely accessible over its API. For instance, if you attempt to retrieve all of your connections data over the API, you may receive a 403 ("Forbidden") error. LinkedIn still permits you to download an archive of all of your member data, which we'll discuss in "Downloading LinkedIn Connections as a CSV File" on page 125. This is the same data you would be able to access as an authenticated user navigating LinkedIn's website in your browser.

 Be careful when tinkering around with LinkedIn's API: the rate limits don't reset until midnight UTC, and one buggy loop could potentially blow your plans for the next 24 hours if you aren't careful.

For example, Example 4-2 shows how to fetch your own profile's complete job position history.

Example 4-2. Displaying job position history for your profile and a connection's profile

```python
import json

# See https://developer.linkedin.com/docs/fields/positions for details
# on additional field selectors that can be passed in for retrieving
# additional profile information.

# Display your own positions...
my_positions = app.get_profile(selectors=['positions'])
print(json.dumps(my_positions, indent=1))
```

Sample output reveals a number of interesting details about each position, including the company name, industry, summary of efforts, and employment dates:

```json
{
 "positions": {
  "_total": 10,
  "values": [
   {
    "startDate": {
     "year": 2013,
     "month": 2
    },
    "title": "Chief Technology Officer",
    "company": {
     "industry": "Computer Software",
     "name": "Digital Reasoning Systems"
    },
    "summary": "I lead strategic technology efforts...",
    "isCurrent": true,
    "id": 370675000
   },
   {
    "startDate": {
```

```
        "year": 2009,
        "month": 10
    }
    ...
  }
 ]
 }
}
```

As might be expected, some API responses may not necessarily contain all of the information that you want to know, and some responses may contain more information than you need. Instead of making multiple API calls to piece together information or potentially stripping out information you don't want to keep, you could take advantage of the field selector syntax (*http://bit.ly/2E7vahT*) to customize the response details. Example 4-3 shows how you can retrieve only the name, industry, and id fields for companies as part of a response for profile positions.

Example 4-3. Using field selector syntax to request additional details for APIs

```
# See http://bit.ly/2E7vahT for more information on the field selector syntax

my_positions = app.get_profile(selectors=['positions:(company:(name,industry,id))'])
print json.dumps(my_positions, indent=1)
```

Once you're familiar with the basic APIs that are available to you, have a few handy pieces of documentation bookmarked, and have made a few API calls to familiarize yourself with the basics, you're up and running with LinkedIn.

4.2.2 Downloading LinkedIn Connections as a CSV File

While using the API provides programmatic access to many things that would be visible to you as an authenticated user browsing profiles at *http://linkedin.com*, you can get all of the job title details you'll need for much of this chapter by exporting your LinkedIn connections as address book data in a CSV file format. To initiate the export, navigate to your LinkedIn Settings & Privacy page and find the "Download your data" option, or navigate directly to the Export LinkedIn Connections dialog (*http://linkd.in/1a1m4ho*) illustrated in Figure 4-2.

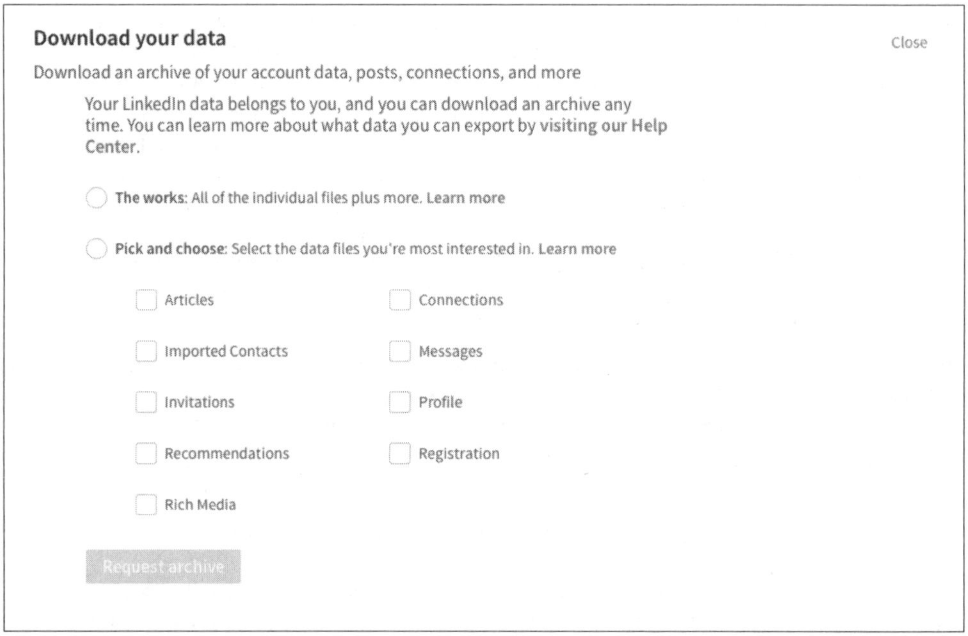

Figure 4-2. A lesser-known feature of LinkedIn is that you can export all of your connections in a convenient and portable CSV format

4.3 Crash Course on Clustering Data

Now that you have a basic understanding of how to access LinkedIn's API, let's dig into some more specific analysis with what will turn out to be a fairly thorough discussion of *clustering*,[1] an unsupervised machine learning technique that is a staple in any data mining toolkit. Clustering involves taking a collection of items and partitioning them into smaller collections (clusters) according to some heuristic that is usually designed to compare items in the collection.

---

1 Without splitting hairs over technical nuances, it's also commonly referred to as *approximate matching, fuzzy matching*, and/or *deduplication*, among many other names.

Clustering is a fundamental data mining technique, and as part of a proper introduction to it, this chapter includes some footnotes and interlaced discussion of a somewhat mathematical nature that undergirds the problem. Although you should strive to eventually understand these details, you don't need to grasp all of the finer points to successfully employ clustering techniques, and you certainly shouldn't feel any pressure to understand them the first time that you encounter them. It may take a little bit of reflection to digest some of the discussion, especially if you don't have a mathematical background.

For example, if you were considering a geographic relocation, you might find it useful to cluster your LinkedIn connections into some number of geographic regions in order to better understand the economic opportunities available. We'll revisit this concept momentarily, but first let's take a moment to briefly discuss some nuances associated with clustering.

When implementing solutions to problems that lend themselves to clustering on LinkedIn or elsewhere, you'll repeatedly encounter at least two primary themes (see "The Role of Dimensionality Reduction in Clustering" on page 128 for a discussion of a third) as part of a clustering analysis:

Data normalization

> Even when you're retrieving data from a nice API, it's usually not the case that the data will be provided to you in exactly the format you'd like—it often takes more than a little bit of munging to get the data into a form suitable for analysis. For example, LinkedIn members can enter in text that describes their job titles, so you won't always end up with perfectly normalized job titles. One executive might choose the title "Chief Technology Officer," while another may opt for the more ambiguous "CTO," and still others may choose other variations of the same role. We'll revisit the data normalization problem and implement a pattern for handling certain aspects of it for LinkedIn data momentarily.

Similarity computation

> Assuming you have reasonably well-normalized items, you'll need to measure similarity between any two of them, whether they're job titles, company names, professional interests, geographic labels, or any other field you can enter in as variable-free text, so you'll need to define a heuristic that can approximate the similarity between any two values. In some situations computing a similarity heuristic can be quite obvious, but in others it can be tricky.

For example, comparing the combined years of career experience for two people might be as simple as some addition operations, but comparing a broad professional element such as "leadership aptitude" in a fully automated manner could be quite a challenge.

The Role of Dimensionality Reduction in Clustering

Although data normalization and similarity computation are two overarching themes that you'll encounter in clustering at an abstract level, dimensionality reduction is a third theme that soon emerges once the scale of the data you are working with becomes nontrivial. To cluster all of the items in a set using a similarity metric, you would ideally compare every member to every other member. Thus, for a set of n members in a collection, you would perform somewhere on the order of n^2 similarity computations in your algorithm for the worst-case scenario because you have to compare each of the n items to $n-1$ other items.

Computer scientists call this predicament an *n-squared problem* and generally use the nomenclature $O(n^2)$ to describe it; conversationally, you'd say it's a "Big-O of n-squared" problem. $O(n^2)$ problems become intractable for very large values of n, and most of the time, the use of the term *intractable* means you'd have to wait "too long" for a solution to be computed. "Too long" might be minutes, years, or eons, depending on the nature of the problem and its constraints.

An exploration of dimensionality reduction techniques is beyond the scope of the current discussion, but suffice it to say that a typical dimensionality reduction technique involves using a function to organize "similar enough" items into a fixed number of bins so that the items within each bin can then be more exhaustively compared to one another. Dimensionality reduction is often as much art as it is science, and is frequently considered proprietary information or a trade secret by organizations that successfully employ it to gain a competitive advantage.

Techniques for clustering are a fundamental part of any legitimate data miner's tool belt, because in nearly any sector of any industry—ranging from defense intelligence to fraud detection at a bank to landscaping—there can be a truly immense amount of semistandardized relational data that needs to be analyzed, and the rise of data scientist job opportunities over the previous years has been a testament to this.

What generally happens is that a company establishes a database for collecting some kind of information, but not every field is enumerated into some predefined universe of valid answers. Whether it's because the application's user interface logic wasn't designed properly, because some fields just don't lend themselves to having static predetermined values, or because it was critical to the user experience that users be allowed to enter whatever they'd like into a text box, the result is always the same: you eventually end up with a lot of semistandardized data, or "dirty records." While there might be a total of N distinct string values for a particular field, some number of these string values will actually relate the same concept. Duplicates can occur for various reasons, such as misspellings, abbreviations or shorthand, and differences in the case of words.

As hinted at previously, this is a classic situation we're faced with in mining LinkedIn data: LinkedIn members are able to enter in their professional information as free text, which results in a certain amount of unavoidable variation. For example, if you wanted to examine your professional network and try to determine where most of your connections work, you'd need to consider common variations in company names. Even the simplest of company names has a few common variations you'll almost certainly encounter (e.g., "Google" is an abbreviated form of "Google, Inc."), but even these kinds of simple variations in naming conventions must be explicitly accounted for during standardization efforts. In standardizing company names, a good starting point is to first consider suffixes such as LLC and Inc.

4.3.1 Normalizing Data to Enable Analysis

As a necessary and helpful interlude toward building a working knowledge of clustering algorithms, let's explore a few of the typical situations you may face in normalizing LinkedIn data. In this section, we'll implement a common pattern for normalizing company names and job titles. As a more advanced exercise, we'll also briefly divert and discuss the problem of disambiguating and geocoding geographic references from LinkedIn profile information. (In other words, we'll attempt to convert labels from LinkedIn profiles such as "Greater Nashville Area" to coordinates that can be plotted on a map.)

 The chief artifact of data normalization efforts is that you can count and analyze important features of the data and enable advanced data mining techniques such as clustering. In the case of LinkedIn data, we'll be examining entities such as companies' job titles and geographic locations.

Normalizing and counting companies

Let's take a stab at standardizing company names from your professional network. Recall that the two primary ways you can access your LinkedIn data are either by using the LinkedIn API to programmatically retrieve the relevant fields or by employing a slightly lesser-known mechanism that allows you to export your professional network as address book data, which includes basic information such as name, job title, company, and contact information.

Assuming you have a CSV file of contacts that you've exported from LinkedIn, you could normalize and display selected entities from a histogram, as illustrated in Example 4-4.

 As you'll notice in the opening comments of code listings such as Example 4-4, you'll need to copy and rename the CSV file of your LinkedIn connections that you exported to a particular directory in your source code checkout, per the guidance provided in "Downloading LinkedIn Connections as a CSV File" on page 125.

Example 4-4. Simple normalization of company suffixes from address book data

```python
import os
import csv
from collections import Counter
from operator import itemgetter
from prettytable import PrettyTable

# Download your LinkedIn data from: https://www.linkedin.com/psettings/member-data.
# Once requested, LinkedIn will prepare an archive of your profile data,
# which you can then download. Place the contents of the archive in a
# subfolder, e.g., resources/ch03-linkedin/.

CSV_FILE = os.path.join("resources", "ch03-linkedin", 'Connections.csv')

# Define a set of transforms that convert the first item
# to the second item. Here, we're simply handling some
# commonly known abbreviations, stripping off common suffixes,
# etc.

transforms = [(', Inc.', ''), (', Inc', ''), (', LLC', ''), (', LLP', ''),
              (' LLC', ''), (' Inc.', ''), (' Inc', '')]

companies = [c['Company'].strip() for c in contacts if c['Company'].strip() != '']

for i, _ in enumerate(companies):
    for transform in transforms:
        companies[i] = companies[i].replace(*transform)
```

```
pt = PrettyTable(field_names=['Company', 'Freq'])
pt.align = 'l'
c = Counter(companies)

[pt.add_row([company, freq]) for (company, freq) in
    sorted(c.items(), key=itemgetter(1), reverse=True) if freq > 1]

print(pt)
```

The following illustrates typical results for frequency analysis:

```
+------------------------------+------+
| Company                      | Freq |
+------------------------------+------+
| Digital Reasoning Systems    | 31   |
| O'Reilly Media               | 19   |
| Google                       | 18   |
| Novetta Solutions            | 9    |
| Mozilla Corporation          | 9    |
| Booz Allen Hamilton          | 8    |
| ...                          | ...  |
+------------------------------+------+
```

 Python allows you to pass arguments to a function by *dereferencing* a list and dictionary as parameters, which is sometimes convenient, as illustrated in Example 4-4. For example, calling `f(*args, **kw)` is equivalent to calling `f(1,7, x=23)` so long as `args` is defined as `[1,7]` and `kw` is defined as `{'x' : 23}`. See Appendix C for more Python tips.

Keep in mind that you'll need to get a little more sophisticated to handle more complex situations, such as the various manifestations of company names—like O'Reilly Media—that have evolved over the years. For example, you might see this company's name represented as O'Reilly & Associates, O'Reilly Media, O'Reilly, Inc., or just O'Reilly.[2]

Normalizing and counting job titles

As might be expected, the same problem that occurs with normalizing company names presents itself when considering job titles, except that it can get a lot messier because job titles are so much more variable. Table 4-1 lists a few job titles you're likely to encounter in a software company that include a certain amount of natural variation. How many distinct roles do you see for the 10 distinct titles that are listed?

---

2 If you think this is starting to sound complicated, just consider the work taken on by Dun & Bradstreet (*http://bit.ly/1a1m4Om*), the "Who's Who" of company information, blessed with the challenge of maintaining a worldwide directory that identifies companies spanning multiple languages from all over the globe.

Table 4-1. Example job titles for the technology industry

Job title
Chief Executive Officer
President/CEO
President & CEO
CEO
Developer
Software Developer
Software Engineer
Chief Technical Officer
President
Senior Software Engineer

While it's certainly possible to define a list of aliases or abbreviations that equates titles like CEO and Chief Executive Officer, it may not be practical to manually define lists that equate titles such as Software Engineer and Developer for the general case in all possible domains. However, for even the messiest of fields in a worst-case scenario, it shouldn't be too difficult to implement a solution that condenses the data to the point that it's manageable for an expert to review it and then feed it back into a program that can apply it in much the same way that the expert would have done. More times than not, this is actually the approach that organizations prefer since it allows humans to briefly insert themselves into the loop to perform quality control.

Recall that one of the most obvious starting points when working with any data set is to count things, and this situation is no different. Let's reuse the same concepts from normalizing company names to implement a pattern for normalizing common job titles and then perform a basic frequency analysis on those titles as an initial basis for clustering. Assuming you have a reasonable number of exported contacts, the minor nuances among job titles that you'll encounter may actually be surprising—but before we get into that, let's introduce some sample code that establishes some patterns for normalizing record data and takes a basic inventory sorted by frequency.

Example 4-5 inspects job titles and prints out frequency information for the titles themselves and for individual tokens that occur in them.

Example 4-5. Standardizing common job titles and computing their frequencies

```
import os
import csv
from operator import itemgetter
from collections import Counter
from prettytable import PrettyTable
```

```
# Point this to your 'Connections.csv' file
CSV_FILE = os.path.join('resources', 'ch03-linkedin', 'Connections.csv')

csvReader = csv.DictReader(open(CSV_FILE), delimiter=',', quotechar='"')
contacts = [row for row in csvReader]

transforms = [
    ('Sr.', 'Senior'),
    ('Sr', 'Senior'),
    ('Jr.', 'Junior'),
    ('Jr', 'Junior'),
    ('CEO', 'Chief Executive Officer'),
    ('COO', 'Chief Operating Officer'),
    ('CTO', 'Chief Technology Officer'),
    ('CFO', 'Chief Finance Officer'),
    ('VP', 'Vice President'),
    ]

# Read in a list of titles and split apart
# any combined titles like "President/CEO."
# Other variations could be handled as well, such
# as "President & CEO", "President and CEO", etc.

titles = []
for contact in contacts:
    titles.extend([t.strip() for t in contact['Position'].split('/')
                   if contact['Position'].strip() != ''])

# Replace common/known abbreviations

for i, _ in enumerate(titles):
    for transform in transforms:
        titles[i] = titles[i].replace(*transform)

# Print out a table of titles sorted by frequency

pt = PrettyTable(field_names=['Job Title', 'Freq'])
pt.align = 'l'
c = Counter(titles)
[pt.add_row([title, freq])
 for (title, freq) in sorted(c.items(), key=itemgetter(1), reverse=True)
    if freq > 1]
print(pt)

# Print out a table of tokens sorted by frequency

tokens = []
for title in titles:
    tokens.extend([t.strip(',') for t in title.split()])
pt = PrettyTable(field_names=['Token', 'Freq'])
pt.align = 'l'
c = Counter(tokens)
```

```
[pt.add_row([token, freq])
 for (token, freq) in sorted(c.items(), key=itemgetter(1), reverse=True)
     if freq > 1 and len(token) > 2]
print(pt)
```

In short, the code reads in CSV records and makes a mild attempt at normalizing them by splitting apart combined titles that use the forward slash (like a title of "President/CEO") and replacing known abbreviations. Beyond that, it just displays the results of a frequency distribution of both full job titles and individual tokens contained in the job titles.

This is not all that different from the previous exercise with company names, but it serves as a useful starting template and provides you with some reasonable insight into how the data breaks down.

Sample results follow:

```
+----------------------------------------+------+
| Title                                  | Freq |
+----------------------------------------+------+
| Chief Executive Officer                | 19   |
| Senior Software Engineer               | 17   |
| President                              | 12   |
| Founder                                | 9    |
| ...                                    | ...  |
+----------------------------------------+------+

+---------------+------+
| Token         | Freq |
+---------------+------+
| Engineer      | 43   |
| Chief         | 43   |
| Senior        | 42   |
| Officer       | 37   |
| ...           | ...  |
+---------------+------+
```

One thing that's notable about the sample results is that the most common job title based on exact matches is "Chief Executive Officer," which is closely followed by other senior positions such as "President" and "Founder." Hence, the ego of this professional network has reasonably good access to entrepreneurs and business leaders. The most common tokens from within the job titles are "Engineer" and "Chief." The "Chief" token correlates back to the previous thought about connections to higher-ups in companies, while the token "Engineer" provides a slightly different clue into the nature of the professional network. Although "Engineer" is not a constituent token of the most common job title, it does appear in a large number of job titles (such as "Senior Software Engineer" and "Software Engineer") that show up near the top of the job titles list. Therefore, the ego of this network appears to have connections to technical practitioners as well.

In job title or address book data analysis, this is precisely the kind of insight that motivates the need for an approximate matching or clustering algorithm. The next section investigates further.

Normalizing and counting locations

Although LinkedIn includes general contact information about your connections, you can no longer export general geographic information. This leads us to a general problem in data science, which is what to do about missing information. And what if a piece of geographic information is ambiguous, or has multiple possible representations? For example, "New York," "New York City," "NYC," "Manhattan," and "New York Metropolitan Area" are all related to the same geographic location, but might need to be normalized for proper counting.

As a generalized problem, disambiguating geographic references is quite difficult. The population of New York City might be high enough that you can reasonably infer that "New York" refers to New York City, New York, but what about "Smithville"? There are many Smithvilles in the United States, and with most states having several of them, geographic context beyond the surrounding state is needed to make the right determination. It won't be the case that a highly ambiguous place like "Greater Smithville Area" is something you'll see on LinkedIn, but it serves to illustrate the general problem of disambiguating a geographic reference so that it can be resolved to a specific set of coordinates.

Disambiguating and geocoding the whereabouts of LinkedIn connections is slightly easier than the most generalized form of the problem because most professionals tend to identify with the larger metropolitan area that they're associated with, and there are a relatively finite number of these regions. Although not always the case, you can generally employ the crude assumption that the location referred to in a LinkedIn profile is a relatively well-known location and is likely to be the "most popular" metropolitan region by that name.

In cases where precise information is missing, is it possible to make reasonable estimates? Now that LinkedIn doesn't export the locations of your connections, is there another way of perhaps inferring where your contacts are living and working?

It turns out that we can make educated guesses for any connection by noting the company at which they work and running a geographic lookup on the company's address. This approach may fail for companies that do not list an address publicly. Another failure mode exists when our connection's employer has offices in multiple cities and our geographic lookup returns the wrong address. Nevertheless, as a first approach, we can begin to learn about the geographic locations of our contacts this way.

You can install a Python package called geopy via **pip install geopy**; it provides a generalized mechanism for passing in labels for locations and getting back lists of coordinates that might match. The geopy package itself is a proxy to multiple web services providers such as Bing and Google that perform the geocoding, and an advantage of using it is that it provides a standardized API for interfacing with various geocoding services so that you don't have to manually craft requests and parse responses. The geopy GitHub code repository (*http://bit.ly/1a1m7Ka*) is a good starting point for reading the documentation that's available online.

Example 4-6 illustrates how to use geopy with the Google Maps geocoding API. To run the script, you will need to request an API key from the Google Developers Console (*http://bit.ly/2EGbF15*).

Example 4-6. Geocoding locations with the Google Maps API

```
from geopy import geocoders # pip install geopy

GOOGLEMAPS_APP_KEY = '' # Obtain your key at https://console.developers.google.com/
g = geocoders.GoogleV3(GOOGLEMAPS_APP_KEY)

location = g.geocode("O'Reilly Media")
print(location)
print('Lat/Lon: {0}, {1}'.format(location.latitude,
                                 location.longitude))
print('https://www.google.ca/maps/@{0},{1},17z'.format(location.latitude,
                                                        location.longitude))
```

Next we loop over all our connections and perform a geographic lookup of the name in the "Company" column in the CSV file, as shown in Example 4-7. Sample results from this script follow and illustrate the nature of using an ambiguous label like "Nashville" to resolve a set of coordinates:

```
[(u'Nashville, TN, United States', (36.16783905029297, -86.77816009521484)),
 (u'Nashville, AR, United States', (33.94792938232422, -93.84703826904297)),
 (u'Nashville, GA, United States', (31.206039428710938, -83.25031280517578)),
 (u'Nashville, IL, United States', (38.34368133544922, -89.38263702392578)),
 (u'Nashville, NC, United States', (35.97433090209961, -77.96495056152344))]
```

Example 4-7. Geocoding company names

```
import os
import csv
from geopy import geocoders # pip install geopy

GOOGLEMAPS_APP_KEY = '' # Obtain your key at https://console.developers.google.com/
g = geocoders.GoogleV3(GOOGLEMAPS_APP_KEY)

# Point this to your 'Connections.csv' file
```

```
CSV_FILE = os.path.join('resources', 'ch03-linkedin', 'Connections.csv')

csvReader = csv.DictReader(open(CSV_FILE), delimiter=',', quotechar='"')
contacts = [row for row in csvReader]

for i, c in enumerate(contacts):
    progress = '{0:3d} of {1:3d} - '.format(i+1,len(contacts))
    company = c['Company']
    try:
        location = g.geocode(company, exactly_one=True)
    except:
        print('... Failed to get a location for {0}'.format(company))
        location = None

    if location != None:
        c.update([('Location', location)])
        print(progress + company[:50] + ' -- ' + location.address)
    else:
        c.update([('Location', None)])
        print(progress + company[:50] + ' -- ' + 'Unknown Location')
```

A sample of the output of running Example 4-7 looks like this:

```
40 of 500 - TE Connectivity Ltd. -- 250 Eddie Jones Way, Oceanside, CA...
41 of 500 - Illinois Tool Works -- 1568 Barclay Blvd, Buffalo Grove, IL...
42 of 500 - Hewlett Packard Enterprise -- 15555 Cutten Rd, Houston, TX...
... Failed to get a location for International Business Machines
43 of 500 - International Business Machines -- Unknown Location
44 of 500 - Deere & Co. -- 1 John Deere Pl, Moline, IL 61265, USA
... Failed to get a location for Affiliated Managers Group Inc
45 of 500 - Affiliated Managers Group Inc -- Unknown Location
46 of 500 - Mettler Toledo -- 1900 Polaris Pkwy, Columbus, OH 43240, USA
```

Later in this chapter, we'll use the locations returned from geocoding as part of a clustering algorithm that can be a good way to analyze your professional network. First, we'll look at another useful visualization called a *cartogram* that may be of interest.

Depending on the number of API calls that needed to be processed, running the code in Example 4-7 may have taken some time. Now is a good time to save this processed data. JSON is a useful universal format for doing so, and the code in Example 4-8 illustrates how.

Example 4-8. Saving processed data as JSON

```
CONNECTIONS_DATA = 'linkedin_connections.json'

# Loop over contacts and update the location information to store the
# string address, also adding latitude and longitude information
def serialize_contacts(contacts, output_filename):
    for c in contacts:
        location = c['Location']
```

```
    if location != None:
        # Convert the location to a string for serialization
        c.update([('Location', location.address)])
        c.update([('Lat', location.latitude)])
        c.update([('Lon', location.longitude)])

f = open(output_filename, 'w')
f.write(json.dumps(contacts, indent=1))
f.close()
return

serialize_contacts(contacts, CONNECTIONS_DATA)
```

In "k-means clustering" on page 153 we'll start by reading in this saved data.

Visualizing locations with cartograms

A cartogram (*http://bit.ly/1a1m5Ss*) is a visualization that displays a geography by scaling geographic boundaries according to an underlying variable. For example, a map of the United States might scale the size of each state so that it is larger or smaller than it should be based upon a variable such as obesity rate, poverty level, number of millionaires, or any other variable. The resulting visualization would not necessarily present a fully integrated view of the geography since the individual states would no longer fit together due to their scaling. Still, you'd have an idea about the overall status of the variable that led to the scaling for each state.

A specialized variation of a cartogram called a *Dorling cartogram* (*http://stanford.io/1a1m5SA*) substitutes a shape, such as a circle, for each unit of area on a map in its approximate location and scales the size of the shape according to the value of the underlying variable. Another way to describe a Dorling cartogram is as a "geographically clustered bubble chart." It's a great visualization tool because it allows you to use your instincts about where information should appear on a 2D mapping surface, and it's able to encode parameters using intuitive properties of shapes, like area and color.

Given that the Google Maps geocoding service returns results that include the state for each city that is geocoded, let's take advantage of this information and build a Dorling cartogram of your professional network where we'll scale the size of each state according to the number of contacts you have there. The D3 (*http://bit.ly/1a1kGvo*) cutting-edge visualization toolkit, includes most of the machinery for a Dorling cartogram and provides a highly customizable means of extending the visualization to include other variables if you'd like to do so. D3 also includes several other visualizations that convey geographical information, such as heatmaps, symbol maps, and choropleth maps, that should be easily adaptable to the working data.

There's really just one data munging task that needs to be performed in order to visualize your contacts by state, and that's parsing the states from the geocoder responses.

The Google Maps geocoder returns structured output that allows us to extract the state name from each result.

Example 4-9 illustrates how to parse the geocoder response and write out a JSON file that can be loaded by a D3-powered Dorling cartogram visualization. Since the data visualization we are preparing is focused only on US states, we need to filter out locations from other countries. To do this we've written a helper function, checkIfUSA, that returns a Boolean True if the location is within the United States.

Example 4-9. Parsing out states from the Google Maps geocoder results using a regular expression

```
def checkIfUSA(loc):
    if loc == None: return False
    for comp in loc.raw['address_components']:
        if 'country' in comp['types']:
            if comp['short_name'] == 'US':
                return True
            else:
                return False


def parseStateFromGoogleMapsLocation(loc):
    try:
        address_components = loc.raw['address_components']
        for comp in address_components:
            if 'administrative_area_level_1' in comp['types']:
                return comp['short_name']
    except:
        return None

results = {}
for c in contacts:
    loc = c['Location']
    if loc == None: continue
    if not checkIfUSA(loc): continue
    state = parseStateFromGoogleMapsLocation(loc)
    if state == None: continue
    results.update({loc.address : state})

print(json.dumps(results, indent=1))
```

Sample results follow and illustrate the efficacy of this technique:

```
{
 "1 Amgen Center Dr, Thousand Oaks, CA 91320, USA": "CA",
 "1 Energy Plaza, Jackson, MI 49201, USA": "MI",
 "14460 Qorvo Dr, Farmers Branch, TX 75244, USA": "TX",
 "1915 Rexford Rd, Charlotte, NC 28211, USA": "NC",
 "1549 Ringling Blvd, Sarasota, FL 34236, USA": "FL",
```

```
    "539 S Main St, Findlay, OH 45840, USA": "OH",
    "1 Ecolab Place, St Paul, MN 55102, USA": "MN",
    "N Eastman Rd, Kingsport, TN 37664, USA": "TN",
    ...
}
```

With the ability to distill reliable state abbreviations from your LinkedIn contacts, you can now compute the frequency at which each state appears, which is all that is needed to drive a turnkey Dorling cartogram visualization with D3. A sample visualization for a professional network is displayed in Figure 4-3. Despite the fact that the visualization is just a lot of carefully displayed circles on a map, it's relatively obvious which circles correspond to which states (note that in many cartograms Alaska and Hawaii are displayed in the lower-left corner of the visualization, as is the case with many maps that display them as inlays). Hovering over circles produces tool tips that display the name of the state by default, and additional customization would not be difficult to implement by observing standard D3 best practices. The process of generating the final output for consumption by D3 involves little more than generating a frequency distribution by state and serializing it out as JSON.

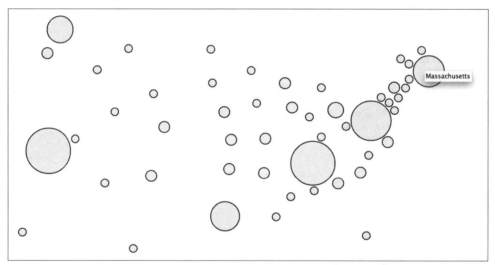

Figure 4-3. A Dorling Cartogram of locations resolved from a LinkedIn professional network—tool tips display the name of each state when the circles are hovered over (in this particular figure, the state of Massachusetts is being hovered over with the mouse)

Some of the code for creating a Dorling cartogram from your LinkedIn connections is omitted from this section for brevity, but it is included as a completely turnkey example with the Jupyter Notebook for this chapter.

4.3.2 Measuring Similarity

With an appreciation for some of the subtleties that are required to normalize data, let us now turn our attention to the problem of computing similarity, which is the principal basis of clustering. The most substantive decision we need to make in clustering a set of strings—job titles, in this case—in a useful way is which underlying similarity metric to use. There are myriad string similarity metrics available, and choosing the one that's most appropriate for your situation largely depends on the nature of your objective.

Although these similarity measurements are not difficult to define and compute ourselves, I'll take this opportunity to introduce the Natural Language Toolkit (NLTK) (*http://bit.ly/1a1mc0m*), a Python toolkit that you'll be glad to have in your arsenal for mining the social web. As with other Python packages, you can simply run **pip install nltk** to install NLTK.

 Depending on your use of NLTK, you may find that you also need to download some additional data sets that aren't packaged with it by default. If you're not employing the book's virtual machine, running the command **nltk.download()** downloads all of NLTK's data add-ons. You can read more about it in the documentation (*http://bit.ly/1a1mcgV*).

Here are a few of the common similarity metrics that might be helpful in comparing job titles that are implemented in NLTK:

Edit distance

The edit distance, also known as Levenshtein distance (*http://bit.ly/1JtgTWJ*), is a simple measure of how many insertions, deletions, and replacements it would take to convert one string into another. For example, the cost of converting *dad* into *bad* would be one replacement operation (substituting the first *d* with a *b*) and would yield a value of 1. NLTK provides an implementation of edit distance via the nltk.metrics.distance.edit_distance function.

The actual edit distance between two strings is quite different from the number of operations required to *compute* the edit distance; computation of edit distance is usually on the order of $M*N$ operations for strings of length M and N. In other words, computing edit distance can be a computationally intense operation, so use it wisely on nontrivial amounts of data.

n-gram similarity

An *n*-gram is just a terse way of expressing each possible consecutive sequence of *n* tokens from a text, and it provides the foundational data structure for computing collocations. There are many variations of *n*-gram similarity, but consider the straightforward case of computing all possible bigrams (two-grams) for the tokens of two strings, and scoring the similarity between the strings by counting the number of common bigrams between them, as demonstrated in Example 4-10.

 An extended discussion of *n*-grams and collocations is presented in "Analyzing Bigrams in Human Language" on page 187.

Example 4-10. Using NLTK to compute bigrams

```
from nltk.util import bigrams

ceo_bigrams = list(bigrams("Chief Executive Officer".split(),
                           pad_left=True, pad_right=True))
cto_bigrams = list(bigrams("Chief Technology Officer".split(),
                           pad_left=True, pad_right=True))

print(ceo_bigrams)
print(cto_bigrams)

print(len(set(ceo_bigrams).intersection(set(cto_bigrams))))
```

The following sample results illustrate the computation of bigrams and the set intersection of bigrams between two different job titles:

```
[(None, 'Chief'), ('Chief', 'Executive'), ('Executive', 'Officer'),
('Officer', None)]
[(None, 'Chief'), ('Chief', 'Technology'), ('Technology', 'Officer'),
('Officer', None)]
2
```

The use of the keyword arguments `pad_right` and `pad_left` intentionally allows for leading and trailing tokens to match. The effect of padding is to allow bigrams such as `(None, 'Chief')` to emerge, which are important matches across job titles. NLTK provides a fairly comprehensive array of bigram and trigram (three-gram) scoring functions via the `BigramAssociationMeasures` and `TrigramAssociationMeasures` classes defined in its `nltk.metrics.association` module.

Jaccard distance

More often than not, similarity can be computed between two sets of things, where a *set* is just an unordered collection of items. The Jaccard similarity metric expresses the similarity of two sets and is defined by the intersection of the sets divided by the union of the sets. Mathematically, the Jaccard similarity is written as:

$$\frac{|Set1 \cap Set2|}{|Set1 \cup Set2|}$$

which is the number of items in common between the two sets (the cardinality of their set intersection) divided by the total number of distinct items in the two sets (the cardinality of their union). The intuition behind this ratio is that calculating the number of unique items that are common to both sets divided by the number of total unique items is a reasonable way to derive a normalized score for computing similarity. In general, you'll compute Jaccard similarity by using n-grams, including unigrams (single tokens), to measure the similarity of two strings.

Given that the Jaccard similarity metric measures how close two sets are to one another, you can measure the dissimilarity between them by subtracting this value from 1.0 to arrive at what is known as the Jaccard distance.

 In addition to these handy similarity measurements and among its other numerous utilities, NLTK provides a class you can access as nltk.FreqDist. This produces a frequency distribution similar to the way that we've been using collections.Counter from Python's standard library.

Calculating similarity is a critical aspect of any clustering algorithm, and it's easy enough to try out different similarity heuristics as part of your work in data science once you have a better feel for the data you're mining. The next section works up a script that clusters job titles using Jaccard similarity.

4.3.3 Clustering Algorithms

With the prerequisite appreciation for data normalization and similarity heuristics in place, let's now collect some real-world data from LinkedIn and compute some meaningful clusters to gain a few more insights into the dynamics of your professional network. Whether you want to take an honest look at whether your networking skills have been helping you to meet the "right kinds of people," you want to approach contacts who will most likely fit into a certain socioeconomic bracket with a particular kind of business inquiry or proposition, or you want to determine if there's a better place you could live or open a remote office to drum up business, there's bound to be something valuable in a professional network rich with high-quality data. The remainder of this section illustrates a few different clustering approaches by further considering the problem of grouping together job titles that are similar.

Greedy clustering

Given that we have insight suggesting that overlap in titles is important, let's try to cluster job titles by comparing them to one another as an extension of Example 4-5 using Jaccard distance. Example 4-11 clusters similar titles and then displays your contacts accordingly. Skim the code—especially the nested loop invoking the DIS TANCE function—and then we'll discuss.

Example 4-11. Clustering job titles using a greedy heuristic

```
import os
import csv
from nltk.metrics.distance import jaccard_distance

# Point this to your 'Connections.csv' file
CSV_FILE = os.path.join('resources', 'ch03-linkedin', 'Connections.csv')

# Tweak this distance threshold and try different distance calculations
# during experimentation
DISTANCE_THRESHOLD = 0.6
DISTANCE = jaccard_distance

def cluster_contacts_by_title():

    transforms = [
        ('Sr.', 'Senior'),
        ('Sr', 'Senior'),
        ('Jr.', 'Junior'),
        ('Jr', 'Junior'),
        ('CEO', 'Chief Executive Officer'),
        ('COO', 'Chief Operating Officer'),
        ('CTO', 'Chief Technology Officer'),
        ('CFO', 'Chief Finance Officer'),
        ('VP', 'Vice President'),
        ]

    separators = ['/', ' and ', ' & ', '|', ',']

    # Normalize and/or replace known abbreviations
    # and build up a list of common titles.

    all_titles = []
    for i, _ in enumerate(contacts):
        if contacts[i]['Position'] == '':
            contacts[i]['Position'] = ['']
            continue
        titles = [contacts[i]['Position']]
        # flatten list
        titles = [item for sublist in titles for item in sublist]
        for separator in separators:
            for title in titles:
```

```
            if title.find(separator) >= 0:
                titles.remove(title)
                titles.extend([title.strip() for title in
                    title.split(separator) if title.strip() != ''])

        for transform in transforms:
            titles = [title.replace(*transform) for title in titles]

        contacts[i]['Position'] = titles
        all_titles.extend(titles)

    all_titles = list(set(all_titles))

    clusters = {}
    for title1 in all_titles:
        clusters[title1] = []
        for title2 in all_titles:
            if title2 in clusters[title1] or title2 in clusters and title1
                in clusters[title2]:
                continue
            distance = DISTANCE(set(title1.split()), set(title2.split()))

            if distance < DISTANCE_THRESHOLD:
                clusters[title1].append(title2)

    # Flatten out clusters

    clusters = [clusters[title] for title in clusters if len(clusters[title]) > 1]

    # Round up contacts who are in these clusters and group them together

    clustered_contacts = {}
    for cluster in clusters:
        clustered_contacts[tuple(cluster)] = []
        for contact in contacts:
            for title in contact['Position']:
                if title in cluster:
                    clustered_contacts[tuple(cluster)].append('{0} {1}.'.format(
                        contact['FirstName'], contact['LastName'][0]))

    return clustered_contacts


clustered_contacts = cluster_contacts_by_title()

for titles in clustered_contacts:
    common_titles_heading = 'Common Titles: ' + ', '.join(titles)

    descriptive_terms = set(titles[0].split())
    for title in titles:
        descriptive_terms.intersection_update(set(title.split()))
    if len(descriptive_terms) == 0: descriptive_terms = ['***No words in common***']
```

```
descriptive_terms_heading = 'Descriptive Terms: '
    + ', '.join(descriptive_terms)
print(common_titles_heading)
print('\n'+descriptive_terms_heading)
print('-' * 70)
print('\n'.join(clustered_contacts[titles]))
print()
```

The code listing starts by separating out combined titles using a list of common conjunctions and then normalizes common titles. Then, a nested loop iterates over all of the titles and clusters them together according to a thresholded Jaccard similarity metric as defined by DISTANCE where the assignment of jaccard_distance to DISTANCE, was chosen to make it easy to swap in a different distance calculation for experimentation. This tight loop is where most of the real action happens in the listing: it's where each title is compared to each other title.

If the distance between any two titles as determined by a similarity heuristic is "close enough," we *greedily* group them together. In this context, being "greedy" means that the first time we are able to determine that an item might fit in a cluster, we go ahead and assign it without further considering whether there might be a better fit, or making any attempt to account for such a better fit if one appears later. Although incredibly pragmatic, this approach produces very reasonable results. Clearly, the choice of an effective similarity heuristic is critical to its success, but given the nature of the nested loop, the fewer times we have to invoke the scoring function, the faster the code executes (a principal concern for nontrivial sets of data). More will be said about this consideration in the next section, but do note that we use some conditional logic to try to avoid repeating unnecessary calculations if possible.

The rest of the listing just looks up contacts with a particular job title and groups them for display, but there is one other nuance involved in computing clusters: *you often need to assign each cluster a meaningful label.* The working implementation computes labels by taking the setwise intersection of terms in the job titles for each cluster, which seems reasonable given that it's the most obvious common thread. Your mileage is sure to vary with other approaches.

The types of results you might expect from this code are useful in that they group together individuals who are likely to share common responsibilities in their job duties. As previously noted, this information might be useful for a variety of reasons, whether you're planning an event that includes a "CEO Panel," trying to figure out who can best help you to make your next career move, or trying to determine whether you are *really* well enough connected to other similar professionals given your own job responsibilities and future aspirations. Abridged results for a sample professional network follow:

```
Common Titles: Sociology Professor, Professor
```

```
Descriptive Terms: Professor
-----------------------------------------------------------------------
Kurtis R.
Patrick R.
Gerald D.
April P.
...


Common Titles: Petroleum Engineer, Engineer

Descriptive Terms: Engineer
-----------------------------------------------------------------------
Timothy M.
Eileen V.
Lauren G.
Erin C.
Julianne M.
...
```

Runtime analysis.

This section contains a relatively advanced discussion about the computational details of clustering and should be considered optional reading, as it may not appeal to everyone. If this is your first reading of this chapter, feel free to skip this section and peruse it upon encountering it a second time.

In the *worst case*, the nested loop executing the DISTANCE calculation from Example 4-11 would require it to be invoked in what we've already mentioned is $O(n^2)$ time complexity—in other words, len(all_titles)*len(all_titles) times. A nested loop that compares every single item to every single other item for clustering purposes is *not* a scalable approach for a very large value of *n*, but given that the unique number of titles for your professional network is not likely to be very large, it shouldn't impose a performance constraint. It may not seem like a big deal—after all, it's just a nested loop—but the crux of an $O(n^2)$ algorithm is that the number of comparisons required to process an input set increases exponentially in proportion to the number of items in the set. For example, a small input set of 100 job titles would require only 10,000 scoring operations, while 10,000 job titles would require 100,000,000 scoring operations. The math doesn't work out so well and eventually buckles, even when you have a lot of hardware to throw at it.

Your initial reaction when faced with what seems like a predicament that doesn't scale will probably be to try to reduce the value of *n* as much as possible. But most of the time you won't be able to reduce it enough to make your solution scalable as the size of your input grows, because you still have an $O(n^2)$ algorithm. What you really want to do is come up with an algorithm that's on the order of $O(k*n)$, where *k* is much smaller than *n* and represents a manageable amount of overhead that grows much more slowly than the rate of *n*'s growth. As with any other engineering decision, there are performance and quality trade-offs to be made in all corners of the real world, and *it can be quite challenging* to strike the right balance. In fact, many data mining companies that have successfully implemented scalable record-matching analytics at a high degree of fidelity consider their specific approaches to be proprietary information (trade secrets), since they result in definite business advantages.

For situations in which an $O(n^2)$ algorithm is simply unacceptable, one variation to the working example that you might try is rewriting the nested loops so that a random sample is selected for the scoring function, which would effectively reduce it to $O(k*n)$, if *k* were the sample size. As the value of the sample size approaches *n*, however, you'd expect the runtime to begin approaching the $O(n^2)$ runtime. The following amendments to Example 4-11 show how that sampling technique might look in code; the key changes to the previous listing are highlighted in bold. The core takeaway is that for each invocation of the outer loop, we're executing the inner loop a much smaller, fixed number of times:

```
# ... snip ...

all_titles = list(set(all_titles))
clusters = {}
for title1 in all_titles:
    clusters[title1] = []
    for sample in range(SAMPLE_SIZE):
        title2 = all_titles[random.randint(0, len(all_titles)-1)]
        if title2 in clusters[title1] or clusters.has_key(title2) and title1
            in clusters[title2]:
            continue
        distance = DISTANCE(set(title1.split()), set(title2.split()))
        if distance < DISTANCE_THRESHOLD:
            clusters[title1].append(title2)

# ... snip ...
```

Another approach you might consider is to randomly sample the data into *n* bins (where *n* is some number that's generally less than or equal to the square root of the number of items in your set), perform clustering within each of those individual bins, and then optionally merge the output. For example, if you had 1 million items, an $O(n^2)$ algorithm would take a trillion logical operations, whereas binning the 1 million items into 1,000 bins containing 1,000 items each and clustering each individual bin would require only a billion operations. (That's 1,000*1,000 comparisons for each bin for all 1,000 bins.) A billion is still a large number, but it's three orders of magnitude smaller than a trillion, and that's a substantial improvement (although it still may not be enough in some situations).

There are many other approaches in the literature besides sampling or binning that could be far better at reducing the dimensionality of a problem. For example, you'd ideally compare every item in a set, and at the end of the day, the particular technique you'll end up using to avoid an $O(n^2)$ situation for a large value of n will vary based upon real-world constraints and insights you're likely to gain through experimentation and domain-specific knowledge. As you consider the possibilities, keep in mind that the field of machine learning offers many techniques that are designed to combat exactly these types of scale problems by using various sorts of probabilistic models and sophisticated sampling techniques. In "k-means clustering" on page 153, you'll be introduced to a fairly intuitive and well-known clustering algorithm called k-means, which is a general-purpose unsupervised approach for clustering a multidimensional space. We'll be using this technique later to cluster your contacts by geographic location.

Hierarchical clustering

Example 4-11 introduced an intuitive, greedy approach to clustering, principally as part of an exercise to teach you about the underlying aspects of the problem. With a proper appreciation for the fundamentals now in place, it's time to introduce you to two common clustering algorithms that you'll routinely encounter throughout your data mining career and apply in a variety of situations: hierarchical clustering and k-means clustering.

Hierarchical clustering is superficially similar to the greedy heuristic we have been using, while k-means clustering is radically different. We'll primarily focus on k-means throughout the rest of this chapter, but it's worthwhile to briefly introduce the theory behind both of these approaches since you're very likely to encounter them during literature review and research. An excellent implementation of both of these approaches is available via the `cluster` module that you can install via **pip install cluster**.

Hierarchical clustering is a deterministic technique in that it computes the full matrix[3] of distances between all items and then walks through the matrix clustering items that meet a minimum distance threshold. It's *hierarchical* in that walking over the matrix and clustering items together produces a tree structure that expresses the relative distances between items. In the literature, you may see this technique called *agglomerative* because it constructs a tree by arranging individual data items into clusters, which hierarchically merge into other clusters until the entire data set is clustered at the top of the tree. The leaf nodes on the tree represent the data items that are

---

3 The computation of a full matrix implies a polynomial runtime. For agglomerative clustering, the runtime is often on the order of $O(n^3)$.

being clustered, while intermediate nodes in the tree hierarchically agglomerate these items into clusters.

To conceptualize the idea of agglomeration, take a look ahead at Figure 4-4 and observe that people such as "Andrew O." and "Matthias B." are leaves on the tree that are clustered, while nodes such as "Chief, Technology, Officer" agglomerate these leaves into a cluster. Although the tree in the dendogram is only two levels deep, it's not hard to imagine an additional level of agglomeration that conceptualizes something along the lines of a business executive with a label like "Chief, Officer" and agglomerates the "Chief, Technology, Officer" and "Chief, Executive, Officer" nodes.

Agglomeration is a technique that is similar to but not fundamentally the same as the approach used in Example 4-11, which uses a greedy heuristic to cluster items instead of successively building up a hierarchy. As such, the amount of time it takes for the code to run for hierarchical clustering may be considerably longer, and you may need to tweak your scoring function and distance threshold accordingly.[4] Oftentimes, agglomerative clustering is not appropriate for large data sets because of its impractical runtimes.

If we were to rewrite Example 4-11 to use the `cluster` package, the nested loop performing the clustering DISTANCE computation would be replaced with something like the following code:

```
# ... snip ...

# Define a scoring function
def score(title1, title2):
    return DISTANCE(set(title1.split()), set(title2.split()))

# Feed the class your data and the scoring function
hc = HierarchicalClustering(all_titles, score)

# Cluster the data according to a distance threshold
clusters = hc.getlevel(DISTANCE_THRESHOLD)

# Remove singleton clusters
clusters = [c for c in clusters if len(c) > 1]

# ... snip ...
```

---

[4] The use of dynamic programming (*http://bit.ly/1a1maFO*) and other clever bookkeeping techniques can result in substantial savings in execution time, and one of the advantages of using a well-implemented toolkit is that these clever optimizations often are already implemented for you. For example, given that the distance between two items such as job titles is almost certainly going to be symmetric, you should have to compute only one-half of the distance matrix instead of the full matrix. Therefore, even though the time complexity of the algorithm as a whole is still $O(n^2)$, only $n^2/2$ units of work are being performed instead of n^2 units of work.

If you're interested in variations on hierarchical clustering, be sure to check out the HierarchicalClustering class's setLinkageMethod method, which provides some subtle variations on how the class can compute distances between clusters. For example, you can specify whether distances between clusters should be determined by calculating the shortest, longest, or average distance between any two clusters. Depending on the distribution of your data, choosing a different linkage method can potentially produce quite different results.

Figures 4-4 and 4-5 display a slice from a professional network as a dendogram and a node-link tree layout, respectively, using D3 (*http://bit.ly/1a1kGvo*), the state-of-the-art visualization toolkit introduced earlier. The node-link tree layout is more space-efficient and probably a better choice for this particular data set, while a dendogram (*http://bit.ly/1a1md4B*) would be a great choice if you needed to easily find correlations between each level in the tree (which would correspond to each level of agglomeration in hierarchical clustering) for a more complex set of data. If the hierarchical layout were deeper, the dendogram would have obvious benefits, but the current clustering approach is just a couple of levels deep, so the particular advantages of one layout versus the other may be mostly aesthetic for this particular data set. As these visualizations show, an amazing amount of information becomes apparent when you are able to look at a simple image of your professional network.

 The code for creating node-link tree and dendogram visualizations with D3 is omitted from this section for brevity but is included as a completely turnkey example with the Jupyter Notebook for this chapter.

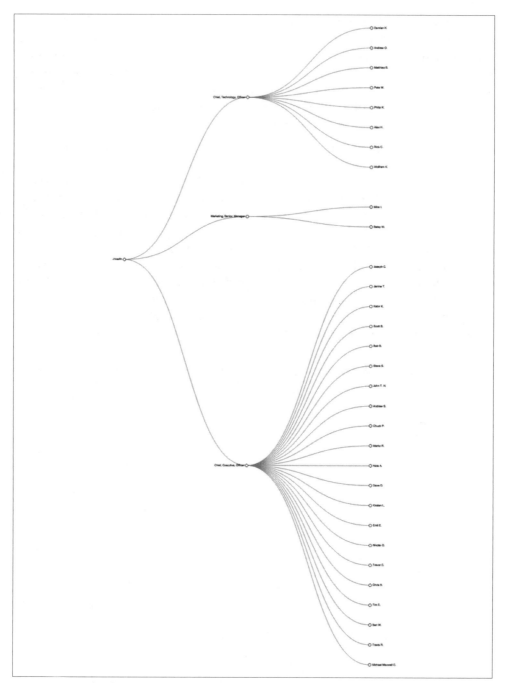

Figure 4-4. A dendogram layout of contacts clustered by job title—dendograms are typically presented in an explicitly hierarchical manner

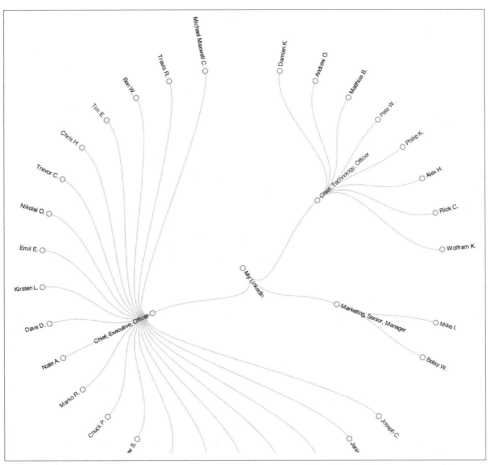

Figure 4-5. A node-link tree layout of contacts clustered by job title that conveys the same information as the dendogram in Figure 4-4—node-link trees tend to provide a more aesthetically pleasing layout when compared to dendograms

k-means clustering

Whereas hierarchical clustering is a deterministic technique that exhausts the possibilities and is often an expensive computation on the order of $O(n^3)$, k-means clustering generally executes on the order of $O(k*n)$ times. Even for large values of k, the savings are substantial. The savings in performance come at the expense of results that are approximate, but they still have the potential to be quite good. The idea is that you generally have a multidimensional space containing n points, which you cluster into k clusters through the following series of steps:

1. Randomly pick k points in the data space as initial values that will be used to compute the k clusters: $K_1, K_2, ..., K_k$.

2. Assign each of the *n* points to a cluster by finding the nearest K_n—effectively creating *k* clusters and requiring *k*n* comparisons.

3. For each of the *k* clusters, calculate the *centroid (http://bit.ly/1a1mbcW)*, or the mean of the cluster, and reassign its K_i value to be that value. (Hence, you're computing "*k*-means" during each iteration of the algorithm.)

4. Repeat steps 2–3 until the members of the clusters do not change between iterations. Generally speaking, relatively few iterations are required for convergence.

Because *k*-means may not be all that intuitive at first glance, Figure 4-6 displays each step of the algorithm as presented in the online "Tutorial on Clustering Algorithms," (*http://bit.ly/1a1mbtp*) which features an interactive Java applet. The sample parameters used involve 100 data points and a value of 3 for the parameter *k*, which means that the algorithm will produce three clusters. The important thing to note at each step is the location of the squares, and which points are included in each of those three clusters as the algorithm progresses. The algorithm takes only nine steps to complete.

Although you could run *k*-means on points in two dimensions or two thousand dimensions, the most common range is usually somewhere on the order of tens of dimensions, with the most common cases being two or three dimensions. When the dimensionality of the space you're working in is relatively small, *k*-means can be an effective clustering technique because it executes fairly quickly and is capable of producing very reasonable results. You do, however, need to pick an appropriate value for *k*, which is not always obvious.

The remainder of this section demonstrates how to geographically cluster and visualize your professional network by applying *k*-means and rendering the output with Google Maps (*http://bit.ly/1a1mdRV*) or Google Earth (*http://bit.ly/1a1meFC*).

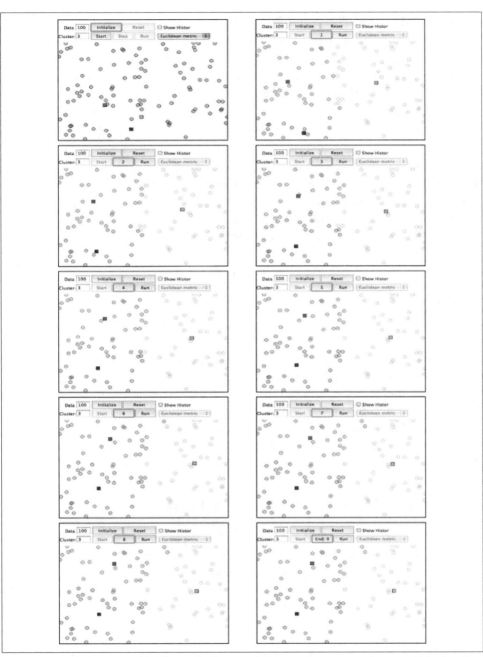

Figure 4-6. Progression of k-means for k=3 with 100 points—notice how quickly the clusters emerge in the first few steps of the algorithm, with the remaining steps primarily affecting the data points around the edges of the clusters

Visualizing geographic clusters with Google Earth

A worthwhile exercise to see *k*-means in action is to use it to visualize and cluster your professional LinkedIn network by plotting it in two-dimensional space. In addition to the insight gained by visualizing how your contacts are spread out and noting any patterns or anomalies, you can analyze clusters by using your contacts, the distinct employers of your contacts, or the distinct metro areas in which your contacts reside as a basis. All three approaches might yield results that are useful for different purposes.

Recalling that through the LinkedIn API you can fetch location information that describes the major metropolitan area, such as "Greater Nashville Area," we'll be able to geocode the locations into coordinates and emit them in an appropriate format (such as KML (*http://bit.ly/1a1meWb*)) that we can plot in a tool like Google Earth, which provides an interactive user experience.

> Google's new Maps Engine also provides various means of uploading data (*http://bit.ly/1a1mep1*) for visualization purposes.

The primary things that you must do in order to convert your LinkedIn contacts to a format such as KML include parsing out the geographic location from each of your connections' profiles and constructing the KML for a visualization such as Google Earth. Example 4-7 demonstrated how to geocode profile information and provides a working foundation for gathering the data we'll need. The KMeansClustering class of the cluster package can calculate clusters for us, so all that's really left is to munge the data and clustering results into KML, which is a relatively rote exercise with XML tools.

As in Example 4-11, most of the work involved in getting to the point where the results can be visualized is data-processing boilerplate. The most interesting details are tucked away inside of KMeansClustering's getclusters method call. The approach demonstrated groups your contacts by location, clusters them, and then uses the results of the clustering algorithm to compute the centroids. Figure 4-7 and Figure 4-8 illustrate sample results from running the code in Example 4-12. The example begins by reading in the geocoded contact information we saved as a JSON object in Example 4-8.

Example 4-12. Clustering your LinkedIn professional network based upon the locations of your connections and emitting KML output for visualization with Google Earth

```
import simplekml # pip install simplekml
from cluster import KMeansClustering
```

```
from cluster.util import centroid

# Load this data from where you've previously stored it
CONNECTIONS_DATA = 'linkedin_connections.json'

# Open up your saved connections with extended profile information
# or fetch them again from LinkedIn if you prefer
connections = json.loads(open(CONNECTIONS_DATA).read())


# A KML object for storing all your contacts
kml_all = simplekml.Kml()

for c in connections:
    location = c['Location']
    if location is not None:
        lat, lon = c['Lat'], c['Lon']
        kml_all.newpoint(name='{} {}'.format(c['FirstName'], c['LastName']),
                         coords=[(lon,lat)]) # coords reversed

kml_all.save('resources/ch03-linkedin/viz/connections.kml')


# Now cluster your contacts using the k-means algorithm into K clusters

K = 10

cl = KMeansClustering([(c['Lat'], c['Lon']) for c in connections
                      if c['Location'] is not None])

# Get the centroids for each of the K clusters
centroids = [centroid(c) for c in cl.getclusters(K)]

# A KML object for storing the locations of each of the clusters
kml_clusters = simplekml.Kml()

for i, c in enumerate(centroids):
    kml_clusters.newpoint(name='Cluster {}'.format(i),
                          coords=[(c[1],c[0])]) # coords reversed

kml_clusters.save('resources/ch03-linkedin/viz/kmeans_centroids.kml')
```

Figure 4-7. Geospatial visualization of the locations of all contacts

Figure 4-8. Geospatial visualization of the locations of the centroids from a k-means clustering

The code in Example 4-12 makes use of the `simplekml` Python library, which simplifies the creation of KML objects. Two KML files get written to disk, which can be loaded into geospatial applications such as Google Earth. The first of these is a file containing the estimated locations of all of your LinkedIn connections for which locations could be guessed by a geocoder, based on your connections' declared employer.

Next, after performing *k*-means clustering, you write the locations of 10 centroids to a KML file. You can compare the two files in Google Earth and see where the cluster centroids are positioned relative the individual connections. What you might find is that the centroids sit on or near the locations of major cities. Try playing around with different values of *K* and see which value best summarizes the geographic distribution of your LinkedIn connections.

Just visualizing your network can provide previously unknown insights, but computing the geographic centroids of your professional network can also open up some intriguing possibilities. For example, you might want to compute candidate locations for a series of regional workshops or conferences. Alternatively, if you're in the consulting business and have a hectic travel schedule, you might want to plot out some good locations for renting a little home away from home. Or maybe you want to map out professionals in your network according to their job duties, or the socioeconomic bracket they're likely to fit into based on their job titles and experience. Beyond the numerous options opened up by visualizing your professional network's location data, geographic clustering lends itself to many other possibilities, such as supply chain management and traveling salesman (*http://bit.ly/1a1mhkF*) types of problems in which it is necessary to minimize the expenses involved in traveling or moving goods from point to point.

4.4 Closing Remarks

This chapter covered some serious ground, introducing the fundamental concept of clustering and demonstrating a variety of ways to apply it to your professional network data on LinkedIn. It was without a doubt more advanced than the preceding chapters in terms of core content, in that it began to address common problems such as normalization of (somewhat) messy data, similarity computation on normalized data, and concerns related to the computational efficiency of approaches for a common data mining technique. Although it might be difficult to process all of the material in a single reading, don't be discouraged if you feel a bit overwhelmed. It may take a couple of readings to fully absorb the details introduced in this chapter.

Also keep in mind that a working knowledge of how to employ clustering doesn't necessarily require an advanced understanding of the theory behind it, although in general you should strive to understand the fundamentals that undergird the techniques you employ when mining the social web. As in the other chapters, you could easily make the case that we've just barely touched the tip of the iceberg; there are many other interesting things that you can do with your LinkedIn data that were not introduced in this chapter, many of which involve basic frequency analysis and do not require clustering at all. That said, you do have a pretty nice power tool in your belt now.

 The source code outlined for this chapter and all other chapters is available on GitHub (*http://bit.ly/Mining-the-Social-Web-3E*) in a convenient Jupyter Notebook format that you're highly encouraged to try out from the comfort of your own web browser.

4.5 Recommended Exercises

- Take some time to explore the extended profile information that you have available. It could be fun to try to correlate where people work versus where they went to school and/or to analyze whether people tend to relocate into and out of certain areas.

- Try employing an alternative visualization from D3, such as a choropleth map (*http://bit.ly/1a1mg0a*), to visualize your professional network.

- Read up on the new and exciting geoJSON specification (*http://bit.ly/1a1mggF*) and how you can easily create interactive visualizations at GitHub by generating geoJSON data. Try to apply this technique to your professional network as an alternative to using Google Earth.

- Take a look at `geodict` (*http://bit.ly/1a1mgxd*) and some of the other geo utilities in the Data Science Toolkit (*http://bit.ly/1a1mgNK*). Can you extract locations from arbitrary prose and visualize them in a meaningful way to gain insight into what's happening in the data without having to read through all of it?

- Mine Twitter or Facebook profiles for geo information and visualize it in a meaningful way. Tweets and Facebook posts often contain geocodes as part of their structured metadata.

- The LinkedIn API provides a means of retrieving a connection's Twitter handle. How many of your LinkedIn connections have Twitter accounts associated with their professional profiles? How active are their accounts? How *professional* are their online Twitter personalities from the perspective of a potential employer?

- Apply clustering techniques from this chapter to tweets. Given a user's tweets, can you extract meaningful tweet entities, define a meaningful similarity computation, and cluster tweets in a meaningful way?

- Apply clustering techniques from this chapter to Facebook data such as likes or posts. Given a collection of Facebook likes for a friend, can you define a meaningful similarity computation, and cluster the likes in a meaningful way? Given all of the likes for all of your friends, can you cluster the likes (or your friends) in a meaningful way?

4.6 Online Resources

The following list of links from this chapter may be useful for review:

- Bing Maps portal (*http://bit.ly/1a1m5lq*)
- Centroid (*http://bit.ly/1a1mbcW*)
- D3.js examples gallery (*http://bit.ly/1a1lMal*)
- Data Science Toolkit (*http://bit.ly/1a1mgNK*)
- Dendrogram (*http://bit.ly/1a1md4B*)
- geopy GitHub code repository (*http://bit.ly/1a1m7Ka*)
- Google Maps APIs (*http://bit.ly/2GN6QU5*)
- Keyhole Markup Language (KML) (*http://bit.ly/1a1meWb*)
- Levenshtein distance (*http://bit.ly/1JtgTWJ*)
- LinkedIn API field selector syntax (*http://bit.ly/2E7vahT*)
- LinkedIn Data Export (*http://linkd.in/1a1m4ho*)
- LinkedIn REST API documentation (*http://linkd.in/1a1lZuj*)
- Mapping geoJSON files on GitHub (*http://bit.ly/1a1mp3J*)
- python3-linkedin PyPi page (*http://bit.ly/2nNViqS*)
- Traveling salesman problem (*http://bit.ly/1a1mhkF*)
- Tutorial on Clustering Algorithms (*http://bit.ly/1a1mbtp*)

## CHAPTER 5

Mining Text Files: Computing Document Similarity, Extracting Collocations, and More

This chapter introduces some fundamental concepts from text mining[1] and is somewhat of an inflection point in this book. Whereas we started the book with basic frequency analyses of Twitter data and gradually worked up to more sophisticated clustering analyses of messier data from LinkedIn profiles, this chapter begins munging and making sense of textual information in documents by introducing information retrieval theory fundamentals such as TF-IDF, cosine similarity, and collocation detection. Accordingly, its content is a bit more complex than that of the chapters before it, and it may be helpful to have worked through those chapters before picking up here.

Previous editions of this book featured the now defunct Google+ product as the basis of this chapter. Although Google+ is no longer featured as the basis of examples, the core concepts are preserved and introduced in nearly the same way as before. For continuity, the examples in this chapter continue to reflect Tim O'Reilly's Google+ posts as with previous editions. An archive of these posts is provided with the book's example code on GitHub.

---

1 This book avoids splitting hairs over exactly what differences could be implied by common phrases such as *text mining, unstructured data analytics* (UDA), or *information retrieval*, and simply treats them as essentially the same thing.

Wherever possible we won't reinvent the wheel and implement analysis tools from scratch, but we will take a couple of "deep dives" when particularly foundational topics come up that are essential to an understanding of text mining. The Natural Language Toolkit (NLTK) is a powerful technology that you may recall from Chapter 4; it provides many of the tools we'll use in this chapter. Its rich suites of APIs can be a bit overwhelming at first, but don't worry: while text analytics is an incredibly diverse and complex field of study, there are lots of powerful fundamentals that can take you a long way without too significant of an investment. This chapter and the chapters after it aim to hone in on those fundamentals. (A full-blown introduction to NLTK is outside the scope of this book, but you can review the full text of *Natural Language Processing with Python: Analyzing Text with the Natural Language Toolkit* [O'Reilly] at the NLTK website (*http://bit.ly/1a1mtAk*).)

 Always get the latest bug-fixed source code for this chapter (and every other chapter) on GitHub (*http://bit.ly/Mining-the-Social-Web-3E*). Be sure to also take advantage of this book's virtual machine experience, as described in Appendix A, to maximize your enjoyment of the sample code.

5.1 Overview

This chapter uses a small corpus of text files similar to blog posts to begin our journey in analyzing human language data. In this chapter you'll learn about:

- TF-IDF (Term Frequency–Inverse Document Frequency), a fundamental technique for analyzing words in documents
- How to apply NLTK to the problem of understanding human language
- How to apply cosine similarity to common problems such as querying documents by keyword
- How to extract meaningful phrases from human language data by detecting collocation patterns

5.2 Text Files

Although audio and video content is now pervasive, text continues to be the dominant form of communication throughout the digital world, and the situation is unlikely to change anytime soon. Developing even a minimum set of skills for compiling and extracting meaningful statistics from the human language in text data equips you with significant leverage on a variety of problems that you'll face throughout your experiences on the social web and elsewhere in professional life. In general, you should assume that the textual data exposed through social web APIs could be full-fledged HTML or contain some basic markup, such as <br /> tags and escaped HTML entities for apostrophes. So as a best practice, you'll need to do a little bit of additional filtering to clean it up. Example 5-1 provides an example of how to distill plain text from the content field of a note by introducing a function called cleanHtml. It takes advantage of a handy package for manipulating HTML, called BeautifulSoup, that converts HTML entities back to plain text. If you haven't already encountered BeautifulSoup, it's a package that you won't want to live without once you've added it to your toolbox—it has the ability to process HTML in a reasonable way even if it is invalid and violates standards or other reasonable expectations (à la web data). You should install the package via **pip install beautifulsoup4** if you haven't already.

Example 5-1. Cleaning HTML content by stripping out HTML tags and converting HTML entities back to plain-text representations

```
from bs4 import BeautifulSoup # pip install beautifulsoup4

def cleanHtml(html):
    if html == "": return ""

    return BeautifulSoup(html, 'html5lib').get_text()

txt = "Don&#39;t forget about HTML entities and <strong>markup</strong> when "+\
    "mining text!<br />"

print(cleanHtml(txt))
```

 Don't forget that pydoc can be helpful for gathering clues about a package, class, or method in a terminal as you are learning it. The help function in a standard Python interpreter is also useful. Recall that appending ? to a method name in IPython is a shortcut for displaying its docstring.

The output from the most sane HTML content, once cleansed with cleanHtml, is relatively clean text that can be further refined as needed to remove additional noise. As you'll learn in this chapter and follow-on chapters about text mining, reduction of noise in text content is a critical aspect of improving accuracy. Here's another example from one of Tim O'Reilly's online musings about privacy.

Here's some raw content:

```
This is the best piece about privacy that I&#39;ve read in a long time!
If it doesn&#39;t change how you think about the privacy issue, I&#39;ll be
surprised.  It opens:<br /><br />&quot;Many governments (including our own,
here in the US) would have its citizens believe that privacy is a switch (that
is, you either reasonably expect it, or you don't). This has been demonstrated
```

```
in many legal tests, and abused in many circumstances ranging from spying
on electronic mail, to drones in our airspace monitoring the movements of
private citizens. But privacy doesn't work like a switch - at least it shouldn't
for a country that recognizes that privacy is an inherent right. In fact,
privacy, like other components to security, works in layers...&quot;<br /><br />
Please read!
```

And here's the content rendered after cleansing with the function cleanHtml():

```
This is the best piece about privacy that I've read in a long time!  If it
doesn't change how you think about the privacy issue, I'll be surprised.  It
opens: "Many governments (including our own, here in the US) would have its
citizens believe that privacy is a switch (that is, you either reasonably expect it,
or you don't). This has been demonstrated in many legal tests, and abused
in many circumstances ranging from spying on electronic mail, to drones in our
airspace monitoring the movements of private citizens. But privacy doesn't work like
a switch - at least it shouldn't for a country that recognizes that privacy is an
inherent right. In fact, privacy, like other components to security, works in
layers..." Please read!
```

The ability to manipulate clean text from nearly any social web API or corpus you could compile by any alternative means is the basis for the remainder of the text mining exercises in this chapter. The next section introduces one of the most classic starting points for understanding statistics about human language data.

5.3 A Whiz-Bang Introduction to TF-IDF

Although rigorous approaches to natural language processing (NLP) that include such things as sentence segmentation, tokenization, word chunking, and entity detection are necessary in order to achieve the deepest possible understanding of textual data, it's helpful to first introduce some fundamentals from information retrieval theory. The remainder of this chapter introduces some of its more foundational aspects, including TF-IDF, the cosine similarity metric, and some of the theory behind collocation detection. Chapter 6 provides a deeper discussion of NLP as a logical continuation of this discussion.

 If you want to dig deeper into IR theory, the full text of Christopher Manning, Prabhakar Raghavan, and Hinrich Schütze's *Introduction to Information Retrieval* (Cambridge University Press) is available online (*http://stanford.io/1a1mAvP*) and provides more information than you could (probably) ever want to know about the field.

Information retrieval is an extensive field with many specialties. This discussion narrows in on TF-IDF, one of the most fundamental techniques for retrieving relevant documents from a corpus (collection). TF-IDF stands for *term frequency–inverse document frequency* and can be used to query a corpus by calculating normalized scores that express the relative importance of terms in the documents.

Mathematically, TF-IDF is expressed as the product of the term frequency and the inverse document frequency, $tf\_idf = tf*idf$, where the term tf represents the importance of a term in a specific document and idf represents the importance of a term relative to the entire corpus. Multiplying these terms together produces a score that accounts for both factors and has been an integral part of every major search engine at some point in its existence. To get a more intuitive idea of how TF-IDF works, let's walk through each of the calculations involved in computing the overall score.

5.3.1 Term Frequency

For simplicity in illustration, suppose you have a corpus containing three sample documents and terms are calculated by simply breaking on whitespace, as illustrated in Example 5-2 as ordinary Python code.

Example 5-2. Sample data structures used in illustrations for the rest of this chapter

```
corpus = {
 'a' : "Mr. Green killed Colonel Mustard in the study with the candlestick. \
Mr. Green is not a very nice fellow.",
 'b' : "Professor Plum has a green plant in his study.",
 'c' : "Miss Scarlett watered Professor Plum's green plant while he was away \
from his office last week."
}
terms = {
 'a' : [ i.lower() for i in corpus['a'].split() ],
 'b' : [ i.lower() for i in corpus['b'].split() ],
 'c' : [ i.lower() for i in corpus['c'].split() ]
 }
```

A term's frequency could simply be represented as the number of times it occurs in the text, but it is more commonly the case that you normalize it by taking into account the total number of terms in the text, so that the overall score accounts for document length relative to a term's frequency. For example, "green" (once normalized to lowercase) occurs twice in corpus['a'] and only once in corpus['b'], so corpus['a'] would produce a higher score if frequency were the only scoring criterion. However, if you normalize for document length, corpus['b'] would have a slightly higher term frequency score for "green" (1/9) than corpus['a'] (2/19), because corpus['b'] is shorter than corpus['a']. A common technique for scoring a compound query such as "Mr. Green" is to sum the term frequency scores for each of the query terms in each document, and return the documents ranked by the summed term frequency score.

Let's illustrate how term frequency works by querying our sample corpus for "Mr. Green," which would produce the normalized scores reported in Table 5-1 for each document.

Table 5-1. Sample term frequency scores for "Mr. Green"

Document	tf(mr.)	tf(green)	Sum
corpus['a']	2/19	2/19	4/19 (0.2105)
corpus['b']	0	1/9	1/9 (0.1111)
corpus['c']	0	1/16	1/16 (0.0625)

For this contrived example, a cumulative term frequency scoring scheme works out and returns corpus['a'] (the document that we'd expect it to return), since corpus['a'] is the only one that contains the compound token "Mr. Green." However, a number of problems could have emerged, because the term frequency scoring model looks at each document as an unordered collection of words. For example, queries for "Green Mr." or "Green Mr. Foo" would have returned the exact same scores as the query for "Mr. Green," even though neither of those phrases appears in the sample sentences. Additionally, there are a number of scenarios that we could easily contrive to illustrate fairly poor results from the term frequency ranking technique given that trailing punctuation is not handled properly, and that the context around tokens of interest is not taken into account by the calculations.

Considering term frequency alone turns out to be a common source of problems when scoring on a document-by-document basis, because it doesn't account for very frequent words, called *stopwords*,[2] that are common across many documents. In other words, all terms are weighted equally, regardless of their actual importance. For example, "the green plant" contains the stopword "the," which skews overall term frequency scores in favor of corpus['a'] because "the" appears twice in that document, as does "green." In contrast, in corpus['c'] "green" and "plant" each appear only once.

Consequently, the scores would break down as shown in Table 5-2, with corpus['a'] ranked as more relevant than corpus['c'], even though intuition might lead you to believe that ideal query results probably shouldn't have turned out that way. (Fortunately, however, corpus['b'] still ranks highest.)

Table 5-2. Sample term frequency scores for "the green plant"

Document	tf(the)	tf(green)	tf(plant)	Sum
corpus['a']	2/19	2/19	0	4/19 (0.2105)
corpus['b']	0	1/9	1/9	2/9 (0.2222)
corpus['c']	0	1/16	1/16	1/8 (0.125)

---

2 Stopwords are words that appear frequently in text but usually relay little information. Common examples of stopwords are *a*, *an*, *the*, and other determinants.

5.3.2 Inverse Document Frequency

Toolkits such as NLTK provide lists of stopwords that can be used to filter out terms such as *and*, *a*, and *the*, but keep in mind that there may be terms that evade even the best stopword lists and yet still are quite common to specialized domains. Although you can certainly customize a list of stopwords with domain knowledge, the inverse document frequency metric is a calculation that provides a generic normalization metric for a corpus. It works in the general case by accounting for the appearance of common terms across a set of documents by considering the total number of documents in which a query term ever appears.

The intuition behind this metric is that it produces a higher value if a term is somewhat uncommon across the corpus than if it is common, which helps to account for the problem with stopwords we just investigated. For example, a query for "green" in the corpus of sample documents should return a lower inverse document frequency score than a query for "candlestick," because "green" appears in every document while "candlestick" appears in only one. Mathematically, the only nuance of interest for the inverse document frequency calculation is that a logarithm is used to reduce the result into a compressed range, since its usual application is in multiplying it against term frequency as a scaling factor. For reference, a logarithm function is shown in Figure 5-1; as you can see, the logarithm function grows very slowly as values for its domain increase, effectively "squashing" its input.

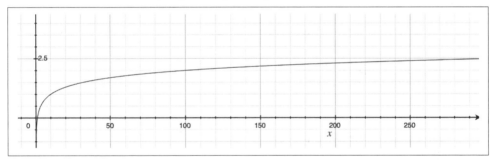

Figure 5-1. The logarithm function "squashes" a large range of values into a more compressed space—notice how slowly the y values grow as the values of x increase

Table 5-3 provides inverse document frequency scores that correspond to the term frequency scores in the previous section. Example 5-3 in the next section presents source code that shows how to compute these scores. In the meantime, you can notionally think of the IDF score for a term as the logarithm of a quotient that is defined by the number of documents in the corpus divided by the number of texts in the corpus that contain the term. When viewing these tables, keep in mind that whereas a term frequency score is calculated on a per-document basis, an inverse document frequency score is computed on the basis of the entire corpus. Hopefully this makes sense given that its purpose is to act as a normalizer for common words across the entire corpus.

Table 5-3. Sample inverse document frequency scores for terms appearing in "mr. green" and "the green plant"

idf(mr.)	idf(green)	idf(the)	idf(plant)
1+ log(3/1) = 2.0986	1 + log(3/3) = 1.0	1 + log(3/1) = 2.0986	1 + log(3/2) = 1.4055

5.3.3 TF-IDF

At this point, we've come full circle and devised a way to compute a score for a multi-term query that accounts for the frequency of terms appearing in a document, the length of the document in which any particular term appears, and the overall uniqueness of the terms across documents in the entire corpus. We can combine the concepts behind term frequency and inverse document frequency into a single score by multiplying them together, so that *TF–IDF = TF*IDF*. Example 5-3 is a naive implementation of this discussion that should help solidify the concepts described. Take a moment to review it, and then we'll discuss a few sample queries.

Example 5-3. Running TF-IDF on sample data

```
from math import log

# Enter in a query term from the corpus variable
QUERY_TERMS = ['mr.', 'green']

def tf(term, doc, normalize=True):
    doc = doc.lower().split()
    if normalize:
        return doc.count(term.lower()) / float(len(doc))
    else:
        return doc.count(term.lower()) / 1.0


def idf(term, corpus):
    num_texts_with_term = len([True for text in corpus if term.lower()
                              in text.lower().split()])

    # tf-idf calc involves multiplying against a tf value less than 0, so it's
    # necessary to return a value greater than 1 for consistent scoring.
    # (Multiplying two values less than 1 returns a value less than each of
    # them.)

    try:
        return 1.0 + log(float(len(corpus)) / num_texts_with_term)
    except ZeroDivisionError:
        return 1.0
```

```python
def tf_idf(term, doc, corpus):
    return tf(term, doc) * idf(term, corpus)


corpus = \
    {'a': 'Mr. Green killed Colonel Mustard in the study with the candlestick. \
Mr. Green is not a very nice fellow.',
     'b': 'Professor Plum has a green plant in his study.',
     'c': "Miss Scarlett watered Professor Plum's green plant while he was away \
from his office last week."}

for (k, v) in sorted(corpus.items()):
    print(k, ':', v)
print()

# Score queries by calculating cumulative tf_idf score for each term in query

query_scores = {'a': 0, 'b': 0, 'c': 0}
for term in [t.lower() for t in QUERY_TERMS]:
    for doc in sorted(corpus):
        print('TF({0}): {1}'.format(doc, term), tf(term, corpus[doc]))
    print('IDF: {0}'.format(term), idf(term, corpus.values()))
    print()

    for doc in sorted(corpus):
        score = tf_idf(term, corpus[doc], corpus.values())
        print('TF-IDF({0}): {1}'.format(doc, term), score)
        query_scores[doc] += score
    print()

print("Overall TF-IDF scores for query '{0}'".format(' '.join(QUERY_TERMS)))
for (doc, score) in sorted(query_scores.items()):
    print(doc, score)
```

Sample output follows:

```
a : Mr. Green killed Colonel Mustard in the study...
b : Professor Plum has a green plant in his study.
c : Miss Scarlett watered Professor Plum's green...

TF(a): mr. 0.105263157895
TF(b): mr. 0.0
TF(c): mr. 0.0
IDF: mr. 2.09861228867

TF-IDF(a): mr. 0.220906556702
TF-IDF(b): mr. 0.0
TF-IDF(c): mr. 0.0

TF(a): green 0.105263157895
TF(b): green 0.111111111111
```

```
TF(c): green 0.0625
IDF: green 1.0

TF-IDF(a): green 0.105263157895
TF-IDF(b): green 0.111111111111
TF-IDF(c): green 0.0625

Overall TF-IDF scores for query 'mr. green'
a 0.326169714597
b 0.111111111111
c 0.0625
```

Although we're working on a trivially small scale, the calculations involved work the same for larger data sets. Table 5-4 is a consolidated adaptation of the program's output for three sample queries that involve four distinct terms:

- "green"
- "mr. green"
- "the green plant"

Even though the IDF calculations for terms are computed on the basis of the entire corpus, they are displayed on a per-document basis so that you can easily verify TF-IDF scores by skimming a single row and multiplying two numbers. As you work through the query results, you'll find that it's remarkable just how powerful TF-IDF is, given that it doesn't account for the proximity or ordering of words in a document.

Table 5-4. Calculations involved in TF-IDF sample queries, as computed by Example 5-3

Document	tf(mr.)	tf(green)	tf(the)	tf(plant)
corpus['a']	0.1053	0.1053	0.1053	0
corpus['b']	0	0.1111	0	0.1111
corpus['c']	0	0.0625	0	0.0625

idf(mr.)	idf(green)	idf(the)	idf(plant)
2.0986	1.0	2.099	1.4055

	tf-idf(mr.)	tf-idf(green)	tf-idf(the)	tf-idf(plant)
corpus['a']	0.1053*2.0986 = 0.2209	0.1053*1.0 = 0.1053	0.1053*2.099 = 0.2209	0*1.4055 = 0
corpus['b']	0*2.0986 = 0	0.1111*1.0 = 0.1111	0*2.099 = 0	0.1111*1.4055 = 0.1562
corpus['c']	0*2.0986 = 0	0.0625*1.0 = 0.0625	0*2.099 = 0	0.0625*1.4055 = 0.0878

The same results for each query are shown in Table 5-5, with the TF-IDF values summed on a per-document basis.

Table 5-5. Summed TF-IDF values for sample queries as computed by Example 5-3 (values in bold are the maximum scores for each of the three queries)

Query	corpus['a']	corpus['b']	corpus['c']
green	0.1053	**0.1111**	0.0625
Mr. Green	0.2209 + 0.1053 = **0.3262**	0 + 0.1111 = 0.1111	0 + 0.0625 = 0.0625
the green plant	0.2209 + 0.1053 + 0 = **0.3262**	0 + 0.1111 + 0.1562 = 0.2673	0 + 0.0625 + 0.0878 = 0.1503

From a qualitative standpoint, the query results are quite reasonable. The `corpus['b']` document is the winner for the query "green," with `corpus['a']` just a hair behind. In this case, the deciding factor was the length of `corpus['b']` being much smaller than that of `corpus['a']`—the normalized TF score tipped the results in favor of `corpus['b']` for its one occurrence of "green," even though "Green" appeared in `corpus['a']` two times. Since "green" appears in all three documents, the net effect of the IDF term in the calculations was a wash.

Do note, however, that if we had returned 0.0 instead of 1.0 for "green," as is done in some IDF implementations, the TF-IDF scores for "green" would have been 0.0 for all three documents due the effect of multiplying the TF score by zero. Depending on the particular situation, it may be better to return 0.0 for the IDF scores rather than 1.0. For example, if you had 100,000 documents and "green" appeared in all of them, you'd almost certainly consider it to be a stopword and want to remove its effects in a query entirely.

For the query "Mr. Green," the clear and appropriate winner is the `corpus['a']` document. However, this document also comes out on top for the query "the green plant." A worthwhile exercise is to consider why `corpus['a']` scored highest for this query as opposed to `corpus['b']`, which at first blush might have seemed a little more obvious.

A final nuanced point to observe is that the sample implementation provided in Example 5-3 adjusts the IDF score by adding a value of 1.0 to the logarithm calculation, for the purposes of illustration and because we're dealing with a trivial document set. Without the 1.0 adjustment in the calculation, it would be possible to have the `idf` function return values that are less than 1.0, which would result in two fractions being multiplied in the TF-IDF calculation. Since multiplying two fractions together results in a value smaller than either of them, this turns out to be an easily overlooked edge case in the TF-IDF calculation. Recall that the intuition behind the TF-IDF calculation is that we'd like to be able to multiply two terms in a way that consistently produces larger TF-IDF scores for more relevant queries than for less relevant queries.

5.4 Querying Human Language Data with TF-IDF

Let's take the theory that you just learned about in the previous section and put it to work. In this section you'll get officially introduced to NLTK, a powerful toolkit for processing natural language, and use it to support the analysis of human language data.

5.4.1 Introducing the Natural Language Toolkit

If you have not done so already, you should install Python's Natural Language Toolkit (NLTK) via **pip install nltk** now. NLTK is written such that you can explore data easily and begin to form some impressions without a lot of upfront investment. Before skipping ahead, though, consider following along with the interpreter session in Example 5-4 to get a feel for some of the powerful functionality that NLTK provides right out of the box. Since you may not have done much work with NLTK before, don't forget that you can use the built-in help function to get more information whenever you need it. For example, help(nltk) would provide documentation on the NLTK package in an interpreter session.

Not all of the functionality from NLTK is intended for incorporation into production software, since output is written to the console and not capturable into a data structure such as a list. In that regard, methods such as nltk.text.concordance are considered "demo functionality." Speaking of which, many of NLTK's modules have a demo function that you can call to get some idea of how to use the functionality they provide, and the source code for these demos is a great starting point for learning how to use new APIs. For example, you could run nltk.text.demo() in the interpreter to get some additional insight into the capabilities provided by the nltk.text module.

Example 5-4 demonstrates some good starting points for exploring the data with sample output included as part of an interactive interpreter session, and the same commands to explore the data are included in the Jupyter Notebook for this chapter. Please follow along with this example and examine the outputs of each step along the way. Are you able to follow along and understand the investigative flow of the interpreter session? Take a look, and we'll discuss some of the details after the example.

 The next example includes stopwords, which—as noted earlier— are words that appear frequently in text but usually relay very little information (e.g., *a*, *an*, *the*, and other determinants).

Example 5-4. Exploring text data with NLTK

```python
# Explore some of NLTK's functionality by exploring the data.
# Here are some suggestions for an interactive interpreter session.

import json
import nltk

# Download ancillary nltk packages if not already installed
nltk.download('stopwords')

# Load in human language data from wherever you've saved it
DATA = 'resources/ch05-textfiles/ch05-timoreilly.json'
data = json.loads(open(DATA).read())

# Combine titles and post content
all_content = " ".join([ i['title'] + " " + i['content'] for i in data ])

# Approximate bytes of text
print(len(all_content))

tokens = all_content.split()
text = nltk.Text(tokens)

# Examples of the appearance of the word "open"
text.concordance("open")

# Frequent collocations in the text (usually meaningful phrases)
text.collocations()

# Frequency analysis for words of interest
fdist = text.vocab()
print(fdist["open"])
print(fdist["source"])
print(fdist["web"])
print(fdist["2.0"])

# Number of words in the text
print('Number of tokens:', len(tokens))

# Number of unique words in the text
print('Number of unique words:', len(fdist.keys()))

# Common words that aren't stopwords
print('Common words that aren\'t stopwords')
print([w for w in list(fdist.keys())[:100]
    if w.lower() not in nltk.corpus.stopwords.words('english')])

# Long words that aren't URLs
print('Long words that aren\'t URLs')
print([w for w in fdist.keys() if len(w) > 15 and 'http' not in w])
```

```
# Number of URLs
print('Number of URLs: ',len([w for w in fdist.keys() if 'http' in w]))

# Top 10 Most Common Words
print('Top 10 Most Common Words')
print(fdist.most_common(10))
```

 The examples throughout this chapter, including the prior example, use the split method to tokenize text. Tokenization isn't quite as simple as splitting on whitespace, however, and Chapter 6 introduces more sophisticated approaches for tokenization that work better for the general case.

The last command in the interpreter session lists the words from the frequency distribution, sorted by frequency. Not surprisingly, stopwords like *the*, *to*, and *of* are the most frequently occurring, but there's a steep decline and the distribution has a very long tail. We're working with a small sample of text data, but this same property will hold true for any frequency analysis of natural language.

Zipf's law (*http://bit.ly/1a1mCUD*), a well-known empirical law of natural language, asserts that a word's frequency within a corpus is inversely proportional to its rank in the frequency table. What this means is that if the most frequently occurring term in a corpus accounts for *N*% of the total words, the second most frequently occurring term in the corpus should account for (*N*/2)% of the words, the third most frequent term for (*N*/3)% of the words, and so on. When graphed, such a distribution (even for a small sample of data) shows a curve that hugs each axis, as you can see in Figure 5-2.

Though perhaps not initially obvious, most of the area in such a distribution lies in its tail, and for a corpus large enough to span a reasonable sample of a language, the tail is always quite long. If you were to plot this kind of distribution on a chart where each axis was scaled by a logarithm, the curve would approach a straight line for a representative sample size.

Zipf's law gives you insight into what a frequency distribution for words appearing in a corpus should look like, and it provides some rules of thumb that can be useful in estimating frequency. For example, if you know that there are a million (nonunique) words in a corpus, and you assume that the most frequently used word (usually *the*, in English) accounts for 7% of the words,[3] you could derive the total number of logical calculations an algorithm performs if you were to consider a particular slice of the terms from the frequency distribution. Sometimes this kind of simple, back-of-the-

---

[3] The word *the* accounts for 7% of the tokens in the Brown Corpus (*http://bit.ly/1a1mB2X*) and provides a reasonable starting point for a corpus if you don't know anything else about it.

napkin arithmetic is all that it takes to sanity-check assumptions about a long-running wall-clock time, or confirm whether certain computations on a large enough data set are even tractable.

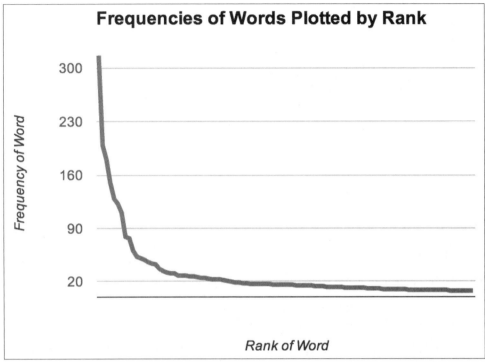

Figure 5-2. The frequency distribution for terms appearing in a small sample of data "hugs" each axis closely; plotting it on a log-log scale would render it as something much closer to a straight line with a negative slope

 Can you graph the same kind of curve shown in Figure 5-2 for text content from your own small corpus using the techniques introduced in this chapter combined with IPython's plotting functionality, as introduced in Chapter 1?

5.4.2 Applying TF-IDF to Human Language

Let's apply TF-IDF to the sample text data and see how it works out as a tool for querying the data. NLTK provides some abstractions that we can use instead of rolling our own, so there's actually very little to do now that you understand the underlying theory. The listing in Example 5-5 assumes you are working with the sample data provided with the sample code for this chapter as a JSON file, and it allows you to pass in multiple query terms that are used to score the documents by relevance.

Example 5-5. Querying text data with TF-IDF

```
import json
import nltk

# Provide your own query terms here

QUERY_TERMS = ['Government']

# Load in human language data from wherever you've saved it
DATA = 'resources/ch05-textfiles/ch05-timoreilly.json'
data = json.loads(open(DATA).read())

activities = [post['content'].lower().split()
                for post in data
                    if post['content'] != ""]

# TextCollection provides tf, idf, and tf_idf abstractions so
# that we don't have to maintain/compute them ourselves

tc = nltk.TextCollection(activities)

relevant_activities = []

for idx in range(len(activities)):
    score = 0
    for term in [t.lower() for t in QUERY_TERMS]:
        score += tc.tf_idf(term, activities[idx])
    if score > 0:
        relevant_activities.append({'score': score, 'title': data[idx]['title']})

# Sort by score and display results

relevant_activities = sorted(relevant_activities,
                            key=lambda p: p['score'], reverse=True)
for activity in relevant_activities:
    print('Title: {0}'.format(activity['title']))
    print('Score: {0}'.format(activity['score']))
    print()
```

Sample query results for "Government" from some of Tim O'Reilly's online musings are as follows:

```
Title: Totally hilarious and spot-on. Has to be the best public service video...
Score: 0.106601312641

Title: Excellent set of principles for digital government. Echoes those put...
Score: 0.102501262155

Title: "We need to show every American competent government services they can...
Score: 0.0951797434292
```

```
Title: If you're interested about the emerging startup ecosystem around...
Score: 0.091897683311

Title: I'm proud to be a judge for the new +Code for America tech awards. If...
Score: 0.0873781251154

...
```

Given a search term, being able to zero in on content ranked by relevance is of tremendous benefit when analyzing unstructured text data. Try out some other queries and qualitatively review the results to see for yourself how well the TF-IDF metric works, keeping in mind that the absolute values of the scores aren't really important—it's the ability to find and sort documents by relevance that matters. Then, begin to ponder the countless ways that you could tune or augment this metric to be even more effective. One obvious improvement that's left as an exercise for the reader is to stem verbs so that variations in elements such as tense and grammatical role resolve to the same stem and can be more accurately accounted for in similarity calculations. The `nltk.stem` module provides easy-to-use implementations for several common stemming algorithms.

Now let's take our new tools and apply them to the foundational problem of finding similar documents. After all, once you've zeroed in on a document of interest, the next natural step is to discover other content that might be of interest.

5.4.3 Finding Similar Documents

Once you've queried and discovered relevant documents, one of the next things you might want to do is find similar documents. Whereas TF-IDF can provide the means to narrow down a corpus based on search terms, cosine similarity is one of the most common techniques for comparing documents to one another, which is the essence of finding a similar document. An understanding of cosine similarity requires a brief introduction to vector space models, which is the topic of the next section.

The theory behind vector space models and cosine similarity

While it has been emphasized that TF-IDF models documents as unordered collections of words, another convenient way to model documents is with a model called a *vector space*. The basic theory behind a vector space model is that you have a large multidimensional space that contains one vector for each document, and the distance between any two vectors indicates the similarity of the corresponding documents. One of the most beautiful things about vector space models is that you can also represent a query as a vector and discover the most relevant documents for the query by finding the document vectors with the shortest distance to the query vector.

Although it's virtually impossible to do this subject justice in a short section, it's important to have a basic understanding of vector space models if you have any interest at all in text mining or the IR field. If you're not interested in the background theory and want to jump straight into implementation details on good faith, feel free to skip ahead to the next section.

 This section assumes a basic understanding of trigonometry. If your trigonometry skills are a little rusty, consider this section a great opportunity to brush up on high school math. If you're not feeling up to it, just skim this section and rest assured that there is some mathematical rigor that backs the similarity computation we'll be employing to find similar documents.

First, it might be helpful to clarify exactly what is meant by the term *vector*, since there are so many subtle variations associated with it across various fields of study. Generally speaking, a vector is a list of numbers that expresses both a direction relative to an origin and a magnitude, which is the distance from that origin. A vector can naturally be represented as a line segment drawn between the origin and a point in an *N*-dimensional space.

To illustrate, imagine a document that is defined by only two terms ("Open" and "Web"), with a corresponding vector of (*0.45, 0.67*), where the values in the vector are values such as TF-IDF scores for the terms. In a vector space, this document could be represented in two dimensions by a line segment extending from the origin at (*0, 0*) to the point at (*0.45, 0.67*). In reference to an x/y plane, the x-axis would represent "Open," the y-axis would represent "Web," and the vector from (*0, 0*) to (*0.45, 0.67*) would represent the document in question. Nontrivial documents generally contain hundreds of terms at a minimum, but the same fundamentals apply for modeling documents in these higher-dimensional spaces; it's just harder to visualize.

Try making the transition from visualizing a document represented by a vector with two components to a document represented by three dimensions, such as "Open," "Web," and "Government." Then consider taking a leap of faith and accepting that although it's hard to visualize, it is still possible to have a vector represent additional dimensions that you can't easily sketch out or see. If you're able to do that, you should have no problem believing that the same vector operations that can be applied to a 2-dimensional space can be applied equally well to a 10-dimensional space or a 367-dimensional space. Figure 5-3 shows an example vector in 3-dimensional space.

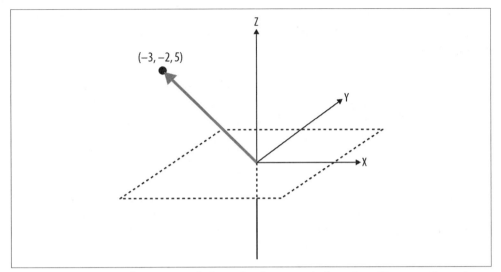

Figure 5-3. An example vector with the value (–3, –2, 5) plotted in 3D space; from the origin, move to the left three units, move down two units, and move up five units to arrive at the point

Given that it's possible to model documents as term-centric vectors, with each term in the document represented by its corresponding TF-IDF score, the task is to determine what metric best represents the similarity between two documents. As it turns out, the cosine of the angle between any two vectors is a valid metric for comparing them and is known as the *cosine similarity* of the vectors. Although it's perhaps not yet intuitive, years of scientific research have demonstrated that computing the cosine similarity of documents represented as term vectors is a very effective metric. (It does suffer from many of the same problems as TF-IDF, though; see "Closing Remarks" for a brief synopsis.) Building up a rigorous proof of the details behind the cosine similarity metric would be beyond the scope of this book, but the gist is that the cosine of the angle between any two vectors indicates the similarity between them and is equivalent to the dot product (*http://bit.ly/1a1mBjn*) of their unit vectors.

Intuitively, it might be helpful to consider that the closer two vectors are to one another, the smaller the angle between them will be, and thus the larger the cosine of the angle between them will be. Two identical vectors would have an angle of 0 degrees and a similarity metric of 1.0, while two vectors that are orthogonal to one another would have an angle of 90 degrees and a similarity metric of 0.0. The following sketch attempts to demonstrate:

$\vec{doc1} \cdot \vec{doc2} = \lVert doc1 \rVert \cdot \lVert doc2 \rVert \cdot \cos\Theta$	Given (by trigonometry)
$\dfrac{\vec{doc1} \cdot \vec{doc2}}{\lVert doc1 \rVert \cdot \lVert doc2 \rVert} = \cos\Theta$	By division
$\hat{doc1} \cdot \hat{doc2} = \cos\Theta$	By definition of "unit vector"
$\hat{doc1} \cdot \hat{doc2} = \text{Similarity (doc1, doc2)}$	By substitution (assume: $\cos\Theta$ = Similarity (doc1, doc2)

Recalling that a unit vector has a length of 1.0 (by definition), you can see that the beauty of computing document similarity with unit vectors is that they're already normalized against what might be substantial variations in length. We'll put all of this newly found knowledge to work in the next section.

Clustering posts with cosine similarity

One of the most important points to internalize from the previous discussion is that *to compute the similarity between two documents, you really just need to produce a term vector for each document and compute the dot product of the unit vectors for those documents*. Conveniently, NLTK exposes the `nltk.cluster.util.cosine_dis tance(v1,v2)` function for computing cosine similarity, so it really is pretty straightforward to compare documents. As the upcoming Example 5-6 shows, all of the work involved is in producing the appropriate term vectors; in short, it computes term vectors for a given pair of documents by assigning TF-IDF scores to each component in the vectors. Because the exact vocabularies of the two documents are probably not identical, however, placeholders with a value of 0.0 must be left in each vector for words that are missing from the document at hand but present in the other one. The net effect is that you end up with two vectors of identical length with components ordered identically that can be used to perform the vector operations.

For example, suppose *document1* contained the terms *(A, B, C)* and had the corresponding vector of TF-IDF weights *(0.10, 0.15, 0.12)*, while *document2* contained the terms *(C, D, E)* with the corresponding vector of TF-IDF weights *(0.05, 0.10, 0.09)*. The derived vector for *document1* would be *(0.10, 0.15, 0.12, 0.0, 0.0)*, and the derived vector for *document2* would be *(0.0, 0.0, 0.05, 0.10, 0.09)*. Each of these vectors could be passed into NLTK's `cosine_distance` function, which yields the cosine similarity. Internally, `cosine_distance` uses the `numpy` module to *very* efficiently compute the dot product of the unit vectors, and that's the result.

Although the code in this section reuses the TF-IDF calculations that were introduced previously, the exact scoring function could be any useful metric. TF-IDF (or some variation thereof), however, is quite common for many implementations and provides a great starting point.

Example 5-6 illustrates an approach for using cosine similarity to find the most similar document to each document in a corpus. It should apply equally well to any other type of human language data, such as blog posts or books.

Example 5-6. Finding similar documents using cosine similarity

```
import json
import nltk
import nltk.cluster

# Load in human language data from wherever you've saved it
DATA = 'resources/ch05-textfiles/ch05-timoreilly.json'
data = json.loads(open(DATA).read())

all_posts = [ (i['title'] + " " + i['content']).lower().split() for i in data ]

# Provides tf, idf, and tf_idf abstractions for scoring

tc = nltk.TextCollection(all_posts)

# Compute a term-document matrix such that td_matrix[doc_title][term]
# returns a tf-idf score for the term in the document

td_matrix = {}
for idx in range(len(all_posts)):
    post = all_posts[idx]
    fdist = nltk.FreqDist(post)

    doc_title = data[idx]['title'].replace('\n', '')
    td_matrix[doc_title] = {}

    for term in fdist.keys():
        td_matrix[doc_title][term] = tc.tf_idf(term, post)

# Build vectors such that term scores are in the same positions...

distances = {}
for title1 in td_matrix.keys():

    distances[title1] = {}
    (min_dist, most_similar) = (1.0, ('', ''))

    for title2 in td_matrix.keys():
```

```
# Take care not to mutate the original data structures
# since we're in a loop and need the originals multiple times

terms1 = td_matrix[title1].copy()
terms2 = td_matrix[title2].copy()

# Fill in "gaps" in each map so vectors of the same length can be computed
for term1 in terms1:
    if term1 not in terms2:
        terms2[term1] = 0

for term2 in terms2:
    if term2 not in terms1:
        terms1[term2] = 0

# Create vectors from term maps
v1 = [score for (term, score) in sorted(terms1.items())]
v2 = [score for (term, score) in sorted(terms2.items())]

# Compute similarity amongst documents
distances[title1][title2] = nltk.cluster.util.cosine_distance(v1, v2)

if title1 == title2:
    #print distances[title1][title2]
    continue

if distances[title1][title2] < min_dist:
    (min_dist, most_similar) = (distances[title1][title2], title2)

print(u'Most similar (score: {})\n{}\n{}\n'.format(1-min_dist, title1,
                                                    most_similar))
```

If you've found this discussion of cosine similarity interesting, it might at first seem almost magical when you realize that *the best part is that querying a vector space is the same operation as computing the similarity between documents, except that instead of comparing just document vectors, you compare your query vector and the document vectors.* Take a moment to think about it: it's a rather profound insight that the mathematics work out that way.

In terms of implementing a program to compute similarity across an entire corpus, however, take note that the naive approach means constructing a vector containing your query terms and comparing it to every single document in the corpus. Clearly, the approach of directly comparing a query vector to every possible document vector is not a good idea for even a corpus of modest size, and you'd need to make some good engineering decisions involving the appropriate use of indexes to achieve a scalable solution.

We briefly touched upon the fundamental problem of needing a dimensionality reduction as a common staple in clustering in Chapter 4, and here we see the same concept emerge. *Any time you encounter a similarity computation, you will almost imminently encounter the need for a dimensionality reduction to make the computation tractable.*

Visualizing document similarity with a matrix diagram

The approach for visualizing similarity between items as introduced in this section is by using use graph-like structures, where a link between documents encodes a measure of the similarity between them. This situation presents an excellent opportunity to introduce more data visualizations using `matplotlib` (*https://matplotlib.org*), a popular library for creating high-quality figures in Python. If you are working through the code examples in a Jupyter Notebook, data visualizations can be rendered directly within the notebook with the `%matplotlib inline` declaration.

Example 5-7 shows the code required to generate a visualization of the matrix of document similarities, which is shown in Figure 5-4. The cosine similarity between every pair of documents is analyzed and stored so cell *(i,j)* in the matrix encodes 1.0 minus the cosine distance between documents *i* and *j*. The `distances` array was already computed in Example 5-6. The sample code contains the `%matplotlib` "magic command" with the `inline` parameter. This line of code only makes sense in the Jupyter Notebook environment, where it instructs the software to draw the images directly inline between the cells of the Notebook.

Example 5-7. Generating a figure to visually display the cosine similarity between documents

```python
import numpy as np
import matplotlib.pyplot as plt # pip install matplotlib
%matplotlib inline

max_articles = 15

# Get the titles - the keys to the 'distances' dict
keys = list(distances.keys())

# Extract the article titles
titles = [l[:40].replace('\n',' ')+'...' for l in list(distances.keys())]

n_articles = len(titles) if len(titles) < max_articles else max_articles

# Initialize the matrix of appropriate size to store similarity scores
similarity_matrix = np.zeros((n_articles, n_articles))

# Loop over the cells in the matrix
for i in range(n_articles):
```

```
    for j in range(n_articles):
        # Retrieve the cosine distance between articles i and j
        d = distances[keys[i]][keys[j]]

        # Store the 'similarity' between articles i and j, defined as 1.0 - distance
        similarity_matrix[i, j] = 1.0 - d


# Create a figure and axes
fig = plt.figure(figsize=(8,8), dpi=300)
ax = fig.add_subplot(111)

# Visualize the matrix with colored squares indicating similarity
ax.matshow(similarity_matrix, cmap='Greys', vmin = 0.0, vmax = 0.2)

# Set regular ticks, one for each article in the collection
ax.set_xticks(range(n_articles))
ax.set_yticks(range(n_articles))

# Set the tick labels as the article titles
ax.set_xticklabels(titles)
ax.set_yticklabels(titles)

# Rotate the labels on the x-axis by 90 degrees
plt.xticks(rotation=90);
```

The code produces the matrix diagram in Figure 5-4 (although the text labels have been abridged somewhat). The prominent black diagonal encodes the self-similarity of the documents in the corpus.

Figure 5-4. A matrix diagram displaying linkages extracted from text content

5.4.4 Analyzing Bigrams in Human Language

As previously mentioned, one issue that is frequently overlooked in unstructured text processing is the tremendous amount of information gained when you're able to look at more than one token at a time, because so many concepts we express are phrases and not just single words. For example, if someone were to tell you that a few of the most common terms in a post are "open," "source," and "government," could you necessarily say that the text is probably about "open source," "open government," both, or neither? If you had a priori knowledge of the author or content, you could probably make a good guess, but if you were relying totally on a machine to try to *classify* a document as being about collaborative software development or transformational government, you'd need to go back to the text and somehow determine which of the other two words most frequently occurs after "open"—that is, you'd like to find the *collocations* that start with the token "open."

Recall from Chapter 4 that an *n*-gram is just a terse way of expressing each possible consecutive sequence of *n* tokens from a text, and it provides the foundational data structure for computing collocations. There are always *n*–1 *n*-grams for any value of *n*, and if you were to consider all of the bigrams (two-grams) for the sequence of tokens ["Mr.", "Green", "killed", "Colonel", "Mustard"], you'd have four possibilities: [("Mr.", "Green"), ("Green", "killed"), ("killed", "Colonel"), ("Colonel", "Mustard")]. You'd need a larger sample of text than just our sample sentence to determine collocations, but assuming you had background knowledge or additional text, the next step would be to statistically analyze the bigrams in order to determine which of them are likely to be collocations.

Storage Requirements for N-Grams

It's worth noting that the storage necessary for persisting an *n*-gram model requires space for $(T–1)*n$ tokens (which is practically $T*n$), where T is the number of tokens in question and *n* is defined by the size of the desired *n*-gram. As an example, assume a document contains 1,000 tokens and requires around 8 KB of storage. Storing all bigrams for the text would require roughly double the original storage, or 16 KB, as you would be storing 999*2 tokens plus overhead. Storing all trigrams for the text (998*3 tokens plus overhead) would require roughly triple the original storage, or 24 KB. Thus, without devising specialized data structures or compression schemes, the storage costs for *n*-grams can be estimated as *n* times the original storage requirement for any value of *n*.

---

n-grams are very simple yet very powerful as a technique for clustering commonly co-occurring words. If you compute all of the *n*-grams for even a small value of *n*, you're likely to discover that some interesting patterns emerge from the text itself with no additional work required. (Typically, bigrams and trigrams are what you'll often see used in practice for data mining exercises.) For example, in considering the bigrams for a sufficiently long text, you're likely to discover the proper names, such as "Mr. Green" and "Colonel Mustard," concepts such as "open source" or "open government," and so forth. In fact, computing bigrams in this way produces essentially the same results as the `collocations` function that you ran earlier, except that some additional statistical analysis takes into account the use of rare words. Similar patterns emerge when you consider frequent trigrams and *n*-grams for values of *n* slightly larger than three. As you already know from Example 5-4, NLTK takes care of most of the effort in computing *n*-grams, discovering collocations in a text, discovering the context in which a token has been used, and more. Example 5-8 demonstrates.

Example 5-8. Using NLTK to compute bigrams and collocations for a sentence

```
import nltk

sentence = "Mr. Green killed Colonel Mustard in the study with the " + \
           "candlestick. Mr. Green is not a very nice fellow."

print([bg for bg in nltk.ngrams(sentence.split(), 2)])
txt = nltk.Text(sentence.split())

txt.collocations()
```

A drawback to using built-in "demo" functionality such as `nltk.Text.collocations` is that these functions don't usually return data structures that you can store and manipulate. Whenever you run into such a situation, just take a look at the underlying source code, which is usually pretty easy to learn from and adapt for your own purposes. Example 5-9 illustrates how you could compute the collocations and concordance indexes for a collection of tokens and maintain control of the results.

 In a Python interpreter, you can usually find the source directory for a package on disk by accessing the package's __file__ attribute. For example, try printing out the value of `nltk.__file__` to find where NLTK's source is at on disk. In IPython or Jupyter Notebook, you could use the "double question mark magic" function to preview the source code on the spot by executing `nltk??`.

Example 5-9. Using NLTK to compute collocations in a similar manner to the nltk.Text.collocations demo functionality

```
import json
import nltk
from nltk.metrics import association

# Load in human language data from wherever you've saved it
DATA = 'resources/ch05-textfiles/ch05-timoreilly.json'
data = json.loads(open(DATA).read())

# Number of collocations to find

N = 25

all_tokens = [token for post in data for token in post['content'].lower().split()]

finder = nltk.BigramCollocationFinder.from_words(all_tokens)
finder.apply_freq_filter(2)
finder.apply_word_filter(lambda w: w in nltk.corpus.stopwords.words('english'))
scorer = association.BigramAssocMeasures.jaccard
collocations = finder.nbest(scorer, N)
```

```
for collocation in collocations:
    c = ' '.join(collocation)
    print(c)
```

In short, the implementation loosely follows NLTK's `collocations` demo function. It filters out bigrams that don't appear more than a minimum number of times (two, in this case) and then applies a scoring metric to rank the results. In this instance, the scoring function is the well-known Jaccard similarity we discussed in Chapter 4, as defined by `nltk.metrics.association.BigramAssocMeasures.jaccard`. A *contingency table* is used by the `BigramAssocMeasures` class to rank the co-occurrence of terms in any given bigram as compared to the possibilities of other words that could have appeared in the bigram. Conceptually, the Jaccard similarity measures similarity of sets, and in this case, the sample sets are specific comparisons of bigrams that appeared in the text.

While arguably an advanced topic, the next section, "Contingency tables and scoring functions" on page 192, provides an extended discussion of the details of how contingency tables and Jaccard values are calculated, since this is foundational to a deeper understanding of collocation detection.

In the meantime, though, let's examine some output from Tim O'Reilly's posts that makes it pretty apparent that returning scored bigrams is immensely more powerful than returning only tokens, because of the additional context that grounds the terms in meaning:

```
brett goldstein
cabo pulmo
nick hanauer
wood fired
yuval noah
child welfare
silicon valley
jennifer pahlka
barre historical
computational biologist
drm-free ebooks
mikey dickerson
saul griffith
bay mini
credit card
east bay
on-demand economy
white house
inca trail
italian granite
private sector
weeks ago
```

Keeping in mind that no special heuristics or tactics that could have inspected the text for proper names based on Title Case were employed, it's actually quite amazing that so many proper names and common phrases were sifted out of the data. Although you could have read through the content and picked those names out for yourself, it's remarkable that a machine could do it for you as a means of bootstrapping your own more focused analysis.

There's still a certain amount of inevitable noise in the results because we have not yet made any effort to clean punctuation from the tokens, but for the small amount of work we've put in, the results are really quite good. This might be the right time to mention that even if reasonably good natural language processing capabilities were employed, it might still be difficult to eliminate all the noise from the results of textual analysis. Getting comfortable with the noise and finding heuristics to control it is a good idea until you get to the point where you're willing to make a significant investment in obtaining the perfect results that a well-educated human would be able to pick out from the text.

Hopefully, the primary observation you're making at this point is that with very little effort and time invested, we've been able to use another basic technique to draw out some powerful meaning from some free text data, and *the results seem to be pretty representative of what we already suspect should be true*. This is encouraging, because it suggests that applying the same technique to any other kind of unstructured text would potentially be just as informative, giving you a quick glimpse into key items that are being discussed. And just as importantly, while the data in this case probably confirms a few things you may already know about Tim O'Reilly, you may have learned a couple of new things, as evidenced by the people who showed up at the top of the collocations list. While it would be easy enough to use the `concordance` method, a regular expression, or even the Python string type's built-in `find` method to find posts relevant to "Brett Goldstein," let's instead take advantage of the code we developed in Example 5-5 and use TF-IDF to query for [*brett, goldstein*] Here's what comes back:

```
Title: Brett Goldstein gives some excellent advice on basic security hygiene...
Score: 0.19612432637
```

And there you have it: the targeted query leads us to some content about security advice. You've effectively started with a nominal (if that) understanding of the text, zeroed in on some interesting topics using collocation analysis, and searched the text for one of those topics using TF-IDF. There's no reason you couldn't also use cosine similarity at this point to find the most similar post to anything else it is that you're keen to investigate).

Contingency tables and scoring functions

 This section dives into some of the more technical details of how `BigramCollocationFinder`—the Jaccard scoring function from Example 5-9—works. If this is your first reading of the chapter or you're not interested in these details, feel free to skip this section and come back to it later. It's arguably an advanced topic, and you don't need to fully understand it to effectively employ the techniques from this chapter.

A common data structure that's used to compute metrics related to bigrams is the *contingency table*. The purpose of a contingency table is to compactly express the frequencies associated with the various possibilities for the appearance of different terms of a bigram. Take a look at the bold entries in Table 5-6, where *token1* expresses the existence of *token1* in the bigram, and *~token1* expresses that *token1* does not exist in the bigram.

Table 5-6. Contingency table example—values in italics represent "marginals," and values in bold represent frequency counts of bigram variations

	token1	~token1	
token2	**frequency(token1, token2)**	**frequency(~token1, token2)**	frequency(*, token2)
~token2	**frequency(token1, ~token2)**	**frequency(~token1, ~token2)**	
	frequency(token1, *)		frequency(*, *)

Although there are a few details associated with which cells are significant for which calculations, hopefully it's not difficult to see that the four middle cells in the table express the frequencies associated with the appearance of various tokens in the bigram. The values in these cells can compute different similarity metrics that can be used to score and rank bigrams in order of likely significance, as was the case with the previously introduced Jaccard similarity, which we'll dissect in just a moment. First, however, let's briefly discuss how the terms for the contingency table are computed.

The way that the various entries in the contingency table are computed is directly tied to which data structures you have precomputed or otherwise have available. If you assume that you have available only a frequency distribution for the various bigrams in the text, the way to calculate *frequency(token1, token2)* is a direct lookup, but what about *frequency(~token1, token2)*? With no other information available, you'd need to scan *every single bigram* for the appearance of *token2* in the second slot and subtract *frequency(token1, token2)* from that value. (Take a moment to convince yourself that this is true if it isn't obvious.)

However, if you assume that you have a frequency distribution available that counts the occurrences of each individual token in the text (the text's unigrams) in addition to a frequency distribution of the bigrams, there's a *much less expensive* shortcut you can take that involves two lookups and an arithmetic operation. Subtract the number of times that *token2* appeared as a unigram from the number of times the bigram *(token1, token2)* appeared, and you're left with the number of times the bigram *(~token1, token2)* appeared. For example, if the bigram *("mr.", "green")* appeared three times and the unigram *("green")* appeared seven times, it must be the case that the bigram *(~ "mr.", "green")* appeared four times (where ~ *"mr."* literally means "any token other than *'mr.'"*). In Table 5-6, the expression *frequency(*, token2)* represents the unigram *token2* and is referred to as a *marginal* because it's noted in the margin of the table as a shortcut. The value for *frequency(token1, *)* works the same way in helping to compute *frequency(token1, ~token2)*, and the expression *frequency(*, *)* refers to any possible unigram and is equivalent to the total number of tokens in the text. Given *frequency(token1, token2)*, *frequency(token1, ~token2)*, and *frequency(~token1, token2)*, the value of *frequency(*, *)* is necessary to calculate *frequency(~token1, ~token2)*.

Although this discussion of contingency tables may seem somewhat tangential, it's an important foundation for understanding different scoring functions. For example, consider the Jaccard similarity as introduced back in Chapter 4. Conceptually, it expresses the similarity of two sets and is defined by:

$$\frac{|Set1 \cap Set2|}{|Set1 \cup Set2|}$$

In other words, that's the number of items in common between the two sets divided by the total number of distinct items in the combined sets. It's worth taking a moment to ponder this simple yet effective calculation. If *Set1* and *Set2* were identical, the union and the intersection of the two sets would be equivalent to one another, resulting in a ratio of 1.0. If both sets were completely different, the numerator of the ratio would be 0, resulting in a value of 0.0. Then there's everything else in between.

The Jaccard similarity as applied to a particular bigram expresses the ratio between the frequency of a particular bigram and the sum of the frequencies with which any bigram containing a term in the bigram of interest appears. One interpretation of that metric might be that the higher the ratio is, the more likely it is that *(token1, token2)* appears in the text, and hence the more likely it is that the collocation "token1 token2" expresses a meaningful concept.

The selection of the most appropriate scoring function is usually determined based upon knowledge about the characteristics of the underlying data, some intuition, and sometimes a bit of luck. Most of the association metrics defined in the module `nltk.metrics.association` are discussed in Chapter 5 of Christopher Manning and Hinrich Schütze's *Foundations of Statistical Natural Language Processing* (MIT Press), which is conveniently available online (*http://stanford.io/1a1mBQy*) and serves as a useful reference for the descriptions that follow.

Is Being "Normal" Important?

One of the most fundamental concepts in statistics is a normal distribution. This type of distribution, often referred to as a *bell curve* because of its shape, is called a "normal" distribution because it is often the basis (or norm) against which other distributions are compared. It is a symmetric distribution that is perhaps the most widely used in statistics. One reason that its significance is so profound is because it provides a model for the variation that is regularly encountered in many natural phenomena in the world, ranging from physical characteristics of populations to defects in manufacturing processes and the rolling of dice.

A rule of thumb that shows why the normal distribution can be so useful is the so-called *68–95–99.7 rule* (*http://bit.ly/1a1mEf0*), a handy heuristic that can be used to answer many questions about approximately normal distributions. For a normal distribution, it turns out that virtually all (99.7%) of the data lies within three standard deviations of the mean, 95% of it lies within two standard deviations, and 68% of it lies within one standard deviation. Thus, if you know that a distribution that explains some real-world phenomenon is approximately normal for some characteristic and its mean and standard deviation are defined, you can reason about it to answer many useful questions. Figure 5-5 illustrates the 68–95–99.7 rule.

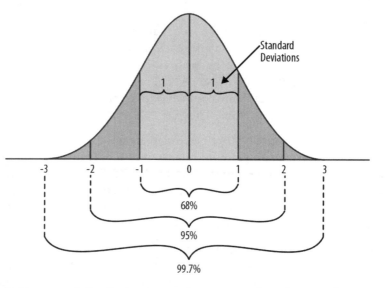

Figure 5-5. The normal distribution is a staple in statistical mathematics because it models variance in so many natural phenomena

Khan Academy's "Introduction to the Normal Distribution" (*http://bit.ly/1a1mCnm*) provides an excellent 30-minute overview of the normal distribution; you might also enjoy the 10-minute segment on the central limit theorem (*http://bit.ly/1a1mCnA*), which is an equally profound concept in statistics in which the normal distribution emerges in a surprising (and amazing) way.

A thorough discussion of these metrics is outside the scope of this book, but the promotional chapter just mentioned provides a detailed account with in-depth examples. The Jaccard similarity, Dice's coefficient, and the likelihood ratio are good starting points if you find yourself needing to build your own collocation detector. They are described, along with some other key terms, in the list that follows:

Raw frequency
As its name implies, raw frequency is the ratio expressing the frequency of a particular *n*-gram divided by the frequency of all *n*-grams. It is useful for examining the overall frequency of a particular collocation in a text.

Jaccard similarity
The Jaccard similarity is a ratio that measures the similarity between sets. As applied to collocations, it is defined as the frequency of a particular collocation divided by the total number of collocations that contain at least one term in the collocation of interest. It is useful for determining the likelihood of whether the given terms actually form a collocation, as well as ranking the likelihood of probable collocations. Using notation consistent with previous explanations, this formulation would be mathematically defined as:

$$\frac{freq(term1, term2)}{freq(term1, term2) + freq(\sim term1, term2) + freq(term1, \sim term2)}$$

Dice's coefficient
Dice's coefficient is extremely similar to the Jaccard similarity. The fundamental difference is that it weights agreements among the sets twice as heavily as Jaccard. It is defined mathematically as:

$$\frac{2 * freq(term1, term2)}{freq(*, term2) + freq(term1, *)}$$

Mathematically, it can be shown fairly easily that:

$$Dice = \frac{2 * Jaccard}{1 + Jaccard}$$

You'd likely choose to use this metric instead of the Jaccard similarity when you'd like to boost the score to favor overlap between sets, which may be handy when one or more of the differences between the sets are high. The reason is that a Jaccard score inherently diminishes as the cardinality of the set differences increases in size, since the union of the set is in the denominator of the Jaccard score.

Student's t-score

Traditionally, Student's *t*-score has been used for hypothesis testing, and as applied to *n*-gram analysis, *t*-scores can be used for testing the hypothesis of whether two terms are collocations. The statistical procedure for this calculation uses a standard distribution per the norm for *t*-testing. An advantage of the *t*-score values as opposed to raw frequencies is that a *t*-score takes into account the frequency of a bigram relative to its constituent components. This characteristic facilitates ranking the strengths of collocations. A criticism of the *t*-test is that it necessarily assumes that the underlying probability distribution for collocations is normal, which is not often the case.

Chi-square

Like Student's *t*-score, this metric is commonly used for testing independence between two variables and can be used to measure whether two tokens are collocations based upon Pearson's chi-square test of statistical significance. Generally speaking, the differences obtained from applying the *t*-test and chi-square test are not substantial. The advantage of chi-square testing is that unlike *t*-testing, it does not assume an underlying normal distribution; for this reason, chi-square testing is more commonly used.

Likelihood ratio

This metric is yet another approach to hypothesis testing that is used to measure the independence between terms that may form a collocation. It's been shown to be a more appropriate approach for collocation discovery than the chi-square test in the general case, and it works well on data that includes many infrequent collocations. The particular calculations involved in computing likelihood estimates for collocations as implemented by NLTK assume a binomial distribution (*http://bit.ly/1a1mEMj*), where the parameters governing the distribution are calculated based upon the number of occurrences of collocations and constituent terms.

Pointwise Mutual Information

Pointwise Mutual Information (PMI) is a measure of how much information is gained about a particular word if you also know the value of a neighboring word. To put it another way, it refers to how much one word can tell you about another. Ironically (in the context of the current discussion), the calculations involved in computing the PMI lead it to score high-frequency words lower than low-frequency words, which is the opposite of the desired effect. Therefore, it is a good measure of independence but not a good measure of dependence (i.e., it's a less-than-ideal choice for scoring collocations). It has also been shown that sparse data is a particular stumbling block for PMI scoring, and that other techniques such as the likelihood ratio tend to outperform it.

Evaluating and determining the best method to apply in any particular situation is often as much art as science. Some problems are fairly well studied and provide a foundation that guides additional work, while some circumstances often require more novel research and experimentation. For most nontrivial problems, you'll want to consider exploring the latest scientific literature (whether it be a textbook or a whitepaper from academia that you find with Google Scholar (*http://bit.ly/1a1mHYk*)) to determine if a particular problem you are trying to solve has been well studied.

5.4.5 Reflections on Analyzing Human Language Data

This chapter has introduced a variety of tools and processes for analyzing human language data, and some closing reflections may be helpful in synthesizing its content:

Context drives meaning

While TF-IDF is a powerful tool that's easy to use, our specific implementation of it has a few important limitations that we've conveniently overlooked but that you should consider. One of the most fundamental is that it treats a document as a "bag of words," which means that the order of terms in both the document and the query itself does not matter. For example, querying for "Green Mr." would return the same results as "Mr. Green" if we didn't implement logic to take the query term order into account or interpret the query as a phrase as opposed to a pair of independent terms. But obviously, the order in which terms appear is very important.

In performing an *n*-gram analysis to account for collocations and term ordering, we still face the underlying issue that TF-IDF assumes that all tokens with the same text value mean the same thing. Clearly, however, this need not be the case. A homonym (*http://bit.ly/1a1mFzJ*) is a word that has identical spellings and pronunciations to another word but whose meaning is driven entirely by context, and any homonym of your choice is a counterexample. Homonyms such as *book*, *match*, *cave*, and *cool* are a few examples that should illustrate the importance of context in determining the meaning of a word.

Cosine similarity suffers from many of the same flaws as TF-IDF. It does not take into account the context of the document or the term order from the *n*-gram analysis, and it assumes that terms appearing close to one another in vector space are necessarily similar, which is certainly not always the case. As with TF-IDF, the obvious counterexample is homonyms. Our particular implementation of cosine similarity also hinges on TF-IDF scoring as its means of computing the relative importance of words in documents, so the TF-IDF errors have a cascading effect.

Human language is overloaded with context

You've probably noticed that there can be a lot of pesky details that have to be managed in analyzing unstructured text, and these details turn out to be pretty important for competitive implementations. For example, string comparisons are case-sensitive, so it's important to normalize terms so that frequencies can be calculated as accurately as possible. However, blindly normalizing to lowercase can also complicate the situation since the case used in certain words and phrases can be important.

"Mr. Green" and "Web 2.0" are two examples worth considering. In the case of "Mr. Green," maintaining the title case in "Green" could potentially be advantageous since it could provide a useful clue to a query algorithm that this term is not referring to an adjective and is likely part of a noun phrase. We'll briefly touch on this topic again in Chapter 6 when NLP is discussed, since it's ultimately the *context* in which "Green" is being used that is lost with the bag-of-words approach, whereas more advanced parsing with NLP has the potential to preserve that context.

Parsing context from human language isn't easy

Another consideration that's rooted more in our particular implementation than a general characteristic of TF-IDF itself is that our use of `split` to tokenize the text may leave trailing punctuation on tokens that can affect tabulating frequencies. For example, in Example 5-2, `corpus['b']` ends with the token "study."; this is not the same as the token "study" that appears in `corpus['a']` (the token that someone would probably be more likely to query). In this instance, the trailing period on the token affects both the TF and the IDF calculations. Something as seemingly simple as a period signaling the end of a sentence is context that our brain processes trivially, but it's much more difficult for a machine to do this with the same level of accuracy.

Writing software to help machines better understand the context of words as they appear in human language data is a very active area of research and has tremendous potential for the future of search technology, the web, and artificial intelligence.

5.5 Closing Remarks

This chapter introduced some ways to cleanse human language data and spent some time learning about a few of the fundamentals of IR theory, TF-IDF, cosine similarity, and collocations as the means of analyzing the data we collect. Eventually we worked up to the point where we were considering some of the same problems that any search engine provider has had to consider to build a successful technology product. However, even though I hope this chapter has given you some good insight into how to extract useful information from unstructured text, it's barely scratched the surface of the most fundamental concepts, both in terms of theory and engineering considerations. Information retrieval is literally a multibillion-dollar industry, so you can only imagine the amount of combined investment that goes into both the theory and implementations that work at scale to power search engines such as Google and Bing.

Given the immense power of search providers like Google, it's easy to forget that these foundational search techniques even exist. However, understanding them yields insight into the assumptions and limitations of the commonly accepted status quo for search, while also clearly differentiating the state-of-the-art, entity-centric techniques that are emerging. Chapter 6 introduces a fundamental paradigm shift away from some of the techniques in this chapter. There are lots of exciting opportunities for technology-driven companies that can effectively analyze human language data.

 The source code outlined for this chapter and all other chapters is available on GitHub (*http://bit.ly/Mining-the-Social-Web-3E*) in a convenient Jupyter Notebook format that you're highly encouraged to try out from the comfort of your own web browser.

5.6 Recommended Exercises

- Take advantage of Jupyter Notebook's plotting features, introduced in Chapter 1, to graph Zipf's curve for the tokens from a corpus.

- If you'd like to try applying the techniques from this chapter to the web (in general), you might want to check out Scrapy (*http://bit.ly/1a1mG6P*), an easy-to-use and mature web scraping and crawling framework that can help you to harvest web pages.

- Spend some time and add interactive capabilities to the matrix diagram presented in this chapter. Can you add event handlers to automatically take you to the post when text is clicked on? Can you conceive of any meaningful ways to order the rows and columns so that it's easier to identify patterns?

- Update the code that emits the JSON that drives the matrix diagram so that it computes similarity differently and thus correlates documents differently from the default implementation.

- What additional features from the text can you think of that would make computing similarity across documents more accurate?

- Spend some time really digging into the theory presented in this chapter for the underlying IR concepts that were presented.

5.7 Online Resources

The following list of links from this chapter may be useful for review:

- 68-95-99.7 rule (*http://bit.ly/1a1mEf0*)
- Binomial distribution (*http://bit.ly/1a1mEMj*)
- Brown Corpus (*http://bit.ly/1a1mB2X*)
- Central limit theorem (*http://bit.ly/1a1mCnA*)
- HTTP API Overview (*http://bit.ly/1a1mAfm*)
- *Introduction to Information Retrieval* (*http://stanford.io/1a1mAvP*)
- "Introduction to the Normal Distribution" (*http://bit.ly/1a1mCnm*)
- *Foundations of Statistical Natural Language Processing*, Chapter 5 ("Collocations") (*http://stanford.io/1a1mBQy*)
- `matplotlib` (*https://matplotlib.org*)
- NLTK online book (*http://bit.ly/1a1mtAk*)
- Scrapy (*http://bit.ly/1a1mG6P*)
- Zipf's law (*http://bit.ly/1a1mCUD*)

## CHAPTER 6

Mining Web Pages: Using Natural Language Processing to Understand Human Language, Summarize Blog Posts, and More

This chapter follows closely on the heels of the chapter before it and is a modest attempt to introduce natural language processing (NLP) and apply it to the vast source of human language[1] data that you'll encounter on the social web (or elsewhere). The previous chapter introduced some foundational techniques from information retrieval (IR) theory, which generally treats text as document-centric "bags of words" (unordered collections of words) that can be modeled and manipulated as vectors. Although these models often perform remarkably well in many circumstances, a recurring shortcoming is that they do not maximize cues from the immediate context that ground words in meaning.

This chapter employs different techniques that are more context-driven and delves deeper into the semantics of human language data. Social web APIs that return data conforming to a well-defined schema are essential, but the most basic currency of human communication is natural language data such as the words that you are reading on this page, Facebook posts, web pages linked into tweets, and so forth. Human language is by far the most ubiquitous kind of data available to us, and the future of data-driven innovation depends largely upon our ability to effectively harness machines to understand digital forms of human communication.

---

[1] Throughout this chapter, the phrase *human language data* refers to the object of natural language processing and is intended to convey the same meaning as *natural language data* or *unstructured data*. No particular distinction is intended to be drawn by this choice of words other than its precision in describing the data itself.

It is highly recommended that you have a good working knowledge of the content in the previous chapter before you dive into this chapter. A good understanding of NLP presupposes an appreciation and working knowledge of some of the fundamental strengths and weaknesses of TF-IDF, vector space models, and so on. In that regard, this chapter and the one before it have a somewhat tighter coupling than most other chapters in this book.

In the spirit of the prior chapters, we'll attempt to cover the minimal level of detail required to empower you with a solid general understanding of an inherently complex topic, while also providing enough of a technical drill-down that you'll be able to immediately get to work mining some data. While continuing to cut corners and attempting to give you the crucial 20% of the skills that you can use to do 80% of the work (no single chapter out of any book—or small multivolume set of books, for that matter—could possibly do the topic of NLP justice), the content in this chapter is a pragmatic introduction that'll give you enough information to do some pretty amazing things with the human language data that you'll find all over the social web. Although we'll be focused on extracting human language data from web pages and feeds, keep in mind that just about every social website with an API is going to return human language, so these techniques generalize to just about any social website.

 Always get the latest bug-fixed source code for this chapter (and every other chapter) online at *http://bit.ly/Mining-the-Social-Web-3E*. Be sure to also take advantage of this book's virtual machine experience, as described in Appendix A, to maximize your enjoyment of the sample code.

6.1 Overview

This chapter continues our journey in analyzing human language data and uses arbitrary web pages and feeds as a basis. In this chapter you'll learn about:

- Fetching web pages and extracting the human language data from them
- Leveraging NLTK for completing fundamental tasks in natural language processing
- Contextually driven analysis in NLP
- Using NLP to complete analytical tasks such as generating document abstracts
- Metrics for measuring quality for domains that involve predictive analysis

6.2 Scraping, Parsing, and Crawling the Web

Although it's trivial to use a programming language or terminal utility such as `curl` or `wget` to fetch an arbitrary web page, extracting the isolated text that you want from the page isn't quite as trivial. Although the text is certainly in the page, so is lots of other "boilerplate" content such as navigation bars, headers, footers, advertisements, and other sources of noise that you probably don't care about. Hence, the bad news is that the solution isn't quite as simple as just stripping out the HTML tags and processing the text that is left behind, because the removal of HTML tags will have done nothing to remove the boilerplate itself. In some cases, there may actually be more boilerplate in the page that contributes noise than the signal you were looking for in the first place.

The good news is that the tools for helping to identify the content you're interested in have continued to mature over the years, and there are some excellent options for isolating the material that you'd want for text mining purposes. Additionally, the relative ubiquity of feeds such as RSS and Atom can often aid the process of retrieving clean text without all of the cruft that's typically in web pages, if you have the foresight to fetch the feeds while they are available.

 It's often the case that feeds are published only for "recent" content, so you may sometimes have to process web pages even if feeds are available. If given the choice, you'll probably want to prefer the feeds over arbitrary web pages, but you'll need to be prepared for both.

One excellent tool for *web scraping* (the process of extracting text from a web page) is the Java-based `boilerpipe` (*http://bit.ly/2MzPXhy*) library, which is designed to identify and remove the boilerplate from web pages. The library is based on a published paper entitled "Boilerplate Detection Using Shallow Text Features," (*http://bit.ly/1a1mN21*) which explains the efficacy of using supervised machine learning (*http://bit.ly/1a1mPHr*) techniques to bifurcate the boilerplate and the content of the page. Supervised learning techniques involve a process that creates a predictive model from training samples that are representative of its domain, and thus `boilerpipe` is customizable should you desire to tweak it for increased accuracy.

There's a default extractor that works for the general case, an extractor that has been trained for web pages containing articles, and an extractor that is trained to extract the largest body of text on a page, which might be suitable for web pages that tend to have just one large block of text. In any case, there may still be some light postprocessing required on the text, depending on what other features you can identify that may be noise or require attention, but employing `boilerpipe` to do the heavy lifting is just about as easy as it should be.

Even though the library is Java-based, it's useful and popular enough that a Python 3 package wrapper (*http://bit.ly/2sCIFET*) is available. Installation of this package is predictable: use `pip install boilerpipe3`. Assuming you have a relatively recent version of Java on your system, that's all that should be required to use `boilerpipe`.

Example 6-1 demonstrates a sample script that illustrates its rather straightforward usage for the task of extracting the body content of an article, as denoted by the `Arti cleExtractor` parameter that's passed into the `Extractor` constructor. You can also try out a hosted version of `boilerpipe` (*http://bit.ly/1a1mSTF*) online to see the difference between this and some of its other provided extractors, such as the `Large stContentExtractor` or `DefaultExtractor`.

Example 6-1. Using boilerpipe to extract the text from a web page

```
from boilerpipe.extract import Extractor

URL='http://radar.oreilly.com/2010/07/louvre-industrial-age-henry-ford.html'

extractor = Extractor(extractor='ArticleExtractor', url=URL)

print(extractor.getText())
```

Although web scraping used to be the only way to fetch content from websites, there's potentially an easier way to harvest content, especially if it's content that's coming from a news source, blog, or other syndicated source. But before we get into that, let's take a quick trip down memory lane.

If you've been using the web long enough, you may remember a time in the late 1990s when news readers didn't exist. Back then, if you wanted to know what the latest changes to a website were, you just had to go to the site and see if anything had changed. As a result, syndication formats took advantage of the self-publishing movement with blogs and formats such as RSS (Really Simple Syndication) and Atom built upon the evolving XML (*http://bit.ly/18RFKaW*) specifications that were growing in popularity to handle content providers publishing content and consumers subscribing to it. Parsing feeds is an easier problem to solve since the feeds are well-formed (*http://bit.ly/1a1mQLr*) XML data that validates (*http://bit.ly/1a1mTqE*) to a published schema, whereas web pages may or may not be well formed, be valid, or even conform to best practices.

The commonly used Python package `feedparser` is an essential utility to have on hand for parsing feeds. You can install it with `pip` using the standard `pip install feedparser` approach in a terminal, and Example 6-2 illustrates minimal usage to extract the text, title, and source URL for an entry in an RSS feed.

Example 6-2. Using feedparser to extract the text (and other fields) from an RSS or Atom feed

```
import feedparser

FEED_URL='http://feeds.feedburner.com/oreilly/radar/atom'

fp = feedparser.parse(FEED_URL)

for e in fp.entries:
    print(e.title)
    print(e.links[0].href)
    print(e.content[0].value)
```

HTML, XML, and XHTML

As the early web evolved, the difficulty of separating the content in a page from its presentation quickly became recognized as a problem, and XML was (in part) a solution. The idea was that content creators could publish data in an XML format and use a stylesheet to transform it into XHTML for presentation to an end user. XHTML is essentially just HTML that is written as well-formed XML: each tag is defined in lowercase, tags are properly nested as a tree structure, and either tags are self-closing (such as <br />) or each opening tag (e.g., <p>) has a corresponding closing tag (</p>).

In the context of web scraping, these conventions have the added benefit of making each web page much easier to process with a parser, and in terms of design, it appeared that XHTML was exactly what the web needed. There was a lot to gain and virtually nothing to lose from the proposition: *well-formed* XHTML content could be proven *valid* against an XML schema and enjoy all of the other perks of XML, such as custom attributes using namespaces (a device that semantic web technologies such as RDFa rely upon).

The problem was that it just didn't catch on. As a result, we now live in a world where semantic markup based on the HTML 4.01 standard that's over a decade old continues to thrive, while XHTML and XHTML-based technologies such as RDFa remain on the fringe. (In fact, libraries such as BeautifulSoup (*http://bit.ly/1a1mRit*) are designed with the specific intent of being able to reasonably process HTML that probably isn't well-formed or even sane.) Most of the web development world is holding its breath and hoping that HTML5 (*http://bit.ly/1a1mRz5*) will indeed create a long-overdue convergence as technologies like microdata (*http://bit.ly/1a1mRPA*) catch on and publishing tools modernize. The HTML article on Wikipedia (*http://bit.ly/1a1mS66*) is worth reading if you find this kind of history interesting.

Crawling websites is a logical extension of the same concepts already presented in this section: it typically consists of fetching a page, extracting the hyperlinks in the page, and then systematically fetching all of the linked-to pages. This process is repeated to an arbitrary depth, depending on your objective. This very process is the way that the earliest search engines used to work, and the way most search engines that index the web still continue to work today. Although a crawl of the web is far outside our scope, it is helpful to have a working knowledge of the problem, so let's briefly think about the computational complexity of harvesting all of those pages.

In terms of implementing your own web crawl, should you ever desire to do so, Scrapy (*http://bit.ly/1a1mG6P*) is a Python-based framework for web scraping that serves as an excellent resource. The documentation is excellent and includes all of the tutelage you'll need to get a targeted web crawl going with little effort up front. The next section is a brief aside that discusses the computational complexity of how web crawls are typically implemented so that you can better appreciate what you may be getting yourself into.

Nowadays, you can get a periodically updated crawl of the web that's suitable for most research purposes from a source such as Amazon's Common Crawl corpus (*http://amzn.to/1a1mXXb*), which features more than 5 billion web pages and checks in at over 81 terabytes of data!

6.2.1 Breadth-First Search in Web Crawling

This section contains some detailed content and analysis about how web crawls can be implemented and is not essential to your understanding of the content in this chapter (although you will likely find it interesting and edifying). If this is your first reading of the chapter, feel free to save it for next time.

The basic algorithm for a web crawl can be framed as a *breadth-first search* (*http://bit.ly/1a1mYdG*), which is a fundamental technique for exploring a space that's typically modeled as a tree or a graph given a starting node and no other known information except a set of possibilities. In our web crawl scenario, our starting node would be the initial web page and the set of neighboring nodes would be the other pages that are hyperlinked.

There are alternative ways to search the space, including a *depth-first search* (*http://bit.ly/1a1mVPd*). The particular choice of one technique versus another often depends on available computing resources, specific domain knowledge, and even theoretical considerations. A breadth-first search is a reasonable approach for exploring a sliver of the web. Example 6-3 presents some pseudocode that illustrates how it works.

Example 6-3. Pseudocode for a breadth-first search

```
Create an empty graph
Create an empty queue to keep track of nodes that need to be processed

Add the starting point to the graph as the root node
Add the root node to a queue for processing

Repeat until some maximum depth is reached or the queue is empty:
  Remove a node from the queue
  For each of the node's neighbors:
    If the neighbor hasn't already been processed:
      Add it to the queue
      Add it to the graph
      Create an edge in the graph that connects the node and its neighbor
```

We generally haven't taken quite this long of a pause to analyze an approach, but breadth-first search is a fundamental tool you'll want to have in your belt and understand well. In general, there are two criteria for examination that you should always consider for an algorithm: efficiency and effectiveness (or, to put it another way: performance and quality).

Standard performance analysis of any algorithm generally involves examining its worst-case time and space complexity—in other words, the amount of time it would take the program to execute, and the amount of memory required for execution over a very large data set. The breadth-first approach we've used to frame a web crawl is essentially a breadth-first search, except that we're not actually searching for anything in particular because there are no exit criteria beyond expanding the graph out either to a maximum depth or until we run out of nodes. If we were searching for something specific instead of just crawling links indefinitely, that would be considered an actual breadth-first search. Thus, a more common variation of a breadth-first search is called a *bounded breadth-first search*, which imposes a limit on the maximum depth of the search just as we do in this example.

For a breadth-first search (or breadth-first crawl), both the time and space complexity can be bounded in the worst case by b^d, where b is the branching factor of the graph and d is the depth. If you sketch out an example on paper, as in Figure 6-1, and think about it, this analysis quickly becomes more apparent.

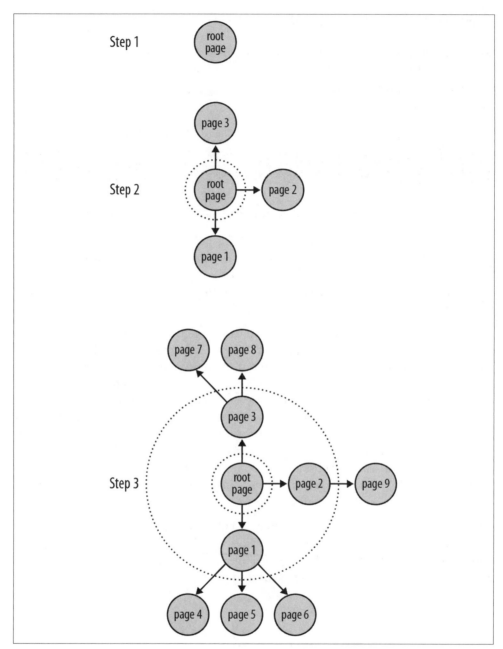

Figure 6-1. In a breadth-first search, each step of the search expands the depth by one level until a maximum depth or some other termination criterion is reached

If every node in a graph had 5 neighbors, and you only went out to a depth of a, you'd end up with 6 nodes in all: the root node and its 5 neighbors. If all 5 of those neighbors had 5 neighbors too and you expanded out another level, you'd end up with 31 nodes in all: the root node, the root node's 5 neighbors, and 5 neighbors for each of the root node's neighbors. Table 6-1 provides an overview of how b^d grows for a few sizes of b and d.

Table 6-1. Example branching factor calculations for graphs of varying depths

Branching factor	Nodes for depth = 1	Nodes for depth = 2	Nodes for depth = 3	Nodes for depth = 4	Nodes for depth = 5
2	3	7	15	31	63
3	4	13	40	121	364
4	5	21	85	341	1,365
5	6	31	156	781	3,906
6	7	43	259	1,555	9,331

Figure 6-2 provides a visual for the values displayed in Table 6-1.

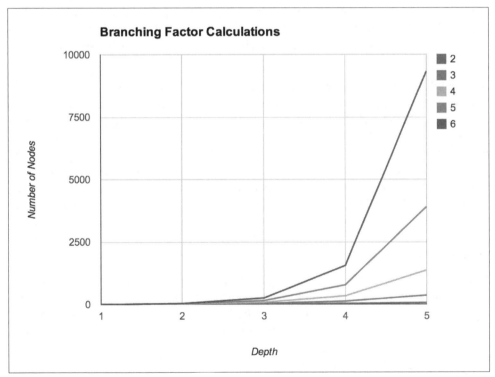

Figure 6-2. The growth in the number of nodes as the depth of a breadth-first search increases

While the previous comments pertain primarily to the theoretical bounds of the algorithm, one final consideration worth noting is the practical performance of the algorithm for a data set of a fixed size. Mild profiling of a breadth-first implementation that fetches web pages would likely reveal that the code is primarily *I/O bound* from the standpoint that the vast majority of time is spent waiting for a library call to return content to be processed. In situations in which you are I/O bound, a thread pool (*http://bit.ly/1a1mW5M*) is a common technique for increasing performance.

6.3 Discovering Semantics by Decoding Syntax

You may recall from the previous chapter that perhaps the most fundamental weaknesses of TF-IDF and cosine similarity are that these models inherently don't leverage a deep semantic understanding of the data and throw away a lot of critical context. Quite the contrary, the examples in that chapter took advantage of very basic syntax that separated tokens by whitespace to break an otherwise opaque document into a bag of words (*http://bit.ly/1a1lHDF*) and used frequency and simple statistical similarity metrics to determine which tokens were likely to be important in the data. Although you can do some really amazing things with these techniques, they don't really give you any notion of what any given token means in the context in which it appears in the document. Look no further than a sentence containing a homograph (*http://bit.ly/1a1mWCL*) such as *fish*, *bear*, or even *google* as a case in point; either one could be a noun or a verb.[2]

NLP is inherently complex and difficult to do even reasonably well, and completely nailing it for a large set of commonly spoken languages may well be the problem of the century. Despite what many believe, it's far from being a solved problem, and it is already the case that we are starting to see a rising interest in a "deeper understanding" of the web with initiatives such as Google's Knowledge Graph (*http://bit.ly/ 2NKhEZz*), which is being promoted as "the future of search." After all, a complete mastery of NLP is essentially a plausible strategy for acing the Turing test (*http:// bit.ly/1a1mZON*), and to the most careful observer, a computer program that achieves this level of "understanding" demonstrates an uncanny amount of human-like intelligence even if it is through a brain that's mathematically modeled in software as opposed to a biological one.

Whereas structured or semistructured sources are essentially collections of records with some presupposed meaning given to each field that can immediately be analyzed, there are subtler considerations to be handled with human language data for even the seemingly simplest of tasks. For example, let's suppose you're given a docu-

---

2 A homonym is a special case of a homograph. Two words are homographs if they have the same spelling. Two words are homonyms if they have the same spelling and the same pronunciation. For some reason, *homonym* seems more common in parlance than *homograph*, even if it's being misused.

ment and asked to count the number of sentences in it. It's a trivial task if you're a human and have just a basic understanding of English grammar, but it's another story entirely for a machine, which will require a complex and detailed set of instructions to complete the same task.

The encouraging news is that machines can detect the ends of sentences in relatively well-formed data quickly and with nearly perfect accuracy. Even if you've accurately detected all of the sentences, though, there's still a lot that you probably don't know about the ways that words or phrases are used in those sentences. Look no further than sarcasm or other forms of ironic language as cases in point. Even with perfect information about the structure of a sentence, you often still need additional context outside the sentence to properly interpret it.

Thus, as an overly broad generalization, we can say that NLP is fundamentally about taking an opaque document that consists of an ordered collection of symbols adhering to proper *syntax* and a reasonably well-defined *grammar*, and deducing the *semantics* associated with those symbols.

Let's get back to the task of detecting sentences, the first step in most NLP pipelines, to illustrate some of the complexity involved in NLP. It's deceptively easy to overestimate the utility of simple rule-based heuristics, and it's important to work through an exercise so that you realize what some of the key issues are and don't waste time trying to reinvent the wheel.

Your first attempt at solving the sentence detection problem might be to just count the periods, question marks, and exclamation points in the text. That's the most obvious heuristic for starting out, but it's quite crude and has the potential for producing an extremely high margin of error. Consider the following (relatively unambiguous) accusation:

> Mr. Green killed Colonel Mustard in the study with the candlestick. Mr. Green is not a very nice fellow.

Simply tokenizing the text by splitting on punctuation (specifically, periods) would produce the following result:

```
>>> txt = "Mr. Green killed Colonel Mustard in the study with the \
... candlestick. Mr. Green is not a very nice fellow."
>>> txt.split(".")
['Mr', 'Green killed Colonel Mustard in the study with the candlestick',
 'Mr', 'Green is not a very nice fellow', '']
```

It should be immediately obvious that performing sentence detection by blindly breaking on periods without incorporating some notion of context or higher-level information is insufficient. In this case, the problem is the use of "Mr.," a valid abbreviation that's commonly used in the English language. Although we already know from the previous chapter that *n*-gram analysis of this sample would likely tell us that "Mr. Green" is really one compound token called a collocation or *chunk*, if we had a larger amount of text to analyze, it's not hard to imagine other edge cases that would be difficult to detect based on the appearance of collocations. Thinking ahead a bit, it's also worth pointing out that finding the key topics in a sentence isn't easy to accomplish with trivial logic either. As an intelligent human, you can easily discern that the key topics in our sample might be "Mr. Green," "Colonel Mustard," "the study," and "the candlestick," but training a machine to tell you the same things without human intervention is a complex task.

Take a moment to think about how you might write a computer program to solve the problem before continuing in order to get the most out of the remainder of this discussion.

A few obvious possibilities are probably occurring to you, such as doing some "Title Case" detection with a regular expression, constructing a list of common abbreviations to parse out the proper noun phrases, and applying some variation of that logic to the problem of finding end-of-sentence (EOS) boundaries to prevent yourself from getting into trouble on that front. OK, sure. Those things will work for some examples, but what's the margin of error going to be like for *arbitrary* English text? How forgiving is your algorithm for poorly formed English text; highly abbreviated information such as text messages or tweets; or (gasp) other romantic languages, such as Spanish, French, or Italian? There are no simple answers here, and that's why text analytics is such an important topic in an age where the amount of digitally available human language data is literally increasing every second.

6.3.1 Natural Language Processing Illustrated Step-by-Step

Let's prepare to step through a series of examples that illustrate NLP with NLTK. The NLP pipeline we'll examine involves the following steps:

1. EOS detection
2. Tokenization
3. Part-of-speech tagging
4. Chunking
5. Extraction

The following NLP pipeline is presented as though it is unfolding in a Python interpreter session for clarity and ease of illustration of the input and expected output of each step. However, each step of the pipeline is preloaded into this chapter's Jupyter Notebook so that you can follow along per the norm with all the other examples.

We'll continue to use the following sample text from the previous chapter for the purposes of illustration: "Mr. Green killed Colonel Mustard in the study with the candlestick. Mr. Green is not a very nice fellow." Remember that even though you have already read the text and understand its underlying grammatical structure, it's merely an opaque string value to a machine at this point. Let's look at the steps we need to work through in more detail:

EOS detection
> This step breaks a text into a collection of meaningful sentences. Since sentences generally represent logical units of thought, they tend to have a predictable syntax that lends itself well to further analysis. Most NLP pipelines you'll see begin with this step because tokenization (the next step) operates on individual sentences. Breaking the text into paragraphs or sections might add value for certain types of analysis, but it is unlikely to aid in the overall task of EOS detection. In the interpreter, you'd parse out a sentence with NLTK like so:

```
>>> import nltk
>>> txt = "Mr. Green killed Colonel Mustard in the study with the  \
... candlestick. Mr. Green is not a very nice fellow."
>>> txt = "Mr. Green killed Colonel Mustard in the study with the \
... candlestick. Mr. Green is not a very nice fellow."
>>> sentences = nltk.tokenize.sent_tokenize(txt)
>>> sentences
['Mr. Green killed Colonel Mustard in the study with the candlestick.',
 'Mr. Green is not a very nice fellow.']
```

> We'll talk a little bit more about what is happening under the hood with sent_tokenize in the next section. For now, we'll accept at face value that proper sentence detection has occurred for arbitrary text—a clear improvement over breaking on characters that are likely to be punctuation marks.

Tokenization
> This step operates on individual sentences, splitting them into tokens. Following along in the example interpreter session, you'd do the following:

```
>>> tokens = [nltk.tokenize.word_tokenize(s) for s in sentences]
>>> tokens
[['Mr.', 'Green', 'killed', 'Colonel', 'Mustard', 'in', 'the', 'study',
  'with', 'the', 'candlestick', '.'],
 ['Mr.', 'Green', 'is', 'not', 'a', 'very', 'nice', 'fellow', '.']]
```

Note that for this simple example, tokenization appeared to do the same thing as splitting on whitespace, with the exception that it tokenized out EOS markers (the periods) correctly. As we'll see in a later section, though, it can do a bit more if we give it the opportunity, and we already know that distinguishing between whether a period is an EOS marker or part of an abbreviation isn't always trivial. As an anecdotal note, some written languages, such as ones that use pictograms as opposed to letters, don't necessarily even require whitespace to separate the tokens in sentences and require the reader (or machine) to distinguish the boundaries.

POS tagging

This step assigns part-of-speech (POS) information to each token. In the example interpreter session, you'd run the tokens through one more step to have them decorated with tags:

```
>>> pos_tagged_tokens = [nltk.pos_tag(t) for t in tokens]
>>> pos_tagged_tokens
[[('Mr.', 'NNP'), ('Green', 'NNP'), ('killed', 'VBD'), ('Colonel', 'NNP'),
  ('Mustard', 'NNP'), ('in', 'IN'), ('the', 'DT'), ('study', 'NN'),
  ('with', 'IN'), ('the', 'DT'), ('candlestick', 'NN'), ('.', '.')],
 [('Mr.', 'NNP'), ('Green', 'NNP'), ('is', 'VBZ'), ('not', 'RB'),
  ('a', 'DT'), ('very', 'RB'), ('nice', 'JJ'), ('fellow', 'JJ'),
  ('.', '.')]]
```

You may not intuitively understand all of these tags, but they do represent POS information. For example, 'NNP' indicates that the token is a noun that is part of a noun phrase, 'VBD' indicates a verb that's in simple past tense, and 'JJ' indicates an adjective. The Penn Treebank Project (*http://bit.ly/2C5ecDq*) provides a full summary (*http://bit.ly/1a1n05o*) of the POS tags that could be returned. With POS tagging completed, it should be getting pretty apparent just how powerful analysis can become. For example, by using the POS tags, we'll be able to chunk together nouns as part of noun phrases and then try to reason about what types of entities they might be (e.g., people, places, or organizations). If you never thought that you'd need to apply those exercises from elementary school regarding parts of speech, think again: it's essential to a proper application of natural language processing.

Chunking

This step involves analyzing each tagged token within a sentence and assembling compound tokens that express logical concepts—quite a different approach than statistically analyzing collocations. It is possible to define a custom grammar through NLTK's chunk.regexp.RegexpParser, but that's beyond the scope of this chapter; see Chapter 9 of Edward Loper, Ewan Klein, and Steven Bird's *Natural Language Processing with Python* (*http://bit.ly/2szE1HW*) (O'Reilly) for full details. Besides, NLTK exposes a function that combines chunking with named entity extraction, which is the next step.

Extraction

This step involves analyzing each chunk and further tagging the chunks as named entities, such as people, organizations, locations, etc. The continuing saga of NLP in the interpreter demonstrates:

```
>>> ne_chunks = list(nltk.chunk.ne_chunk_sents(pos_tagged_tokens))
>>> print(ne_chunks)
[Tree('S', [Tree('PERSON', [('Mr.', 'NNP')]),
 Tree('PERSON', [('Green', 'NNP')]), ('killed', 'VBD'),
 Tree('ORGANIZATION', [('Colonel', 'NNP'), ('Mustard', 'NNP')]),
      ('in', 'IN'), ('the', 'DT'), ('study', 'NN'), ('with', 'IN'),
      ('the', 'DT'), ('candlestick', 'NN'), ('.', '.')]),
 Tree('S', [Tree('PERSON', [('Mr.', 'NNP')]),
                  Tree('ORGANIZATION',
                      [('Green', 'NNP')]), ('is', 'VBZ'), ('not', 'RB'),
                      ('a', 'DT'), ('very', 'RB'), ('nice', 'JJ'),
                      ('fellow', 'JJ'), ('.', '.')])]
>>> ne_chunks[0].pprint() # You can pretty-print each chunk in the tree

(S
  (PERSON Mr./NNP)
  (PERSON Green/NNP)
  killed/VBD
  (ORGANIZATION Colonel/NNP Mustard/NNP)
  in/IN
  the/DT
  study/NN
  with/IN
  the/DT
  candlestick/NN
  ./.)
```

Don't get too wrapped up in trying to decipher exactly what the tree output means just yet. In short, it has chunked together some tokens and attempted to classify them as being certain types of entities. (You may be able to discern that it has identified "Mr. Green" as a person, but unfortunately categorized "Colonel Mustard" as an organization.) Figure 6-3 illustrates output in the Jupyter Notebook.

As worthwhile as it would be to continue exploring natural language with NLTK, that level of engagement isn't really our purpose here. The background in this section is provided to motivate an appreciation for the difficulty of the task and to encourage you to review the NLTK book (*http://bit.ly/1a1mtAk*) or one of the many other plentiful resources available online if you'd like to pursue the topic further.

Given that it's possible to customize certain aspects of NLTK, the remainder of this chapter assumes you'll be using NLTK "as is" unless otherwise noted.

With that brief introduction to NLP concluded, let's get to work mining some blog data.

```
In [34]: # Downloading nltk packages used in this example
         nltk.download('maxent_ne_chunker')
         nltk.download('words')

         ne_chunks = list(nltk.chunk.ne_chunk_sents(pos_tagged_tokens))
         print(ne_chunks)
         ne_chunks[0].pprint()

[nltk_data] Downloading package maxent_ne_chunker to
[nltk_data]     /Users/mikhail/nltk_data...
[nltk_data]   Package maxent_ne_chunker is already up-to-date!
[nltk_data] Downloading package words to /Users/mikhail/nltk_data...
[nltk_data]   Package words is already up-to-date!
[Tree('S', [Tree('PERSON', [('Mr.', 'NNP')]), Tree('PERSON', [('Green', 'NNP')]), ('killed', 'VBD'), Tree('ORGANIZATI
ON', [('Colonel', 'NNP'), ('Mustard', 'NNP')]), ('in', 'IN'), ('the', 'DT'), ('study', 'NN'), ('with', 'IN'), ('the',
'DT'), ('candlestick', 'NN'), ('.', '.')]), Tree('S', [Tree('PERSON', [('Mr.', 'NNP')]), Tree('ORGANIZATION', [('Gree
n', 'NNP')]), ('is', 'VBZ'), ('not', 'RB'), ('a', 'DT'), ('very', 'RB'), ('nice', 'JJ'), ('fellow', 'NN'), ('.', '.')
])]
(S
  (PERSON Mr./NNP)
  (PERSON Green/NNP)
  killed/VBD
  (ORGANIZATION Colonel/NNP Mustard/NNP)
  in/IN
  the/DT
  study/NN
  with/IN
  the/DT
  candlestick/NN
  ./.)
```

Figure 6-3. Using NLTK to chunk tokens and classify them as named entities

6.3.2 Sentence Detection in Human Language Data

Given that sentence detection is probably the first task you'll want to ponder when building an NLP stack, it makes sense to start there. Even if you never complete the remaining tasks in the pipeline, it turns out that EOS detection alone yields some powerful possibilities, such as document summarization, which we'll be considering as a follow-up exercise in the next section. But first, we'll need to fetch some clean human language data. Let's use the tried-and-true feedparser package, along with some utilities introduced in the previous chapter that are based on nltk and Beauti fulSoup, to fetch some posts from the O'Reilly Ideas (*http://oreil.ly/2QwxDch*) and clean up any HTML formatting that may appear in the content. The listing in Example 6-4 fetches a few posts and saves them to a local file as JSON.

Example 6-4. Harvesting blog data by parsing feeds

```python
import os
import sys
import json
import feedparser
from bs4 import BeautifulSoup
from nltk import clean_html

FEED_URL = 'http://feeds.feedburner.com/oreilly/radar/atom'

def cleanHtml(html):
    if html == "": return ""

    return BeautifulSoup(html, 'html5lib').get_text()
```

```
fp = feedparser.parse(FEED_URL)

print("Fetched {0} entries from '{1}'".format(len(fp.entries[0].title),
    fp.feed.title))

blog_posts = []
for e in fp.entries:
    blog_posts.append({'title': e.title, 'content'
                       : cleanHtml(e.content[0].value), 'link': e.links[0].href})

out_file = os.path.join('feed.json')
f = open(out_file, 'w+')
f.write(json.dumps(blog_posts, indent=1))
f.close()

print('Wrote output file to {0}'.format(f.name))
```

Obtaining human language data from a reputable source affords us the luxury of assuming good English grammar; hopefully this also means that one of NLTK's out-of-the-box sentence detectors will work reasonably well. There's no better way to find out than hacking some code to see what happens, so go ahead and review the code listing in Example 6-5. It introduces the sent_tokenize and word_tokenize methods, which are aliases for NLTK's currently recommended sentence detector and word tokenizer. A brief discussion of the listing is provided afterward.

Example 6-5. Using NLTK's NLP tools to process human language in blog data

```
import json
import nltk

BLOG_DATA = "resources/ch06-webpages/feed.json"

blog_data = json.loads(open(BLOG_DATA).read())

# Download nltk packages used in this example
nltk.download('stopwords')

# Customize your list of stopwords as needed. Here, we add common
# punctuation and contraction artifacts.

stop_words = nltk.corpus.stopwords.words('english') + [
    '.',
    ',',
    '--',
    '\'s',
    '?',
    ')',
    '(',
    ':',
    '\'',
```

```
        '\'re',
        '"',
        '-',
        '}',
        '{',
        u'—',
        ']',
        '[',
        '...'
    ]

for post in blog_data:
    sentences = nltk.tokenize.sent_tokenize(post['content'])

    words = [w.lower() for sentence in sentences for w in
                nltk.tokenize.word_tokenize(sentence)]

    fdist = nltk.FreqDist(words)

    # Remove stopwords from fdist
    for sw in stop_words:
        del fdist[sw]

    # Basic stats

    num_words = sum([i[1] for i in fdist.items()])
    num_unique_words = len(fdist.keys())

    # Hapaxes are words that appear only once
    num_hapaxes = len(fdist.hapaxes())

    top_10_words_sans_stop_words = fdist.most_common(10)

    print(post['title'])
    print('\tNum Sentences:'.ljust(25), len(sentences))
    print('\tNum Words:'.ljust(25), num_words)
    print('\tNum Unique Words:'.ljust(25), num_unique_words)
    print('\tNum Hapaxes:'.ljust(25), num_hapaxes)
    print('\tTop 10 Most Frequent Words (sans stop words):\n\t\t',
        '\n\t\t'.join(['{0} ({1})'.format(w[0], w[1])
        for w in top_10_words_sans_stop_words]))
    print()
```

NLTK provides several options for tokenization, but it provides "recommendations" as to the best available via the sent_tokenize and word_tokenize aliases. At the time of this writing (you can double-check this with pydoc or with a command like nltk.tokenize.sent_tokenize? in IPython or the Jupyter Notebook at any time), the sentence detector is the PunktSentenceTokenizer and the word tokenizer is the TreebankWordTokenizer. Let's take a brief look at each of these.

Internally, the `PunktSentenceTokenizer` relies heavily on being able to detect abbreviations as part of collocation patterns, and it uses some regular expressions to try to intelligently parse sentences by taking into account common patterns of punctuation usage. A full explanation of the innards of the `PunktSentenceTokenizer`'s logic is outside the scope of this book, but Tibor Kiss and Jan Strunk's original paper "Unsupervised Multilingual Sentence Boundary Detection" (*http://bit.ly/2EzWCEZ*) discusses its approach in a highly readable way, and you should take some time to review it.

As we'll see in a bit, it is possible to instantiate the `PunktSentenceTokenizer` with sample text that it trains on to try to improve its accuracy. The type of underlying algorithm that's used is an *unsupervised learning algorithm*; it does not require you to explicitly mark up the sample training data in any way. Instead, the algorithm inspects certain *features* that appear in the text itself, such as the use of capitalization and the co-occurrences of tokens, to derive suitable parameters for breaking the text into sentences.

While NLTK's `WhitespaceTokenizer`, which creates tokens by breaking a piece of text on whitespace, would have been the simplest word tokenizer to introduce, you're already familiar with some of the shortcomings of blindly breaking on whitespace. Instead, NLTK currently recommends the `TreebankWordTokenizer`, a word tokenizer that operates on sentences and uses the same conventions as the Penn Treebank Project (*http://bit.ly/2C5ecDq*).[3] The one thing that may catch you off guard is that the `TreebankWordTokenizer`'s tokenization (*http://bit.ly/2EBDPNQ*) does some less-than-obvious things, such as separately tagging components in contractions and nouns having possessive forms. For example, the parsing for the sentence "I'm hungry" would yield separate components for "I" and "'m," maintaining a distinction between the subject and verb for the two words conjoined in the contraction "I'm." As you might imagine, finely grained access to this kind of grammatical information can be quite valuable when it's time to do advanced analysis that scrutinizes relationships between subjects and verbs in sentences.

Given a sentence tokenizer and a word tokenizer, we can first parse the text into sentences and then parse each sentence into tokens. While this approach is fairly intuitive, its Achilles' heel is that errors produced by the sentence detector propagate forward and can potentially bound the upper limit of the quality that the rest of the NLP stack can produce. For example, if the sentence tokenizer mistakenly breaks a sentence on the period after "Mr." that appears in a section of text such as "Mr. Green killed Colonel Mustard in the study with the candlestick," it may not be possible to

---

3 *Treebank* is a very specific term that refers to a corpus that's been specially tagged with advanced linguistic information. In fact, the reason such a corpus is called a treebank is to emphasize that it's a bank (think: collection) of sentences that have been parsed into trees adhering to a particular grammar.

extract the entity "Mr. Green" from the text unless specialized repair logic is in place. Again, it all depends on the sophistication of the full NLP stack and how it accounts for error propagation.

The out-of-the-box `PunktSentenceTokenizer` is trained on the Penn Treebank corpus and performs quite well. The end goal of the parsing is to instantiate an `nltk.FreqDist` object (which is like a slightly more sophisticated `collections.Counter`), which expects a list of tokens. The remainder of the code in Example 6-5 is a straightforward usage of a few of the commonly used NLTK APIs.

> If you have a lot of trouble with advanced word tokenizers such as NLTK's `TreebankWordTokenizer` or `PunktWordTokenizer`, it's fine to default to the `WhitespaceTokenizer` until you decide whether it's worth the investment to use a more advanced tokenizer. In fact, using a more straightforward tokenizer can often be advantageous. For example, using an advanced tokenizer on data that frequently inlines URLs might be a bad idea.

The aim of this section was to familiarize you with the first step involved in building an NLP pipeline. Along the way, we developed a few metrics that make a feeble attempt at characterizing some blog data. Our pipeline doesn't involve part-of-speech tagging or chunking (yet), but it should give you a basic understanding of some concepts and get you thinking about some of the subtler issues involved. While it's true that we could have simply split on whitespace, counted terms, tallied the results, and still gained a lot of information from the data, it won't be long before you'll be glad that you took these initial steps toward a deeper understanding of the data. To illustrate one possible application for what you've just learned, in the next section we'll look at a simple document summarization algorithm that relies on little more than sentence segmentation and frequency analysis.

6.3.3 Document Summarization

Being able to perform reasonably good sentence detection as part of an NLP approach to mining unstructured data can enable some pretty powerful text mining capabilities, such as crude but very reasonable attempts at document summarization. There are numerous possibilities and approaches, but one of the simplest to get started with dates all the way back to the April 1958 issue of *IBM Journal*. In the seminal article entitled "The Automatic Creation of Literature Abstracts," (*http://bit.ly/1a1n4Cj*) H.P. Luhn describes a technique that essentially boils down to filtering out sentences containing frequently occurring words that appear near one another.

The original paper is easy to understand and rather interesting; Luhn actually describes how he prepared punch cards in order to run various tests with different parameters! It's amazing to think that what we can implement in a few dozen lines of

Python on a cheap piece of commodity hardware, he probably labored over for hours and hours to program into a gargantuan mainframe. Example 6-6 provides a basic implementation of Luhn's algorithm for document summarization. A brief analysis of the algorithm appears in the next section. Before skipping ahead to that discussion, first take a moment to trace through the code to learn more about how it works.

 Example 6-6 uses the numpy package (a collection of highly optimized numeric operations), which should have been installed alongside nltk. If for some reason you are not using the virtual machine and need to install it, just use **pip install numpy**.

Example 6-6. A document summarization algorithm based principally upon sentence detection and frequency analysis within sentences

```
import json
import nltk
import numpy

BLOG_DATA = "resources/ch06-webpages/feed.json"

blog_data = json.loads(open(BLOG_DATA).read())

N = 100  # Number of words to consider
CLUSTER_THRESHOLD = 5  # Distance between words to consider
TOP_SENTENCES = 5  # Number of sentences to return for a "top n" summary

# Extend the stopwords somewhat
stop_words = nltk.corpus.stopwords.words('english') + [
    '.',
    ',',
    '--',
    '\'s',
    '?',
    ')',
    '(',
    ':',
    '\'',
    '\'re',
    '"',
    '-',
    '}',
    '{',
    u'—',
    '>',
    '<',
    '...'
    ]

# Approach taken from "The Automatic Creation of Literature Abstracts" by H.P. Luhn
```

```
def _score_sentences(sentences, important_words):
    scores = []
    sentence_idx = 0

    for s in [nltk.tokenize.word_tokenize(s) for s in sentences]:

        word_idx = []

        # For each word in the word list...
        for w in important_words:
            try:
                # Compute an index for where any important words occur in
                # the sentence
                word_idx.append(s.index(w))
            except ValueError: # w not in this particular sentence
                pass

        word_idx.sort()

        # It is possible that some sentences may not contain any important
        # words at all
        if len(word_idx)== 0: continue

        # Using the word index, compute clusters by using a max distance threshold
        # for any two consecutive words

        clusters = []
        cluster = [word_idx[0]]
        i = 1
        while i < len(word_idx):
            if word_idx[i] - word_idx[i - 1] < CLUSTER_THRESHOLD:
                cluster.append(word_idx[i])
            else:
                clusters.append(cluster[:])
                cluster = [word_idx[i]]
            i += 1
        clusters.append(cluster)

        # Score each cluster. The max score for any given cluster is the score
        # for the sentence.

        max_cluster_score = 0

        for c in clusters:
            significant_words_in_cluster = len(c)
            # True clusters also contain insignificant words, so we get
            # the total cluster length by checking the indices
            total_words_in_cluster = c[-1] - c[0] + 1
            score = 1.0 * significant_words_in_cluster**2 / total_words_in_cluster

            if score > max_cluster_score:
                max_cluster_score = score
```

```
            scores.append((sentence_idx, max_cluster_score))
            sentence_idx += 1

    return scores

def summarize(txt):
    sentences = [s for s in nltk.tokenize.sent_tokenize(txt)]
    normalized_sentences = [s.lower() for s in sentences]

    words = [w.lower() for sentence in normalized_sentences for w in
                nltk.tokenize.word_tokenize(sentence)]

    fdist = nltk.FreqDist(words)

    # Remove stopwords from fdist
    for sw in stop_words:
        del fdist[sw]

    top_n_words = [w[0] for w in fdist.most_common(N)]

    scored_sentences = _score_sentences(normalized_sentences, top_n_words)

    # Summarization Approach 1:
    # Filter out nonsignificant sentences by using the average score plus a
    # fraction of the std dev as a filter

    avg = numpy.mean([s[1] for s in scored_sentences])
    std = numpy.std([s[1] for s in scored_sentences])
    mean_scored = [(sent_idx, score) for (sent_idx, score) in scored_sentences
                    if score > avg + 0.5 * std]

    # Summarization Approach 2:
    # Another approach would be to return only the top N ranked sentences

    top_n_scored = sorted(scored_sentences, key=lambda s: s[1])[-TOP_SENTENCES:]
    top_n_scored = sorted(top_n_scored, key=lambda s: s[0])

    # Decorate the post object with summaries

    return dict(top_n_summary=[sentences[idx] for (idx, score) in top_n_scored],
                mean_scored_summary=[sentences[idx] for (idx, score) in mean_scored])

blog_data = json.loads(open(BLOG_DATA).read())

for post in blog_data:

    post.update(summarize(post['content']))

    print(post['title'])
    print('=' * len(post['title']))
    print()
```

```
print('Top N Summary')
print('-------------')
print(' '.join(post['top_n_summary']))
print()
print('Mean Scored Summary')
print('-------------------')
print(' '.join(post['mean_scored_summary']))
print()
```

As example input/output, we'll use Tim O'Reilly's Radar post, "The Louvre of the Industrial Age." (*http://oreil.ly/1a1n4SO*) It's around 460 words long and is reprinted here so that you can compare the sample output from the two summarization attempts in the listing:

> This morning I had the chance to get a tour of The Henry Ford Museum in Dearborn, MI, along with Dale Dougherty, creator of Make: and Makerfaire, and Marc Greuther, the chief curator of the museum. I had expected a museum dedicated to the auto industry, but it's so much more than that. As I wrote in my first stunned tweet, "it's the Louvre of the Industrial Age."
>
> When we first entered, Marc took us to what he said may be his favorite artifact in the museum, a block of concrete that contains Luther Burbank's shovel, and Thomas Edison's signature and footprints. Luther Burbank was, of course, the great agricultural inventor who created such treasures as the nectarine and the Santa Rosa plum. Ford was a farm boy who became an industrialist; Thomas Edison was his friend and mentor. The museum, opened in 1929, was Ford's personal homage to the transformation of the world that he was so much a part of. This museum chronicles that transformation.
>
> The machines are astonishing—steam engines and coal-fired electric generators as big as houses, the first lathes capable of making other precision lathes (the makerbot of the 19th century), a ribbon glass machine that is one of five that in the 1970s made virtually all of the incandescent lightbulbs in the world, combine harvesters, railroad locomotives, cars, airplanes, even motels, gas stations, an early McDonalds' restaurant and other epiphenomena of the automobile era.
>
> Under Marc's eye, we also saw the transformation of the machines from purely functional objects to things of beauty. We saw the advances in engineering—the materials, the workmanship, the design, over a hundred years of innovation. Visiting The Henry Ford, as they call it, is a truly humbling experience. I would never in a hundred years have thought of making a visit to Detroit just to visit this museum, but knowing what I know now, I will tell you confidently that it is as worth your while as a visit to Paris just to see the Louvre, to Rome for the Vatican Museum, to Florence for the Uffizi Gallery, to St. Petersburg for the Hermitage, or to Berlin for the Pergamon Museum. This is truly one of the world's great museums, and the world that it chronicles is our own.
>
> I am truly humbled that the Museum has partnered with us to hold Makerfaire Detroit on their grounds. If you are anywhere in reach of Detroit this weekend, I heartily recommend that you plan to spend both days there. You can easily spend a day at Makerfaire, and you could easily spend a day at The Henry Ford. P.S. Here are some of my

photos from my visit. (More to come soon. Can't upload many as I'm currently on a plane.)

Filtering sentences using an average score and standard deviation yields a summary of around 170 words:

> This morning I had the chance to get a tour of The Henry Ford Museum in Dearborn, MI, along with Dale Dougherty, creator of Make: and Makerfaire, and Marc Greuther, the chief curator of the museum. I had expected a museum dedicated to the auto industry, but it's so much more than that. As I wrote in my first stunned tweet, "it's the Louvre of the Industrial Age. This museum chronicles that transformation. The machines are astonishing - steam engines and coal fired electric generators as big as houses, the first lathes capable of making other precision lathes (the makerbot of the 19th century), a ribbon glass machine that is one of five that in the 1970s made virtually all of the incandescent lightbulbs in the world, combine harvesters, railroad locomotives, cars, airplanes, even motels, gas stations, an early McDonalds' restaurant and other epiphenomena of the automobile era. You can easily spend a day at Makerfaire, and you could easily spend a day at The Henry Ford.

An alternative summarization approach, which considers only the top N sentences (where $N = 5$ in this case), produces a slightly more abridged result of around 90 words. It's even more succinct, but arguably still a pretty informative distillation:

> This morning I had the chance to get a tour of The Henry Ford Museum in Dearborn, MI, along with Dale Dougherty, creator of Make: and Makerfaire, and Marc Greuther, the chief curator of the museum. I had expected a museum dedicated to the auto industry, but it's so much more than that. As I wrote in my first stunned tweet, "it's the Louvre of the Industrial Age. This museum chronicles that transformation. You can easily spend a day at Makerfaire, and you could easily spend a day at The Henry Ford.

As in any other situation involving analysis, there's a lot of insight to be gained from visually inspecting the summarizations in relation to the full text.

Outputting a simple markup format that can be opened by virtually any web browser is as simple as adjusting the final portion of the script that performs the output to do some string substitution. Example 6-7 illustrates one possibility for visualizing the output of document summarization by presenting the full text of the article with the sentences that are included as part of the summary in bold so that it's easy to see what was included in the summary and what wasn't. The script saves a collection of HTML files to disk that you can view within your Jupyter Notebook session or open in a browser without the need for a web server.

Example 6-7. Visualizing document summarization results with HTML output

```
import os
from IPython.display import IFrame
from IPython.core.display import display

HTML_TEMPLATE = """<html>
```

```
    <head>
        <title>{0}</title>
        <meta http-equiv="Content-Type" content="text/html; charset=UTF-8"/>
    </head>
    <body>{1}</body>
</html>"""

for post in blog_data:

    # Uses previously defined summarize function
    post.update(summarize(post['content']))

    # You could also store a version of the full post with key sentences marked up
    # for analysis with simple string replacement

    for summary_type in ['top_n_summary', 'mean_scored_summary']:
        post[summary_type + '_marked_up'] = '<p>{0}</p>'.format(post['content'])

        for s in post[summary_type]:
            post[summary_type + '_marked_up'] =
            post[summary_type + '_marked_up'].replace(s,
            '<strong>{0}</strong>'.format(s))

        filename = post['title'].replace("?", "") + '.summary.' + summary_type +
        '.html'

        f = open(os.path.join(filename), 'wb')
        html = HTML_TEMPLATE.format(post['title'] + ' Summary',
        post[summary_type + '_marked_up'])
        f.write(html.encode('utf-8'))
        f.close()

        print("Data written to", f.name)

# Display any of these files with an inline frame. This displays the
# last file processed by using the last value of f.name
print()
print("Displaying {0}:".format(f.name))
display(IFrame('files/{0}'.format(f.name), '100%', '600px'))
```

The resulting output is the full text of the document with sentences composing the summary highlighted in bold, as displayed in Figure 6-4. As you explore alternative techniques for summarization, a quick glance between browser tabs can give you an intuitive feel for the similarity between the summarization techniques. The primary difference illustrated here is a fairly long (and descriptive) sentence near the middle of the document, beginning with the words "The machines are astonishing."

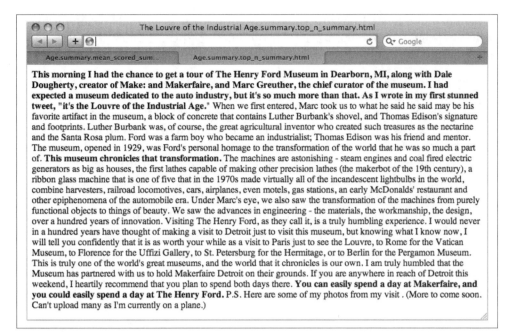

Figure 6-4. A visualization of the text from an O'Reilly Radar blog post with the most important sentences as determined by a summarization algorithm conveyed in bold

The next section presents a brief discussion of Luhn's document summarization approach.

Analysis of Luhn's summarization algorithm

This section provides an analysis of Luhn's summarization algorithm. It aims to broaden your understanding of techniques in processing human language data but is certainly not a requirement for mining the social web. If you find yourself getting lost in the details, feel free to skip this section and return to it at a later time.

The basic premise behind Luhn's algorithm is that the important sentences in a document will be the ones that contain frequently occurring words. However, there are a few details worth pointing out. First, not all frequently occurring words are important; generally speaking, stopwords are filler and are hardly ever of interest for analysis. Keep in mind that although we do filter out common stopwords in the sample implementation, it may be possible to create a custom list of stopwords for any given blog or domain with additional a priori knowledge, which might further bolster the strength of this algorithm or any other algorithm that assumes stopwords have been filtered. For example, a blog written exclusively about baseball might so commonly use the word *baseball* that you should consider adding it to a stopword list, even though it's not a general-purpose stopword. (As a side note, it would be interesting to incorporate TF-IDF into the scoring function for a particular data source as a means of accounting for common words in the parlance of the domain.)

Assuming that a reasonable attempt to eliminate stopwords has been made, the next step in the algorithm is to choose a reasonable value for N and choose the top N words as the basis of analysis. The latent assumption behind this algorithm is that these top N words are sufficiently descriptive to characterize the nature of the document, and that for any two sentences in the document, the sentence that contains more of these words will be considered more descriptive. All that's left after determining the "important words" in the document is to apply a heuristic to each sentence and filter out some subset of sentences to use as a summarization or abstract of the document. Scoring each sentence takes place in the function score_sentences. This is where most of the action happens in the listing.

In order to score each sentence, the algorithm in score_sentences applies a simple distance threshold to cluster tokens and scores each cluster according to the following formula:

$$\frac{(significant\ words\ in\ cluster)^2}{total\ words\ in\ cluster}$$

The final score for each sentence is equal to the highest score for any cluster appearing in the sentence. Let's consider the high-level steps involved in score_sentences for an example sentence to see how this approach works in practice:

Input: Sample sentence
```
['Mr.', 'Green', 'killed', 'Colonel', 'Mustard', 'in', 'the',
'study', 'with', 'the', 'candlestick', '.']
```

Input: List of important words
```
['Mr.', 'Green', 'Colonel', 'Mustard', 'candlestick']
```

Input/assumption: Cluster threshold (distance)
```
3
```

Intermediate computation: Clusters detected
```
[ ['Mr.', 'Green', 'killed', 'Colonel', 'Mustard'], ['candle
stick'] ]
```

Intermediate computation: Cluster scores
```
[ 3.2, 1 ] # Computation: [ (4*4)/5, (1*1)/1]
```

Output: Sentence score
```
3.2 # max([3.2, 1])
```

The actual work done in `score_sentences` is just bookkeeping to detect the clusters in the sentence. A *cluster* is defined as a sequence of words containing two or more important words, where each important word is within a distance threshold of its nearest neighbor. While Luhn's paper suggests a value of 4 or 5 for the distance threshold, we used a value of 3 for simplicity in this example; thus, the distance between `'Green'` and `'Colonel'` was sufficiently bridged, and the first cluster detected consisted of the first five words in the sentence. Had the word *study* also appeared in the list of important words, the entire sentence (except the final punctuation) would have emerged as a cluster.

Once each sentence has been scored, all that's left is to determine which sentences to return as a summary. The sample implementation provides two approaches. The first approach uses a statistical threshold to filter out sentences by computing the mean and standard deviation for the scores obtained, while the latter simply returns the top *N* sentences. Depending on the nature of the data, your mileage will vary, but you should be able to tune the parameters to achieve reasonable results with either. One nice thing about using the top *N* sentences is that you have a pretty good idea about the maximum length of the summary. Using the mean and standard deviation could potentially return more sentences than you'd prefer, if a lot of sentences contain scores that are relatively close to one another.

Luhn's algorithm is simple to implement and plays to the usual strength of frequently appearing words being descriptive of the overall document. However, keep in mind that like many of the approaches based on the classic information retrieval concepts we explored in the previous chapter, Luhn's algorithm itself makes no attempt to understand the data at a deeper semantic level—although it does depend on more than just a "bag of words." It directly computes summarizations as a function of frequently occurring words, and it isn't terribly sophisticated in how it scores sentences, but (as was the case with TF-IDF) this just makes it all the more amazing that it can perform as well as it seems to perform on randomly selected blog data.

When you're weighing the pros and cons of implementing a much more complicated approach, it's worth reflecting on the effort that would be required to improve upon a reasonable summarization such as that produced by Luhn's algorithm. Sometimes, a crude heuristic is all you really need to accomplish your goal. At other times, however, you may need something more cutting-edge. The tricky part is computing the cost-benefit analysis of migrating from the crude heuristic to the state-of-the-art solution. Many of us tend to be overly optimistic about the relative effort involved.

6.4 Entity-Centric Analysis: A Paradigm Shift

Throughout this chapter, it's been implied that analytic approaches that exhibit a deeper understanding of the data can be dramatically more powerful than approaches that simply treat each token as an opaque symbol. But what does a "deeper understanding" of the data really mean?

One interpretation is being able to detect the entities in documents and using those entities as the basis of analysis, as opposed to doing document-centric analysis involving keyword searches or interpreting a search input as a particular type of entity and customizing the results accordingly. Although you may not have thought about it in those terms, this is precisely what emerging technologies such as Wolfram|Alpha (*http://bit.ly/2xtPzM7*) do at the presentation layer. For example, a search for "tim o'reilly" in Wolfram|Alpha returns results that imply an understanding that the entity being searched for is a person; you don't just get back a list of documents containing the keywords (see Figure 6-5). Regardless of the internal technique that's used to accomplish this end, the resulting user experience is dramatically more powerful because the results conform to a format that more closely satisfies the user's expectations.

Although we can't ponder all of the various possibilities of entity-centric analysis in the current discussion, it's well within our reach and quite appropriate to present a means of extracting the entities from a document, which can then be used for various analytic purposes. Assuming the sample flow of an NLP pipeline as presented earlier in this chapter, you could simply extract all the nouns and noun phrases from the document and index them as entities appearing in the documents—the important underlying assumption being that nouns and noun phrases (or some carefully constructed subset thereof) qualify as entities of interest. This is actually a fair assumption to make and a good starting point for entity-centric analysis, as the following sample listing demonstrates. Note that for results annotated according to Penn Treebank conventions, any tag beginning with 'NN' is some form of a noun or noun phrase. A full listing of the Penn Treebank tags (*http://bit.ly/2obCDGA*) is available online.

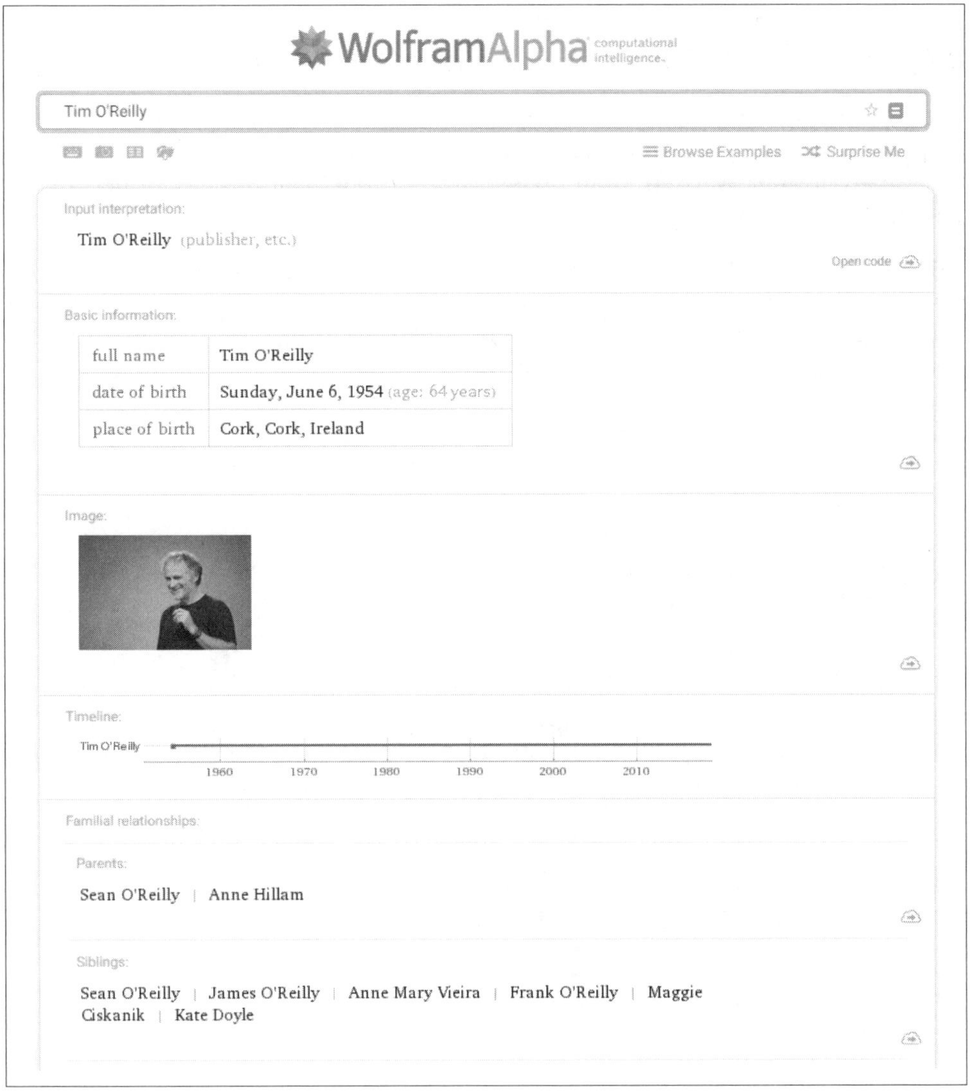

Figure 6-5. Sample results for a "tim o'reilly" query with Wolfram|Alpha

Example 6-8 analyzes the part-of-speech tags that are applied to tokens, and identifies nouns and noun phrases as entities. In data mining parlance, finding the entities in a text is called *entity extraction* or *named entity recognition*, depending on the nuances of exactly what you are trying to accomplish.

Example 6-8. Extracting entities from a text with NLTK

```python
import nltk
import json

BLOG_DATA = "resources/ch06-webpages/feed.json"

blog_data = json.loads(open(BLOG_DATA).read())

for post in blog_data:

    sentences = nltk.tokenize.sent_tokenize(post['content'])
    tokens = [nltk.tokenize.word_tokenize(s) for s in sentences]
    pos_tagged_tokens = [nltk.pos_tag(t) for t in tokens]

    # Flatten the list since we're not using sentence structure
    # and sentences are guaranteed to be separated by a special
    # POS tuple such as ('.', '.')

    pos_tagged_tokens = [token for sent in pos_tagged_tokens for token in sent]

    all_entity_chunks = []
    previous_pos = None
    current_entity_chunk = []
    for (token, pos) in pos_tagged_tokens:

        if pos == previous_pos and pos.startswith('NN'):
            current_entity_chunk.append(token)
        elif pos.startswith('NN'):

            if current_entity_chunk != []:

                # Note that current_entity_chunk could be a duplicate when appended,
                # so frequency analysis again becomes a consideration

                all_entity_chunks.append((' '.join(current_entity_chunk), pos))
            current_entity_chunk = [token]

        previous_pos = pos

    # Store the chunks as an index for the document
    # and account for frequency while we're at it...

    post['entities'] = {}
    for c in all_entity_chunks:
        post['entities'][c] = post['entities'].get(c, 0) + 1

    # For example, we could display just the title-cased entities

    print(post['title'])
    print('-' * len(post['title']))
    proper_nouns = []
```

```
for (entity, pos) in post['entities']:
    if entity.istitle():
        print('\t{0} ({1})'.format(entity, post['entities'][(entity, pos)]))
print()
```

 You may recall from the description of "extraction" in "Natural Language Processing Illustrated Step-by-Step" on page 212 that NLTK provides an nltk.batch_ne_chunk function that attempts to extract named entities from POS-tagged tokens. You're welcome to use this capability directly, but you may find that your mileage varies with the out-of-the-box models provided with the NLTK implementation.

Sample output for the listing is presented next and conveys results that are quite meaningful and could be used in a variety of ways. For example, they would make great suggestions for tagging posts by an intelligent blogging platform like a WordPress plug-in:

```
The Louvre of the Industrial Age
--------------------------------
        Paris (1)
        Henry Ford Museum (1)
        Vatican Museum (1)
        Museum (1)
        Thomas Edison (2)
        Hermitage (1)
        Uffizi Gallery (1)
        Ford (2)
        Santa Rosa (1)
        Dearborn (1)
        Makerfaire (1)
        Berlin (1)
        Marc (2)
        Makerfaire (1)
        Rome (1)
        Henry Ford (1)
        Ca (1)
        Louvre (1)
        Detroit (2)
        St. Petersburg (1)
        Florence (1)
        Marc Greuther (1)
        Makerfaire Detroit (1)
        Luther Burbank (2)
        Make (1)
        Dale Dougherty (1)
        Louvre (1)
```

Statistical artifacts often have different purposes and consumers. A text summary is meant to be read, whereas a list of extracted entities like the preceding one lends itself to being scanned quickly for patterns. For a larger corpus than we're working with in this example, a tag cloud (*http://bit.ly/1a1n5pO*) could be an obvious candidate for visualizing the data.

 Try reproducing these results by scraping the text from the web page *http://oreil.ly/1a1n4SO*.

Could we have discovered the same list of terms by more blindly analyzing the lexical characteristics (such as use of capitalization) of the sentence? Perhaps, but keep in mind that this technique can also capture nouns and noun phrases that are not indicated by title case. Case is indeed an important feature of the text that can generally be exploited to great benefit, but there are other intriguing entities in the sample text that are all lowercase (for example, "chief curator," "locomotives," and "lightbulbs").

Although the list of entities certainly doesn't convey the overall meaning of the text as effectively as the summary we computed earlier, identifying these entities can be extremely valuable for analysis since *they have meaning at a semantic level and are not just frequently occurring words*. In fact, the frequencies of most of the terms displayed in the sample output are quite low. Nevertheless, they're important because they have a grounded meaning in the text—namely, they're people, places, things, or ideas, which are generally the substantive information in the data.

6.4.1 Gisting Human Language Data

It's not much of a leap at this point to think that it would be another major step forward to take into account the verbs and compute triples of the form *(subject, predicate, object)* so that you know which entities are interacting with which other entities, and the nature of those interactions. Such triples would lend themselves to visualizing object graphs of documents, which we could potentially skim much faster than we could read the documents themselves. Better yet, imagine taking multiple object graphs derived from a set of documents and merging them to get the gist of the larger corpus. This exact technique is an area of active research and has tremendous applicability for virtually any situation suffering from the information-overload problem. But as will be illustrated, it's an excruciating problem for the general case and not for the faint of heart.

Assuming a part-of-speech tagger has identified the parts of speech from a sentence and emitted output such as [('Mr.', 'NNP'), ('Green', 'NNP'), ('killed', 'VBD'), ('Colonel', 'NNP'), ('Mustard', 'NNP'), …], an index storing *(subject, predicate, object)* tuples of the form ('Mr. Green', 'killed', 'Colonel Mustard') would be easy to compute. However, the reality of the situation is that you're unlikely to run across actual POS-tagged data with that level of simplicity—unless you're planning to mine children's books (not actually a bad starting point for testing toy ideas). For example, consider the tagging emitted from NLTK for the first sentence from the blog post printed earlier in this chapter as an arbitrary and realistic piece of data you might like to translate into an object graph:

> This morning I had the chance to get a tour of The Henry Ford Museum in Dearborn, MI, along with Dale Dougherty, creator of Make: and Makerfaire, and Marc Greuther, the chief curator of the museum.

The simplest possible triple that you might expect to distill from that sentence is ('I', 'get', 'tour'), but even if you got that back, it wouldn't convey that Dale Dougherty also got the tour, or that Marc Greuther was involved. The POS-tagged data should make it pretty clear that it's not quite so straightforward to arrive at any of those interpretations, either, because the sentence has a very rich structure:

```
[(u'This', 'DT'), (u'morning', 'NN'), (u'I', 'PRP'), (u'had', 'VBD'),
(u'the', 'DT'), (u'chance', 'NN'), (u'to', 'TO'), (u'get', 'VB'),
(u'a', 'DT'), (u'tour', 'NN'), (u'of', 'IN'), (u'The', 'DT'),
(u'Henry', 'NNP'), (u'Ford', 'NNP'), (u'Museum', 'NNP'), (u'in', 'IN'),
(u'Dearborn', 'NNP'), (u',', ','), (u'MI', 'NNP'), (u',', ','),
(u'along', 'IN'), (u'with', 'IN'), (u'Dale', 'NNP'), (u'Dougherty', 'NNP'),
(u',', ','), (u'creator', 'NN'), (u'of', 'IN'), (u'Make', 'NNP'), (u':', ':'),
(u'and', 'CC'), (u'Makerfaire', 'NNP'), (u',', ','), (u'and', 'CC'),
(u'Marc', 'NNP'), (u'Greuther', 'NNP'), (u',', ','), (u'the', 'DT'),
(u'chief', 'NN'), (u'curator', 'NN'), (u'of', 'IN'), (u'the', 'DT'),
(u'museum', 'NN'), (u'.', '.')]
```

It's doubtful that a high-quality open source NLP toolkit would be capable of emitting meaningful triples in this case, given the complex nature of the predicate "had a chance to get a tour" and that the other actors involved in the tour are listed in a phrase appended to the end of the sentence.

If you'd like to pursue strategies for constructing these triples, you should be able to use reasonably accurate POS tagging information to take a good initial stab at it. Advanced tasks in manipulating human language data can be a lot of work, but the results are satisfying and have the potential to be quite disruptive (in a good way).

The good news is that you can actually do a lot of fun things by distilling just the entities from text and using them as the basis of analysis, as demonstrated earlier. You can easily produce triples from text on a per-sentence basis, where the "predicate" of each triple is a notion of a generic relationship signifying that the subject and object "interacted" with each other. Example 6-9 is a refactoring of Example 6-8 that collects entities on a per-sentence basis, which could be quite useful for computing the interactions between entities using a sentence as a context window.

Example 6-9. Discovering interactions between entities

```python
import nltk
import json

BLOG_DATA = "resources/ch06-webpages/feed.json"

def extract_interactions(txt):
    sentences = nltk.tokenize.sent_tokenize(txt)
    tokens = [nltk.tokenize.word_tokenize(s) for s in sentences]
    pos_tagged_tokens = [nltk.pos_tag(t) for t in tokens]

    entity_interactions = []
    for sentence in pos_tagged_tokens:

        all_entity_chunks = []
        previous_pos = None
        current_entity_chunk = []

        for (token, pos) in sentence:

            if pos == previous_pos and pos.startswith('NN'):
                current_entity_chunk.append(token)
            elif pos.startswith('NN'):
                if current_entity_chunk != []:
                    all_entity_chunks.append((' '.join(current_entity_chunk),
                                pos))
                current_entity_chunk = [token]

            previous_pos = pos

        if len(all_entity_chunks) > 1:
            entity_interactions.append(all_entity_chunks)
        else:
            entity_interactions.append([])

    assert len(entity_interactions) == len(sentences)

    return dict(entity_interactions=entity_interactions,
                sentences=sentences)

blog_data = json.loads(open(BLOG_DATA).read())

# Display selected interactions on a per-sentence basis

for post in blog_data:

    post.update(extract_interactions(post['content']))

    print(post['title'])
    print('-' * len(post['title']))
    for interactions in post['entity_interactions']:
```

```
    print('; '.join([i[0] for i in interactions]))
  print()
```

The following results from this listing highlight something important about the nature of unstructured data analysis: it's messy!

```
The Louvre of the Industrial Age
--------------------------------
morning; chance; tour; Henry Ford Museum; Dearborn; MI; Dale Dougherty; creator;
Make; Makerfaire; Marc Greuther; chief curator

tweet; Louvre

"; Marc; artifact; museum; block; contains; Luther Burbank; shovel; Thomas Edison

Luther Burbank; course; inventor; treasures; nectarine; Santa Rosa

Ford; farm boy; industrialist; Thomas Edison; friend

museum; Ford; homage; transformation; world

machines; steam; engines; coal; generators; houses; lathes; precision; lathes;
makerbot; century; ribbon glass machine; incandescent; lightbulbs; world;
combine; harvesters; railroad; locomotives; cars; airplanes; gas; stations;
McDonalds; restaurant; epiphenomena

Marc; eye; transformation; machines; objects; things

advances; engineering; materials; workmanship; design; years

years; visit; Detroit; museum; visit; Paris; Louvre; Rome; Vatican Museum;
Florence; Uffizi Gallery; St. Petersburg; Hermitage; Berlin

world; museums

Museum; Makerfaire Detroit

reach; Detroit; weekend

day; Makerfaire; day
```

A certain amount of noise in the results is almost inevitable, but realizing results that are highly intelligible and useful—even if they do contain a manageable amount of noise—is a worthy aim. The amount of effort required to achieve pristine results that are nearly noise-free can be immense. In fact, in most situations, this is downright impossible because of the inherent complexity involved in natural language and the limitations of most currently available toolkits, including NLTK. If you are able to make certain assumptions about the domain of the data or have expert knowledge of the nature of the noise, you may be able to devise heuristics that are effective without risking an unacceptable amount of information loss—but it's a fairly difficult proposition.

Still, the interactions do provide a certain amount of "gist" that's valuable. For example, how closely would your interpretation of "morning; chance; tour; Henry Ford Museum; Dearborn; MI; Dale Dougherty; creator; Make; Makerfaire; Marc Greuther; chief curator" align with the meaning in the original sentence?

As was the case with our previous adventure in summarization, displaying markup that can be visually skimmed for inspection is also quite handy. A simple modification to Example 6-9's output, as shown in Example 6-10, is all that's necessary to produce the results shown in Figure 6-6.

Example 6-10. Visualizing interactions between entities with HTML output

```python
import os
import json
import nltk
from IPython.display import IFrame
from IPython.core.display import display

BLOG_DATA = "resources/ch06-webpages/feed.json"

HTML_TEMPLATE = """<html>
    <head>
        <title>{0}</title>
        <meta http-equiv="Content-Type" content="text/html; charset=UTF-8"/>
    </head>
    <body>{1}</body>
</html>"""

blog_data = json.loads(open(BLOG_DATA).read())

for post in blog_data:

    post.update(extract_interactions(post['content']))

    # Display output as markup with entities presented in bold text

    post['markup'] = []

    for sentence_idx in range(len(post['sentences'])):

        s = post['sentences'][sentence_idx]
        for (term, _) in post['entity_interactions'][sentence_idx]:
            s = s.replace(term, '<strong>{0}</strong>'.format(term))

        post['markup'] += [s]

    filename = post['title'].replace("?", "") + '.entity_interactions.html'
```

```
f = open(os.path.join(filename), 'wb')
html = HTML_TEMPLATE.format(post['title'] + ' Interactions',
    ' '.join(post['markup']))
f.write(html.encode('utf-8'))
f.close()

print('Data written to', f.name)

# Display any of these files with an inline frame. This displays the
# last file processed by using the last value of f.name

print('Displaying {0}:'.format(f.name))
display(IFrame('files/{0}'.format(f.name), '100%', '600px'))
```

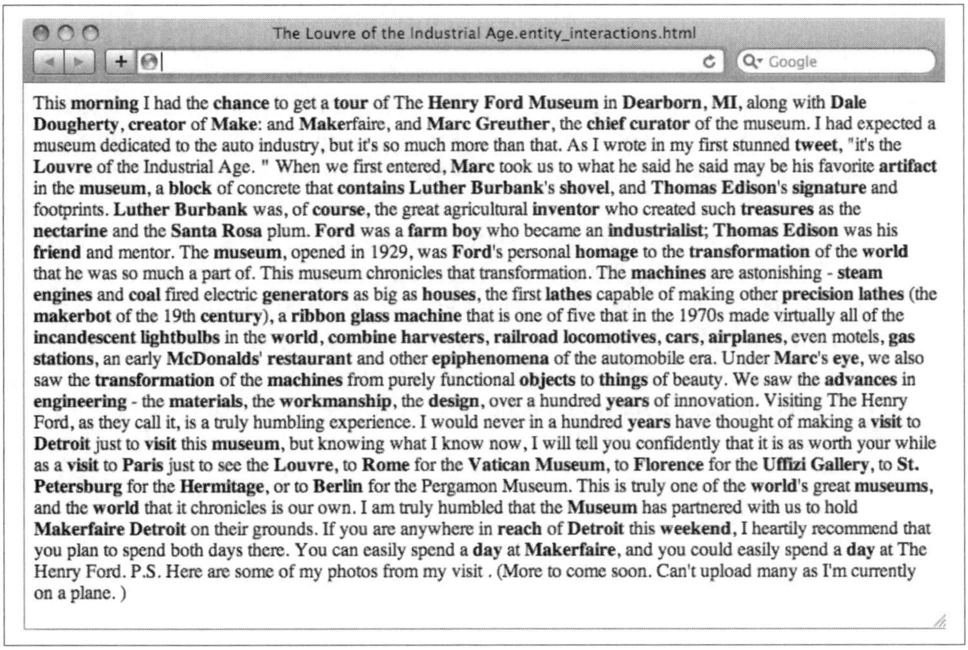

Figure 6-6. Sample HTML output that displays entities identified in the text in bold so that it's easy to visually skim the content for its key concepts

It could also be fruitful to perform additional analyses to identify the sets of interactions for a larger body of text and to find and visualize co-occurrences in the interactions. The code involving force-directed graphs illustrated in Example 8-16 would make a good starting template for visualization, but even without knowing the specific nature of the interaction, there's still a lot of value in just knowing the subject and the object. If you're feeling ambitious, you should attempt to complete the tuples with the missing verbs.

6.5 Quality of Analytics for Processing Human Language Data

When you've done even a modest amount of text mining, you'll eventually want to start quantifying the quality of your analytics. How accurate is your end-of-sentence detector? How accurate is your part-of-speech tagger? For example, if you began customizing the basic algorithm for extracting the entities from unstructured text, how would you know whether your algorithm was getting more or less performant with respect to the quality of the results? While you could manually inspect the results for a small corpus and tune the algorithm until you were satisfied with them, you'd still have a devil of a time determining whether your analytics would perform well on a much larger corpus or a different class of document altogether—hence, the need for a more automated process.

An obvious starting point is to randomly sample some documents and create a "golden set" of entities that you believe are absolutely crucial for a good algorithm to extract from them, and then use this list as the basis of evaluation. (((("confidence intervals")))Depending on how rigorous you'd like to be, you might even be able to compute the sample error and use a statistical device called a *confidence interval* (*http://bit.ly/1a1n8BW*) to ((("true error")))predict the true error with a sufficient degree of confidence for your needs. However, what exactly is the calculation you should be performing based on the results of your extractor and golden set in order to compute accuracy? ((("F1 score")))A very common calculation for measuring accuracy is called the *F1 score*, which is defined in terms of two concepts called *precision* and *recall*[4] as:

$$F = 2 * \frac{precision * recall}{precision + recall}$$

where:

$$precision = \frac{TP}{TP + FP}$$

and:

---

4 More precisely, F1 is said to be the *harmonic mean* of precision and recall, where the harmonic mean of any two numbers x and y is defined as:

$$H = 2 * \frac{x * y}{x + y}$$

You can read more about why it's the "harmonic" mean by reviewing the definition of a *harmonic number* (*http://bit.ly/1a1n6tJ*).

$$recall = \frac{TP}{TP + FN}$$

In the current context, precision is a measure of exactness that reflects false positives, and recall is a measure of completeness that reflects true positives. The following list clarifies the meaning of these terms in relation to the current discussion in case they're unfamiliar or confusing:

True positives (TP)
Terms that were correctly identified as entities

False positives (FP)
Terms that were identified as entities but should not have been

True negatives (TN)
Terms that were not identified as entities and should not have been

False negatives (FN)
Terms that were not identified as entities but should have been

Given that precision is a measure of exactness that quantifies false positives, it is defined as *TP / (TP + FP)*. Intuitively, if the number of false positives is zero, the exactness of the algorithm is perfect and the precision yields a value of 1.0. Conversely, if the number of false positives is high and begins to approach or surpass the number of true positives, precision is poor and the ratio approaches zero. As a measure of completeness, recall is defined as *TP / (TP + FN)* and yields a value of 1.0, indicating perfect recall, if the number of false negatives is zero. As the number of false negatives increases, recall approaches zero. By definition, F1 yields a value of 1.0 when precision and recall are both perfect, and approaches zero when both precision and recall are poor.

Of course, what you'll find out in the wild is that it's a trade-off as to whether you want to boost precision or recall, because it's difficult to have both. If you think about it, this makes sense because of the trade-offs involved with false positives and false negatives (see Figure 6-7).

To put all of this into perspective, let's consider the sentence "Mr. Green killed Colonel Mustard in the study with the candlestick" one last time and assume that an expert has determined that the key entities in the sentence are "Mr. Green," "Colonel Mustard," "study," and "candlestick." Assuming your algorithm identified these four terms and only these four terms, you'd have four true positives, zero false positives, five true negatives ("killed," "with," "the," "in," "the"), and zero false negatives. That's perfect precision and perfect recall, which yields an F1 score of 1.0. Substituting various values into the precision and recall formulas is straightforward and a worthwhile exercise if this is your first time encountering these terms.

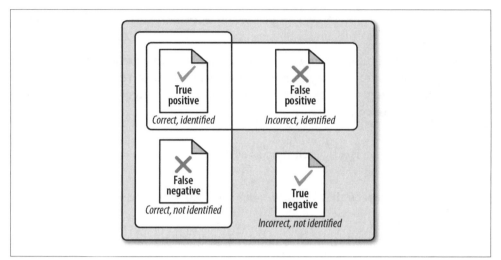

Figure 6-7. The intuition behind true positives, false positives, true negatives, and false negatives from the standpoint of predictive analytics

 What would the precision, recall, and F1 score have been if your algorithm had identified "Mr. Green," "Colonel," "Mustard," and "candlestick"?

Many of the most compelling technology stacks used by commercial businesses in the NLP space use advanced statistical models to process natural language according to supervised learning algorithms. Given our discussion earlier in this chapter, you know that a supervised learning algorithm is essentially an approach in which you provide training samples that comprise inputs and expected outputs such that the model is able to predict the tuples with reasonable accuracy. The tricky part is ensuring that the trained model generalizes well to inputs that have not yet been encountered. If the model performs well for training data but poorly on unseen samples, it's usually said to suffer from the problem of *overfitting* the training data. A common approach for measuring the efficacy of a model is called *cross-validation*. With this approach, a portion of the training data (say, one-third) is reserved exclusively for the purpose of testing the model, and only the remainder is used for training the model.

6.6 Closing Remarks

This chapter introduced the fundamentals of unstructured data analytics, and demonstrated how to use NLTK and put together the rest of an NLP pipeline to extract entities from text. The emerging field of understanding human language data is incredibly interdisciplinary and still quite nascent despite our collective attempts, and nailing the problem of NLP for most of the world's most commonly spoken languages is arguably the problem of this century (or at least the first half of it).

Push NLTK to its limits, and when you need more performance or quality, consider rolling up your sleeves and digging into some of the academic literature. It's admittedly a daunting task at first, but a truly worthy problem if you are interested in tackling it. There's only so much that one chapter out of any book can teach you, but the possibilities are vast, open source toolkits are a good starting point, and there's a bright future ahead for those who can master the science and art of processing human language data.

 The source code outlined for this chapter and all other chapters is available on GitHub (*http://bit.ly/Mining-the-Social-Web-3E*) in a convenient Jupyter Notebook format that you're highly encouraged to try out from the comfort of your own web browser.

6.7 Recommended Exercises

- Adapt the code from this chapter to collect a few hundred high-quality articles or blog posts from the web and summarize the content.

- Build a hosted web app with a toolkit such as Google App Engine to build an online summarization tool. (Given that Yahoo! once acquired a company called Summly (*http://tcrn.ch/1a1n70L*) that summarizes news for readers, you may find this exercise particularly inspiring. The acquisition was reportedly worth something close to $30 million.)

- Consider using NLTK's word-stemming tools to try to compute *(entity, stemmed predicate, entity)* tuples, building upon the code in Example 6-9.

- Look into WordNet (*http://bit.ly/1a1n7hj*), a tool that you'll undoubtedly run into sooner rather than later, to discover additional meaning about predicate phrases you will encounter during NLP.

- Visualize entities extracted from text with a tag cloud (*http://bit.ly/1a1n5pO*).

- Try writing your own end-of-sentence detector as a deterministic parser based upon logic you can encode as rules in `if-then` statements and compare it to the facilities in NLTK. Is it appropriate to try to model language with deterministic rules?

- Use Scrapy to crawl a small sample of news articles or blog posts and extract the text for processing.

- Explore NLTK's Bayesian classifier (*http://bit.ly/1a1n9Wt*), a supervised learning technique that can be used to label training samples such as documents. Can you train a classifier to label documents as "sports," "editorial," and "other" from a small crawl with Scrapy? Measure your accuracy as an F1 score.

- Are there situations in which a harmonic mean between precision and recall is not desirable? When might you want higher precision at the cost of recall? When might you want higher recall at the cost of precision?

- Can you apply the techniques from this chapter to Twitter data? The GATE Twitter part-of-speech tagger (*http://bit.ly/1a1nad2*) and Carnegie Mellon's Twitter NLP and part-of-speech tagging (*http://bit.ly/1a1n84Y*) libraries make a great starting point.

6.8 Online Resources

The following list of links from this chapter may be useful for review:

- "The Automatic Creation of Literature Abstracts" (*http://bit.ly/1a1n4Cj*)
- Bag-of-words model (*http://bit.ly/1a1lHDF*)
- Bayesian classifier (*http://bit.ly/1a1n9Wt*)
- BeautifulSoup (*http://bit.ly/1a1mRit*)
- boilerpipe3 (*http://bit.ly/2sCIFET*)
- "Boilerplate Detection Using Shallow Text Features" (*http://bit.ly/1a1mN21*)
- Breadth-first search (*http://bit.ly/1a1mYdG*)
- Depth-first search (*http://bit.ly/1a1mVPd*)
- Carnegie Mellon's Twitter NLP and part-of-speech tagger (*http://bit.ly/1a1n84Y*)
- Common Crawl corpus (*http://amzn.to/1a1mXXb*)
- Confidence interval (*http://bit.ly/1a1n8BW*)
- d3-cloud GitHub repository (*http://bit.ly/1a1n5pO*)
- GATE Twitter part-of-speech tagger (*http://bit.ly/1a1nad2*)
- Hosted version of boilerpipe (*http://bit.ly/1a1mSTF*)
- HTML5 (*http://bit.ly/1a1mRz5*)
- Microdata (*http://bit.ly/1a1mRPA*)
- NLTK book (*http://bit.ly/1a1mtAk*)
- Penn Treebank Project (*http://bit.ly/2C5ecDq*)
- Scrapy (*http://bit.ly/1a1mG6P*)
- Supervised learning (*http://bit.ly/1a1mPHr*)
- Thread pool (*http://bit.ly/1a1mW5M*)

- Turing test (*http://bit.ly/1a1mZON*)
- "Unsupervised Multilingual Sentence Boundary Detection" (*http://bit.ly/2EzWCEZ*)
- WordNet (*http://bit.ly/1a1n7hj*)

## CHAPTER 7

Mining Mailboxes: Analyzing Who's Talking to Whom About What, How Often, and More

Mail archives are arguably the ultimate kind of social web data and the basis of the earliest online social networks. Mail data is ubiquitous, and each message is inherently social, involving conversations and interactions among two or more people. Furthermore, each message consists of human language data that's inherently expressive, and is laced with structured metadata fields that anchor the human language data in particular timespans and unambiguous identities. Mining mailboxes certainly provides an opportunity to synthesize all of the concepts you've learned in previous chapters and opens up incredible opportunities for discovering valuable insights.

Whether you are the CIO of a corporation and want to analyze corporate communications for trends and patterns, you have a keen interest in mining online mailing lists for insights, or you'd simply like to explore your own mailbox for patterns as part of quantifying yourself (*http://bit.ly/1a1niJw*), the following discussion provides a primer to help you get started. This chapter introduces some fundamental tools and techniques for exploring mailboxes to answer questions such as:

- Who sends mail to whom (and how much/often)?

- Is there a particular time of the day (or day of the week) when the most mail chatter happens?

- Which people send the most messages to one another?

- What are the subjects of the liveliest discussion threads?

Although social media sites are racking up petabytes of near-real-time social data, there is still the significant drawback that social networking data is centrally managed by a service provider that gets to create the rules about exactly how you can access it and what you can and can't do with it. Mail archives, on the other hand, are decentralized and scattered across the web in the form of rich mailing list discussions about a litany of topics, as well as the many thousands of messages that people have tucked away in their own accounts. When you take a moment to think about it, it seems as though being able to effectively mine mail archives could be one of the most essential capabilities in your data mining toolbox.

Although it's not always easy to find realistic social data sets for purposes of illustration, this chapter showcases the fairly well-studied Enron corpus (*http://bit.ly/ 1a1nj01*) as its basis in order to maximize the opportunity for analysis without introducing any legal[1] or privacy concerns. We'll standardize the data set into the well-known Unix mailbox (mbox) format so that we can employ a common set of tools to process it. Finally, although we could just opt to process the data in a JSON format that we store in a flat file, we'll take advantage of the powerful `pandas` (*http://bit.ly/ 2Fjxgwq*) data analysis library that we introduced in Chapter 2, which allows us to form powerful indexing and query operations against our data.

 Always get the latest bug-fixed source code for this chapter (and every other chapter) on GitHub (*http://bit.ly/Mining-the-Social-Web-3E*). Be sure to also take advantage of this book's virtual machine experience, as described in Appendix A, to maximize your enjoyment of the sample code.

7.1 Overview

Mail data is incredibly rich and presents opportunities for analysis involving everything you've learned about so far in this book. In this chapter you'll learn about:

- The process of standardizing mail data to a convenient and portable format
- `pandas`, a powerful data analysis library for Python for performing operations on tabular data
- The Enron corpus, a public data set consisting of the contents of employee mailboxes from around the time of the Enron scandal

---

[1] Should you want to analyze mailing list data, be advised that most service providers (such as Google and Yahoo!) restrict your use of this data if you retrieve it using their APIs, but you can easily enough collect and archive mailing list data yourself by subscribing to a list and waiting for your mailbox to start filling up. You might also be able to ask the list owner or members of the list to provide you with an archive as another option.

- Using pandas to query the Enron corpus in arbitrary ways
- Tools for accessing and exporting your own mailbox data for analysis

7.2 Obtaining and Processing a Mail Corpus

This section illustrates how to obtain a mail corpus, convert it into the standardized Unix mbox format, and then import the mbox into a pandas DataFrame, which will serve as a general-purpose object for storing and querying the data. We'll start out by analyzing a small fictitious mailbox and then proceed to processing the Enron corpus.

7.2.1 A Primer on Unix Mailboxes

An mbox is really just a large text file of concatenated mail messages that are easily accessible by text-based tools. Mail tools and protocols have long since evolved beyond mboxes, but it's usually the case that you can use this format as a lowest common denominator to easily process the data and feel confident that if you share or distribute the data it'll be just as easy for someone else to process it. In fact, most mail clients provide an "export" or "save as" option to export data to this format (even though the verbiage may vary), as illustrated in Figure 7-5 in the section "Analyzing Your Own Mail Data".

In terms of specification, the beginning of each message in an mbox is signaled by a special *From_* line formatted to the pattern From *user@example.com asctime*, where *asctime* (*http://bit.ly/1a1nmcl*) is a standardized fixed-width representation of a time-stamp in the form Fri Dec 25 00:06:42 2009. The boundary between messages is determined by a *From_* line preceded (except for the first occurrence) by exactly two newline characters. (Visually, as shown in the following example, this appears as though there is a single blank line that precedes the *From_* line.) A small slice from a fictitious mbox containing two messages follows:

```
From santa@northpole.example.org Fri Dec 25 00:06:42 2009
Message-ID: <16159836.1075855377439@mail.northpole.example.org>
References: <88364590.8837464573838@mail.northpole.example.org>
In-Reply-To: <194756537.0293874783209@mail.northpole.example.org>
Date: Fri, 25 Dec 2001 00:06:42 -0000 (GMT)
From: St. Nick <santa@northpole.example.org>
To: rudolph@northpole.example.org
Subject: RE: FWD: Tonight
Mime-Version: 1.0
Content-Type: text/plain; charset=us-ascii
Content-Transfer-Encoding: 7bit

Sounds good. See you at the usual location.
```

Thanks,
-S

-----Original Message-----
From: Rudolph
Sent: Friday, December 25, 2009 12:04 AM
To: Claus, Santa
Subject: FWD: Tonight

Santa -

Running a bit late. Will come grab you shortly. Stand by.

Rudy

Begin forwarded message:

> Last batch of toys was just loaded onto sleigh.
>
> Please proceed per the norm.
>
> Regards,
> Buddy
>
> --
> Buddy the Elf
> Chief Elf
> Workshop Operations
> North Pole
> buddy.the.elf@northpole.example.org

From buddy.the.elf@northpole.example.org Fri Dec 25 00:03:34 2009
Message-ID: <88364590.8837464573838@mail.northpole.example.org>
Date: Fri, 25 Dec 2001 00:03:34 -0000 (GMT)
From: Buddy <buddy.the.elf@northpole.example.org>
To: workshop@northpole.example.org
Subject: Tonight
Mime-Version: 1.0
Content-Type: text/plain; charset=us-ascii
Content-Transfer-Encoding: 7bit

Last batch of toys was just loaded onto sleigh.

Please proceed per the norm.

Regards,
Buddy

--
Buddy the Elf
Chief Elf
Workshop Operations

```
North Pole
buddy.the.elf@northpole.example.org
```

In the preceding sample we see two messages, although there is evidence of at least one other message that was replied to that might exist elsewhere in the mbox. Chronologically, the first message was authored by a fellow named Buddy and was sent out to *workshop@northpole.example.org* to announce that the toys had just been loaded. The other message in the mbox is a reply from Santa to Rudolph. Not shown in the sample mbox is an intermediate message in which Rudolph forwarded Buddy's message to Santa with a note saying that he was running late. Although we could infer these things by reading the text of the messages themselves as humans with contextualized knowledge, the `Message-ID`, `References`, and `In-Reply-To` headers also provide important clues that can be analyzed.

These headers are pretty intuitive and provide the basis for algorithms that display threaded discussions and things of that nature. We'll look at a well-known algorithm that uses these fields to thread messages a bit later, but the gist is that each message has a unique message ID, contains a reference to the exact message that is being replied to in the case of it being a reply, and can reference multiple other messages in the reply chain that are part of the larger discussion thread at hand.

 Because we'll be employing some Python modules to do much of the tedious work for us, we won't need to digress into discussions concerning the nuances of email messages, such as multipart content, MIME types (*http://bit.ly/1a1nmsJ*), and 7-bit content transfer encoding.

These headers are vitally important. Even with this simple example, you can already see how things can get quite messy when you're parsing the actual body of a message: Rudolph's client quoted forwarded content with > characters, while the mail client Santa used to reply apparently didn't quote anything, but instead included a human-readable message header.

Most mail clients have an option to display extended mail headers beyond the ones you normally see, if you're interested in a technique that's a little more accessible than digging into raw storage when you want to view this kind of information. Figure 7-1 shows sample headers as displayed by Apple Mail.

From:	Matthew Russell
Subject:	**Message to self**
Date:	September 28, 2010 9:31:01 PM CDT
To:	Matthew Russell
Return-Path:	<matthew@zaffra.com>
X-Spam-Checker-Version:	SpamAssassin 3.1.9 (2007-02-13) on mail2.webfaction.com
X-Spam-Level:	
X-Spam-Status:	No, score=-2.6 required=5.0 tests=BAYES_00 autolearn=ham version=3.1.9
Received:	from smtp.webfaction.com (mail6.webfaction.com [74.55.86.74]) by mail2.webfaction.com (8.13.1/8.13.3) with ESMTP id o8T2V254026699 for <matthew@zaffra.com>; Tue, 28 Sep 2010 21:31:02 -0500
Received:	from [192.168.1.67] (99-0-32-163.lightspeed.nsvltn.sbcglobal.net [99.0.32.163]) by smtp.webfaction.com (Postfix) with ESMTP id 9CE61324B7D for <matthew@zaffra.com>; Tue, 28 Sep 2010 21:31:02 -0500 (CDT)
Message-Id:	<D9A2277D-A6A1-4CD2-B891-C0A1E4C6C6CD@zaffra.com>
Content-Type:	text/plain; charset=US-ASCII; format=flowed
Content-Transfer-Encoding:	7bit
Mime-Version:	1.0 (Apple Message framework v936)
X-Mailer:	Apple Mail (2.936)

Hello Matthew!

Regards - Matthew

---
http://www.linkedin.com/in/ptwobrussell

Figure 7-1. Most mail clients allow you to view the extended headers through an options menu

Luckily, there's a lot you can do without having to essentially reimplement a mail client. Besides, if all you wanted to do was browse the mailbox, you'd simply import it into a mail client and browse away, right?

 It's worth taking a moment to explore whether your mail client has an option to import/export data in the mbox format so that you can use the tools in this chapter to manipulate it.

To get the ball rolling on some data processing, Example 7-1 illustrates a routine that makes numerous simplifying assumptions about an mbox to introduce the `mailbox` package that is part of Python's standard library.

Example 7-1. Converting a toy mailbox to JSON

```
import mailbox # pip install mailbox
import json

MBOX = 'resources/ch07-mailboxes/data/northpole.mbox'

# A routine that makes a ton of simplifying assumptions
# about converting an mbox message into a Python object
# given the nature of the northpole.mbox file in order
# to demonstrate the basic parsing of an mbox with mail
```

```
# utilities

def objectify_message(msg):

    # Map in fields from the message
    o_msg = dict([ (k, v) for (k,v) in msg.items() ])

    # Assume one part to the message and get its content
    # and its content type

    part = [p for p in msg.walk()][0]
    o_msg['contentType'] = part.get_content_type()
    o_msg['content'] = part.get_payload()

    return o_msg

# Create an mbox that can be iterated over and transform each of its
# messages to a convenient JSON representation

mbox = mailbox.mbox(MBOX)

messages = []

for msg in mbox:
    messages.append(objectify_message(msg))

print(json.dumps(messages, indent=1))
```

Although this little script for processing an mbox file seems pretty clean and produces reasonable results, trying to parse arbitrary mail data or determine the exact flow of a conversation from mailbox data for the general case can be a tricky enterprise. Many factors contribute to this, such as the ambiguity involved and the variation that can occur in how humans embed replies and comments into reply chains, how different mail clients handle messages and replies, etc.

Table 7-1 illustrates the message flow and explicitly includes the third message that was referenced but not present in *northpole.mbox* to highlight this point. Truncated sample output from the script follows:

```
[
 {
  "From": "St. Nick <santa@northpole.example.org>",
  "Content-Transfer-Encoding": "7bit",
  "content": "Sounds good. See you at the usual location.\n\nThanks,...",
  "To": "rudolph@northpole.example.org",
  "References": "<88364590.8837464573838@mail.northpole.example.org>",
  "Mime-Version": "1.0",
  "In-Reply-To": "<194756537.0293874783209@mail.northpole.example.org>",
  "Date": "Fri, 25 Dec 2001 00:06:42 -0000 (GMT)",
  "contentType": "text/plain",
  "Message-ID": "<16159836.1075855377439@mail.northpole.example.org>",
```

```
    "Content-Type": "text/plain; charset=us-ascii",
    "Subject": "RE: FWD: Tonight"
  },
  {
    "From": "Buddy <buddy.the.elf@northpole.example.org>",
    "Subject": "Tonight",
    "Content-Transfer-Encoding": "7bit",
    "content": "Last batch of toys was just loaded onto sleigh. \n\nPlease...",
    "To": "workshop@northpole.example.org",
    "Date": "Fri, 25 Dec 2001 00:03:34 -0000 (GMT)",
    "contentType": "text/plain",
    "Message-ID": "<88364590.8837464573838@mail.northpole.example.org>",
    "Content-Type": "text/plain; charset=us-ascii",
    "Mime-Version": "1.0"
  }
]
```

Table 7-1. Message flow from northpole.mbox

Date	Message activity
Fri, 25 Dec 2001 00:03:34 -0000 (GMT)	Buddy sends a message to the workshop
Friday, December 25, 2009 12:04 AM	Rudolph forwards Buddy's message to Santa with an additional note
Fri, 25 Dec 2001 00:06:42 -0000 (GMT)	Santa replies to Rudolph

With a basic appreciation for mailboxes in place, let's now shift our attention to converting the Enron corpus to an mbox so that we can leverage Python's standard library as much as possible.

7.2.2 Getting the Enron Data

The full Enron data set (*http://bit.ly/1a1nmsU*) is available in multiple formats requiring various amounts of processing. We'll opt to start with the original raw form of the data set, which is essentially a set of folders that organizes a collection of mailboxes by person and folder. Data standardization and cleansing is a routine problem, and this section should give you some perspective and some appreciation for it.

If you are taking advantage of the virtual machine experience for this book, the Jupyter Notebook for this chapter provides a script that downloads the data to the proper working location for you to seamlessly follow along with these examples. The full Enron corpus is approximately 450 MB in the compressed form in which you would download it to follow along with these exercises.

The initial processing steps can take a while. If time is a significant factor and you can't let this script run at an opportune time, you could opt to skip them; the refined version of the data, as produced from Example 7-2, is checked in with the source code and available at *ipynb3e/resources/ch07-mailboxes/data/enron.mbox*.bz2. See the notes in the Jupyter Notebook for this chapter for more details.

> The download and decompression of the file are relatively fast compared to the time that it takes to synchronize the high number of files that decompress with the host machine, and at the time of this writing, there isn't a known workaround that will speed this up for all platforms.

The annotated output from the following terminal session illustrates the basic structure of the corpus once you've downloaded and unarchived it.

> If you are working on a Windows system or are not comfortable working in a terminal, you can poke around in the *ipynb/resources/ch06-mailboxes/data* folder, which will be synchronized onto your host machine if you are taking advantage of the virtual machine experience for this book.

It's worthwhile to explore the data in a terminal session for a few minutes once you've downloaded it to familiarize yourself with what's there and learn how to navigate through it:

```
$ cd enron_mail_20110402/maildir # Go into the mail directory

maildir $ ls # Show folders/files in the current directory

allen-p         crandell-s      gay-r           horton-s
lokey-t         nemec-g         rogers-b        slinger-r
tycholiz-b      arnold-j        cuilla-m        geaccone-t
hyatt-k         love-p          panus-s         ruscitti-k
smith-m         ward-k          arora-h         dasovich-j
germany-c       hyvl-d          lucci-p         parks-j
sager-e         solberg-g       watson-k        badeer-r
corman-s        gang-l          holst-k         lokay-m

                ...directory listing truncated...

neal-s          rodrique-r      skilling-j      townsend-j

$ cd allen-p/ # Go into the allen-p folder

allen-p $ ls # Show files in the current directory

_sent_mail      contacts        discussion_threads notes_inbox
```

```
    sent_items          all_documents      deleted_items       inbox
    sent                straw

allen-p $ cd inbox/ # Go into the inbox for allen-p

inbox $ ls # Show the files in the inbox for allen-p

1.  11. 13. 15. 17. 19. 20. 22. 24. 26. 28. 3.  31. 33. 35. 37. 39. 40.
42. 44. 5.  62. 64. 66. 68. 7.  71. 73. 75. 79. 83. 85. 87. 10. 12. 14.
16. 18. 2.  21. 23. 25. 27. 29. 30. 32. 34. 36. 38. 4.  41. 43. 45. 6.
63. 65. 67. 69. 70. 72. 74. 78. 8.  84. 86. 9.

inbox $ head -20 1. # Show the first 20 lines of the file named "1."

Message-ID: <16159836.1075855377439.JavaMail.evans@thyme>
Date: Fri, 7 Dec 2001 10:06:42 -0800 (PST)
From: heather.dunton@enron.com
To: k..allen@enron.com
Subject: RE: West Position
Mime-Version: 1.0
Content-Type: text/plain; charset=us-ascii
Content-Transfer-Encoding: 7bit
X-From: Dunton, Heather </O=ENRON/OU=NA/CN=RECIPIENTS/CN=HDUNTON>
X-To: Allen, Phillip K. </O=ENRON/OU=NA/CN=RECIPIENTS/CN=Pallen>
X-cc:
X-bcc:
X-Folder: \Phillip_Allen_Jan2002_1\Allen, Phillip K.\Inbox
X-Origin: Allen-P
X-FileName: pallen (Non-Privileged).pst


Please let me know if you still need Curve Shift.

Thanks,
```

The final command in the terminal session shows that mail messages are organized into files and contain metadata in the form of headers that can be processed along with the content of the data itself. The data is in a fairly consistent format, but not necessarily a well-known format with great tools for processing it. So, let's do some preprocessing on the data and convert a portion of it to the well-known Unix mbox format in order to illustrate the general process of standardizing a mail corpus to a format that is widely known and well tooled.

7.2.3 Converting a Mail Corpus to a Unix Mailbox

Example 7-2 illustrates an approach that searches the directory structure of the Enron corpus for folders named "inbox" and adds messages contained in them to a single output file that's written out as *enron.mbox*. To run this script, you will need to download the Enron corpus and unarchive it to the path specified by MAILDIR in the script.

The script takes advantage of a package called dateutil to handle the parsing of dates into a standard format. We didn't do this earlier, and it's slightly trickier than it may sound given the room for variation in the general case. You can install this package with **pip install python_dateutil**. (In this particular instance, the package name that pip tries to install is slightly different than what you import in your code.) Otherwise, the script is just using some tools from Python's standard library to munge the data into an mbox. Although not analytically interesting, the script provides reminders of how to use regular expressions, uses the email package that we'll continue to see, and illustrates some other concepts that may be useful for general data processing. Be sure that you understand how Example 7-2 works to broaden your overall working knowledge and data mining toolchain.

 This script may take 10–15 minutes to run on the entire Enron corpus, depending on your hardware. The Jupyter Notebook will indicate that it is still processing data by displaying a "Kernel Busy" message in the upper-right corner of the user interface.

Example 7-2. Converting the Enron corpus to a standardized mbox format

```
import re
import email
from time import asctime
import os
import sys
from dateutil.parser import parse # pip install python_dateutil

# Download the Enron corpus to resources/ch07-mailboxes/data
# and unarchive it there

MAILDIR = 'resources/ch07-mailboxes/data/enron_mail_20110402/maildir'

# Where to write the converted mbox
MBOX = 'resources/ch07-mailboxes/data/enron.mbox'

# Create a file handle that we'll be writing into
mbox = open(MBOX, 'w+')

# Walk the directories and process any folder named 'inbox'

for (root, dirs, file_names) in os.walk(MAILDIR):

    if root.split(os.sep)[-1].lower() != 'inbox':
        continue

    # Process each message in 'inbox'

    for file_name in file_names:
```

```
        file_path = os.path.join(root, file_name)
        message_text = open(file_path, errors='ignore').read()

        # Compute fields for the From_ line in a traditional mbox message
        _from = re.search(r"From: ([^\r\n]+)", message_text).groups()[0]
        _date = re.search(r"Date: ([^\r\n]+)", message_text).groups()[0]

        # Convert _date to the asctime representation for the From_ line
        _date = asctime(parse(_date).timetuple())

        msg = email.message_from_string(message_text)
        msg.set_unixfrom('From {0} {1}'.format(_from, _date))

        mbox.write(msg.as_string(unixfrom=True) + "\n\n")

mbox.close()
```

If you peek at the mbox file that you've just created, you'll see that it looks quite similar to the mail format you saw earlier, except that it now conforms to well-known specifications and is a single file.

 Keep in mind that you could just as easily create separate mbox files for each individual person or a particular group of people if you preferred to analyze a more focused subset of the Enron corpus.

7.2.4 Converting Unix Mailboxes to pandas DataFrames

Having an mbox file is especially convenient because of the variety of tools available to process it across computing platforms and programming languages. In this section we'll look at eliminating many of the simplifying assumptions from Example 7-1, to the point that we can robustly process the Enron mailbox and take into account several of the common issues that you'll likely encounter with mailbox data from the wild.

The mbox data structure is fairly versatile, but to do more powerful data manipulations, queries, and data visualizations, we are going to convert it into a data structure we introduced in Chapter 2—the pandas DataFrame.

pandas, just to refresh your memory, is a software library written for Python that allows for versatile data analysis. It should be a part of every data scientist's toolbox. pandas introduces a data structure called a DataFrame, which is a way of holding labeled two-dimensional data tables. You can think of them like spreadsheets, where every column has a name. The data types of each column do not need to be all the same. You can have a column of dates, another column with string data, and a third column of floating-point numbers, all inhabiting the same DataFrame.

Email data lends itself to being stored in a DataFrame. You can have one column containing the *From* field, another column holding the subject line, and so on. Once the data has been stored and indexed in a DataFrame, you can perform queries ("Which emails contained a specific keyword?") or calculate statistics ("How much email was sent in the month of April?"). pandas makes performing these operations relatively simple.

In Example 7-3 we first convert the Enron email corpus from its mbox format to a Python dictionary. The mbox_dict variable holds all the emails as individual key/value pairs, with each email itself being structured as a Python dictionary where the keys are the headers (To, From, Subject, etc.), and finally the body content of the email itself. This Python dictionary is then easily loaded into a DataFrame with the from_dict method.

Example 7-3. Converting an mbox to a Python dict structure and then importing into a pandas DataFrame

```
import pandas as pd # pip install pandas
import mailbox

MBOX = 'resources/ch07-mailboxes/data/enron.mbox'
mbox = mailbox.mbox(MBOX)

mbox_dict = {}
for i, msg in enumerate(mbox):
    mbox_dict[i] = {}
    for header in msg.keys():
        mbox_dict[i][header] = msg[header]
    mbox_dict[i]['Body'] = msg.get_payload().replace('\n', ' ')
        .replace('\t', ' ').replace('\r', ' ').strip()

df = pd.DataFrame.from_dict(mbox_dict, orient='index')
```

The first five rows of the DataFrame can be inspected using the head method. Figure 7-2 shows what the output of this command looks like.

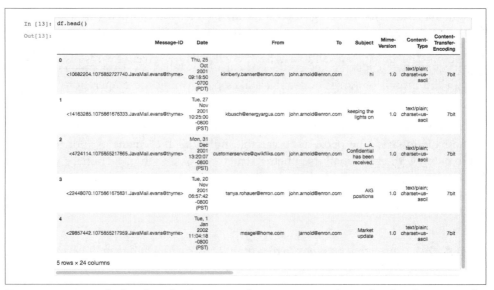

In [13]: df.head()

Out[13]:

	Message-ID	Date	From	To	Subject	Mime-Version	Content-Type	Content-Transfer-Encoding
0	<10682204.1075852727740.JavaMail.evans@thyme>	Thu, 25 Oct 2001 09:18:50 -0700 (PDT)	kimberly.banner@enron.com	john.arnold@enron.com	hi	1.0	text/plain; charset=us-ascii	7bit
1	<14163285.1075861676333.JavaMail.evans@thyme>	Tue, 27 Nov 2001 10:25:00 -0800 (PST)	kbusch@energyargus.com	john.arnold@enron.com	keeping the lights on	1.0	text/plain; charset=us-ascii	7bit
2	<4724114.1075855217865.JavaMail.evans@thyme>	Mon, 31 Dec 2001 13:20:07 -0800 (PST)	customerservice@qwikfliks.com	john.arnold@enron.com	L.A. Confidential has been received.	1.0	text/plain; charset=us-ascii	7bit
3	<22448070.1075861675831.JavaMail.evans@thyme>	Tue, 20 Nov 2001 06:57:42 -0800 (PST)	tanya.rohauer@enron.com	john.arnold@enron.com	AIG positions	1.0	text/plain; charset=us-ascii	7bit
4	<29857442.1075855217959.JavaMail.evans@thyme>	Tue, 1 Jan 2002 11:04:18 -0800 (PST)	msagel@home.com	jarnold@enron.com	Market update	1.0	text/plain; charset=us-ascii	7bit

5 rows × 24 columns

Figure 7-2. Using the head method on a pandas DataFrame shows the first five rows of the DataFrame and is a handy way to quickly inspect your data

There is a lot of information in the email header. Each header is now its own column in the `DataFrame`. To see a list of column names, the `df.columns` command may be used.

We may not be interested in keeping all of these columns for our analysis, so let's settle on a few and make the `DataFrame` a little more compact. We'll keep only the *From*, *To*, *Cc*, *Bcc*, *Subject*, and *Body* columns.

One other advantage of `DataFrames` is that we can choose how they ought to be indexed. The choice of index will dramatically affect the speed at which certain queries can be performed. If we can imagine ourselves asking a lot of questions about *when* emails were being sent, then it may make the most sense to set the index of the `DataFrame` to be a `DatetimeIndex`. This will sort the `DataFrame` by date and time, which allows for very fast searches against email timestamps. The code in Example 7-4 shows how the index of the `DataFrame` can be reset and how we can choose a subset of the `DataFrame`'s columns to keep.

Example 7-4. Setting the index of the DataFrame and selecting a subset of the columns to keep

```
df.index = df['Date'].apply(pd.to_datetime)

# Remove nonessential columns
```

```
cols_to_keep = ['From', 'To', 'Cc', 'Bcc', 'Subject', 'Body']
df = df[cols_to_keep]
```

Inspecting the `DataFrame` with the `head` method now gives the results shown in Figure 7-3.

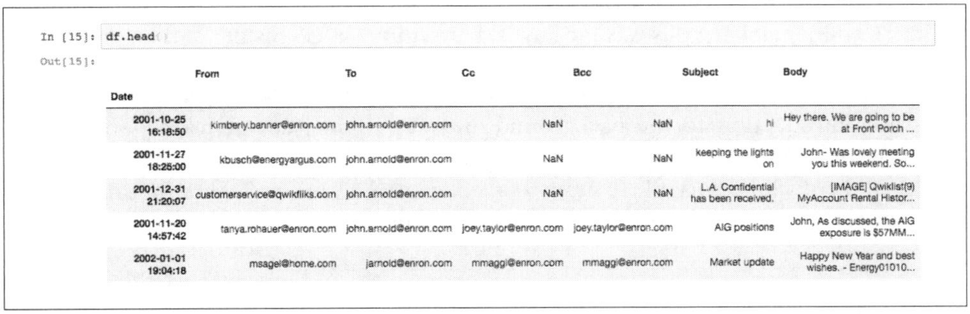

Figure 7-3. Output of the head method after making the changes in Example 7-4

With the email data now converted from an mbox to a `pandas DataFrame`, the columns of interest selected, and a `DatetimeIndex` set, we are now ready to proceed with our analysis.

7.3 Analyzing the Enron Corpus

Having invested a significant amount of energy and attention in the problem of getting the Enron data into a convenient format that we can query, let's now embark upon a quest to begin understanding the data. As you know from previous chapters, counting things is usually one of the first exploratory tasks you'll want to consider when faced with a new data set of any kind, because it can tell you so much with so little effort. This section investigates a couple of ways you can use `pandas` to query a mailbox for various combinations of fields and criteria with minimal effort required, as an extension of the working discussion.

Overview of the Enron Scandal

Although not entirely necessary, you will likely learn more in this chapter if you are notionally familiar with the Enron scandal, which is the subject of the mail data that we'll be analyzing. Following are a few key facts about Enron that will be helpful in understanding the context as we analyze the data for this chapter:

- Enron was a Texas-based energy company that grew to a multibillion-dollar company between its founding in 1985 and the scandal revealed in October 2001.

- Kenneth Lay was the CEO of Enron and the subject of many Enron-related discussions.

- The substance of the Enron scandal involved the use of financial instruments (referred to as *raptors*) to effectively hide accounting losses.

- Arthur Andersen, once a prestigious accounting firm, was responsible for performing the financial audits. It closed shortly after the Enron scandal.

- Soon after the scandal was revealed, Enron filed bankruptcy to the tune of over $60 billion dollars; this was the largest bankruptcy in US history at the time.

The Wikipedia article on the Enron scandal (*http://bit.ly/1a1nuZo*) provides an easy-to-read introduction to the background and key events, and it takes only a few minutes to read enough of it to get the gist of what happened. If you'd like to dig deeper, the documentary film *Enron: The Smartest Guys in the Room* (*http://imdb.to/1a1nvwd*) provides all the background you'll ever need.

The website *http://www.enron-mail.com* hosts a version of the Enron mail data that you may find helpful as you initially get acquainted with the Enron corpus.

7.3.1 Querying by Date/Time Range

In Example 7-4 we changed the index of the `DataFrame` from merely being a row number to being the date and time at which the email was sent. This allows us to rapidly retrieve rows from the `DataFrame` based on the email's timestamp, making it easy to answer questions like:

- How much email was sent on November 1, 2001?
- Which month saw the highest email volume?
- What was the total number of emails sent by week in 2002?

`pandas` comes with a handful of useful indexing functions (*http://bit.ly/2HGyotX*), the most important of which are the `loc` and `iloc` methods. The `loc` method is primarily a label-based selection, allowing you to perform queries such as

```
df.loc[df.From == 'kenneth.lay@enron.com']
```

This command returns all emails sent by Kenneth Lay within the `DataFrame`. The returned data structure is also a `pandas DataFrame`, so it can be assigned to a variable to be used in other ways later.

The `iloc` method is primarily for position-based selections, which is useful if you know exactly which rows are of interest to you. This allows for queries such as:

```
df.iloc[10:15]
```

which would return a slice of the data set containing rows 10 through 15.

Suppose, though, that we wanted to retrieve all email sent or received between two exact dates. This is where our DatetimeIndex comes in really handy. As Example 7-5 shows, we can easily retrieve all emails sent between two dates and then perform handy operations on that data slice, such as counting the number of emails sent by month.

Example 7-5. Retrieving a selection of the data using the DatetimeIndex, then counting the number of emails sent by month

```
start_date = '2000-1-1'
stop_date = '2003-1-1'

datemask = (df.index > start_date) & (df.index <= stop_date)
vol_by_month = df.loc[datemask].resample('1M').count()['To']

print(vol_by_month)
```

What we have done here is create a Boolean mask that returns True when a row in the DataFrame satisfies the dual constraint of having a date after start_date but before end_date. This selection is then resampled on one-month intervals and counted.

The output of Example 7-5 looks like this:

```
Date
2000-12-31       1
2001-01-31       3
2001-02-28       2
2001-03-31      21
2001-04-30     720
2001-05-31    1816
2001-06-30    1423
2001-07-31     704
2001-08-31    1333
2001-09-30    2897
2001-10-31    9137
2001-11-30    8569
2001-12-31    4167
2002-01-31    3464
2002-02-28    1897
2002-03-31     497
2002-04-30      88
2002-05-31      82
2002-06-30     158
2002-07-31       0
2002-08-31       0
2002-09-30       0
2002-10-31       1
```

```
2002-11-30     0
2002-12-31     1
Freq: M, Name: To, dtype: int64
```

Let's clean this up a little so that it becomes easier to read. We can use `prettytable` like we've done in the past to quickly create a text-based table to cleanly represent our output. We do this in Example 7-6.

Example 7-6. Representing monthly email volume using prettytable

```
from prettytable import PrettyTable

pt = PrettyTable(field_names=['Year', 'Month', 'Num Msgs'])
pt.align['Num Msgs'], pt.align['Month'] = 'r', 'r'
[ pt.add_row([ind.year, ind.month, vol])
  for ind, vol in zip(vol_by_month.index, vol_by_month)]

print(pt)
```

This produces as output:

```
+------+-------+----------+
| Year | Month | Num Msgs |
+------+-------+----------+
| 2000 |    12 |        1 |
| 2001 |     1 |        3 |
| 2001 |     2 |        2 |
| 2001 |     3 |       21 |
| 2001 |     4 |      720 |
| 2001 |     5 |     1816 |
| 2001 |     6 |     1423 |
| 2001 |     7 |      704 |
| 2001 |     8 |     1333 |
| 2001 |     9 |     2897 |
| 2001 |    10 |     9137 |
| 2001 |    11 |     8569 |
| 2001 |    12 |     4167 |
| 2002 |     1 |     3464 |
| 2002 |     2 |     1897 |
| 2002 |     3 |      497 |
| 2002 |     4 |       88 |
| 2002 |     5 |       82 |
| 2002 |     6 |      158 |
| 2002 |     7 |        0 |
| 2002 |     8 |        0 |
| 2002 |     9 |        0 |
| 2002 |    10 |        1 |
| 2002 |    11 |        0 |
| 2002 |    12 |        1 |
+------+-------+----------+
```

Of course, it may be even better to visualize this table as a graph, which we can do pretty quickly with the built-in plotting commands that are already a part of pandas. The code in Example 7-7 shows how to create a quick horizontal bar chart of email volume by month.

Example 7-7. Representing monthly email volume using a horizontal bar chart

```
vol_by_month[::-1].plot(kind='barh', figsize=(5,8), title='Email Volume by Month')
```

The output of this can be seen in Figure 7-4.

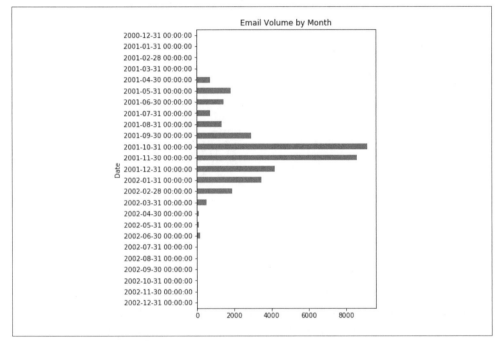

Figure 7-4. A horizontal bar chart of monthly email volume based on the code in Example 7-7

 It is easiest to follow along with these examples by using the latest code from *http://bit.ly/Mining-the-Social-Web-3E*. Running this code inside the Jupyter Notebook environment makes it easier to try out the different ways of querying pandas DataFrames. The Jupyter Notebook is a great tool for exploring data.

7.3.2 Analyzing Patterns in Sender/Recipient Communications

Other metrics, such as how many messages a given person originally authored or how many direct communications occurred between any given group of people, are highly relevant statistics to consider as part of email analysis. However, before you start analyzing who is communicating with whom, you may first want to simply enumerate all of the possible senders and receivers, optionally constraining the query by a criterion such as the domain from which the emails originated or to which they were delivered. As a starting point in this illustration, let's calculate the number of distinct email addresses that sent or received messages, as demonstrated in Example 7-8.

Example 7-8. Enumerating senders and receivers of messages

```
senders = df['From'].unique()
receivers = df['To'].unique()
cc_receivers = df['Cc'].unique()
bcc_receivers = df['Bcc'].unique()

print('Num Senders:', len(senders))
print('Num Receivers:', len(receivers))
print('Num CC Receivers:', len(cc_receivers))
print('Num BCC Receivers:', len(bcc_receivers))
```

Sample output for the working data set follows:

```
Num Senders: 7678
Num Receivers: 10556
Num CC Receivers: 5449
Num BCC Receivers: 5449
```

Even without any other information, these counts of senders and receivers are fairly interesting to consider. On average, each message was sent to 1.4 people, with a fairly substantial number of courtesy copies (CCs) and blind courtesy copies (BCCs) on the messages. The next step might be to winnow down the data and use basic set operations (*http://bit.ly/1a1l2Sw*) (as introduced back in Chapter 1) to determine what kind of overlap exists between various combinations of these criteria. To do that, we'll simply need to cast the lists that contain each unique value to sets so that we can make various kinds of set comparisons (*http://bit.ly/2IzBW2j*), including intersections, differences, and unions. Table 7-2 illustrates these basic operations over this small universe of senders and receivers to show you how this will work on the data:

```
Senders = {Abe, Bob}, Receivers = {Bob, Carol}
```

Table 7-2. Sample set operations

Operation	Operation name	Result	Comment
Senders ∪ Receivers	Union	Abe, Bob, Carol	All unique senders and receivers of messages
Senders ∩ Receivers	Intersection	Bob	Senders who were also receivers of messages
Senders - Receivers	Difference	Abe	Senders who did not receive messages
Receivers - Senders	Difference	Carol	Receivers who did not send messages

Example 7-9 shows how to employ set operations in Python to compute on data.

Example 7-9. Generating lists of the top email senders and receivers in the Enron corpus

```
senders = set(senders)
receivers = set(receivers)
cc_receivers = set(cc_receivers)
bcc_receivers = set(bcc_receivers)

# Find the number of senders who were also direct receivers

senders_intersect_receivers = senders.intersection(receivers)

# Find the senders that didn't receive any messages

senders_diff_receivers = senders.difference(receivers)

# Find the receivers that didn't send any messages

receivers_diff_senders = receivers.difference(senders)

# Find the senders who were any kind of receiver by
# first computing the union of all types of receivers

all_receivers = receivers.union(cc_receivers, bcc_receivers)
senders_all_receivers = senders.intersection(all_receivers)

print("Num senders in common with receivers:", len(senders_intersect_receivers))
print("Num senders who didn't receive:", len(senders_diff_receivers))
print("Num receivers who didn't send:", len(receivers_diff_senders))
print("Num senders in common with *all* receivers:", len(senders_all_receivers))
```

The following sample output from this script reveals some additional insight about
the nature of the mailbox data:

```
Num senders in common with receivers: 3220
Num senders who didn't receive: 4445
Num receivers who didn't send: 18942
Num senders in common with all receivers: 3440
```

Another question of interest might be who is sending or receiving the most email. Suppose we would like to produce a ranked list of the top senders and top receivers of email within our corpus. How would we go about this? We might consider taking the entire data set, grouping it by either sender or receiver, and then counting the number of emails in each group. A group represents all the email one sender has sent or one receiver has received, and thus we can create ranked lists of top senders and top receivers.

This type of grouping operation is a common task in relational databases, and it has been implemented in pandas. In Example 7-10 we use its groupby operation (*http:// bit.ly/2FRGnno*) to create these groupings.

Example 7-10. Generating lists of the top email senders and receivers in the Enron corpus

```
import numpy as np

top_senders = df.groupby('From')
top_receivers = df.groupby('To')

top_senders = top_senders.count()['To']
top_receivers = top_receivers.count()['From']

# Get the ordered indices of the top senders and receivers in descending order
top_snd_ord = np.argsort(top_senders)[::-1]
top_rcv_ord = np.argsort(top_receivers)[::-1]

top_senders = top_senders[top_snd_ord]
top_receivers = top_receivers[top_rcv_ord]
```

After creating these ranked lists, we can use the prettytable package to output the results. Example 7-11 shows how to produce a text-based table of the top 10 highest-volume email senders in our corpus.

Example 7-11. Finding the top 10 highest-volume email senders in the Enron corpus

```
from prettytable import PrettyTable

top10 = top_senders[:10]
pt = PrettyTable(field_names=['Rank', 'Sender', 'Messages Sent'])
pt.align['Messages Sent'] = 'r'
[ pt.add_row([i+1, email, vol]) for i, email, vol in zip(range(10),
    top10.index.values, top10.values)]

print(pt)
```

The output of running this code is:

```
+------+----------------------------------+---------------+
| Rank |             Sender               | Messages Sent |
+------+----------------------------------+---------------+
|  1   |        pete.davis@enron.com      |      722      |
|  2   |   announcements.enron@enron.com  |      372      |
|  3   |        jae.black@enron.com       |      322      |
|  4   | enron_update@concureworkplace.com|      213      |
|  5   |        feedback@intcx.com        |      209      |
|  6   |     chairman.ken@enron.com       |      197      |
|  7   |   arsystem@mailman.enron.com     |      192      |
|  8   |     mike.grigsby@enron.com       |      191      |
|  9   |       soblander@carrfut.com      |      186      |
|  10  |        mary.cook@enron.com       |      186      |
+------+----------------------------------+---------------+
```

We can produce a similar table of results for receivers. Example 7-12 shows how this can be done.

Example 7-12. Finding the top 10 highest-volume email receivers in the Enron corpus

```python
from prettytable import PrettyTable

top10 = top_receivers[:10]
pt = PrettyTable(field_names=['Rank', 'Receiver', 'Messages Received'])
pt.align['Messages Sent'] = 'r'
[ pt.add_row([i+1, email, vol]) for i, email, vol in zip(range(10),
    top10.index.values, top10.values)]

print(pt)
```

The output looks like this:

```
+------+----------------------------+-------------------+
| Rank |          Receiver          | Messages Received |
+------+----------------------------+-------------------+
|  1   |    pete.davis@enron.com    |        721        |
|  2   |   gerald.nemec@enron.com   |        677        |
|  3   |   kenneth.lay@enron.com    |        608        |
|  4   | sara.shackleton@enron.com  |        453        |
|  5   |  jeff.skilling@enron.com   |        420        |
|  6   | center.dl-portland@enron.com |      394        |
|  7   |  jeff.dasovich@enron.com   |        346        |
|  8   |    tana.jones@enron.com    |        303        |
|  9   |     rick.buy@enron.com     |        286        |
|  10  |  barry.tycholiz@enron.com  |        280        |
+------+----------------------------+-------------------+
```

7.3.3 Searching Emails by Keywords

pandas features a number of powerful indexing capabilities (*http://bit.ly/2HGyotX*) that can also be used to construct search queries.

For example, in an mbox, if you were searching for an email address you might want to query the *To* and *From* fields first, then later inspect the *Cc* or *Bcc* fields. If you were searching for keywords, you would perform string matching inside the subject line or the body of the mail message.

In the context of Enron, *raptors* (*http://bit.ly/1a1nFE6*) were financial devices that were used to hide hundreds of millions of dollars in debt, from an accounting standpoint. If we were doing an audit, we would want tools for quickly searching through an entire corpus of emails or documents. We've already done the work of reading the entire corpus into a format (the pandas DataFrame) that facilitates easy data analysis from within a Python environment. Now we just need to learn how to perform searches for specific words, such as "raptor." The sample code in Example 7-13 shows one such way.

Example 7-13. Querying a pandas DataFrame to look for a search term in the subject line or email body and printing the first 10 results

```
import textwrap

search_term = 'raptor'

query = (df['Body'].str.contains(search_term, case=False) |
    df['Subject'].str.contains(search_term, case=False))

results = df[query]

print('{0} results found.'.format(query.sum()))
print('Printing first 10 results...')
for i in range(10):
    subject, body = results.iloc[i]['Subject'], results.iloc[i]['Body']
    print()
    print('SUBJECT: ', subject)
    print('-'*20)
    for line in textwrap.wrap(body, width=70, max_lines=5):
        print(line)
```

In Example 7-13, we create a Boolean logical expression that we save in the query variable. That query inspects the bodies and subject lines of the emails in our Data Frame for strings containing the search term, which we've saved to the search_term variable. The case=False keyword ensures that we return results irrespective of how "raptor" is capitalized.

The query variable is a series of True and False values that, when passed to the Data Frame df, returns the rows that match True to our search query (i.e., the rows in which the subject or body contains the word "raptor"). We store those rows in the variable results.

The `for` loop later in the sample code then prints the first 10 matching rows. We use the `textwrap` library to print out the first five lines of each matching email. This helps us inspect the output quickly. Following are truncated sample query results:

```
SUBJECT:  RE: Pricing of restriction on Enron stock
--------------------
Vince, I just spoke with Rakesh.  I believe that there is some
confusion regarding which part of that Raptor transaction we are
talking about.  There are actually two different sets of forwards: one
for up to 18MM shares contingently based on price as an offset to the
Whitewing forward shortfall, and the other was for 12MM shares [...]

SUBJECT:  FW: Note on Valuation
--------------------
Vince,  I have it.  Rakesh  -----Original Message----- From: Kaminski,
Vince J  Sent: Monday, October 22, 2001 2:39 PM To: Bharati, Rakesh;
Shanbhogue, Vasant Cc: Kaminski, Vince J;
'kimberly.r.scardino@us.andersen.com' Subject: RE: Note on Valuation
Rakesh,  I have informed Ryan Siurek (cc Rick Buy) on Oct 4 that [...]

SUBJECT:  FW: Raptors
--------------------
I am forwarding a copy of a message I sent some time ago to the same
address. The lawyer representing the Special Committee (David Cohen)
could not locate it. The message disappeared as well form my mailbox.
Fortunately, I have preserved another copy.  Vince Kaminski
-----Original Message----- From:  VKaminski@aol.com@ENRON [...]

SUBJECT:  Raptors
--------------------
David,  I am forwarding to you, as promised, the text of the
10/04/2001  message to Ryan Siurek regarding Raptor valuations. The
message is stored on my PC at home. It disappeared from my mailbox on
the Enron system.  Vince Kaminski  **********************************
***************************************** Subj:   FW: [...]
```

These snippets contain interesting pieces of information in a larger puzzle. You now have the tools and the know-how to dig deeper and find out more.

7.4 Analyzing Your Own Mail Data

The Enron mail data makes for great illustrations in a chapter on mail analysis, but you'll probably also want to take a closer look at your own mail data. Fortunately, many popular mail clients provide an "export to mbox" option, which makes it pretty simple to get your mail data into a format that lends itself to analysis by the techniques described in this chapter.

For example, in Apple Mail, you can export your entire mailbox in mbox format using the Export Mailbox command in the Mailbox menu. You can also export individual emails by selecting them and then choosing Save As from the File menu. Select

Raw Message Source as the formatting option for the file (see Figure 7-5). A little bit of searching should turn up results for how to do this in most other major clients.

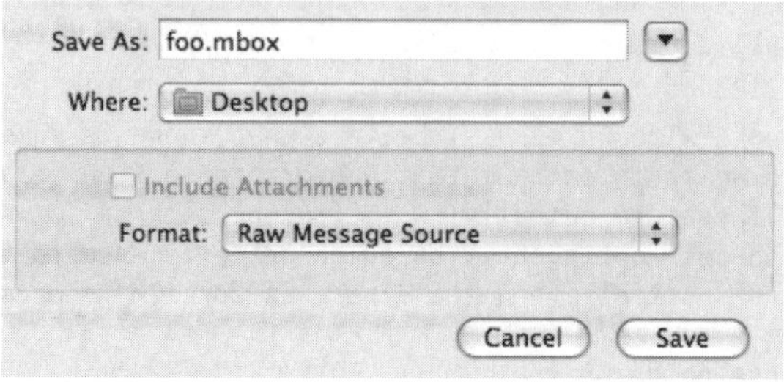

Figure 7-5. Most mail clients provide an option for exporting your mail data to an mbox archive

If you exclusively use an online mail client, you could opt to pull your data down into a mail client and export it, but you might prefer to fully automate the creation of an mbox file by pulling the data directly from the server. Just about any online mail service will support POP3 (*http://bit.ly/1a1nHvx*) (Post Office Protocol, version 3) and most also support IMAP (*http://bit.ly/2MXFFvF*), and it's not hard to whip up Python scripts for pulling down your mail.

One particularly robust command-line tool that you can use to pull mail data from just about anywhere is `getmail` (*http://bit.ly/1a1nKaL*), which turns out to be written in Python. Two modules included in Python's standard library, `poplib` (*http://bit.ly/1a1nI2G*) and `imaplib` (*http://bit.ly/1a1nIj5*), provide a terrific foundation, so you're also likely to run across lots of useful scripts if you do a bit of searching online. `get mail` is particularly easy to get up and running. To retrieve your Gmail inbox data, for example, you just download and install it, then set up a *getmailrc* configuration file.

The following sample settings demonstrate some settings for a *nix environment. Windows users would need to change the [`destination`] `path` and [`options`] `mes sage_log` values to valid paths, but keep in mind that you could opt to run the script on the virtual machine for this book if you needed a quick fix for a *nix environment:

```
[retriever]
type = SimpleIMAPSSLRetriever
server = imap.gmail.com
username = ptwobrussell
password = xxx

[destination]
type = Mboxrd
path = /tmp/gmail.mbox

[options]
```

```
verbose = 2
message_log = ~/.getmail/gmail.log
```

With a configuration in place, simply invoking `getmail` from a terminal does the rest. Once you have a local mbox on hand, you can analyze it using the techniques you've learned in this chapter. Here's what `getmail` looks like while it's in action slurping down your mail data:

```
$ getmail
getmail version 4.20.0
Copyright (C) 1998-2009 Charles Cazabon.  Licensed under the GNU GPL version 2.
SimpleIMAPSSLRetriever:ptwobrussell@imap.gmail.com:993:
  msg    1/10972 (4227 bytes) from ... delivered to Mboxrd /tmp/gmail.mbox
  msg    2/10972 (3219 bytes) from ... delivered to Mboxrd /tmp/gmail.mbox
  ...
```

7.4.1 Accessing Your Gmail with OAuth

In early 2010, Google announced OAuth access to IMAP and SMTP in Gmail (*http://bit.ly/1a1nIzH*). This was a significant announcement because it officially opened the door to "Gmail as a platform," enabling third-party developers to build apps that can access your Gmail data without you needing to give them your username and password. This section won't get into the particular nuances of how OAuth 2.0 (*http://bit.ly/2GoT1Pl*) works (see Appendix B for a terse introduction to OAuth in general);. Instead, it focuses on getting you up and running so that you can access your Gmail data, which involves a few steps:

1. Use the Google Developer Console (*http://bit.ly/2ImRDZM*) to create or select a project. Turn on the Gmail API.

2. Select the Credentials tab, click "Create credentials," and select "OAuth client ID."

3. Select the application type Other, enter the name "Gmail API Quickstart," and click the Create button.

4. Click OK to dismiss the resulting dialog.

5. Click the file download button next to your newly created credentials to download a JSON file containing them.

6. Move this file to your working directory and rename it *client_secret.json*.

Next you'll need to install the Google Client Library, which is easy to do using `pip`:

```
pip install --upgrade google-api-python-client
```

The library's installation page (*http://bit.ly/2EcUP7P*) contains alternative installation instructions. Once the Python API has been installed and you have your credentials saved locally, you are ready to write code that accesses the Gmail API. The code in Example 7-14 is taken from the Python Quickstart (*http://bit.ly/2GNhSvy*) guide on connecting to Gmail. Save it to a file called *quickstart.py*. If your *client_secrets.json* file is in the same working directory, it should execute successfully, launching a web browser where you will be asked to log into your Gmail account and give your project permission to read your email. The code in the example prints your Gmail labels (if you have created any) to screen.

Example 7-14. Connecting to Gmail with OAuth

```python
import httplib2
import os

from apiclient import discovery
from oauth2client import client
from oauth2client import tools
from oauth2client.file import Storage

try:
    import argparse
    flags = argparse.ArgumentParser(parents=[tools.argparser]).parse_args()
except ImportError:
    flags = None

# If modifying these scopes, delete your previously saved credentials
# at ~/.credentials/gmail-python-quickstart.json
SCOPES = 'https://www.googleapis.com/auth/gmail.readonly'
CLIENT_SECRET_FILE = 'client_secret.json'
APPLICATION_NAME = 'Gmail API Python Quickstart'


def get_credentials():
    """Gets valid user credentials from storage.

    If nothing has been stored, or if the stored credentials are invalid,
    the OAuth2 flow is completed to obtain the new credentials.

    Returns:
        Credentials, the obtained credential.
    """
    home_dir = os.path.expanduser('~')
    credential_dir = os.path.join(home_dir, '.credentials')
    if not os.path.exists(credential_dir):
        os.makedirs(credential_dir)
    credential_path = os.path.join(credential_dir,
                                   'gmail-python-quickstart.json')

    store = Storage(credential_path)
    credentials = store.get()
    if not credentials or credentials.invalid:
        flow = client.flow_from_clientsecrets(CLIENT_SECRET_FILE, SCOPES)
        flow.user_agent = APPLICATION_NAME
```

```
        if flags:
            credentials = tools.run_flow(flow, store, flags)
        else: # Needed only for compatibility with Python 2.6
            credentials = tools.run(flow, store)
        print('Storing credentials to ' + credential_path)
    return credentials

def main():
    """Shows basic usage of the Gmail API.

    Creates a Gmail API service object and outputs a list of label names
    of the user's Gmail account.
    """
    credentials = get_credentials()
    http = credentials.authorize(httplib2.Http())
    service = discovery.build('gmail', 'v1', http=http)

    results = service.users().labels().list(userId='me').execute()
    labels = results.get('labels', [])

    if not labels:
        print('No labels found.')
    else:
      print('Labels:')
      for label in labels:
        print(label['name'])


if __name__ == '__main__':
    main()
```

Example 7-14 serves as a starting point for building more advanced applications that can access your Gmail inbox. Once you're able to programmatically access your mailbox, the next step is to fetch and parse some message data. The great thing about this is that we'll format and export it to exactly the same specification that we've been working with so far in this chapter, so all of your scripts and tools will work on both the Enron corpus and your own mail data!

7.4.2 Fetching and Parsing Email Messages

The IMAP protocol is a fairly finicky and complex beast, but the good news is that you don't have to know much of it to search and fetch mail messages. Furthermore, imaplib-compliant examples are readily available online (*http://bit.ly/1a1nJDG*).

Sticking with the Gmail example, however, you can continue to use OAuth to query your inbox for messages and pull the ones matching a particular search term. Example 7-15 builds on Example 7-14 and assumes you've gone through the steps of setting up a project on the Google Developer Console and activated the Gmail API for your project.

Suppose you wanted to search for email messages containing the term "Alaska." The code in Example 7-15 returns at most 10 matching results (you can change the upper limit of search results to return by changing the max_results variable). A for loop then retrieves the message ID of each search result and fetches the email message corresponding to that ID.

Example 7-15. Query your Gmail inbox and print the message contents

```
import httplib2
import os

from apiclient import discovery
from oauth2client import client
from oauth2client import tools
from oauth2client.file import Storage

# If modifying these scopes, delete your previously saved credentials
# at ~/.credentials/gmail-python-quickstart.json
SCOPES = 'https://www.googleapis.com/auth/gmail.readonly'
CLIENT_SECRET_FILE = 'client_secret.json'
APPLICATION_NAME = 'Gmail API Python Quickstart'


def get_credentials():
    """Gets valid user credentials from storage.

    If nothing has been stored, or if the stored credentials are invalid,
    the OAuth2 flow is completed to obtain the new credentials.

    Returns:
        Credentials, the obtained credential.
    """
    home_dir = os.path.expanduser('~')
    credential_dir = os.path.join(home_dir, '.credentials')
    if not os.path.exists(credential_dir):
        os.makedirs(credential_dir)
    credential_path = os.path.join(credential_dir,
                                   'gmail-python-quickstart.json')

    store = Storage(credential_path)
    credentials = store.get()
    if not credentials or credentials.invalid:
        flow = client.flow_from_clientsecrets(CLIENT_SECRET_FILE, SCOPES)
        flow.user_agent = APPLICATION_NAME
        if flags:
            credentials = tools.run_flow(flow, store, flags)
        else: # Needed only for compatibility with Python 2.6
            credentials = tools.run(flow, store)
        print('Storing credentials to ' + credential_path)
    return credentials
```

```
credentials = get_credentials()
http = credentials.authorize(httplib2.Http())
service = discovery.build('gmail', 'v1', http=http)

results = service.users().labels().list(userId='me').execute()
labels = results.get('labels', [])

if not labels:
    print('No labels found.')
else:
    print('Labels:')
    for label in labels:
        print(label['name'])


query = 'Alaska'
max_results = 10

# Search for Gmail messages containing the query term
results = service.users().messages().list(userId='me', q=query,
            maxResults=max_results).execute()

for result in results['messages']: ·
    print(result['id'])
    # Retrieve the message itself
    msg = service.users().messages().get(userId='me', id=result['id'],
            format='minimal').execute()
    print(msg)
```

To do even more with your Gmail messages, you can read the API documentation (*http://bit.ly/2pYRRzy*). Between the techniques learned in this chapter and the documentation, you should be able to build sophisticated tools for analyzing your Gmail inbox. Of course, depending on the level of support for either IMAP access or an OAuth API, you can write Python code to access other web-based email services besides Gmail.

Once you've successfully parsed out the text from the body of a Gmail message, some additional work will be required to cleanse the text to the point that it's suitable for a nice display or advanced NLP, as illustrated in Chapter 6. However, not much effort is required to get it to the point where it's clean enough for collocation analysis. In fact, the results of Example 7-15 can be fed almost directly into Example 5-9 to produce a list of collocations from the search results. A worthwhile visualization exercise would be to create a graph plotting the strength of linkages between messages based on the number of bigrams they have in common, as determined by a custom metric.

7.4.3 Visualizing Patterns in Email with Immersion

There are several useful toolkits floating around that analyze webmail. One of the most promising to emerge in recent years is Immersion (*http://bit.ly/2q2xUaD*), which was developed at the MIT Media Lab. It promises to take a "people-centric" view of your inbox. You connect your Gmail, Yahoo!, or MS Exchange account with the platform and it generates a data visualization based on the *To*, *From*, *Cc*, and timestamp fields of your email, showing graphs of who you are connected to and other visualizations. Figure 7-6 shows a sample screenshot.

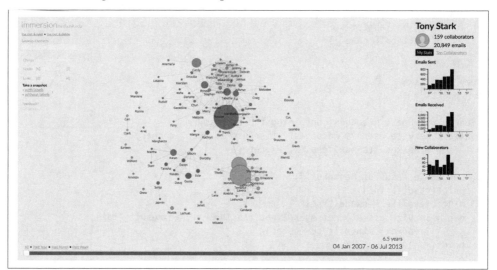

Figure 7-6. A demo of the Immersion email visualization tool

What's especially remarkable is that you can readily reproduce all of the analytics that this extension provides with the techniques you've learned in this chapter plus some supplemental content from earlier chapters, such as the use of a JavaScript visualization library like D3.js or `matplotlib`'s plotting utilities, within the Jupyter Notebook. Your toolbox is full of scripts and techniques that can be readily applied to a data domain to produce a comparable dashboard, whether it be a mailbox, an archive of web pages, or a collection of tweets. You certainly have some careful thinking to do about designing an overall application so that it provides an enjoyable user experience, but the building blocks for the data science and analysis that would be presented to the user are in your grasp.

7.5 Closing Remarks

We've covered a lot of ground in this chapter and synthesized results using many of the tools introduced in previous chapters. Each chapter has successively built upon the earlier ones in an attempt to tell a story about data and its analysis, and we're nearing the end of the book. Although we've barely begun to scratch the surface of what's possible with mail data, you'll surely be able to take advantage of content in the previous chapters to discover amazing insights about your social connections and personal life if you tap into your own mail data, which will add an exciting dimension to the analysis.

Our focus has been on the mbox, a simple and convenient file format that lends itself to high portability and easy analysis by many Python tools and packages, and hopefully you've come to appreciate the value of using a standard and portable format for processing something as complex as a mailbox. There's an incredible amount of open source technology available for mining mboxes, and Python is a terrific language for slicing and dicing them. A small investment in these tools will go a long way in allowing you to focus on the problem at hand.

 The source code outlined for this chapter and all other chapters is available on GitHub (*http://bit.ly/Mining-the-Social-Web-3E*) in a convenient Jupyter Notebook format that you're highly encouraged to try out from the comfort of your own web browser.

7.6 Recommended Exercises

- Identify and hone in on a subset of the original Enron corpus for analysis. For example, do some research on the Enron case by reading about it online or watching a documentary, and then pick 10–15 mailboxes of interest and see what patterns of communication you can identify using the techniques introduced in this chapter.

- Apply text analytics as described in previous chapters to the content of the mail messages. Can you correlate what people are talking about? What are some of the advantages or disadvantages of using a full-text index compared to the information retrieval concepts from earlier chapters?

- Review an email message threading algorithm (*http://bit.ly/1a1nQ23*) that can be used as an effective heuristic for reconstructing mail conversations from mailboxes. A sample implementation (*http://bit.ly/1a1nQ2e*) is available as part of the (now legacy) source code from the first edition of this book.

- Use the SIMILE Timeline (*http://bit.ly/1a1nQz3*) project to visualize message threads from the aforementioned email message threading algorithm. The provided example of plotting mail on Timeline (*http://bit.ly/2Nnj8W1*) just shows the bare minimum to get you up and running; consult the documentation to see what else is possible.

- Run a search for "Enron" on Google Scholar (*http://bit.ly/1a1nR6c*) and review some of the myriad academic papers and studies that have been written about it. Use some of them as inspiration for your own studies.

- Try out the source code from the previous edition of this book for this chapter (*http://bit.ly/2J9gVMv*). Instead of using `pandas`, the Enron corpus is indexed and searched using MongoDB (*https://www.mongodb.com*). The handy `pymongo` (*http://bit.ly/2uBdISn*) library can be used for interfacing with MongoDB databases. Consider the relative advantages and disadvantages of using a full-fledged database versus `pandas` `DataFrames`.

- Check out the blog post (*http://bit.ly/2Iimsiq*) by astrophysicist and data scientist Justin Ellis, who decided to analyze his own Gmail data using `pandas`. If you have a fair amount of email stored in Gmail, see if you can reproduce some of the same data visualizations featured in the article.

- Write some Python code to programmatically access your email. Collect some sample statistics of your own: When you do send and receive the most email? What's the busiest day of the week for email? Or, for a tougher challenge, see if you can determine what types of emails sent are the most likely to receive a reply. Try comparing sent emails of different lengths, or emails sent at different times of the day.

7.7 Online Resources

The following list of links from this chapter may be useful for review:

- Download your Google data (*https://takeout.google.com/*)
- Downloadable Enron corpus (*http://bit.ly/1a1nmsU*)
- Enron corpus (*http://bit.ly/1a1nj01*)
- Enron email corpus and database (public domain) (*http://www.enron-mail.com*)
- Enron scandal (*http://bit.ly/1a1nuZo*)
- Enron whitepapers on Google Scholar (*http://bit.ly/1a1nR6c*)
- `getmail` (*http://bit.ly/1a1nKaL*)
- Git for Windows (*http://bit.ly/2Hiaox1*)
- Immersion: A people-centric view of your email life (*http://bit.ly/2q2xUaD*)
- JWZ's email message threading algorithm (*http://bit.ly/1a1nQ23*)
- MIME types (*http://bit.ly/2Qzxftu*)
- Online demonstrations of SIMILE Timeline (*http://bit.ly/1a1nOr1*)
- "Personal Analytics Part 1: Gmail" (*http://bit.ly/2Iimsiq*)

- SIMILE Timeline (*http://bit.ly/1a1nQz3*)
- Using OAuth 2.0 to Access Google APIs (*http://bit.ly/2GoT1Pl*)

## CHAPTER 8

Mining GitHub: Inspecting Software Collaboration Habits, Building Interest Graphs, and More

GitHub has rapidly evolved in recent years to become the de facto social coding platform with a deceptively simple premise: provide a top-notch hosted solution for developers to create and maintain open source software projects with an open source distributed version control (*http://bit.ly/1a1o1u8*) system called *Git* (*http://bit.ly/16mhOep*). Unlike version control systems such as CVS (*http://bit.ly/1a1nZCI*) or Subversion (*http://bit.ly/2GZy78S*), with Git there is no canonical copy of the code base, per se. All copies are working copies, and developers can commit local changes on a working copy without needing to be connected to a centralized server.

The distributed version control paradigm lends itself exceptionally well to GitHub's notion of *social coding* because it allows developers who are interested in contributing to a project to *fork* a working copy of its code repository and immediately begin working on it in just the same way that the developer who owns the fork works on it. Git not only keeps track of semantics that allow repositories to be forked arbitrarily but also makes it relatively easy to merge changes from a forked *child* repository back into its *parent* repository. Through the GitHub user interface, this workflow is called a *pull request*.

It is a deceptively simple notion, but the ability for developers to create and collaborate on coding projects with elegant workflows that involve minimal overhead (once you understand some fundamental details about how Git works) has certainly streamlined many of the tedious details that have hindered innovation in open source development, including conveniences that transcend into the visualization of data and interoperability with other systems. In other words, think of GitHub as an enabler of open source software development. In the same way, although developers have collaborated on coding projects for decades, a hosted platform like GitHub super-charges collaboration and enables innovation in unprecedented ways by making it easy to create a project, share out its source code, maintain feedback and an issue tracker, accept patches for improvements and bug fixes, and more. More recently, it even appears that GitHub is increasingly catering to nondevelopers (*http://bit.ly/ 1a1o2OZ*)—and becoming one of the hottest social platforms for mainstream collaboration.

Just to be perfectly clear, this chapter does not attempt to provide a tutorial on how to use Git or GitHub as a distributed version control system or even discuss Git software architecture at any level. (See one of the many excellent online Git references, such as *gitscm.com* (*http://bit.ly/1a1o2hZ*), for that kind of instruction.) This chapter does, however, attempt to teach you how to mine GitHub's API to discover patterns of social collaboration in the somewhat niche software development space.

 Always get the latest bug-fixed source code for this chapter (and every other chapter) on GitHub (*http://bit.ly/Mining-the-Social-Web-3E*). Be sure to also take advantage of this book's virtual machine experience, as described in Appendix A, to maximize your enjoyment of the sample code.

8.1 Overview

This chapter provides an introduction to GitHub as a social coding platform and to graph-oriented analysis using NetworkX. In this chapter, you'll learn how to take advantage of GitHub's rich data by constructing a graphical model of the data that can be used in a variety of ways. In particular, we'll treat the relationships between GitHub users, repositories, and programming languages as an interest graph (*http:// bit.ly/1a1o3Cu*), which is a way of interpreting the nodes and links in the graph primarily from the vantage point of people and the things in which they are interested. There is a lot of discussion these days amongst hackers, entrepreneurs, and web mavens as to whether or not the future of the web is largely predicated upon some notion of an interest graph, so now is a fine time to get up to speed on the emerging graph landscape and all that it entails.

In sum, then, this chapter follows the same predictable template as chapters before it and covers:

- GitHub's developer platform and how to make API requests
- Graph schemas and how to model property graphs with NetworkX
- The concept of an interest graph and how to construct an interest graph from GitHub data
- Using NetworkX to query property graphs

- Graph centrality algorithms, including degree, betweenness, and closeness centrality

8.2 Exploring GitHub's API

Like the other social web properties featured in this book, GitHub's developer site (*http://bit.ly/1a1o49k*) offers comprehensive documentation on its APIs, the terms of service governing the use of those APIs, example code, and much more. Although the APIs are fairly rich, we'll be focusing on only the few API calls that we need in order to collect the data for creating some interest graphs that associate software developers, projects, programming languages, and other aspects of software development. The APIs more or less provide you with everything you'd need to build a rich user experience just like *github.com* (*http://bit.ly/1a1kFHM*) offers itself, and there is no shortage of compelling and possibly even lucrative applications that you could build with these APIs.

The most fundamental primitives for GitHub are *users* and *projects*. If you are reading this page, you've probably already managed to pull down this book's source code from its GitHub project page (*http://bit.ly/Mining-the-Social-Web-3E*), so this discussion assumes that you've at least visited a few GitHub project pages, have poked around a bit, and are familiar with the general notion of what GitHub offers.

A GitHub user has a public profile that generally includes one or more code repositories that have either been created or forked from another GitHub user. For example, the GitHub user `ptwobrussell` (*http://bit.ly/1a1o4GC*) owns a couple of GitHub repositories, including one called `Mining-the-Social-Web` (*http://bit.ly/1a1o6Ow*) and another called `Mining-the-Social-Web-2nd-Edition` (*http://bit.ly/1a1kNqy*). `ptwobrussell` has also forked a number of repositories in order to capture a particular working snapshot of certain code bases for development purposes, and these forked projects also appear in his public profile.

Part of what makes GitHub so powerful is that, like any user, `ptwobrussell` is free to do anything he'd like with any of these forked projects (subject to the terms of their software licenses). When a user forks a code repository, that user effectively owns a working copy of the same repository and can do anything from just fiddle around with it to drastically overhaul and create a long-lived fork of the original project that may never be intended to get merged back into the original parent repository. Although most project forks never materialize into derivative works of their own, the effort involved in creating a derivative work is trivial from the standpoint of source code management. It may be short-lived and manifest as a pull request that is merged back into the parent, or it may be long-lived and become an entirely separate project with its own community. The barrier to entry for open source software contribution and other projects that increasingly find themselves appearing on GitHub is low indeed.

In addition to forking projects on GitHub, a user can also bookmark or *star* a project to become what is known as a *stargazer* of the project. Bookmarking a project is essentially the same thing as bookmarking a web page or a tweet. You are signifying interest in the project, and it'll appear on your list of GitHub bookmarks for quick reference. What you'll generally notice is that far fewer people fork code than bookmark it. Bookmarking is an easy and well-understood notion from over a decade of web surfing, whereas forking the code implies having the intent to modify or contribute to it in some way. Throughout the remainder of this chapter, we'll focus primarily on using the list of stargazers for a project as the basis of constructing an interest graph for it.

8.2.1 Creating a GitHub API Connection

Like other social web properties, GitHub implements OAuth, and the steps to gaining API access involve creating an account followed by one of two possibilities: creating an application to use as the consumer of the API or creating a "personal" access token that will be linked directly to your account. In this chapter, we'll opt to use a personal access token, which is as easy as clicking a button in the Personal Access API Tokens section of your account's Applications (*http://bit.ly/1a1o7lw*) menu, as shown in Figure 8-1. (See Appendix B for a more extensive overview of OAuth.)

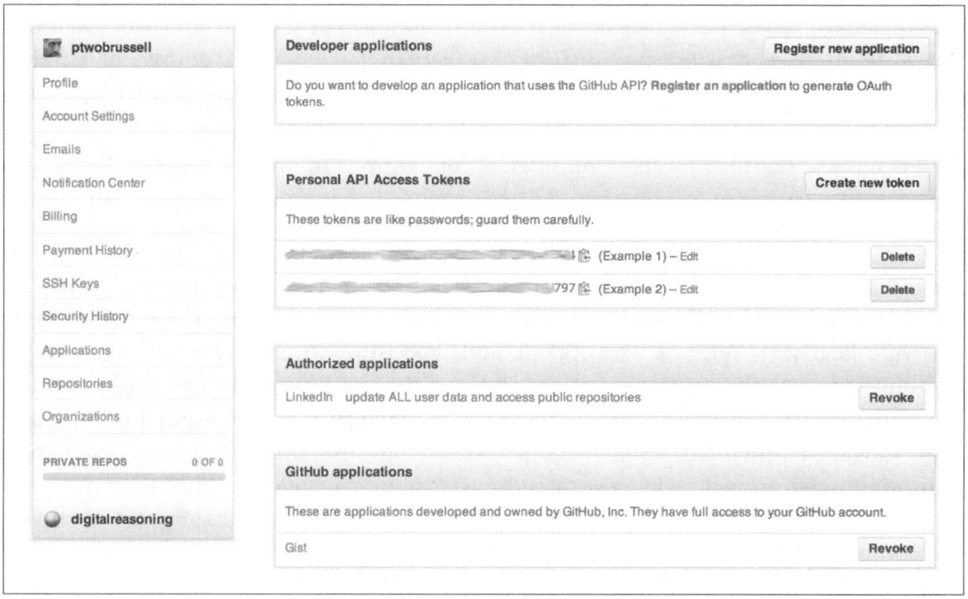

Figure 8-1. Create a personal API access token from the Applications menu in your account and provide a meaningful note so that you'll remember its purpose

A programmatic option for obtaining an access token as opposed to creating one within the GitHub user interface is shown in Example 8-1 as an adaptation of "Creating a personal access token for the command line" (*http://bit.ly/1a1o7lG*) from GitHub's help site. (If you are not taking advantage of the virtual machine experience for this book, as described in Appendix A, you'll need to type **pip install requests** in a terminal prior to running this example.)

Example 8-1. Programmatically obtaining a personal API access token for accessing GitHub's API

```
import requests
import json

username = '' # Your GitHub username
password = '' # Your GitHub password

# Note that credentials will be transmitted over a secure SSL connection
url = 'https://api.github.com/authorizations'
note = 'Mining the Social Web - Mining Github'
post_data = {'scopes':['repo'],'note': note }

response = requests.post(
    url,
    auth = (username, password),
    data = json.dumps(post_data),
    )

print("API response:", response.text)
print()
print("Your OAuth token is", response.json()['token'])

# Go to https://github.com/settings/tokens to revoke this token
```

As is the case with many other social web properties, GitHub's API is built on top of HTTP and accessible through any programming language in which you can make an HTTP request, including command-line tools in a terminal. Following the precedents set by previous chapters, however, we'll opt to take advantage of a Python library so that we can avoid some of the tedious details involved in making requests, parsing responses, and handling pagination. In this particular case, we'll use PyGithub (*http://bit.ly/1a1o7Ca*), which can be installed with the somewhat predictable **pip install PyGithub**. We'll start by taking a look at a couple of examples of how to make GitHub API requests before transitioning into a discussion of graphical models.

Let's seed an interest graph in this chapter from the Mining-the-Social-Web (*http://bit.ly/1a1o6Ow*) GitHub repository and create connections between it and its stargazers. Listing the stargazers for a repository is possible with the List Stargazers API (*http://bit.ly/1a1o9dd*). You could try out an API request to get an idea of what the response type looks like by copying and pasting the following URL in your web browser: *https://api.github.com/repos/ptwobrussell/Mining-the-Social-Web/stargazers.*

 Although you are reading *Mining the Social Web*, 3rd Edition, we'll continue to use the code repository for the first edition in the examples for this chapter, which at the time of this writing has been starred over 1,000 times. Analysis of any repository, including the repositories for the second or third edition of this book, is easy enough to accomplish by simply changing the name of the initial project as introduced in Example 8-3.

The ability to issue an unauthenticated request in this manner is quite convenient as you are exploring the API, and the rate limit of 60 unauthenticated requests per hour is more than adequate for tinkering and exploring. You could, however, append a query string of the form ?access_token=*xxx*, where *xxx* specifies your access token, to make the same request in an authenticated fashion. GitHub's authenticated rate limits are a generous 5,000 requests per hour, as described in the developer documentation for rate limiting (*http://bit.ly/1a1oblo*). Example 8-2 illustrates a sample request and response. (Keep in mind that this is requesting only the first page of results and, as described in the developer documentation for pagination (*http://bit.ly/1a1o9Ki*), metadata information for navigating the pages of results is included in the HTTP headers.)

Example 8-2. Making direct HTTP requests to GitHub's API

```
import json
import requests

# An unauthenticated request that doesn't contain an ?access_token=xxx query string
url = "https://api.github.com/repos/ptwobrussell/Mining-the-Social-Web/stargazers"
response = requests.get(url)

# Display one stargazer
print(json.dumps(response.json()[0], indent=1))
print()

# Display headers
for (k,v) in response.headers.items():
    print(k, "=>", v)
```

Sample output follows:

```
{
 "login": "rdempsey",
 "id": 224,
 "avatar_url": "https://avatars2.githubusercontent.com/u/224?v=4",
 "gravatar_id": "",
```

```
  "url": "https://api.github.com/users/rdempsey",
  "html_url": "https://github.com/rdempsey",
  "followers_url": "https://api.github.com/users/rdempsey/followers",
  "following_url": "https://api.github.com/users/rdempsey/following{/other_user}",
  "gists_url": "https://api.github.com/users/rdempsey/gists{/gist_id}",
  "starred_url": "https://api.github.com/users/rdempsey/starred{/owner}{/repo}",
  "subscriptions_url": "https://api.github.com/users/rdempsey/subscriptions",
  "organizations_url": "https://api.github.com/users/rdempsey/orgs",
  "repos_url": "https://api.github.com/users/rdempsey/repos",
  "events_url": "https://api.github.com/users/rdempsey/events{/privacy}",
  "received_events_url": "https://api.github.com/users/rdempsey/received_events",
  "type": "User",
  "site_admin": false
}

Server => GitHub.com
Date => Fri, 06 Apr 2018 18:41:57 GMT
Content-Type => application/json; charset=utf-8
Transfer-Encoding => chunked
Status => 200 OK
X-RateLimit-Limit => 60
X-RateLimit-Remaining => 55
X-RateLimit-Reset => 1523042441
Cache-Control => public, max-age=60, s-maxage=60
Vary => Accept
ETag => W/"b43b2c639758a6849c9f3f5873209038"
X-GitHub-Media-Type => github.v3; format=json
Link => <https://api.github.com/repositories/1040700/stargazers?page=2>;
rel="next", <https://api.github.com/repositories/1040700/stargazers?page=39>;
rel="last"
Access-Control-Expose-Headers => ETag, Link, Retry-After, X-GitHub-OTP,
X-RateLimit-Limit, X-RateLimit-Remaining, X-RateLimit-Reset,
X-OAuth-Scopes, X-Accepted-OAuth-Scopes, X-Poll-Interval
Access-Control-Allow-Origin => *
Strict-Transport-Security => max-age=31536000; includeSubdomains; preload
X-Frame-Options => deny
X-Content-Type-Options => nosniff
X-XSS-Protection => 1; mode=block
Referrer-Policy => origin-when-cross-origin, strict-origin-when-cross-origin
Content-Security-Policy => default-src 'none'
X-Runtime-rack => 0.057438
Content-Encoding => gzip
X-GitHub-Request-Id => ADE2:10F6:8EC26:1417ED:5AC7BF75
```

As you can see, there's a lot of useful information that GitHub is returning to us that is not in the body of the HTTP response and is instead conveyed as HTTP headers, as outlined in the developer documentation. You should skim and understand what all of the various headers mean, but a few of note include the status header, which tells us that the request was OK with a 200 response; headers that involve the rate limit, such as x-ratelimit-remaining; and the link header, which contains a value such as the following:

```
     https://api.github.com/repositories/1040700/stargazers?page=2; rel="next",
     https://api.github.com/repositories/1040700/stargazers?page=29; rel="last"
```

This gives us a preconstructed URL that can be used to fetch the next page of results, as well as an indication of how many total pages of results there are.

8.2.2 Making GitHub API Requests

Although it's not difficult to use a library like `requests` and make the most of this information by parsing it out ourselves, a library like `PyGithub` makes it that much easier and tackles the abstraction of the implementation details of GitHub's API, leaving us to work with a clean Pythonic API. Better yet, if GitHub changes the underlying implementation of its API, we'll still be able to use `PyGithub` and our code won't break.

Before making a request with `PyGithub`, also take a moment to look at the body of the response itself. It contains some rich information, but the piece we're most interested in is a field called `login`, which is the GitHub username of the user who is stargazing at the repository of interest. This information is the basis of issuing many other queries to other GitHub APIs, such as "List repositories being starred," (*http://bit.ly/1a1oc8X*) an API that returns a list of all repositories a user has starred. This is a powerful pivot because after we have started with an arbitrary repository and queried it for a list of users who are interested in it, we are then able to query those users for additional repositories of interest and potentially discover any patterns that might emerge.

For example, wouldn't it be interesting to know what is the next-most-bookmarked repository among all of the users who have bookmarked Mining-the-Social-Web? The answer to that question could be the basis of an intelligent recommendation that GitHub users would appreciate, and it doesn't take much creativity to imagine different domains in which intelligent recommendations could (and often do) provide enhanced user experiences in applications, as is the case with Amazon and Netflix. At its core, an interest graph inherently lends itself to making such intelligent recommendations, and that's one of the reasons that interest graphs have become such a conversation topic in certain niche circles of late.

Example 8-3 provides an example of how you could use `PyGithub` to retrieve all of the stargazers for a repository to seed an interest graph.

Example 8-3. Using PyGithub to query for stargazers of a particular repository

```
from github import Github # pip install pygithub

# Specify your own access token here

ACCESS_TOKEN = ''
```

```
# Specify a username and a repository of interest for that user

USER = 'ptwobrussell'
REPO = 'Mining-the-Social-Web'
#REPO = 'Mining-the-Social-Web-2nd-Edition'

client = Github(ACCESS_TOKEN, per_page=100)
user = client.get_user(USER)
repo = user.get_repo(REPO)

# Get a list of people who have bookmarked the repo.
# Since you'll get a lazy iterator back, you have to traverse
# it if you want to get the total number of stargazers.

stargazers = [ s for s in repo.get_stargazers() ]
print("Number of stargazers", len(stargazers))
```

Behind the scenes, PyGithub takes care of the API implementation details for you and simply exposes some convenient objects for query. In this case, we create a connection to GitHub and use the per_page keyword parameter to tell it that we'd like to receive the maximum number of results (100) as opposed to the default number (30) in each page of data that comes back. Then, we get a repository for a particular user and query for that repository's stargazers. It is possible for users to have repositories with identical names, so there is not an unambiguous way to query by just a repository's name. Since usernames and repository names could overlap, you need to take special care to specify the kind of object that you are working with when using GitHub's API if using one of these names as an identifier. We'll account for this as we create graphs with node names that may be ambiguous if we do not qualify them as repositories or users.

Finally, PyGithub generally provides "lazy iterators" as results, which in this case means that it does not attempt to fetch all 29 pages of results when the query is issued. Instead, it waits until a particular page is requested when iterating over the data before it retrieves that page. For this reason, we need to exhaust the lazy iterator with a list comprehension in order to actually count the number of stargazers with the API if we want to get an exact count.

PyGithub's documentation (*http://bit.ly/2qaoCtT*) is helpful, its API generally mimics the GitHub API in a predictable way, and you'll usually be able to use its pydoc, such as through the dir and help functions in a Python interpreter. Alternatively, tab completion and "question mark magic" in IPython or the Jupyter Notebook will get you to the same place in figuring out what methods are available to call on what objects. It would be worthwhile to poke around at the GitHub API a bit with PyGithub to better familiarize yourself with some of the possibilities before continuing further. As an exercise to test your skills, can you iterate over Mining-the-Social-Web's stargazers (or some subset thereof) and do some basic frequency analysis that determines which other repositories may be of common interest? You will likely find Python's `collec tions.Counter` or NLTK's `nltk.FreqDist` essential in easily computing frequency statistics.

8.3 Modeling Data with Property Graphs

You may recall from Chapter 2 that graphs were introduced in passing as a means of representing, analyzing, and visualizing social network data from Facebook. This section provides a more thorough discussion and hopefully serves as a useful primer for graph computing. Even though it is still a bit under the radar, the graph computing landscape is emerging rapidly given that graphs are a very natural abstraction for modeling many phenomena in the real world. Graphs offer a flexibility in data representation that is especially hard to beat during data experimentation and analysis when compared to other options, such as relational databases. Graph-centric analyses are certainly not a panacea for every problem, but an understanding of how to model your data with graphical structures is a powerful addition to your toolkit.

 A general introduction to graph theory is beyond the scope of this chapter, and the discussion that follows simply attempts to provide a gentle introduction to key concepts as they arise. You may enjoy the short YouTube video "Graph Theory—An Introduction!" (*http://bit.ly/1a1odto*) if you'd like to accumulate some general background knowledge before proceeding.

The remainder of this section introduces a common kind of graph called a *property graph* for the purpose of modeling GitHub data as an interest graph by way of a Python package called NetworkX (*http://bit.ly/1a1ocFV*). A property graph is a data structure that represents entities with *nodes* and relationships between the entities with *edges*. Each vertex has a unique identifier, a map of properties that are defined as key/value pairs, and a collection of edges. Likewise, edges are unique in that they connect nodes, can be uniquely identified, and can contain properties.

Figure 8-2 shows a trivial example of a property graph with two nodes that are uniquely identified by X and Y with an undescribed relationship between them. This particular graph is called a *digraph* because its edges are directed, which need not be the case unless the directionality of the edge is rooted in meaning for the domain being modeled.

Figure 8-2. A trivial property graph with directed edges

Expressed in code with NetworkX, a trivial property graph could be constructed as shown in Example 8-4. (You can use **pip install networkx** to install this package if you aren't using the book's turnkey virtual machine.)

Example 8-4. Constructing a trivial property graph

```
import networkx as nx # pip install networkx

# Create a directed graph

g = nx.DiGraph()

# Add an edge to the directed graph from X to Y

g.add_edge('X', 'Y')

# Print some statistics about the graph

print(nx.info(g))

# Get the nodes and edges from the graph

print("Nodes:", g.nodes())
print("Edges:", g.edges())
print()

# Get node properties

print("X props:", g.node['X'])
print("Y props:", g.node['Y'])
print()

# Get edge properties

print("X=>Y props:", g['X']['Y'])
print()

# Update a node property

g.node['X'].update({'prop1' : 'value1'})
print("X props:", g.node['X'])
print()

# Update an edge property

g['X']['Y'].update({'label' : 'label1'})
print("X=>Y props:", g['X']['Y'])
```

Sample output from the example follows:

```
Name:
Type: DiGraph
Number of nodes: 2
Number of edges: 1
Average in degree:    0.5000
Average out degree:   0.5000

Nodes: ['Y', 'X']
Edges: [('X', 'Y')]

X props: {}
Y props: {}
X=>Y props: {}

X props: {'prop1': 'value1'}

X=>Y props: {'label': 'label1'}
```

In this particular example, the add_edge method of the digraph adds an edge from a node that's uniquely identified by X to a node that's uniquely identified by Y, resulting in a graph with two nodes and one edge between them. In terms of its unique identifier, this node would be represented by the tuple (X, Y) since both nodes that it connects are uniquely identified themselves. Be aware that adding an edge from Y back to X would create a second edge in the graph, and this second edge could contain its own set of edge properties. In general, you wouldn't want to create this second edge since you can get a node's incoming or outgoing edges and effectively traverse the edge in either direction, but there may be some situations in which it is more convenient to explicitly include the additional edge.

The *degree* of a node in a graph is the number of incident edges to it, and for a directed graph, there is a notion of *in degree* and *out degree* since edges have direction. The average in degree and average out degree values provide a normalized score for the graph that represents the number of nodes that have incoming and outgoing edges. In this particular case, the directed graph has a single directed edge, so there is one node with an outgoing edge and one node with an incoming edge.

The in and out degrees of a node are fundamental concepts in graph theory. Assuming you know the number of vertices in the graph, the average degree provides a measure of the graph's *density*: the number of actual edges compared to the number of possible edges if the graph were fully connected. In a fully connected graph, each node is connected to every other node, and in the case of a directed graph, this means that all nodes have incoming edges from all other nodes.

You calculate the average in degree for an entire graph by summing the values of each node's in degree and dividing the total by the number of nodes in the graph, which is 1 divided by 2 in Example 8-4. The average out degree calculation is computed the same way except that the sum of each node's out degree is used as the value to divide by the number of nodes in the graph. When you're considering an entire directed graph, there will always be an equal number of incoming edges and outgoing edges because each edge connects only two nodes,[1] and the average in degree and average out degree values for the entire graph will be the same.

 In the general case, the maximum values for average in and out degree in a graph are one less than the number of nodes in the graph. Take a moment to convince yourself that this is the case by considering the number of edges that are necessary to fully connect all of the nodes in a graph.

In the next section, we'll construct an interest graph using these same property graph primitives and illustrate these additional methods at work on real-world data. First, take a moment to explore by adding some nodes, edges, and properties to the graph. The NetworkX documentation (*http://bit.ly/1a1ocFV*) provides a number of useful introductory examples that you can also explore if this is one of your first encounters with graphs and you'd like some extra instruction as a primer.

The Rise of Big Graph Databases

This chapter introduces property graphs, versatile data structures that can be used to model complex networks with nodes and edges as simple primitives. We'll be modeling the data according to a flexible graph schema that's based largely on natural intuition, and for a narrowly focused domain, this pragmatic approach is often sufficient. As we'll see throughout the remainder of this chapter, property graphs provide flexibility and versatility in modeling and querying complex data.

NetworkX, the Python-based graph toolkit used throughout this book, provides a powerful toolbox for modeling property graphs. Be aware, however, that NetworkX is an in-memory graph database. The limit of what it can do for you is directly proportional to the amount of working memory that you have on the machine on which you are running it. In many situations, you can work around the memory limitation by constraining the domain to a subset of the data or by using a machine with more working memory. In an increasing number of situations involving "big data" and its burgeoning ecosystem that largely involves Hadoop and NoSQL databases, however, in-memory graphs are simply not an option.

---

1 A more abstract version of a graph called a *hypergraph* (*http://bit.ly/1a1ocWm*) contains *hyperedges* that can connect an arbitrary number of vertices.

8.4 Analyzing GitHub Interest Graphs

Now equipped with the tools to both query GitHub's API and model the data that comes back as a graph, let's put our skills to the test and begin constructing and analyzing an interest graph. We'll start with a repository that will represent a common interest among a group of GitHub users and use GitHub's API to discover the stargazers for this repository. From there, we'll be able to use other APIs to model social connections between GitHub users who follow one another and hone in on other interests that these users might share.

We'll also learn about some fundamental techniques for analyzing graphs called *centrality measures*. Although a visual layout of a graph is tremendously useful, many graphs are simply too large or complex for an effective visual inspection, and centrality measures can be helpful in analytically measuring aspects of the network structure. (But don't worry, we will also visualize a graph before closing this chapter.)

8.4.1 Seeding an Interest Graph

Recall that an interest graph and a social graph (*http://bit.ly/1a1ofl4*) are not the same thing. Whereas a social graph's primary focus is representing connections between people and it generally requires a mutual relationship between the parties involved, an interest graph connects people and interests and involves unidirectional edges. Although the two are by no means totally disjoint concepts, do not confuse the connection between a GitHub user following another GitHub user with a social connection—it is an "interested in" connection because there is not a mutual acceptance criterion involved.

 A classic example of a hybridized graphical model that would qualify as a social interest graph is Facebook. It started primarily as a technology platform based upon the concept of a social graph, but the incorporation of the Like button squarely catapulted it into hybrid territory that could be articulated as a social interest graph. It explicitly represents connections between people as well as connections between people and the things that they are interested in. Twitter has always been a type of interest graph with its asymmetric "following" model, which can be interpreted as a connection between a person and the things (which could be other people) that person is interested in.

Examples 8-5 and 8-6 will introduce code samples to construct the initial "gazes" relationships between users and repositories, demonstrating how to explore the graphical structure that emerges. The graph that is initially constructed can be referred to as an *ego graph* in that there is a central point of focus (an ego) that is the basis for most (in this case, all) of the edges. An ego graph is sometimes called a "hub and spoke graph" or a "star graph" since it resembles a hub with spokes emanating from it and looks like a star when rendered visually.

From the standpoint of a graph schema, the graph contains two types of nodes and one type of edge, as is demonstrated in Figure 8-3.

We'll use the graph schema shown in Figure 8-3 as a starting point and evolve it with modifications throughout the remainder of this chapter.

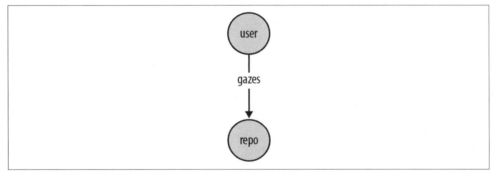

Figure 8-3. The basis of a graph schema that includes GitHub users who are interested in repositories

There is a subtle but important constraint in data modeling that involves the avoidance of naming collisions: usernames and repository names may (and often do) collide with one another. For example, there could be a GitHub user named "ptwobrussell," as well as multiple repositories named "ptwobrussell." Recalling that the add_edge method uses the items passed in as its first two parameters as unique identifiers, we can append either "(user)" or "(repo)" to the items to ensure that all nodes in the graph will be unique. From the standpoint of modeling with NetworkX, appending a type for the node mostly takes care of the problem.

Along the same lines, repositories that are owned by different users can have the same name, whether they are forks of the same code base or entirely different code bases. At the moment this particular detail is of no concern to us, but once we begin to add in other repositories that other GitHub users are stargazing at, the possibility of this kind of collision will increase.

Whether to allow these types of collisions or to implement a graph construction strategy that avoids them is a design decision that carries with it certain consequences. For example, it would probably be desirable to have forks of the same repository collapse into the same node in the graph as opposed to representing them all as different repositories, but you would certainly not want completely different projects that shared a name to collapse into the same node.

 Given the limited scope of the problem that we are solving and that it's initially focusing on a particular repository of interest, we'll opt to avoid the complexity that disambiguating repository names introduces.

With that in mind, take a look at Example 8-5, which constructs an ego graph of a repository and its stargazers, and Example 8-6, which introduces some useful graph operations.

Example 8-5. Constructing an ego graph of a repository and its stargazers

```
# Expand the initial graph with (interest) edges pointing in each direction for
# additional people interested. Take care to ensure that user and repo nodes
# do not collide by appending their type.

import networkx as nx

g = nx.DiGraph()
g.add_node(repo.name + '(repo)', type='repo', lang=repo.language, owner=user.login)

for sg in stargazers:
    g.add_node(sg.login + '(user)', type='user')
    g.add_edge(sg.login + '(user)', repo.name + '(repo)', type='gazes')
```

Example 8-6. Introducing some handy graph operations

```
# Poke around in the current graph to get a better feel for how NetworkX works

print(nx.info(g))
print()
print(g.node['Mining-the-Social-Web(repo)'])
print(g.node['ptwobrussell(user)'])
print()
print(g['ptwobrussell(user)']['Mining-the-Social-Web(repo)'])

# The next line would throw a KeyError since no such edge exists:
# print g['Mining-the-Social-Web(repo)']['ptwobrussell(user)']
print()
print(g['ptwobrussell(user)'])
print(g['Mining-the-Social-Web(repo)'])
```

```
print()
print(g.in_edges(['ptwobrussell(user)']))
print(g.out_edges(['ptwobrussell(user)']))
print()
print(g.in_edges(['Mining-the-Social-Web(repo)']))
print(g.out_edges(['Mining-the-Social-Web(repo)']))
```

The following sample (abbreviated) output demonstrates some of the possibilities based upon the graph operations just shown:

```
Name:
Type: DiGraph
Number of nodes: 1117
Number of edges: 1116
Average in degree:    0.9991
Average out degree:    0.9991

{'lang': u'JavaScript', 'owner': u'ptwobrussell', 'type': 'repo'}
{'type': 'user'}

{'type': 'gazes'}

{u'Mining-the-Social-Web(repo)': {'type': 'gazes'}}
{}

[]
[('ptwobrussell(user)', u'Mining-the-Social-Web(repo)')]

[(u'gregmoreno(user)', 'Mining-the-Social-Web(repo)'),
 (u'SathishRaju(user)', 'Mining-the-Social-Web(repo)'),
 ...
]
[]
```

With an initial interest graph in place, we can get creative in determining which steps might be most interesting to take next. What we know so far is that there are approximately 1,116 users who share a common interest in social web mining, as indicated by their stargazing association to ptwobrussell's Mining-the-Social-Web repository. As expected, the number of edges in the graph is one less than the number of nodes. The reason that this is the case is because there is a one-to-one correspondence at this point between the stargazers and the repository (an edge must exist to connect each stargazer to the repository).

If you recall that the average in degree and average out degree metrics yield a normalized value that provides a measure for the density of the graph, the value of 0.9991 should confirm our intuition. We know that we have 1,117 nodes corresponding to stargazers that each have an out degree equal to 1, and 1 node corresponding to a repository that has an in degree of 1117. In other words, we know that the number of edges in the graph is one less than the number of nodes. The density of edges in the graph is quite low given that the maximum value for the average degree in this case is 1117.

It might be tempting to think about the topology of the graph, knowing that it looks like a star if visually rendered, and try to make some kind of connection to the value of 0.9991. It is true that we have one node that is connected to all other nodes in the graph, but it would be a mistake to generalize and try to make some kind of connection to the average degree being approximately 1.0 based on this single node. It could just as easily have been the case that the 1,117 nodes could have been connected in many other configurations to arrive at a value of 0.9991. To gain insight that would support this kind of conclusion we would need to consider additional analytics, such as the centrality measures introduced in the next section.

8.4.2 Computing Graph Centrality Measures

A centrality measure is a fundamental graph analytic that provides insight into the relative importance of a particular node in a graph. Let's consider the following centrality measures, which will help us more carefully examine graphs to gain insights about networks:

Degree centrality

> The degree centrality of a node in the graph is a measure of the number of incident edges upon it. Think of this centrality measure as a way of tabulating the frequency of incident edges on nodes for the purpose of measuring uniformity among them, finding the nodes with the highest or lowest numbers of incident edges, or otherwise trying to discover patterns that provide insight into the network topology based on number of connections as a primary motivation. The degree centrality of a node is just one facet that is useful in reasoning about its role in a network, and it provides a good starting point for identifying outliers or anomalies with respect to connectedness relative to other nodes in the graph. In aggregate, we also know from our earlier discussion that the average degree centrality tells us something about the density of an overall graph. NetworkX provides networkx.degree_centrality as a built-in function to compute the degree centrality of a graph. It returns a dictionary that maps the ID of each node to its degree centrality.

Betweenness centrality

The betweenness centrality of a node is a measure of how often it connects any other nodes in the graph in the sense of being *in between* other nodes. You might think about betweenness centrality as a measure of how critical a node is in connecting other nodes as a broker or gateway. Although not necessarily the case, the loss of nodes with a high betweenness centrality measure could be quite disruptive to the flow of energy[2] in a graph, and in some circumstances removing nodes with high betweenness centrality can disintegrate a graph into smaller subgraphs. NetworkX provides `networkx.betweenness_centrality` as a built-in function to compute the betweenness centrality of a graph. It returns a dictionary that maps the ID of each node to its betweenness centrality.

Closeness centrality

The closeness centrality of a node is a measure of how highly connected ("close") it is to all other nodes in the graph. This centrality measure is also predicated on the notion of shortest paths in the graph and offers insight into how well connected a particular node is in the graph. Unlike a node's betweenness centrality, which tells you something about how integral it is in connecting nodes as a broker or gateway, a node's closeness centrality accounts more for direct connections. Think of closeness in terms of a node's ability to spread energy to all other nodes in a graph. NetworkX provides `networkx.closeness_centrality` as a built-in function to compute the closeness centrality of a graph. It returns a dictionary that maps the ID of each node to its closeness centrality.

NetworkX provides a number of powerful centrality measures (*http://1.usa.gov/2MC1ZGV*) in its online documentation.

Figure 8-4 shows the Krackhardt kite graph (*http://bit.ly/1a1oixa*), a well-studied graph in social network analysis that illustrates the differences among the centrality measures introduced in this section. It's called a "kite graph" because when rendered visually, it has the appearance of a kite.

---

2 In the current discussion, the term "energy" is used to generically describe flow within an abstract graph.

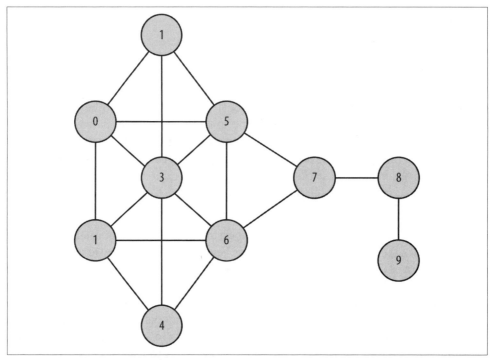

Figure 8-4. The Krackhardt kite graph that will be used to illustrate degree, betweenness, and closeness centrality measures

Example 8-7 shows some code that loads this graph from NetworkX and calculates centrality measures on it, which are reproduced in Table 8-1. Although it has no bearing on the calculations, note that this particular graph is commonly used as a reference in social networking. As such, the edges are not directed since a connection in a social network implies a mutual acceptance criterion. In NetworkX, it is an instance of `networkx.Graph` as opposed to `networkx.DiGraph`.

Example 8-7. Calculating degree, betweenness, and closeness centrality measures on the Krackhardt kite graph

```
from operator import itemgetter
from IPython.display import HTML
from IPython.core.display import display

display(HTML('<img src="resources/ch08-github/kite-graph.png" width="400px">'))

# The classic Krackhardt kite graph
kkg = nx.generators.small.krackhardt_kite_graph()

print("Degree Centrality")
```

```
print(sorted(nx.degree_centrality(kkg).items(),
            key=itemgetter(1), reverse=True))
print()

print("Betweenness Centrality")
print(sorted(nx.betweenness_centrality(kkg).items(),
            key=itemgetter(1), reverse=True))
print()

print("Closeness Centrality")
print(sorted(nx.closeness_centrality(kkg).items(),
            key=itemgetter(1), reverse=True))
```

Table 8-1. Degree, betweenness, and closeness centrality measures for the Krackhardt kite graph (maximum values for each column are presented in bold so that you can easily test your intuition against the graph presented in Figure 8-4)

Node	Degree centrality	Betweenness centrality	Closeness centrality
0	0.44	0.02	0.53
1	0.44	0.02	0.53
2	0.33	0.00	0.50
3	**0.67**	0.10	0.60
4	0.33	0	0.50
5	0.55	0.2	**0.64**
6	0.55	0.2	**0.64**
7	0.33	**0.39**	0.60
8	0.22	0.22	0.43
9	0.11	0.00	0.31

Spend a few moments studying the Krackhardt kite graph and the centrality measures associated with it before moving on to the next section. These centrality measures will remain in our toolbox moving forward through this chapter.

8.4.3 Extending the Interest Graph with "Follows" Edges for Users

In addition to stargazing and forking repositories, GitHub also features a Twitter-esque notion of "following" other users. In this section, we'll query GitHub's API and add "follows" relationships to the graph. Based upon our earlier discussions (such as the one in "Why Is Twitter All the Rage?") about how Twitter is inherently an interest graph, you know that adding these is basically a way of capturing more interest relationships, since a "following" relationship is essentially the same as an "interested in" relationship.

It's a good bet that the owner of a repository is likely to be popular within the community that is stargazing at the repository, but who else might be popular in that community? The answer to this question would certainly be an important insight and provide the basis for a useful pivot into further analysis. Let's answer it by querying GitHub's Followers API (*http://bit.ly/1a1oixo*) for the followers of each user in the graph and adding edges to the graph to indicate follows relationships that exist within it. In terms of our graphical model, these additions only insert additional edges into the graph; no new nodes need to be introduced.

While it would be possible to add all follows relationships that we get back from Git-Hub to the graph, for now we are limiting our analysis to users who have shown an explicit interest in the repository that is the seed of the graph. Example 8-8 illustrates the sample code that adds following edges to the graph, and Figure 8-5 depicts the updated graph schema that now includes following relationships.

 Given GitHub's authenticated rate limit of 5,000 requests per hour, you would need to make more than 80 requests per minute in order to exceed the rate limit. This is somewhat unlikely given the latency incurred with each request, so no special logic is included in this chapter's code samples to cope with the rate limit.

Example 8-8. Adding additional interest edges to the graph through the inclusion of "follows" edges

```
# Add (social) edges from the stargazers' followers. This can take a while
# because of all of the potential API calls to GitHub. The approximate number
# of requests for followers for each iteration of this loop can be calculated as
# math.ceil(sg.get_followers() / 100.0) per the API returning up to 100 items
# at a time.

import sys

for i, sg in enumerate(stargazers):

    # Add "follows" edges between stargazers in the graph if any relationships exist
    try:
        for follower in sg.get_followers():
            if follower.login + '(user)' in g:
                g.add_edge(follower.login + '(user)', sg.login + '(user)',
                        type='follows')
    except Exception as e: #ssl.SSLError
        print("Encountered an error fetching followers for", sg.login,
            "Skipping.", file=sys.stderr)
        print(e, file=sys.stderr)

    print("Processed", i+1, " stargazers. Num nodes/edges in graph",
        g.number_of_nodes(), "/", g.number_of_edges())
    print("Rate limit remaining", client.rate_limiting)
```

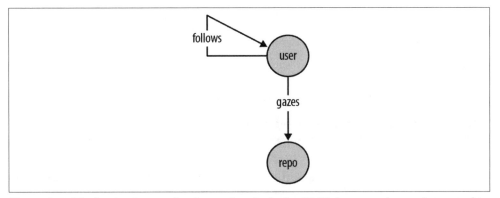

Figure 8-5. The basis of a graph schema that includes GitHub users who are interested in repositories as well as other users

With the incorporation of additional interest data into the graph, the possibilities for analysis become much more interesting. We can now traverse the graph to compute a notion of popularity by counting the number of incoming "follows" edges for a particular user, as demonstrated in Example 8-9. What is so powerful about this analysis is that it enables us to quickly discover who might be the most interesting or influential users to examine for a particular domain of interest.

Example 8-9. Exploring the updated graph's "follows" edges

```
from operator import itemgetter
from collections import Counter

# Let's see how many social edges we added since last time
print(nx.info(g))
print()

# The number of "follows" edges is the difference
print(len([e for e in g.edges_iter(data=True) if e[2]['type'] == 'follows']))
print()

# The repository owner is possibly one of the more popular users in this graph
print(len([e
          for e in g.edges_iter(data=True)
              if e[2]['type'] == 'follows' and e[1] == 'ptwobrussell(user)']))
print()

# Let's examine the number of adjacent edges to each node
print(sorted([n for n in g.degree_iter()], key=itemgetter(1), reverse=True)[:10])
print()

# Consider the ratio of incoming and outgoing edges for a couple of users with
# high node degrees...
```

```
# A user who follows many but is not followed back by many

print(len(g.out_edges('mcanthony(user)')))
print(len(g.in_edges('mcanthony(user)')))
print()

# A user who is followed by many but does not follow back

print(len(g.out_edges('ptwobrussell(user)')))
print(len(g.in_edges('ptwobrussell(user)')))
print()

c = Counter([e[1] for e in g.edges_iter(data=True) if e[2]['type'] == 'follows'])
popular_users = [ (u, f) for (u, f) in c.most_common() if f > 1 ]
print("Number of popular users", len(popular_users))
print("Top 10 popular users:", popular_users[:10])
```

Given that we seeded the graph with the Mining-the-Social-Web repository, a plausible hypothesis is that users who are interested in this topic may have some affiliation with or interest in data mining, and might even have an interest in the Python programming language since its code base is mostly written in Python. Let's explore whether the most popular users, as calculated by Example 8-9, have any affiliation with this programming language.

Sample output follows:

```
Name:
Type: DiGraph
Number of nodes: 1117
Number of edges: 2721
Average in degree:   2.4360
Average out degree:   2.4360

1605

125

[('Mining-the-Social-Web(repo)', 1116),
 ('angusshire(user)', 511),
 ('kennethreitz(user)', 156),
 ('ptwobrussell(user)', 126),
 ('VagrantStory(user)', 106),
 ('beali(user)', 92),
 ('trietptm(user)', 71),
 ('rohithadassanayake(user)', 48),
 ('mcanthony(user)', 37),
 ('daimajia(user)', 36)]

32
5

1
```

```
Number of popular users 270
Top 10 popular users:
[('kennethreitz(user)', 153),
 ('ptwobrussell(user)', 125),
 ('daimajia(user)', 32),
 ('hammer(user)', 21),
 ('isnowfy(user)', 20),
 ('jakubroztocil(user)', 20),
 ('japerk(user)', 19),
 ('angusshire(user)', 18),
 ('dgryski(user)', 12),
 ('tswicegood(user)', 11)]
```

As we might have guessed, the owner of the repository that seeded the original interest graph, ptwobrussell (*http://bit.ly/1a1o4GC*), is among the most popular users in the graph, but another user (kennethreitz) has more, at 153 followers, and there are several other users in the top 10 with a nontrivial number of followers. Among other things, it turns out that kennethreitz (*http://bit.ly/1a1ojkT*) is the author of the popular requests Python package that has been used throughout this book. We also see that mcanthony is a user who follows many users but is not followed back by many users. (We'll return to this latter observation in a moment.)

Application of centrality measures

Before we do any additional work, let's save a view of our graph so that we have a stable snapshot of our current state in case we'd like to tinker with the graph and recover it later, or in case we'd like to serialize and share the data. Example 8-10 demonstrates how to save and restore graphs using NetworkX's built-in pickling capabilities.

Example 8-10. Snapshotting (pickling) the graph's state to disk

```
# Save your work by serializing out (pickling) the graph
nx.write_gpickle(g, "resources/ch08-github/data/github.gpickle.1")

# How to restore the graph...
# import networkx as nx
# g = nx.read_gpickle("resources/ch08-github/data/github.gpickle.1")
```

With a backup of our work saved out to disk, let's now apply the centrality measures from the previous section to this graph and interpret the results. Since we know that Mining-the-Social-Web(repo) is a *supernode* in the graph and connects the majority of the users (all of them in this case), we'll remove it from the graph to get a better view of the network dynamics that might be at play. This leaves behind only GitHub users and the "follows" edges between them. Example 8-11 illustrates some code that provides a starting point for analysis.

Example 8-11. Applying centrality measures to the interest graph

```
from operator import itemgetter

# Create a copy of the graph so that we can iteratively mutate the copy
# as needed for experimentation

h = g.copy()

# Remove the seed of the interest graph, which is a supernode, in order
# to get a better idea of the network dynamics

h.remove_node('Mining-the-Social-Web(repo)')

# Remove any other nodes that appear to be supernodes.
# Filter any other nodes that you can by threshold
# criteria or heuristics from inspection.

# Display the centrality measures for the top 10 nodes


dc = sorted(nx.degree_centrality(h).items(),
            key=itemgetter(1), reverse=True)

print("Degree Centrality")
print(dc[:10])
print()

bc = sorted(nx.betweenness_centrality(h).items(),
            key=itemgetter(1), reverse=True)

print("Betweenness Centrality")
print(bc[:10])
print()

print("Closeness Centrality")
cc = sorted(nx.closeness_centrality(h).items(),
            key=itemgetter(1), reverse=True)
print(cc[:10])
```

Sample results follow:

```
Degree Centrality
[('angusshire(user)', 0.45739910313901344),
 ('kennethreitz(user)', 0.13901345291479822),
 ('ptwobrussell(user)', 0.11210762331838565),
 ('VagrantStory(user)', 0.09417040358744394),
 ('beali(user)', 0.08161434977578476),
```

```
    ('trietptm(user)', 0.06278026905829596),
    ('rohithadassanayake(user)', 0.042152466367713005),
    ('mcanthony(user)', 0.03228699551569507),
    ('daimajia(user)', 0.03139013452914798),
    ('JT5D(user)', 0.029596412556053813)]

Betweenness Centrality
[('angusshire(user)', 0.012199321617913778),
    ('rohithadassanayake(user)', 0.0024989064307240636),
    ('trietptm(user)', 0.0016462150915044311),
    ('douglas(user)', 0.0014378758725072656),
    ('JT5D(user)', 0.00066300082719888302),
    ('mcanthony(user)', 0.0006042022778087548),
    ('VagrantStory(user)', 0.0005563053609377326),
    ('beali(user)', 0.0005419295788331876),
    ('LawrencePeng(user)', 0.0005133545798221231),
    ('frac(user)', 0.0004898921995636457)]

Closeness Centrality
[('angusshire(user)', 0.45124556968457424),
    ('VagrantStory(user)', 0.2824285214515154),
    ('beali(user)', 0.2801929394875192),
    ('trietptm(user)', 0.2665936169015141),
    ('rohithadassanayake(user)', 0.26460080747284836),
    ('mcanthony(user)', 0.255887045941614),
    ('marctmiller(user)', 0.2522401996811634),
    ('cwz8202(user)', 0.24927963395720612),
    ('uetchy(user)', 0.24792169042592171),
    ('LawrencePeng(user)', 0.24734423307244519)]
```

As in our previous analysis, the users ptwobrussell and kennethreitz appear near the top of the list for degree centrality, as expected. However, another user, angusshire, appears at the top of the chart for all centrality measures. This user is a supernode, following and followed by many thousands of other users. If we removed this user from the graph, it would likely change the network dynamics.

Another observation is that the closeness centrality and degree centrality values are much higher than the betweenness centrality value, which is virtually at zero. In the context of "following" relationships, this means that no user in the graph is effectively acting as a bridge in connecting other users in the graph. This makes sense because the original seed of the graph was a repository, which provided a common interest. While it would have been worthwhile to discover that there was a user whose betweenness had a meaningful value, it is not all that unexpected that this was not the case. Had the basis of the interest graph been a particular *user*, the dynamics might have turned out to be different.

Finally, observe that while ptwobrussell and kennethreitz are popular users in the graph, they do not appear in the top 10 users for closeness centrality. Several other users do appear, have a nontrivial value for closeness, and would be interesting to examine. Keep in mind that the dynamic will vary from community to community.

 A worthwhile exercise would be to compare and contrast the network dynamics of two different communities, such as the Ruby on Rails community and the Django community. You might also try comparing the dynamics of a Microsoft-centric community versus a Linux-oriented community.

Adding more repositories to the interest graph

All in all, nothing that interesting turned up in our analysis of the "follows" edges in the graph, which isn't all that surprising when we recall that the seed of the interest graph was a repository that drew in disparate users from all over the world. What might be worthwhile as a next step would be trying to find additional interests for each user in the graph by iterating over them and adding their starred repositories to the graph. Doing this would give us at least two valuable pieces of insight: what other repositories are engaging to this community that is grounded in social web mining (and, to a lesser degree, Python), and what programming languages are popular among this community, given that GitHub attempts to index repositories and determine the programming languages used.

The process of adding repositories and "gazes" edges to the graph is just a simple extension of our previous work in this chapter. GitHub's "List repositories being starred" API (*http://bit.ly/1a1oc8X*) makes it easy enough to get back the list of repositories that a particular user has starred, and we'll just iterate over these results and add the same kinds of nodes and edges to the graph that we added earlier in this chapter. Example 8-12 illustrates the sample code for making this happen. It adds a significant amount of data to the in-memory graph and can take a while to execute. A bit of patience is required if you're working with a repository with more than a few dozen stargazers.

Example 8-12. Adding starred repositories to the graph

```
# Add each stargazer's additional starred repos and add edges
# to find additional interests

MAX_REPOS = 500

for i, sg in enumerate(stargazers):
    print(sg.login)
    try:
        for starred in sg.get_starred()[:MAX_REPOS]: # Slice to avoid supernodes
            g.add_node(starred.name + '(repo)', type='repo', lang=starred.language,
                       owner=starred.owner.login)
            g.add_edge(sg.login + '(user)', starred.name + '(repo)', type='gazes')
```

```
except Exception as e: #ssl.SSLError:
    print("Encountered an error fetching starred repos for", sg.login,
          "Skipping.")

print("Processed", i+1, "stargazers' starred repos")
print("Num nodes/edges in graph", g.number_of_nodes(), "/", g.number_of_edges())
print("Rate limit", client.rate_limiting)
```

One subtle concern with constructing this graph is that while most users have starred a "reasonable" number of repositories, some users may have starred an extremely high number of repositories, falling far outside statistical norms and introducing a highly disproportionate number of edges and nodes to the graph. As previously noted, a node with an extreme number of edges that is an outlier by a large margin is called a *supernode*. It is usually not desirable to model graphs (especially in-memory graphs such as the ones implemented by NetworkX) with supernodes because at best they can significantly complicate traversals and other analytics, and at worst they can cause out-of-memory errors. Your particular situation and objectives will determine whether it's appropriate for you to include supernodes.

A reasonable option that we employ to avoid introducing supernodes into the graph with Example 8-12 is to simply cap the number of repositories that we'll consider for a user. In this particular case, we limit the number of repositories under consideration to a fairly high number (500) by slicing the results of the values being iterated over in the for loop as get_starred()[:500]. Later, if we're interested in revisiting the supernodes, we'll need to query our graph only for nodes that have a high number of outgoing edges in order to discover them.

 Python, including the Jupyter Notebook server kernel, will use as much memory as required as you continue adding data to the graph. If you attempt to create a graph so large that your operating system can no longer function, a kernel supervisor process may kill the offending Python process.

With a graph now constructed that contains additional repositories, we can start having some real fun in querying the graph. There are a number of questions we could now ask and answer beyond the calculation of simple statistics to update us on the overall size of the graph—it might be interesting to zoom in on the user who owns the most repositories that are being watched, for example. Perhaps one of the most pressing questions is what the most popular repositories in the graph are, besides the repository that was used to seed the original interest graph. Example 8-13 demonstrates a sample block of code that answers this question and provides a starting point for further analysis.

Several other useful properties come back from PyGithub's get_starred API call—a wrapper around GitHub's "List repositories being starred" API (*http://bit.ly/1a1oc8X*)—that you might want to consider for future experiments. Be sure to review the API docs so that you don't miss out on anything that might be of use to you in exploring this space.

Example 8-13. Exploring the graph after updates with additional starred repositories

```
# Poke around: how to get users/repos
from operator import itemgetter

print(nx.info(g))
print()

# Get a list of repositories from the graph

repos = [n for n in g.nodes_iter() if g.node[n]['type'] == 'repo']

# Most popular repos

print("Popular repositories")
print(sorted([(n,d)
              for (n,d) in g.in_degree_iter()
                  if g.node[n]['type'] == 'repo'],
             key=itemgetter(1), reverse=True)[:10])
print()

# Projects gazed at by a user

print("Respositories that ptwobrussell has bookmarked")
print([(n,g.node[n]['lang'])
       for n in g['ptwobrussell(user)']
           if g['ptwobrussell(user)'][n]['type'] == 'gazes'])
print()

# Programming languages for each user

print("Programming languages ptwobrussell is interested in")
print(list(set([g.node[n]['lang']
                for n in g['ptwobrussell(user)']
                    if g['ptwobrussell(user)'][n]['type'] == 'gazes'])))
print()

# Find supernodes in the graph by approximating with a high number of
# outgoing edges

print("Supernode candidates")
print(sorted([(n, len(g.out_edges(n)))
              for n in g.nodes_iter()
```

```
                  if g.node[n]['type'] == 'user' and len(g.out_edges(n)) > 500],
              key=itemgetter(1), reverse=True))
```

Sample output follows:

```
Name:
Type: DiGraph
Number of nodes: 106643
Number of edges: 383807
Average in degree:    3.5990
Average out degree:   3.5990

Popular repositories
[('Mining-the-Social-Web(repo)', 1116),
 ('bootstrap(repo)', 246),
 ('d3(repo)', 224),
 ('tensorflow(repo)', 204),
 ('dotfiles(repo)', 196),
 ('free-programming-books(repo)', 179),
 ('Mining-the-Social-Web-2nd-Edition(repo)', 147),
 ('requests(repo)', 138),
 ('storm(repo)', 137),
 ('Probabilistic-Programming-and-Bayesian-Methods-for-Hackers(repo)', 136)]

Respositories that ptwobrussell has bookmarked
[('Mining-the-Social-Web(repo)', 'JavaScript'),
 ('re2(repo)', 'C++'),
 ('google-cloud-python(repo)', 'Python'),
 ('CNTK(repo)', 'C++'),
 ('django-s3direct(repo)', 'Python'),
 ('medium-editor-insert-plugin(repo)', 'JavaScript'),
 ('django-ckeditor(repo)', 'JavaScript'),
 ('rq(repo)', 'Python'),
 ('x-editable(repo)', 'JavaScript'),
 ...
]

Programming languages ptwobrussell is interested in
['Python', 'HTML', 'JavaScript', 'Ruby', 'CSS', 'Common Lisp',
    'CoffeeScript', 'Objective-C', 'PostScript', 'Jupyter
    Notebook', 'Perl', 'C#', 'C', 'C++', 'Lua', 'Java', None, 'Go',
    'Shell', 'Clojure']

Supernode candidates
[('angusshire(user)', 1004),
 ('VagrantStory(user)', 618),
 ('beali(user)', 605),
 ('trietptm(user)', 586),
 ('rohithadassanayake(user)', 579),
 ('zmughal(user)', 556),
 ('LJ001(user)', 556),
 ('JT5D(user)', 554),
 ('kcnickerson(user)', 549),
```

```
    . . .
  ]
```

An initial observation is that the number of edges in the new graph is three orders of magnitude higher than in the previous graph, and the number of nodes is up well over one order of magnitude. This is where analysis can really get interesting because of the complex network dynamics. However, the complex network dynamics also mean that it will take nontrivial amounts of time for NetworkX to compute global graph statistics. Keep in mind that just because the graph is in memory doesn't mean that all computation will necessarily be fast. A basic working knowledge of some fundamental computing principles can be helpful in these circumstances.

Computational considerations

 This brief section contains a somewhat advanced discussion that describes some of the mathematical complexity involved in running graph algorithms. You are encouraged to read it, though you could opt to revisit this later if this is your first reading of this chapter.

For the three centrality measures being computed, we know that the calculation of degree centrality is relatively simple and should be fast, requiring little more than a single pass over the nodes to compute the number of incident edges. Both betweenness and closeness centralities, however, require computation of the minimum spanning tree (*http://bit.ly/1a1omgr*). The underlying NetworkX minimum spanning tree algorithm (*http://bit.ly/2DdURBx*) implements Kruskal's algorithm (*http://bit.ly/ 1a1on3X*), which is a staple in computer science education. In terms of runtime complexity, it takes on the order of $O(E \log E)$, where E represents the number of edges in the graph. Algorithms of this complexity are generally considered efficient, but 100,000 * log(100,000) is still approximately equal to one million operations, so a full analysis can take some time.

The removal of supernodes is critical in achieving reasonable runtimes for network algorithms, and a targeted exploration in which you extract a subgraph (*http://bit.ly/ 2IzO1DQ*) of interest for more thorough analysis is an option to consider. For example, you may want to selectively prune users from the graph based upon filtering criteria such as their number of followers, which could provide a basis for judging their importance to the overall network. You might also consider pruning repositories based on a threshold for a minimum number of stargazers.

When conducting analyses on large graphs, you are advised to examine each of the centrality measures one at a time so that you can more quickly iterate on the results. It is also critical to remove supernodes from the graph in order to achieve reasonable runtimes, since supernodes can easily dominate computation in network algorithms.

Depending on the size of your graph, this may also be a situation in which increasing the amount of memory available to your virtual machine could be beneficial.

8.4.4 Using Nodes as Pivots for More Efficient Queries

Another characteristic of the data to consider is the popularity of programming languages that are employed by users. It could be the case that users star projects that are implemented in programming languages that they are at least loosely interested in and able to use themselves. Although we have the data and the tools to analyze users and popular programming languages with our existing graph, our schema currently has a shortcoming. Since a programming language is modeled as an attribute on a repository, it is necessary to scan all of the repository nodes and either extract or filter by this attribute in order to answer nontrivial questions.

For example, if we wanted to know which programming languages a user programs in using the current schema, we'd need to look up all of the repositories that user gazes at, extract the lang properties, and compute a frequency distribution. This doesn't seem too cumbersome, but what if we wanted to know how many users program in a particular programming language? Although the answer is computable with the existing schema, it requires a scan of every repository node and a count of all of the incoming "gazes" edges. With a modification to the graph schema, however, answering this question could be as simple as accessing a single node in the graph. The modification would involve creating a node in the graph for each programming language that has incoming programs edges that connect users who program in that language, and outgoing implements edges that connect repositories.

Figure 8-6 illustrates our final graph schema, which incorporates programming languages as well as edges between users, repositories, and programming languages. The overall effect of this schema change is that we've taken a property of one node and created an explicit relationship in the graph that was previously implicit. From the standpoint of completeness, there is no new data, but the data that we do have can now be computed on more efficiently for certain queries. Although the schema is fairly simple, the universe of possible graphs adhering to it that could be easily constructed and mined for valuable knowledge is immense.

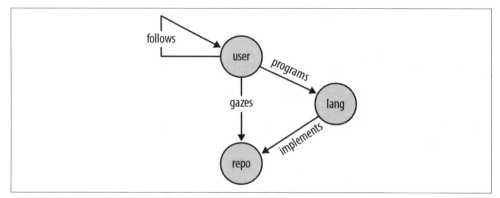

Figure 8-6. A graph schema that includes GitHub users, repositories, and programming languages

Example 8-14 introduces some sample code that constructs the updates as depicted in the final graph schema. Because all of the information that we need to construct the additional nodes and edges is already present in the existing graph (since we have already stored the programming language as a property on the repository nodes), no additional requests to the GitHub API are necessary.

The nice thing about having a single node in the graph that corresponds to a programming language, as opposed to representing a programming language as a property on many nodes, is that a single node acts as a natural point of aggregation. Central points of aggregation can greatly simplify many kinds of queries, such as finding maximal cliques in the graph. For example, finding the maximal clique of users who all follow one another and program with a particular language can be more efficiently computed with NetworkX's clique detection algorithms (*http://bit.ly/2GDgBI6*) since the requirement of a particular programming language node in the clique significantly constrains the search.

Example 8-14. Updating the graph to include nodes for programming languages

```
# Iterate over all of the repos, and add edges for programming languages
# for each person in the graph. We'll also add edges back to repos so that
# we have a good point to "pivot" upon.

repos = [n
        for n in g.nodes_iter()
            if g.node[n]['type'] == 'repo']

for repo in repos:
    lang = (g.node[repo]['lang'] or "") + "(lang)"

    stargazers = [u
                    for (u, r, d) in g.in_edges_iter(repo, data=True)
```

```
                    if d['type'] == 'gazes'
            ]

    for sg in stargazers:
        g.add_node(lang, type='lang')
        g.add_edge(sg, lang, type='programs')
        g.add_edge(lang, repo, type='implements')
```

Our final graph schema is capable of answering a variety of questions. A few questions that seem ripe for investigation at this point include:

- Which languages do particular users program with?
- How many users program in a particular language?
- Which users program in multiple languages, such as Python and JavaScript?
- Which programmer is the most polyglot (programs with the most languages)?
- Is there a higher correlation between particular languages? (For example, given that a programmer programs in Python, is it more likely that this same programmer also programs in JavaScript or with Go based upon the data in this graph?)

Example 8-15 provides some sample code that is a good starting point for answering most of these questions, and others like them.

Example 8-15. Sample queries for the final graph

```
# Some stats

print(nx.info(g))
print()

# What languages exist in the graph?

print([n
       for n in g.nodes_iter()
           if g.node[n]['type'] == 'lang'])
print()

# What languages do users program with?
print([n
       for n in g['ptwobrussell(user)']
           if g['ptwobrussell(user)'][n]['type'] == 'programs'])

print()

# What is the most popular programming language?
print("Most popular languages")
print(sorted([(n, g.in_degree(n))
 for n in g.nodes_iter()
     if g.node[n]['type'] == 'lang'], key=itemgetter(1), reverse=True)[:10])
```

```
print()

# How many users program in a particular language?
python_programmers = [u
                    for (u, l) in g.in_edges_iter('Python(lang)')
                        if g.node[u]['type'] == 'user']
print("Number of Python programmers:", len(python_programmers))
print()

javascript_programmers = [u for
                        (u, l) in g.in_edges_iter('JavaScript(lang)')
                            if g.node[u]['type'] == 'user']
print("Number of JavaScript programmers:", len(javascript_programmers))
print()

# What users program in both Python and JavaScript?
print("Number of programmers who use JavaScript and Python")
print(len(set(python_programmers).intersection(set(javascript_programmers))))

# Programmers who use JavaScript but not Python
print("Number of programmers who use JavaScript but not Python")
print(len(set(javascript_programmers).difference(set(python_programmers))))

# Can you determine who is the most polyglot programmer?
```

Sample output follows:

```
Name:
Type: DiGraph
Number of nodes: 106643
Number of edges: 383807
Average in degree:   3.5990
Average out degree:   3.5990

['JavaScript(lang)', 'Python(lang)', '(lang)', 'Shell(lang)', 'Go(lang)',
 'C++(lang)','HTML(lang)', 'Scala(lang)', 'Objective-C(lang)',
 'TypeScript(lang)', 'Java(lang)', 'C(lang)', 'Jupyter Notebook(lang)',
 'CSS(lang)', 'Ruby(lang)', 'C#(lang)', 'Groovy(lang)', 'XSLT(lang)',
 'Eagle(lang)', 'PostScript(lang)', 'R(lang)', 'PHP(lang)', 'Erlang(lang)',
 'Elixir(lang)', 'CoffeeScript(lang)', 'Matlab(lang)', 'TeX(lang)',
 'VimL(lang)', 'Haskell(lang)', 'Clojure(lang)', 'Makefile(lang)',
 'Emacs Lisp(lang)', 'OCaml(lang)', 'Perl(lang)', 'Swift(lang)', 'Lua(lang)',
 'COBOL(lang)', 'Batchfile(lang)', 'Visual Basic(lang)',
 'Protocol Buffer(lang)', 'Assembly(lang)', 'Arduino(lang)', 'Cuda(lang)',
 'Ada(lang)', 'Rust(lang)', 'HCL(lang)', 'Common Lisp(lang)',
 'Objective-C++(lang)', 'GLSL(lang)', 'D(lang)', 'Dart(lang)',
 'Standard ML(lang)', 'Vim script(lang)', 'Coq(lang)', 'FORTRAN(lang)',
 'Julia(lang)', 'OpenSCAD(lang)', 'Kotlin(lang)', 'Pascal(lang)',
 'Logos(lang)', 'Lean(lang)', 'Vue(lang)', 'Elm(lang)', 'Crystal(lang)',
 'PowerShell(lang)', 'AppleScript(lang)', 'Scheme(lang)', 'Smarty(lang)',
 'PLpgSQL(lang)', 'Groff(lang)', 'Lex(lang)', 'Cirru(lang)',
 'Mathematica(lang)', 'BitBake(lang)', 'Fortran(lang)',
 'DIGITAL Command Language(lang)', 'ActionScript(lang)', 'Smalltalk(lang)',
```

```
'Bro(lang)', 'Racket(lang)', 'Frege(lang)', 'POV-Ray SDL(lang)', 'M(lang)',
'Puppet(lang)', 'GAP(lang)', 'VHDL(lang)', 'Gherkin(lang)',
'Objective-J(lang)', 'Roff(lang)', 'VCL(lang)', 'Hack(lang)',
'MoonScript(lang)', 'Tcl(lang)', 'CMake(lang)', 'Yacc(lang)', 'Vala(lang)',
'ApacheConf(lang)', 'PigLatin(lang)', 'SMT(lang)',
'GCC Machine Description(lang)', 'F#(lang)', 'QML(lang)', 'Monkey(lang)',
'Processing(lang)', 'Parrot(lang)', 'Nix(lang)', 'Nginx(lang)',
'Nimrod(lang)', 'SQLPL(lang)', 'Web Ontology Language(lang)', 'Nu(lang)',
'Arc(lang)', 'Rascal(lang)', "Cap'n Proto(lang)", 'Gosu(lang)', 'NSIS(lang)',
'MTML(lang)', 'ColdFusion(lang)', 'LiveScript(lang)', 'Hy(lang)',
'OpenEdge ABL(lang)', 'KiCad(lang)', 'Perl6(lang)', 'Prolog(lang)',
'XQuery(lang)', 'AutoIt(lang)', 'LOLCODE(lang)', 'Verilog(lang)',
'NewLisp(lang)', 'Cucumber(lang)', 'PureScript(lang)', 'Awk(lang)',
'RAML(lang)', 'Haxe(lang)', 'Thrift(lang)', 'XML(lang)', 'SaltStack(lang)',
'Pure Data(lang)', 'SuperCollider(lang)', 'HaXe(lang)',
'Ragel in Ruby Host(lang)', 'API Blueprint(lang)', 'Squirrel(lang)',
'Red(lang)', 'NetLogo(lang)', 'Factor(lang)', 'CartoCSS(lang)', 'Rebol(lang)',
'REALbasic(lang)', 'Max(lang)', 'ChucK(lang)', 'AutoHotkey(lang)',
'Apex(lang)', 'ASP(lang)', 'Stata(lang)', 'nesC(lang)',
'Gettext Catalog(lang)', 'Modelica(lang)', 'Augeas(lang)', 'Inform 7(lang)',
'APL(lang)', 'LilyPond(lang)', 'Terra(lang)', 'IDL(lang)', 'Brainfuck(lang)',
'Idris(lang)', 'AspectJ(lang)', 'Opa(lang)', 'Nim(lang)', 'SQL(lang)',
'Ragel(lang)', 'M4(lang)', 'Grammatical Framework(lang)', 'Nemerle(lang)',
'AGS Script(lang)', 'MQL4(lang)', 'Smali(lang)', 'Pony(lang)', 'ANTLR(lang)',
'Handlebars(lang)', 'PLSQL(lang)', 'SAS(lang)', 'FreeMarker(lang)',
'Fancy(lang)', 'DM(lang)', 'Agda(lang)', 'Io(lang)', 'Limbo(lang)',
'Liquid(lang)', 'Gnuplot(lang)', 'Xtend(lang)', 'LLVM(lang)',
'BlitzBasic(lang)', 'TLA(lang)', 'Metal(lang)', 'Inno Setup(lang)',
'Diff(lang)', 'SRecode Template(lang)', 'Forth(lang)', 'SQF(lang)',
'PureBasic(lang)', 'Mirah(lang)', 'Bison(lang)', 'Oz(lang)',
'Game Maker Language(lang)', 'ABAP(lang)', 'Isabelle(lang)', 'AMPL(lang)',
'E(lang)', 'Ceylon(lang)', 'WebIDL(lang)', 'GDScript(lang)', 'Stan(lang)',
'Eiffel(lang)', 'Mercury(lang)', 'Delphi(lang)', 'Brightscript(lang)',
'Propeller Spin(lang)', 'Self(lang)', 'HLSL(lang)']

['JavaScript(lang)', 'C++(lang)', 'Java(lang)', 'PostScript(lang)',
'Python(lang)', 'HTML(lang)', 'Ruby(lang)', 'Go(lang)', 'C(lang)', '(lang)',
'Objective-C(lang)', 'Jupyter Notebook(lang)', 'CSS(lang)', 'Shell(lang)',
'Clojure(lang)', 'CoffeeScript(lang)', 'Lua(lang)', 'Perl(lang)',
'C#(lang)', 'Common Lisp(lang)']

Most popular languages
[('JavaScript(lang)', 1115), ('Python(lang)', 1013), ('(lang)', 978),
('Java(lang)', 890), ('HTML(lang)', 873), ('Ruby(lang)', 870),
('C++(lang)', 866), ('C(lang)', 841), ('Shell(lang)', 764),
('CSS(lang)', 762)]

Number of Python programmers: 1013

Number of JavaScript programmers: 1115

Number of programmers who use JavaScript and Python
```

```
1013
Number of programmers who use JavaScript but not Python
102
```

Although the graph schema is conceptually simple, the number of edges has increased by nearly 50% because of the additional programming language nodes! As we see from the output for a few sample queries, there are quite a large number of programming languages in use, and JavaScript and Python top the list. The primary source code for the original repository of interest is written in Python, so the emergence of JavaScript as a more popular programming language among users may be indicative of a web development audience. Of course, it is also the case that JavaScript is just a popular programming language, and there is often a high correlation between JavaScript for a client-side language and Python as a server-side language. The appearance of '(lang)' as the third most popular language is an indication that there are 642 repositories to which GitHub could not assign a programming language, and in aggregate, they rolled up into this single category.

The possibilities are immense for analyzing a graph that expresses people's interests in other people, open source projects in repositories, and programming languages. Whatever analysis you choose to do, think carefully about the nature of the problem and extract only the relevant data from the graph for analysis—either by zeroing in on a set of nodes to extract with the networkx.Graph.subgraph method, or by filtering out nodes by type or frequency threshold.

 A bipartite analysis (*http://bit.ly/1a1oooP*) of users and programming languages would likely be a worthwhile endeavor, given the nature of the relationship between users and programming languages. A bipartite graph involves two disjoint sets of vertices that are connected by edges between the sets. You could easily remove repository nodes from the graph at this point to drastically enhance the efficiency of computing global graph statistics (the number of edges would decrease by over 100,000).

8.4.5 Visualizing Interest Graphs

Although it is exciting to visualize a graph, and a picture really is often worth far more than a thousand words, keep in mind that not all graphs are easily visualized. However, with a little bit of thought you can often extract a subgraph that can be visualized to the extent that it provides some insight or intuition into the problem that you are trying to solve. As you know from our work in this chapter, a graph is just a type of data structure and has no definite visual rendering. To be visualized, a particular type of *layout algorithm* must be applied that maps the nodes and edges to a two- or three-dimensional space for visual consumption.

We'll stick to the core toolkit that we've used throughout the book and lean on NetworkX's ability to export JSON that can be rendered by the JavaScript toolkit D3 (*http://bit.ly/1a1kGvo*), but there are many other toolkits that you could consider when visualizing graphs. Graphviz (*http://bit.ly/1a1ooVG*) is a highly configurable and rather classic tool that can lay out very complex graphs as bitmap images. It has traditionally been used in a terminal setting like other command-line tools, but it also now ships with a user interface for most platforms. Another option is Gephi (*http://bit.ly/1a1opc5*), another popular open source project that provides some powerful interactive possibilities; Gephi has rapidly grown in popularity over the past few years and is an option that's well worth your consideration.

Example 8-16 illustrates a template for extracting a subgraph of the users who gaze at the seed of our original graph (the Mining-the-Social-Web repository) and the "following" connections among them. It extracts the users in the graph with a common interest and visualizes the "follows" edges among them. Keep in mind that the entire graph as constructed in this chapter is quite large and contains tens of thousands of nodes and hundreds of thousands of edges, so you'd need to spend some time better understanding it in order to achieve a reasonable visualization with a tool like Gephi.

Example 8-16. Graph visualization of the social network for the original interest graph

```
import os
import json
from IPython.display import IFrame
from IPython.core.display import display
from networkx.readwrite import json_graph

print("Stats on the full graph")
print(nx.info(g))
print()

# Create a subgraph from a collection of nodes. In this case, the
# collection is all of the users in the original interest graph

mtsw_users = [n for n in g if g.node[n]['type'] == 'user']
h = g.subgraph(mtsw_users)

print("Stats on the extracted subgraph")
print(nx.info(h))

# Visualize the social network of all people from the original interest graph
d = json_graph.node_link_data(h)
json.dump(d, open('force.json', 'w'))


# Jupyter Notebook can serve files and display them into
# inline frames. Prepend the path with the 'files' prefix.
```

```
# A D3 template for displaying the graph data
viz_file = 'force.html'

# Display the D3 visualization

display(IFrame(viz_file, '100%', '500px'))
```

Figure 8-7 shows sample results of running this example code.

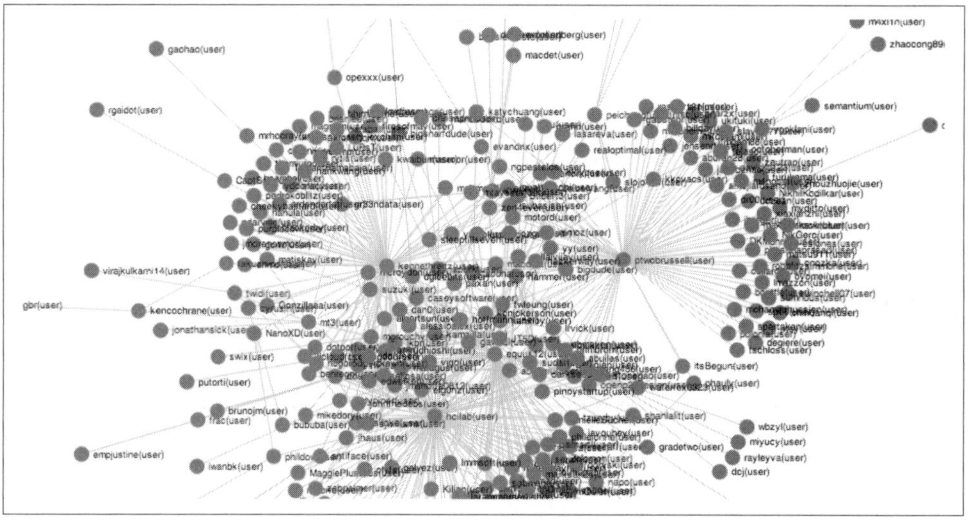

Figure 8-7. An interactive visualization of the "follows" edges among GitHub users for the interest graph—notice the patterns in the visual layout of the graph that correspond to the centrality measures introduced earlier in this chapter

8.5 Closing Remarks

Although various sorts of graphs have been sprinkled throughout earlier chapters in this book, this chapter provided a more substantial introduction to their use as a flexible data structure for representing a network of GitHub users and their common interests in certain software project repositories and programming languages. GitHub's rich API and NetworkX's easy-to-use API are a nice duo for mining some fascinating and often-overlooked social web data in one of the most overtly "social" web properties that's in widespread use across the globe. The notion of an interest graph isn't an entirely new idea, but its application to the social web is a fairly recent development with exciting implications. Whereas interest graphs (or comparable representations) have been used by advertisers to effectively place ads for some time, they're now being used by entrepreneurs and software developers to more effectively target interests and make intelligent recommendations that enhance a product's relevance to users.

Like most of the other chapters in the book, this chapter has served as merely a primer for graphical modeling, interest graphs, GitHub's API, and what you can do with these technologies. You could just as easily apply the graphical modeling techniques in this chapter to other social web properties such as Twitter or Facebook and achieve compelling analytic results, as well as applying other forms of analysis to the rich data that's available from GitHub's API. The possibilities, as always, are quite vast. Our hope first and foremost is that you've enjoyed yourself while working through the exercises in this chapter and learned something new that you can take with you throughout your social web mining journey and beyond.

 The source code outlined for this chapter and all other chapters is available on GitHub (*http://bit.ly/Mining-the-Social-Web-3E*) in a convenient Jupyter Notebook format that you're highly encouraged to try out from the comfort of your own web browser.

8.6 Recommended Exercises

- Repeat the exercises in this chapter, but use a different repository as a starting point. Do the findings from this chapter generally hold true, or are the results of your experiments different in any particular way?

- GitHub has published some data regarding correlations between programming languages (*http://bit.ly/1a1or3Y*). Review and explore the data. Is it any different from what you could collect with the GitHub API?

- NetworkX provides an extensive collection of graph traversal algorithms (*http://bit.ly/2GYXBDn*). Review the documentation and pick a couple of algorithms to run on the data. Centrality measures, cliques, and bipartite algorithms might make a good starting point for inspiration. Can you compute the largest clique of users in the graph? What about the largest clique that shares a common interest, such as a particular programming language?

- The GitHub Archive (*http://bit.ly/1a1orAK*) provides an extensive amount of data about GitHub activity at a global level. Investigate this data, using some of the recommended "big data" tools to explore it.

- Compare data points across two similar GitHub projects. Given the inextricable links between Mining-the-Social-Web and Mining-the-Social-Web-2nd-Edition, these two projects make for a suitable starting point for analysis. Who has bookmarked or forked one but not the other? How do the interest graphs compare? Can you build and analyze an interest graph that contains all of the users who are interested in both editions?

- Use a similarity measurement such as Jaccard similarity (see Chapter 4) to compute the similarity of two arbitrary users on GitHub based upon features such as starred repositories in common, programming languages in common, and other features that you can find in GitHub's API.

- Given users and existing interests, can you design an algorithm that recommends interests for other users? Consider adapting the code from "A Whiz-Bang Introduction to TF-IDF" that uses cosine similarity as a means of predicting relevance.

- Employ a histogram to gain insight into a facet of the interest graph in this chapter, such as the popularity of programming languages.

- Explore graph visualization tools like Graphviz and Gephi to lay out and render a graph for visual inspection.

- Explore the Friendster social network and ground-truth communities (*http://stanford.io/1a1orRr*) data set and use NetworkX algorithms to analyze it.

8.7 Online Resources

The following list of links from this chapter may be useful for review:

- Bipartite graph (*http://bit.ly/1a1oooP*)
- Centrality measures (*http://bit.ly/1a1osEM*)
- "Creating a personal access token for the command line" (*http://bit.ly/1a1o7lG*)
- D3.js (*http://bit.ly/1a1kGvo*)
- Friendster social network and ground-truth communities (*http://stanford.io/1a1orRr*)
- Gephi (*http://bit.ly/1a1opc5*)
- GitHub Archive (*http://bit.ly/1a1orAK*)
- GitHub Developer (*http://bit.ly/1a1o49k*)
- GitHub developer documentation for pagination (*http://bit.ly/1a1o9Ki*)
- GitHub developer documentation for rate limiting (*http://bit.ly/1a1oblo*)
- gitscm.com (online Git book) (*http://bit.ly/1a1o2hZ*)
- Graph Theory—An Introduction! YouTube video (*http://bit.ly/1a1odto*)
- Graphviz (*http://bit.ly/1a1ooVG*)
- Hypergraph (*http://bit.ly/1a1ocWm*)
- Interest graph (*http://bit.ly/1a1o3Cu*)
- Krackhardt kite graph (*http://bit.ly/1a1oixa*)
- Kruskal's algorithm (*http://bit.ly/1a1on3X*)
- Minimum spanning tree (MST) (*http://bit.ly/1a1omgr*)

- NetworkX (*http://bit.ly/1a1ocFV*)
- NetworkX graph traversal algorithms (*http://bit.ly/2GYXBDn*)
- PyGithub GitHub repository (*http://bit.ly/1a1o7Ca*)

## PART II

Twitter Cookbook

Whereas Part I of this book provided a fairly broad overview of a number of social web properties, the remaining chapter comes back full circle to where we started in Part I with Twitter. It is organized as a cookbook and features more than two dozen bite-sized recipes for mining Twitter data. Twitter's accessible APIs, inherent openness, and rampant worldwide popularity make it an ideal social website to zoom in on, but this part of the book aims to create some atomic building blocks that are highly composable to serve a wide variety of purposes. It is designed to narrow the focus on a common set of small problems that you can adapt to other social web properties. Just like any other technical cookbook, these recipes are organized in an easy-to-navigate problem/solution format, and as you are working through them, you are sure to come up with interesting ideas that involve tweaks and modifications.

You are highly encouraged to have as much fun with these recipes as possible, and as you come up with any clever recipes of your own, consider sharing them back with the book's community by sending a pull request to its GitHub repository (*http://bit.ly/ Mining-the-Social-Web-3E*), tweeting about it (mention @SocialWebMining if you want a retweet), or posting about it on *Mining the Social Web*'s Facebook page (*http:// on.fb.me/1a1kHPQ*).

Twitter Cookbook

This cookbook is a collection of recipes for mining Twitter data. Each recipe is designed to solve a particular problem and to be as simple and atomic as possible so that multiple recipes can be composed into more complex recipes with minimal effort. Think of each recipe as being a building block that, while useful in its own right, is even more useful in concert with other building blocks that collectively constitute more complex units of analysis. Unlike the previous chapters, which contain a lot more prose than code, this one provides relatively little discussion and lets the code do more of the talking. The thought is that you'll likely be manipulating and composing the code in various ways to achieve your own particular objectives.

While most recipes involve little more than issuing a parameterized API call and post-processing the response into a convenient format, some recipes are even simpler (involving just a few lines of code), and others are considerably more complex. This cookbook is designed to help you by presenting some common problems and their solutions. In some cases, it may not be common knowledge that the data you desire is really just a couple of lines of code away. The value proposition is in giving you code that you can trivially adapt to suit your own purposes.

One fundamental software dependency you'll need for all of the recipes in this chapter is the `twitter` package, which you can install with `pip` per the rather predictable **pip install twitter** command from a terminal. Other software dependencies will be noted as they are introduced in individual recipes. If you're taking advantage of the book's virtual machine (which you are highly encouraged to do), the `twitter` package and all other dependencies will be preinstalled for you.

As you know from Chapter 1, Twitter's v1.1 API requires all requests to be authenticated, so it's assumed that you will follow the instructions in "Accessing Twitter's API for Development Purposes" or "Doing the OAuth Dance to Access Twitter's API for

Production Purposes" to first gain an authenticated API connector to use in each of the other recipes.

 Always get the latest bug-fixed source code for this chapter (and every other chapter) online at *http://bit.ly/Mining-the-Social-Web-3E*. Be sure to also take advantage of this book's virtual machine experience, as described in Appendix A, to maximize your enjoyment of the sample code.

9.1 Accessing Twitter's API for Development Purposes

9.1.1 Problem

You want to mine your own account data or otherwise gain quick and easy API access for development purposes.

9.1.2 Solution

Use the `twitter` package and the OAuth 2.0 credentials provided in the application's settings to gain API access to your own account without any HTTP redirects.

9.1.3 Discussion

Twitter implements OAuth 2.0 (*http://bit.ly/2IfXIYl*), an authorization mechanism that's expressly designed so that users can grant third parties access to their data without having to do the unthinkable—doling out their usernames and passwords. While you can certainly take advantage of Twitter's OAuth implementation for production situations in which you'll need users to authorize your application to access their accounts, you can also use the credentials in your application's settings to gain instant access for development purposes or to mine the data in your own account.

Register an application under your Twitter account at *http://dev.twitter.com/apps* and take note of the *consumer key*, *consumer secret*, *access token*, and *access token secret*, which constitute the four credentials that any OAuth 2.0–enabled application needs to ultimately gain account access. Figure 9-1 provides a screen capture of a Twitter application's settings. With these credentials in hand, you can use any OAuth 2.0 library to access Twitter's RESTful API (*http://bit.ly/1a1pDEq*), but we'll opt to use the `twitter` package, which provides a minimalist and Pythonic API wrapper around Twitter's RESTful API interface. When registering your application, you don't need to specify the callback URL since we are effectively bypassing the entire OAuth flow and simply using the credentials to immediately access the API. Example 9-1 demonstrates how to use these credentials to instantiate a connector to the API.

Example 9-1. Accessing Twitter's API for development purposes

```
import twitter

def oauth_login():
    # Go to http://twitter.com/apps/new to create an app and get values
    # for these credentials that you'll need to provide in place of the
    # empty string values that are defined as placeholders.
    # See https://dev.twitter.com/docs/auth/oauth for more information
    # on Twitter's OAuth implementation.

    CONSUMER_KEY = ''
    CONSUMER_SECRET = ''
    OAUTH_TOKEN = ''
    OAUTH_TOKEN_SECRET = ''

    auth = twitter.oauth.OAuth(OAUTH_TOKEN, OAUTH_TOKEN_SECRET,
                               CONSUMER_KEY, CONSUMER_SECRET)

    twitter_api = twitter.Twitter(auth=auth)
    return twitter_api

# Sample usage
twitter_api = oauth_login()

# Nothing to see by displaying twitter_api except that it's now a
# defined variable

print(twitter_api)
```

Keep in mind that the credentials used to connect are effectively the same as the username and password combination, so guard them carefully and specify the minimal level of access required in your application's settings. Read-only access is sufficient for mining your own account data.

While convenient for accessing your own data from your own account, this shortcut provides no benefit if your goal is to write a client program for accessing someone else's data. You'll need to perform the full OAuth dance, as demonstrated in Example 9-2, for that situation.

9.2 Doing the OAuth Dance to Access Twitter's API for Production Purposes

9.2.1 Problem

You want to use OAuth so that your application can access another user's account data.

9.2.2 Solution

Implement the "OAuth dance" with the `twitter` package.

9.2.3 Discussion

The `twitter` package provides a built-in implementation of the so-called OAuth dance that works for a console application. It does so by implementing an *out of band* (oob) OAuth flow in which an application that does not run in a browser, such as a Python program, can securely gain these four credentials to access the API, and allows you to easily request access to a particular user's account data as a standard "out of the box" capability. However, if you'd like to write a web application that accesses another user's account data, you may need to lightly adapt its implementation.

Although there may not be many practical reasons to actually implement an OAuth dance from within Jupyter Notebook (unless perhaps you are running a hosted Jupyter Notebook service that's used by other people), this recipe uses Flask as an embedded web server to demonstrate this process using the same toolchain as the rest of the book. It could be easily adapted to work with an arbitrary web application framework of your choice, since the concepts are the same.

Figure 9-1 provides a screen capture of a Twitter application's settings. In an OAuth 2.0 flow, the *consumer key* and *consumer secret* values that were introduced as part of "Accessing Twitter's API for Development Purposes" uniquely identify your application. You provide these values to Twitter when requesting access to a user's data so that Twitter can then prompt the user with information about the nature of your request. Assuming the user approves your application, Twitter redirects back to the callback URL that you specify in your application settings and includes an *OAuth verifier* that is then exchanged for an *access token* and *access token secret, which are used in concert with the consumer key and consumer secret* to ultimately enable your application to access the account data. (For oob OAuth flows, you don't need to include a callback URL; Twitter provides the user with a PIN code as an OAuth verifier that must be copied/pasted back into the application as a manual intervention.) See Appendix B for additional details on the OAuth 2.0 flow.

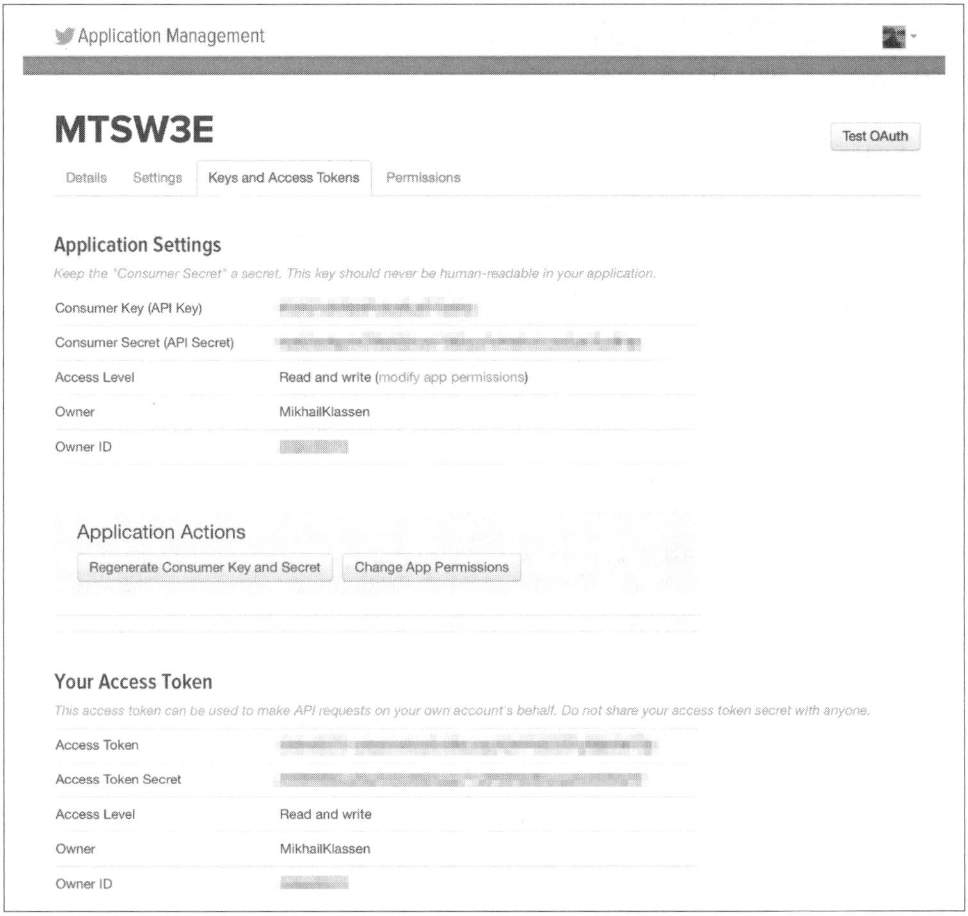

Figure 9-1. Sample OAuth settings for a Twitter application

Example 9-2 illustrates how to use the consumer key and consumer secret to do the OAuth dance with the `twitter` package and gain access to a user's data. The access token and access token secret are written to disk, which streamlines future authorizations. According to Twitter's Developers FAQ (*http://bit.ly/2Lzux3x*), Twitter does not currently expire access tokens, which means that you can reliably store them and use them on behalf of the user indefinitely, as long as you comply with the applicable terms of service (*http://twitter.com/en/tos*).

Example 9-2. Doing the OAuth dance to access Twitter's API for production purposes

```
import json
from flask import Flask, request
import multiprocessing
from threading import Timer
```

```
from IPython.display import IFrame
from IPython.display import display
from IPython.display import Javascript as JS

import twitter
from twitter.oauth_dance import parse_oauth_tokens
from twitter.oauth import read_token_file, write_token_file

# Note: This code is exactly the flow presented in the _AppendixB notebook

OAUTH_FILE = "resources/ch09-twittercookbook/twitter_oauth"

# Go to http://twitter.com/apps/new to create an app and get values
# for these credentials that you'll need to provide in place of the
# empty string values that are defined as placeholders.
# See https://developer.twitter.com/en/docs/basics/authentication/overview/oauth
# for more information on Twitter's OAuth implementation, and ensure that
# *oauth_callback* is defined in your application settings as shown next if
# you are using Flask in this Jupyter Notebook.

# Define a few variables that will bleed into the lexical scope of a couple of
# functions that follow
CONSUMER_KEY = ''
CONSUMER_SECRET = ''
oauth_callback = 'http://127.0.0.1:5000/oauth_helper'

# Set up a callback handler for when Twitter redirects back to us after the user
# authorizes the app

webserver = Flask("TwitterOAuth")
@webserver.route("/oauth_helper")
def oauth_helper():

    oauth_verifier = request.args.get('oauth_verifier')

    # Pick back up credentials from ipynb_oauth_dance
    oauth_token, oauth_token_secret = read_token_file(OAUTH_FILE)

    _twitter = twitter.Twitter(
        auth=twitter.OAuth(
            oauth_token, oauth_token_secret, CONSUMER_KEY, CONSUMER_SECRET),
        format='', api_version=None)

    oauth_token, oauth_token_secret = parse_oauth_tokens(
        _twitter.oauth.access_token(oauth_verifier=oauth_verifier))

    # This web server only needs to service one request, so shut it down
    shutdown_after_request = request.environ.get('werkzeug.server.shutdown')
    shutdown_after_request()

    # Write out the final credentials that can be picked up after the following
    # blocking call to webserver.run()
```

```
    write_token_file(OAUTH_FILE, oauth_token, oauth_token_secret)
    return "%s %s written to %s" % (oauth_token, oauth_token_secret, OAUTH_FILE)

# To handle Twitter's OAuth 1.0a implementation, we'll just need to implement a
# custom "oauth dance" and will closely follow the pattern defined in
# twitter.oauth_dance

def ipynb_oauth_dance():

    _twitter = twitter.Twitter(
        auth=twitter.OAuth('', '', CONSUMER_KEY, CONSUMER_SECRET),
        format='', api_version=None)

    oauth_token, oauth_token_secret = parse_oauth_tokens(
            _twitter.oauth.request_token(oauth_callback=oauth_callback))

    # Need to write these interim values out to a file to pick up on the callback
    # from Twitter that is handled by the web server in /oauth_helper
    write_token_file(OAUTH_FILE, oauth_token, oauth_token_secret)

    oauth_url = ('http://api.twitter.com/oauth/authorize?oauth_token=' + oauth_token)

    # Tap the browser's native capabilities to access the web server through a new
    # window to get user authorization
    display(JS("window.open('%s')" % oauth_url))

# After the webserver.run() blocking call, start the OAuth dance that will
# ultimately cause Twitter to redirect a request back to it. Once that request
# is serviced, the web server will shut down and program flow will resume
# with the OAUTH_FILE containing the necessary credentials.
Timer(1, lambda: ipynb_oauth_dance()).start()

webserver.run(host='0.0.0.0')

# The values that are read from this file are written out at
# the end of /oauth_helper
oauth_token, oauth_token_secret = read_token_file(OAUTH_FILE)

# These four credentials are what is needed to authorize the application
auth = twitter.oauth.OAuth(oauth_token, oauth_token_secret,
                            CONSUMER_KEY, CONSUMER_SECRET)

twitter_api = twitter.Twitter(auth=auth)

print(twitter_api)
```

You should be able to observe that the access token and access token secret that your application retrieves are the same values as the ones in your application's settings, and this is no coincidence. Guard these values carefully, as they are effectively the same thing as a username and password combination.

9.3 Discovering the Trending Topics

9.3.1 Problem

You want to know what is trending on Twitter for a particular geographic area such as the United States, another country or group of countries, or possibly even the entire world.

9.3.2 Solution

Twitter's Trends API (*http://bit.ly/2jSxPmY*) enables you to get the trending topics for geographic areas that are designated by a Where On Earth (WOE) ID (*http://bit.ly/ 2jVIcXo*), originally defined by GeoPlanet and then maintained by Yahoo!

9.3.3 Discussion

A *place* is an essential concept in Twitter's development platform, and trending topics are accordingly constrained by geography to provide the best API possible for querying for trending topics (as shown in Example 9-3). Like all other APIs, it returns the trending topics as JSON data, which can be converted to standard Python objects and then manipulated with list comprehensions or similar techniques. This means it's fairly easy to explore the API responses. Try experimenting with a variety of WOE IDs to compare and contrast the trends from various geographic regions. For example, compare and contrast trends in two different countries, or compare a trend in a particular country to a trend in the world.

Example 9-3. Discovering the trending topics

```python
import json
import twitter

def twitter_trends(twitter_api, woe_id):
    # Prefix ID with the underscore for query string parameterization.
    # Without the underscore, the twitter package appends the ID value
    # to the URL itself as a special-case keyword argument.
    return twitter_api.trends.place(_id=woe_id)

# Sample usage

twitter_api = oauth_login()

# See https://bit.ly/2pdi0tS
# and http://www.woeidlookup.com to look up different Yahoo! Where On Earth IDs

WORLD_WOE_ID = 1
world_trends = twitter_trends(twitter_api, WORLD_WOE_ID)
print(json.dumps(world_trends, indent=1))
```

```
US_WOE_ID = 23424977
us_trends = twitter_trends(twitter_api, US_WOE_ID)
print(json.dumps(us_trends, indent=1))
```

9.4 Searching for Tweets

9.4.1 Problem

You want to search Twitter for tweets using specific keywords and query constraints.

9.4.2 Solution

Use the Search API to perform a custom query.

9.4.3 Discussion

You can use the Search API (*http://bit.ly/2IcgdRL*) to perform a custom query against the entire Twitterverse. Similar to the way that search engines work, Twitter's Search API returns results in batches, and you can configure the number of results per batch to a maximum value of 200 by using the count keyword parameter. It is possible that more than 200 results (or the maximum value that you specify for count) may be available for any given query, and in the parlance of Twitter's API, you'll need to use a *cursor* to navigate to the next batch of results.

Cursors (*http://bit.ly/2IEOvfI*) are a new enhancement to Twitter's v1.1 API and provide a more robust scheme than the pagination paradigm offered by the v1.0 API, which involved specifying a page number and a results-per-page constraint. The essence of the cursor paradigm is that it is able to better accommodate the dynamic and real-time nature of the Twitter platform. For example, Twitter's API cursors are designed to inherently take into account the possibility that updated information may become available in real time while you are navigating a batch of search results. In other words, it could be the case that while you are navigating a batch of query results, relevant information becomes available that you would want to have included in your current results while you are navigating them, rather than needing to dispatch a new query.

Example 9-4 illustrates how to use the Search API and navigate the cursor that's included in a response to fetch more than one batch of results.

Example 9-4. Searching for tweets

```
def twitter_search(twitter_api, q, max_results=200, **kw):

    # See http://bit.ly/2QyGz0P and https://bit.ly/2QyGz0P
    # for details on advanced search criteria that may be useful for
```

```python
        # keyword arguments

        # See https://dev.twitter.com/docs/api/1.1/get/search/tweets
        search_results = twitter_api.search.tweets(q=q, count=100, **kw)

        statuses = search_results['statuses']

        # Iterate through batches of results by following the cursor until we
        # reach the desired number of results, keeping in mind that OAuth users
        # can "only" make 180 search queries per 15-minute interval. See
        # https://developer.twitter.com/en/docs/basics/rate-limits
        # for details. A reasonable number of results is ~1000, although
        # that number of results may not exist for all queries.

        # Enforce a reasonable limit
        max_results = min(1000, max_results)

        for _ in range(10): # 10*100 = 1000
            try:
                next_results = search_results['search_metadata']['next_results']
            except KeyError as e: # No more results when next_results doesn't exist
                break

            # Create a dictionary from next_results, which has the following form:
            # ?max_id=313519052523986943&q=NCAA&include_entities=1
            kwargs = dict([ kv.split('=')
                            for kv in next_results[1:].split("&") ])

            search_results = twitter_api.search.tweets(**kwargs)
            statuses += search_results['statuses']

            if len(statuses) > max_results:
                break

        return statuses

# Sample usage

twitter_api = oauth_login()

q = "CrossFit"
results = twitter_search(twitter_api, q, max_results=10)

# Show one sample search result by slicing the list...
print(json.dumps(results[0], indent=1))
```

9.5 Constructing Convenient Function Calls

9.5.1 Problem

You want to bind certain parameters to function calls and pass around a reference to the bound function in order to simplify coding patterns.

9.5.2 Solution

Use Python's `functools.partial` to create fully or partially bound functions that can be elegantly passed around and invoked by other code without the need to pass additional parameters.

9.5.3 Discussion

Although not a technique that is exclusive to design patterns with the Twitter API, `functools.partial` is a function that you'll find incredibly convenient to use in combination with the `twitter` package and many of the patterns in this cookbook and in your other Python programming experiences. For example, you may find it cumbersome to continually pass around a reference to an authenticated Twitter API connector (`twitter_api`, as illustrated in these recipes, is usually the first argument to most functions) and want to create a function that *partially* satisfies the function arguments so that you can freely pass around a function that can be invoked with its remaining parameters. Similarly, if you get tired of routinely typing `json.dumps({…}, indent=1)`, you could go ahead and partially apply the keyword argument and rename the function to something shorter like `pp` (pretty-print) to save some repetitive typing.

Another example that illustrates the convenience of partially binding parameters is that you may want to bind a Twitter API connector and a WOE ID for a geographic area to the Trends API as a single function call that can be passed around and simply invoked as is. The possibilities are vast, and while you could opt to use Python's `def` keyword to define functions as a possibility that usually achieves the same end, you may find that it's more concise and elegant to use `functools.partial` in some situations. Example 9-5 demonstrates a few cases that you may find useful.

Example 9-5. Constructing convenient function calls

```
from functools import partial

pp = partial(json.dumps, indent=1)

twitter_world_trends = partial(twitter_trends, twitter_api, WORLD_WOE_ID)
```

```
print(pp(twitter_world_trends()))

authenticated_twitter_search = partial(twitter_search, twitter_api)
results = authenticated_twitter_search("iPhone")
print(pp(results))

authenticated_iphone_twitter_search = partial(authenticated_twitter_search, "iPhone")
results = authenticated_iphone_twitter_search()
print(pp(results))
```

9.6 Saving and Restoring JSON Data with Text Files

9.6.1 Problem

You want to store relatively small amounts of data that you've fetched from Twitter's API for recurring analysis or archival purposes.

9.6.2 Solution

Write the data out to a text file in a convenient and portable JSON representation.

9.6.3 Discussion

Although text files won't be appropriate for every occasion, they are a portable and convenient option to consider if you need to just dump some data out to disk to save it for experimentation or analysis. In fact, this could be considered a best practice so that you minimize the number of requests to Twitter's API and avoid the inevitable rate-limiting issues that you'll likely encounter. After all, it certainly would not be in your best interest or Twitter's best interest to repetitively hit the API and request the same data over and over again.

Example 9-6 demonstrates a fairly routine use of Python's io package to ensure that any data that you write to and read from disk is properly encoded and decoded as UTF-8 so that you can avoid the (often dreaded and not often well understood) Unicode deDecodeError exceptions that commonly occur with serialization and deserialization of text data in Python applications.

Example 9-6. Saving and restoring JSON data with text files

```python
import io, json

def save_json(filename, data):
    with open('resources/ch09-twittercookbook/{0}.json'.format(filename),
            'w', encoding='utf-8') as f:
        json.dump(data, f, ensure_ascii=False)
```

```
def load_json(filename):
    with open('resources/ch09-twittercookbook/{0}.json'.format(filename),
            'r', encoding='utf-8') as f:
        return json.load(f)

# Sample usage

q = 'CrossFit'

twitter_api = oauth_login()
results = twitter_search(twitter_api, q, max_results=10)

save_json(q, results)
results = load_json(q)

print(json.dumps(results, indent=1, ensure_ascii=False))
```

9.7 Saving and Accessing JSON Data with MongoDB

9.7.1 Problem

You want to store and access nontrivial amounts of JSON data from Twitter API responses.

9.7.2 Solution

Use a document-oriented database such as MongoDB to store the data in a convenient JSON format.

9.7.3 Discussion

While a directory containing a relatively small number of properly encoded JSON files may work well for trivial amounts of data, you may be surprised at how quickly you start to amass enough data that flat files become unwieldy. Fortunately, document-oriented databases such as MongoDB are ideal for storing Twitter API responses, since they are designed to efficiently store JSON data.

MongoDB is a robust and well-documented database that works well for small or large amounts of data. It provides powerful query operators and indexing capabilities that significantly streamline the amount of analysis that you'll need to do in custom Python code.

 MongoDB can be installed on most platforms (*http://bit.ly/2jUeG3Z*) and there exists excellent online documentation (*http://bit.ly/2Ih7bmn*) for both installation/configuration and query/indexing operations.

In most cases, if you put some thought into how to index and query your data, MongoDB will be able to outperform your custom manipulations through its use of indexes and efficient BSON (*http://bit.ly/1a1pG34*) representation on disk. Example 9-7 illustrates how to connect to a running MongoDB database to save and load data.

 The second edition of this book contained a fairly extensive introduction to MongoDB in Chapter 7, in the context of storing (JSONified mailbox) data and using MongoDB's aggregation framework (*http://bit.ly/1a1pGjv*) to query it in nontrivial ways. This was removed in the current edition in favor of spending more time with the pandas data analysis library, which the authors felt was an important part of any data scientist's toolkit. There will always be multiple ways of solving any problem, and everybody has their own preferred tool.

Example 9-7. Saving and accessing JSON data with MongoDB

```
import json
import pymongo # pip install pymongo

def save_to_mongo(data, mongo_db, mongo_db_coll, **mongo_conn_kw):

    # Connects to the MongoDB server running on
    # localhost:27017 by default

    client = pymongo.MongoClient(**mongo_conn_kw)

    # Get a reference to a particular database

    db = client[mongo_db]

    # Reference a particular collection in the database

    coll = db[mongo_db_coll]

    # Perform a bulk insert and  return the IDs
    try:
        return coll.insert_many(data)
    except:
        return coll.insert_one(data)

def load_from_mongo(mongo_db, mongo_db_coll, return_cursor=False,
                    criteria=None, projection=None, **mongo_conn_kw):

    # Optionally, use criteria and projection to limit the data that is
    # returned as documented in
    # http://docs.mongodb.org/manual/reference/method/db.collection.find/
```

```
    # Consider leveraging MongoDB's aggregations framework for more
    # sophisticated queries

    client = pymongo.MongoClient(**mongo_conn_kw)
    db = client[mongo_db]
    coll = db[mongo_db_coll]

    if criteria is None:
        criteria = {}

    if projection is None:
        cursor = coll.find(criteria)
    else:
        cursor = coll.find(criteria, projection)

    # Returning a cursor is recommended for large amounts of data

    if return_cursor:
        return cursor
    else:
        return [ item for item in cursor ]

# Sample usage

q = 'CrossFit'

twitter_api = oauth_login()
results = twitter_search(twitter_api, q, max_results=10)

ids = save_to_mongo(results, 'search_results', q)

load_from_mongo('search_results', q)
```

Alternatively, if you'd like to store your Twitter data in the form of a `pandas Data Frame`, you can do that too. We provide an example in Example 9-8. For small to medium-sized data mining projects, this might work just fine, but once you start working with more data than can fit into your computer's random access memory (RAM) you will need to find other solutions. And once the amount of data you collect exceeds the capacity of your computer's hard disk, you will need to begin looking into distributed databases. That's the purview of big data.

Example 9-8. Saving and accessing JSON data with pandas

```
import json
import pickle
import pandas as pd

def save_to_pandas(data, fname):
    df = pd.DataFrame.from_records(data)
    df.to_pickle(fname)
```

```
    return df


def load_from_mongo(fname):
    df = pd.read_pickle(fname)
    return df


# Sample usage

q = 'CrossFit'

twitter_api = oauth_login()
results = twitter_search(twitter_api, q, max_results=10)

df = save_to_pandas(results, 'search_results_{}.pkl'.format(q))

df = load_from_mongo('search_results_{}.pkl'.format(q))

# Show some sample output, but just the user and text columns
df[['user','text']].head()
```

9.8 Sampling the Twitter Firehose with the Streaming API

9.8.1 Problem

You want to analyze what people are tweeting about *right now* from a real-time stream of tweets as opposed to querying the Search API for what might be slightly (or very) dated information. Or, you want to begin accumulating nontrivial amounts of data about a particular topic for later analysis.

9.8.2 Solution

Use Twitter's Streaming API (*http://bit.ly/2rDU17W*) to sample public data from the Twitter firehose.

9.8.3 Discussion

Twitter makes up to 1% of all tweets available in real time through a random sampling technique that represents the larger population of tweets and exposes these tweets through the Streaming API. Unless you want to access Twitter's Enterprise API (*http://bit.ly/2KZ1mrJ*) or go to a third-party provider such as DataSift (*http://bit.ly/1a1pGQE*) (which may actually be well worth the cost in many situations), this is about as good as it gets. Although you might think that 1% seems paltry, take a moment to realize that during peak loads, tweet velocity can be tens of thousands of tweets per second. For a broad enough topic, actually storing all of the tweets you sample could quickly become more of a problem than you might think. Access to up to 1% of all public tweets is significant.

Whereas the Search API is a little bit easier to use and queries for "historical" information (which in the Twitterverse could mean data that is minutes or hours old, given how fast trends emerge and dissipate), the Streaming API provides a way to sample from *worldwide information* in as close to real time as you'll ever be able to get. The twitter package exposes the Streaming API in an easy-to-use manner in which you can filter the firehose based upon keyword constraints, which is an intuitive and convenient way to access this information. As opposed to constructing a twitter.Twitter connector, you construct a twitter.TwitterStream connector, which takes a keyword argument that's the same twitter.oauth.OAuth type as previously introduced in "Accessing Twitter's API for Development Purposes" and "Doing the OAuth Dance to Access Twitter's API for Production Purposes".

The sample code in Example 9-9 demonstrates how to get started with Twitter's Streaming API.

Example 9-9. Sampling the Twitter firehose with the Streaming API

```
# Find topics of interest by using the filtering capabilities the API offers

import sys
import twitter

# Query terms

q = 'CrossFit' # Comma-separated list of terms

print('Filtering the public timeline for track={0}'.format(q), file=sys.stderr)
sys.stderr.flush()

# Returns an instance of twitter.Twitter
twitter_api = oauth_login()

# Reference the self.auth parameter
twitter_stream = twitter.TwitterStream(auth=twitter_api.auth)

# See https://developer.twitter.com/en/docs/tutorials/consuming-streaming-data
stream = twitter_stream.statuses.filter(track=q)

# For illustrative purposes, when all else fails, search for Justin Bieber
# and something is sure to turn up (at least, on Twitter)

for tweet in stream:
    print(tweet['text'])
    sys.stdout.flush()

    # Save to a database in a particular collection
```

9.9 Collecting Time-Series Data

9.9.1 Problem

You want to periodically query Twitter's API for specific results or trending topics and store the data for time-series analysis.

9.9.2 Solution

Use Python's built-in `time.sleep` function inside of an infinite loop to issue a query and store the results to a database such as MongoDB if the use of the Streaming API as illustrated in "Sampling the Twitter Firehose with the Streaming API" won't work.

9.9.3 Discussion

Although it's easy to get caught up in pointwise queries on particular keywords at a particular instant in time, the ability to sample data that's collected over time and detect trends and patterns gives us access to a radically powerful form of analysis that is commonly overlooked. Every time you look back and say, "I wish I'd known..." could have been a potential opportunity if you'd had the foresight to preemptively collect data that might have been useful for extrapolation or making predictions about the future (where applicable).

Time-series analysis of Twitter data can be truly fascinating given the ebbs and flows of topics and updates that can occur. Although it may be useful for many situations to sample from the firehose and store the results to a document-oriented database like MongoDB, it may be easier or more appropriate in some situations to periodically issue queries and record the results into discrete time intervals. For example, you might query the trending topics for a variety of geographic regions throughout a 24-hour period and measure the rate at which various trends change, compare rates of change across geographies, find the longest- and shortest-lived trends, and more.

Another compelling possibility that is being actively explored is correlations between sentiment as expressed on Twitter and stock markets. It's easy enough to zoom in on particular keywords, hashtags, or trending topics and later correlate the data against actual stock market changes; this could be an early step in building a bot to make predictions about markets and commodities.

Example 9-10 is essentially a composite of the code from "Accessing Twitter's API for Development Purposes", and Examples 9-3, and 9-7, and it demonstrates how you can use these recipes as primitive building blocks to create more complex scripts with a little bit of creativity and copy/pasting.

Example 9-10. Collecting time-series data

```python
import sys
import datetime
import time
import twitter

def get_time_series_data(api_func, mongo_db_name, mongo_db_coll,
                         secs_per_interval=60, max_intervals=15, **mongo_conn_kw):

    # Default settings of 15 intervals and 1 API call per interval ensure that
    # you will not exceed the Twitter rate limit.

    interval = 0

    while True:

        # A timestamp of the form "2013-06-14 12:52:07"
        now = str(datetime.datetime.now()).split(".")[0]

        response = save_to_mongo(api_func(), mongo_db_name,
                                 mongo_db_coll + "-" + now, **mongo_conn_kw)

        print("Write {0} trends".format(len(response.inserted_ids)), file=sys.stderr)
        print("Zzz...", file=sys.stderr)
        sys.stderr.flush()

        time.sleep(secs_per_interval) # seconds
        interval += 1

        if interval >= 15:
            break

# Sample usage

get_time_series_data(twitter_world_trends, 'time-series', 'twitter_world_trends')
```

9.10 Extracting Tweet Entities

9.10.1 Problem

You want to extract entities such as *@username* mentions, hashtags, and URLs from tweets for analysis.

9.10.2 Solution

Extract the entities from the `entities` field of the tweets.

9.10.3 Discussion

Twitter's API now provides tweet entities as a standard field for most of its API responses, where applicable. The `entities` field, illustrated in Example 9-11, includes user mentions, hashtags, references to URLs, media objects (such as images and videos), and financial symbols such as stock tickers. At the current time, not all fields may apply for all situations. For example, the `media` field will appear and be populated in a tweet only if a user embeds the media using a Twitter client that specifically uses a particular API for embedding the content; simply copying/pasting a link to a YouTube video won't necessarily populate this field.

See the API documentation (*http://bit.ly/2wD3VfB*) for more details, including information on some of the additional fields that are available for each type of entity. For example, in the case of a URL, Twitter offers several variations, including the shortened and expanded forms as well as a value that may be more appropriate for displaying in a user interface for certain situations.

Example 9-11. Extracting tweet entities

```
def extract_tweet_entities(statuses):

    # See https://bit.ly/2MELMkm
    # for more details on tweet entities

    if len(statuses) == 0:
        return [], [], [], [], []

    screen_names = [ user_mention['screen_name']
                        for status in statuses
                            for user_mention in status['entities']['user_mentions'] ]

    hashtags = [ hashtag['text']
                    for status in statuses
                        for hashtag in status['entities']['hashtags'] ]

    urls = [ url['expanded_url']
                for status in statuses
                    for url in status['entities']['urls'] ]

    # In some circumstances (such as search results), the media entity
    # may not appear
    medias = []
    symbols = []
    for status in statuses:
        if 'media' in status['entities']:
            for media in status['entities']['media']:
                medias.append(media['url'])
        if 'symbol' in status['entities']:
            for symbol in status['entities']['symbol']:
```

```
        symbols.append(symbol)

    return screen_names, hashtags, urls, medias, symbols

# Sample usage

q = 'CrossFit'

statuses = twitter_search(twitter_api, q)

screen_names, hashtags, urls, media, symbols = extract_tweet_entities(statuses)

# Explore the first five items for each...

print(json.dumps(screen_names[0:5], indent=1))
print(json.dumps(hashtags[0:5], indent=1))
print(json.dumps(urls[0:5], indent=1))
print(json.dumps(media[0:5], indent=1))
print(json.dumps(symbols[0:5], indent=1))
```

9.11 Finding the Most Popular Tweets in a Collection of Tweets

9.11.1 Problem

You want to determine which tweets are the most popular among a collection of search results or any other batch of tweets, such as a user timeline.

9.11.2 Solution

Analyze the `retweet_count` field of a tweet to determine whether or not the tweet was retweeted and, if so, how many times.

9.11.3 Discussion

Analyzing the `retweet_count` field of a tweet, as shown in Example 9-12, is perhaps the most straightforward measure of popularity because it stands to reason that popular tweets will be shared with others. Depending on your particular interpretation of "popular," however, another possible value that you could incorporate into a formula for determining a tweet's popularity is its `favorite_count`, which is the number of times a user has bookmarked a tweet. For example, you might weight the `retweet_count` at 1.0 and the `favorite_count` at 0.1 to add a marginal amount of weight to tweets that have been both retweeted and favorited if you wanted to use `favorite_count` as a tiebreaker.

The particular choice of values in a formula is entirely up to you and will depend on how important you think each of these fields is in the overall context of the problem that you are trying to solve. Other possibilities, such as incorporating an exponential decay (*http://bit.ly/1a1pHEe*) that accounts for time and weights recent tweets more heavily than less recent tweets, may prove useful in certain analyses.

 See also Recipes 9.14, and 9.15 for some additional discussion that may be helpful in navigating the space of analyzing and applying attribution to retweets, which can be slightly more confusing than it initially seems.

Example 9-12. Finding the most popular tweets in a collection of tweets

```
import twitter

def find_popular_tweets(twitter_api, statuses, retweet_threshold=3):

    # You could also consider using the favorite_count parameter as part of
    # this heuristic, possibly using it to provide an additional boost to
    # popular tweets in a ranked formulation

    return [ status
                for status in statuses
                    if status['retweet_count'] > retweet_threshold ]

# Sample usage

q = "CrossFit"

twitter_api = oauth_login()
search_results = twitter_search(twitter_api, q, max_results=200)

popular_tweets = find_popular_tweets(twitter_api, search_results)

for tweet in popular_tweets:
    print(tweet['text'], tweet['retweet_count'])
```

 The retweeted attribute in a tweet is *not* a shortcut for telling you whether or not a tweet has been retweeted. It is a so-called "perspectival" attribute that tells you whether or not the authenticated user (which would be you in the case that you are analyzing your own data) has retweeted a status, which is convenient for powering markers in user interfaces. It is called a perspectival attribute because it provides perspective from the standpoint of the authenticating user.

9.12 Finding the Most Popular Tweet Entities in a Collection of Tweets

9.12.1 Problem

You'd like to determine if there are any popular tweet entities, such as *@username* mentions, #hashtags, or URLs, that might provide insight into the nature of a collection of tweets.

9.12.2 Solution

Extract the tweet entities with a list comprehension, count them, and filter out any tweet entity that doesn't exceed a minimal threshold.

9.12.3 Discussion

Twitter's API provides access to tweet entities directly in the metadata values of a tweet through the `entities` field, as demonstrated in "Extracting Tweet Entities". After extracting the entities, you can compute the frequencies of each and easily extract the most common entities with a `collections.Counter` (shown in Example 9-13), which is a staple in Python's standard library and a considerable convenience in any frequency analysis experiment with Python. With a ranked collection of tweet entities at your fingertips, all that's left is to apply filtering or other threshold criteria to the collection of tweets in order to zero in on particular tweet entities of interest.

Example 9-13. Finding the most popular tweet entities in a collection of tweets

```python
import twitter
from collections import Counter

def get_common_tweet_entities(statuses, entity_threshold=3):

    # Create a flat list of all tweet entities
    tweet_entities = [ e
                       for status in statuses
                           for entity_type in extract_tweet_entities([status])
                               for e in entity_type
                     ]

    c = Counter(tweet_entities).most_common()

    # Compute frequencies
    return [ (k,v)
             for (k,v) in c
                 if v >= entity_threshold
```

```
        ]

# Sample usage

q = 'CrossFit'

twitter_api = oauth_login()
search_results = twitter_search(twitter_api, q, max_results=100)
common_entities = get_common_tweet_entities(search_results)

print("Most common tweet entities")
print(common_entities)
```

9.13 Tabulating Frequency Analysis

9.13.1 Problem

You'd like to tabulate the results of frequency analysis experiments in order to easily skim the results or otherwise display them in a format that's convenient for human consumption.

9.13.2 Solution

Use the prettytable package to easily create an object that can be loaded with rows of information and displayed as a table with fixed-width columns.

9.13.3 Discussion

The prettytable package is very easy to use and incredibly helpful in constructing an easily readable, text-based output that can be copied and pasted into any report or text file (see Example 9-14). Just use **pip install prettytable** to install the package per the norms for Python package installation. A prettytable.PrettyTable is especially handy when used in tandem with a collections.Counter or other data structure that distills to a list of tuples that can be ranked (sorted) for analysis purposes.

 If you are interested in storing data for consumption in a spreadsheet, you may want to consult the documention on the csv package (*http://bit.ly/2KmFsgz*) that's part of Python's standard library. However, be aware that there are some known issues (as documented) regarding its support for Unicode.

Example 9-14. Tabulating frequency analysis

```
from prettytable import PrettyTable

# Get some frequency data
```

```
twitter_api = oauth_login()
search_results = twitter_search(twitter_api, q, max_results=100)
common_entities = get_common_tweet_entities(search_results)

# Use PrettyTable to create a nice tabular display

pt = PrettyTable(field_names=['Entity', 'Count'])
[ pt.add_row(kv) for kv in common_entities ]
pt.align['Entity'], pt.align['Count'] = 'l', 'r' # Set column alignment
pt._max_width = {'Entity':60, 'Count':10}
print(pt)
```

9.14 Finding Users Who Have Retweeted a Status

9.14.1 Problem

You'd like to discover all of the users who have ever retweeted a particular status.

9.14.2 Solution

Use the GET retweeters/ids API endpoint to determine which users have retweeted the status.

9.14.3 Discussion

Although the GET retweeters/ids API (*http://bit.ly/2jRvjNQ*) returns the IDs of any users who have retweeted a status, there are a couple of subtle caveats that you should know about. In particular, keep in mind that this API reports only users who have retweeted by using Twitter's *native retweet API*, as opposed to users who have copy/ pasted a tweet and prepended it with "RT," appended attribution with "(via *@username*)," or used another common convention.

Most Twitter applications (including the *twitter.com* user interface) use the native retweet API, but some users may still elect to share a status by "working around" the native API for the purposes of attaching additional commentary to a tweet or inserting themselves into a conversation that they'd otherwise be broadcasting only as an intermediary. For example, a user may suffix "< AWESOME!" to a tweet to display like-mindedness about it, and although they may think of this as a retweet, they're actually *quoting* the tweet as far as Twitter's API is concerned. At least part of the reason for the confusion between quoting a tweet and retweeting a tweet is that Twitter has not always offered a native retweet API. In fact, the notion of retweeting is a phenomenon that evolved organically and that Twitter eventually responded to by providing first-class API support back in late 2010.

An illustration may help to drive home this subtle technical detail: suppose that @fperez_org posts a status and then @SocialWebMining retweets it. At this point in time, the `retweet_count` of the status posted by @fperez_org would be equal to 1, and @SocialWebMining would have a tweet in its user timeline that indicates a retweet of @fperez_org's status.

Now let's suppose that @jyeee notices @fperez_org's status by examining @SocialWebMining's user timeline through *twitter.com* or an application like TweetDeck (*http://bit.ly/1a1pIbh*) and clicks the retweet button. At this point in time, @fperez_org's status would have a `retweet_count` equal to 2 and @jyeee would have a tweet in their user timeline (just like @SocialWebMining's last status) indicating a retweet of @fperez_org.

Here's the important point to understand: *from the standpoint of any user browsing @jyeee's timeline, @SocialWebMining's intermediary link between @fperez_org and @jyeee is effectively lost.* In other words, @fperez_org will receive the attribution for the original tweet, regardless of what kind of chain reaction gets set off involving multiple layers of intermediaries for the status.

With the ID values of any user who has retweeted the tweet in hand, it's easy enough to get profile details using the `GET users/lookup` API. See "Resolving User Profile Information" for more details.

Given that Example 9-15 may not fully satisfy your needs, be sure to also carefully consider "Extracting a Retweet's Attribution" as an additional step that you can take to discover broadcasters of a status. It provides an example that uses a regular expression to analyze a tweet's content to extract the attribution information for a *quoted* tweet if you are processing a historical archive of tweets or otherwise want to double-check the content for attribution information.

Example 9-15. Finding users who have retweeted a status

```
import twitter

twitter_api = oauth_login()

print("""User IDs for retweeters of a tweet by @fperez_org
that was retweeted by @SocialWebMining and that @jyeee then retweeted
from @SocialWebMining's timeline\n""")
print(twitter_api.statuses.retweeters.ids(_id=334188056905129984)['ids'])
print(json.dumps(twitter_api.statuses.show(_id=334188056905129984), indent=1))
print()

print("@SocialWeb's retweet of @fperez_org's tweet\n")
print(twitter_api.statuses.retweeters.ids(_id=345723917798866944)['ids'])
print(json.dumps(twitter_api.statuses.show(_id=345723917798866944), indent=1))
print()
```

```
print("@jyeee's retweet of @fperez_org's tweet\n")
print(twitter_api.statuses.retweeters.ids(_id=338835939172417537)['ids'])
print(json.dumps(twitter_api.statuses.show(_id=338835939172417537), indent=1))
```

 Some Twitter users intentionally quote tweets as opposed to using the retweet API in order to inject themselves into conversations and potentially be retweeted themselves, and it is still quite common to see the *RT* and *via* functionality widely used. In fact, popular applications such as TweetDeck include functionality for distinguishing between "Edit & RT" and a native "Retweet," as illustrated in Figure 9-2.

Figure 9-2. Popular applications such as Twitter's own TweetDeck provide "Edit & RT" functionality to "quote" a tweet as well as the newer and more native functionality for "Retweet"

9.15 Extracting a Retweet's Attribution

9.15.1 Problem

You'd like to determine the original attribution of a tweet.

9.15.2 Solution

Analyze the tweet's content with regular expression heuristics for the presence of conventions such as "RT @SocialWebMining" or "(via @SocialWebMining)."

9.15.3 Discussion

Examining the results of Twitter's native retweet API as described in "Finding Users Who Have Retweeted a Status" can provide the original attribution of a tweet in some, but certainly not all, circumstances. As noted in that recipe, it is sometimes the case that users will inject themselves into conversations for various reasons, so it may be necessary to analyze certain tweets in order to discover the original attribution. Example 9-16 demonstrates how to use regular expressions in Python to detect a couple of commonly used conventions that were adopted prior to the release of Twitter's native retweet API and that are still in common use today.

Example 9-16. Extracting a retweet's attribution

```
import re

def get_rt_attributions(tweet):

    # Regex adapted from Stack Overflow (http://bit.ly/1821y0J)

    rt_patterns = re.compile(r"(RT|via)((?:\b\W*@\w+)+)", re.IGNORECASE)
    rt_attributions = []

    # Inspect the tweet to see if it was produced with /statuses/retweet/:id.
    # See https://bit.ly/2BHBEaq

    if 'retweeted_status' in tweet:
        attribution = tweet['retweeted_status']['user']['screen_name'].lower()
        rt_attributions.append(attribution)

    # Also, inspect the tweet for the presence of "legacy" retweet patterns
    # such as "RT" and "via", which are still widely used for various reasons
    # and potentially very useful. See https://bit.ly/2piMo6h
    # for information about retweets

    try:
        rt_attributions += [
                        mention.strip()
                        for mention in rt_patterns.findall(tweet['text'])[0][1].split()
                    ]
    except IndexError as e:
        pass

    # Filter out any duplicates

    return list(set([rta.strip("@").lower() for rta in rt_attributions]))

# Sample usage
twitter_api = oauth_login()

tweet = twitter_api.statuses.show(_id=214746575765913602)
```

```
print(get_rt_attributions(tweet))
print()
tweet = twitter_api.statuses.show(_id=345723917798866944)
print(get_rt_attributions(tweet))
```

9.16 Making Robust Twitter Requests

9.16.1 Problem

In the midst of collecting data for analysis, you encounter unexpected HTTP errors that range from exceeding your rate limits (429 error) to the infamous "fail whale" (503 error) that need to be handled on a case-by-case basis.

9.16.2 Solution

Write a function that serves as a general-purpose API wrapper and provides abstracted logic for handling various HTTP error codes in meaningful ways.

9.16.3 Discussion

Although Twitter's rate limits are arguably adequate for most applications, they are generally inadequate for data mining exercises, so it's common that you'll need to manage the number of requests that you make in a given time period and also account for other types of HTTP failures, such as the infamous "fail whale" or other unexpected network glitches. One approach, shown in Example 9-17, is to write a wrapper function that abstracts away this messy logic and allows you to simply write your script as though rate limits and HTTP errors do not exist for the most part.

See "Constructing Convenient Function Calls" for inspiration on how you could use the standard library's `functools.partial` function to simplify the use of this wrapper function for some situations. Also be sure to review the complete listing of Twitter's HTTP error codes (*http://bit.ly/2rFAjZw*). "Getting All Friends or Followers for a User" provides a concrete implementation that illustrates how to use a function called `make_twitter_request` that should simplify some of the HTTP errors you may experience in harvesting Twitter data.

Example 9-17. Making robust Twitter requests

```
import sys
import time
from urllib.error import URLError
from http.client import BadStatusLine
import json
```

```
import twitter

def make_twitter_request(twitter_api_func, max_errors=10, *args, **kw):

    # A nested helper function that handles common HTTPErrors. Returns an updated
    # value for wait_period if the problem is a 500-level error. Blocks until the
    # rate limit is reset if it's a rate-limiting issue (429 error). Returns None
    # for 401 and 404 errors, which require special handling by the caller.
    def handle_twitter_http_error(e, wait_period=2, sleep_when_rate_limited=True):

        if wait_period > 3600: # Seconds
            print('Too many retries. Quitting.', file=sys.stderr)
            raise e

        # See https://developer.twitter.com/en/docs/basics/response-codes
        # for common codes

        if e.e.code == 401:
            print('Encountered 401 Error (Not Authorized)', file=sys.stderr)
            return None
        elif e.e.code == 404:
            print('Encountered 404 Error (Not Found)', file=sys.stderr)
            return None
        elif e.e.code == 429:
            print('Encountered 429 Error (Rate Limit Exceeded)', file=sys.stderr)
            if sleep_when_rate_limited:
                print("Retrying in 15 minutes...ZzZ...", file=sys.stderr)
                sys.stderr.flush()
                time.sleep(60*15 + 5)
                print('...ZzZ...Awake now and trying again.', file=sys.stderr)
                return 2
            else:
                raise e # Caller must handle the rate-limiting issue
        elif e.e.code in (500, 502, 503, 504):
            print('Encountered {0} Error. Retrying in {1} seconds'\
                .format(e.e.code, wait_period), file=sys.stderr)
            time.sleep(wait_period)
            wait_period *= 1.5
            return wait_period
        else:
            raise e

    # End of nested helper function

    wait_period = 2
    error_count = 0

    while True:
        try:
            return twitter_api_func(*args, **kw)
        except twitter.api.TwitterHTTPError as e:
            error_count = 0
```

```
            wait_period = handle_twitter_http_error(e, wait_period)
            if wait_period is None:
                return
        except URLError as e:
            error_count += 1
            time.sleep(wait_period)
            wait_period *= 1.5
            print("URLError encountered. Continuing.", file=sys.stderr)
            if error_count > max_errors:
                print("Too many consecutive errors...bailing out.", file=sys.stderr)
                raise
        except BadStatusLine as e:
            error_count += 1
            time.sleep(wait_period)
            wait_period *= 1.5
            print("BadStatusLine encountered. Continuing.", file=sys.stderr)
            if error_count > max_errors:
                print("Too many consecutive errors...bailing out.", file=sys.stderr)
                raise

# Sample usage

twitter_api = oauth_login()

# See http://bit.ly/2Gcjfzr for twitter_api.users.lookup

response = make_twitter_request(twitter_api.users.lookup,
                                screen_name="SocialWebMining")

print(json.dumps(response, indent=1))
```

9.17 Resolving User Profile Information

9.17.1 Problem

You'd like to look up profile information for one or more user IDs or screen names.

9.17.2 Solution

Use the GET users/lookup API to exchange as many as 100 IDs or usernames at a time for complete user profiles.

9.17.3 Discussion

Many APIs, such as GET friends/ids and GET followers/ids, return opaque ID values that need to be resolved to usernames or other profile information for meaningful analysis. Twitter provides a GET users/lookup (*https://bit.ly/2Gcjfzr*) API that can be used to resolve as many as 100 IDs or usernames at a time, and a simple pattern can be employed to iterate over larger batches. Although it adds a little bit of complexity to the logic, a single function can be constructed that accepts keyword parameters for your choice of either usernames or IDs that are resolved to user profiles. Example 9-18 illustrates such a function that can be adapted for a large variety of purposes, providing ancillary support for situations in which you'll need to resolve user IDs.

Example 9-18. Resolving user profile information

```python
def get_user_profile(twitter_api, screen_names=None, user_ids=None):

    # Must have either screen_name or user_id (logical xor)
    assert (screen_names != None) != (user_ids != None), \
        "Must have screen_names or user_ids, but not both"

    items_to_info = {}

    items = screen_names or user_ids

    while len(items) > 0:

        # Process 100 items at a time per the API specifications for /users/lookup.
        # See http://bit.ly/2Gcjfzr for details.

        items_str = ','.join([str(item) for item in items[:100]])
        items = items[100:]

        if screen_names:
            response = make_twitter_request(twitter_api.users.lookup,
                                            screen_name=items_str)
        else: # user_ids
            response = make_twitter_request(twitter_api.users.lookup,
                                            user_id=items_str)

        for user_info in response:
            if screen_names:
                items_to_info[user_info['screen_name']] = user_info
            else: # user_ids
                items_to_info[user_info['id']] = user_info

    return items_to_info

# Sample usage

twitter_api = oauth_login()

print(get_user_profile(twitter_api,
    screen_names=["SocialWebMining", "ptwobrussell"]))
#print(get_user_profile(twitter_api, user_ids=[132373965]))
```

9.18 Extracting Tweet Entities from Arbitrary Text

9.18.1 Problem

You'd like to analyze arbitrary text and extract tweet entities, such as *@username* mentions, hashtags, and URLs that may appear within it.

9.18.2 Solution

Use a third-party package like `twitter_text` to extract tweet entities from arbitrary text such as historical tweet archives that may not contain tweet entities as currently provided by the v1.1 API.

9.18.3 Discussion

Twitter has not always extracted tweet entities but you can easily derive them yourself with the help of a third-party package called `twitter_text`, as shown in Example 9-19. You can install `twitter_text` with `pip` using the command **pip install twitter_text**.

Example 9-19. Extracting tweet entities from arbitrary text

```
# pip install twitter_text
import twitter_text

# Sample usage

txt = "RT @SocialWebMining Mining 1M+ Tweets About #Syria http://wp.me/p3QiJd-1I"

ex = twitter_text.Extractor(txt)

print("Screen Names:", ex.extract_mentioned_screen_names_with_indices())
print("URLs:", ex.extract_urls_with_indices())
print("Hashtags:", ex.extract_hashtags_with_indices())
```

9.19 Getting All Friends or Followers for a User

9.19.1 Problem

You'd like to harvest all of the friends or followers for a (potentially very popular) Twitter user.

9.19.2 Solution

Use the `make_twitter_request` function introduced in "Making Robust Twitter Requests" to simplify the process of harvesting IDs by accounting for situations in which the number of followers may exceed what can be fetched within the prescribed rate limits.

9.19.3 Discussion

`GET followers/ids` and `GET friends/ids` provide an API that can be navigated to retrieve all of the follower and friend IDs for a particular user, but the logic involved in retrieving all of the IDs can be nontrivial since each API request returns at most 5,000 IDs at a time. Although most users won't have anywhere near 5,000 friends or followers, some celebrity users, who are often interesting to analyze, will have hundreds of thousands or even millions of followers. Harvesting all of these IDs can be challenging because of the need to walk the cursor for each batch of results and also account for possible HTTP errors along the way. Fortunately, it's not too difficult to adapt `make_twitter_request` and previously introduced logic for walking the cursor of results to systematically fetch all of these IDs.

Techniques similar to those introduced in Example 9-20 could be incorporated into the template supplied in "Resolving User Profile Information" to create a robust function that provides a secondary step, such as resolving a subset (or all) of the IDs for usernames. It is advisable to store the results into a document-oriented database such as MongoDB (as illustrated in "Problem" on page 341) after each result so that no information is ever lost in the event of an unexpected glitch during a large harvesting operation.

 You may be better off paying a third party such as DataSift (*http://bit.ly/1a1pKje*) for faster access to certain kinds of data, such as the complete profiles for all of a very popular user's (say, @ladygaga's) followers. Before you attempt to collect such a vast amount of data, at least do the arithmetic and determine how long it will take, think about the possible (unexpected) errors that may occur along the way for very long-running processes, and consider whether it would be better to acquire the data from another source. What it may cost you in money, it may save you in time.

Example 9-20. Getting all friends or followers for a user

```
from functools import partial
from sys import maxsize as maxint

def get_friends_followers_ids(twitter_api, screen_name=None, user_id=None,
                              friends_limit=maxint, followers_limit=maxint):
```

```
    # Must have either screen_name or user_id (logical xor)
    assert (screen_name != None) != (user_id != None), \
        "Must have screen_name or user_id, but not both"

    # See http://bit.ly/2GcjKJP and http://bit.ly/2rFz90N for details
    # on API parameters

    get_friends_ids = partial(make_twitter_request, twitter_api.friends.ids,
                                count=5000)
    get_followers_ids = partial(make_twitter_request, twitter_api.followers.ids,
                                count=5000)

    friends_ids, followers_ids = [], []

    for twitter_api_func, limit, ids, label in [
                    [get_friends_ids, friends_limit, friends_ids, "friends"],
                    [get_followers_ids, followers_limit, followers_ids, "followers"]
                ]:

        if limit == 0: continue

        cursor = -1
        while cursor != 0:

            # Use make_twitter_request via the partially bound callable
            if screen_name:
                response = twitter_api_func(screen_name=screen_name, cursor=cursor)
            else: # user_id
                response = twitter_api_func(user_id=user_id, cursor=cursor)

            if response is not None:
                ids += response['ids']
                cursor = response['next_cursor']

            print('Fetched {0} total {1} ids for {2}'.format(len(ids),
                    label, (user_id or screen_name)),file=sys.stderr)

            # You may want to store data during each iteration to provide an
            # additional layer of protection from exceptional circumstances

            if len(ids) >= limit or response is None:
                break

    # Do something useful with the IDs, like store them to disk
    return friends_ids[:friends_limit], followers_ids[:followers_limit]

# Sample usage

twitter_api = oauth_login()

friends_ids, followers_ids = get_friends_followers_ids(twitter_api,
```

```
                                       screen_name="SocialWebMining",
                                       friends_limit=10,
                                       followers_limit=10)

print(friends_ids)
print(followers_ids)
```

9.20 Analyzing a User's Friends and Followers

9.20.1 Problem

You'd like to conduct a basic analysis that compares a user's friends and followers.

9.20.2 Solution

Use setwise operations such as intersection and difference to analyze the user's friends and followers.

9.20.3 Discussion

After harvesting all of a user's friends and followers, you can conduct some primitive analyses using only the ID values themselves with the help of setwise operations such as *intersection* and *difference*, as shown in Example 9-21.

Given two sets, the intersection of the sets returns the items that they have in common, whereas the difference between the sets "subtracts" the items in one set from the other, leaving behind the difference. Recall that intersection is a commutative operation, while difference is *not* commutative.[1]

In the context of analyzing friends and followers, the intersection of two sets can be interpreted as "mutual friends," or people a user is following who are also following them back, while the difference of two sets can be interpreted as followers who the user isn't following back or people they are following who aren't following them back, depending on the order of the operands.

Given a complete list of friend and follower IDs, computing these setwise operations is a natural starting point and can be the springboard for subsequent analysis. For example, it probably isn't necessary to use the GET users/lookup API to fetch profiles for millions of followers for a user as an immediate point of analysis. You might instead opt to calculate the results of a setwise operation such as mutual friends (for which there are likely much stronger affinities) and hone in on the profiles of these user IDs before spidering out further.

---

1 A commutative operation is one in which the order of the operands does not matter—the operands can commute—as is the case with addition or multiplication.

Example 9-21. Analyzing a user's friends and followers

```
def setwise_friends_followers_analysis(screen_name, friends_ids, followers_ids):

    friends_ids, followers_ids = set(friends_ids), set(followers_ids)

    print('{0} is following {1}'.format(screen_name, len(friends_ids)))

    print('{0} is being followed by {1}'.format(screen_name, len(followers_ids)))

    print('{0} of {1} are not following {2} back'.format(
            len(friends_ids.difference(followers_ids)),
            len(friends_ids), screen_name))

    print('{0} of {1} are not being followed back by {2}'.format(
            len(followers_ids.difference(friends_ids)),
            len(followers_ids), screen_name))

    print('{0} has {1} mutual friends'.format(
            screen_name, len(friends_ids.intersection(followers_ids))))

# Sample usage

screen_name = "ptwobrussell"

twitter_api = oauth_login()

friends_ids, followers_ids = get_friends_followers_ids(twitter_api,
                                            screen_name=screen_name)
setwise_friends_followers_analysis(screen_name, friends_ids, followers_ids)
```

9.21 Harvesting a User's Tweets

9.21.1 Problem

You'd like to harvest all of a user's most recent tweets for analysis.

9.21.2 Solution

Use the GET statuses/user_timeline API endpoint to retrieve as many as 3,200 of the most recent tweets from a user, preferably with the added help of a robust API wrapper such as make_twitter_request (as introduced in "Making Robust Twitter Requests") since this series of requests may exceed rate limits or encounter HTTP errors along the way.

9.21.3 Discussion

Timelines are a fundamental concept in the Twitter developer ecosystem, and Twitter provides a convenient API endpoint for the purpose of harvesting tweets by user through the concept of a "user timeline." Harvesting a user's tweets, as demonstrated in Example 9-22, is a meaningful starting point for analysis since a tweet is the most fundamental primitive in the ecosystem. A large collection of tweets by a particular user provides an incredible amount of insight into what the person talks (and thus cares) about. With an archive of several hundred tweets for a particular user, you can conduct dozens of experiments, often with little additional API access. Storing the tweets in a particular collection of a document-oriented database such as MongoDB is a natural way to store and access the data during experimentation. For longer-term Twitter users, performing a time-series analysis of how interests or sentiments have changed over time might be a worthwhile exercise.

Example 9-22. Harvesting a user's tweets

```
def harvest_user_timeline(twitter_api, screen_name=None, user_id=None,
    max_results=1000):

    assert (screen_name != None) != (user_id != None), \
    "Must have screen_name or user_id, but not both"

    kw = {  # Keyword args for the Twitter API call
        'count': 200,
        'trim_user': 'true',
        'include_rts' : 'true',
        'since_id' : 1
        }

    if screen_name:
        kw['screen_name'] = screen_name
    else:
        kw['user_id'] = user_id

    max_pages = 16
    results = []

    tweets = make_twitter_request(twitter_api.statuses.user_timeline, **kw)

    if tweets is None: # 401 (Not Authorized) - Need to bail out on loop entry
        tweets = []

    results += tweets

    print('Fetched {0} tweets'.format(len(tweets)), file=sys.stderr)

    page_num = 1

    # Many Twitter accounts have fewer than 200 tweets so you don't want to enter
    # the loop and waste a precious request if max_results = 200.

    # Note: Analogous optimizations could be applied inside the loop to try and
```

```
# save requests (e.g., don't make a third request if you have 287 tweets out of
# a possible 400 tweets after your second request). Twitter does do some post-
# filtering on censored and deleted tweets out of batches of 'count', though,
# so you can't strictly check for the number of results being 200. You might get
# back 198, for example, and still have many more tweets to go. If you have the
# total number of tweets for an account (by GET /users/lookup/), then you could
# simply use this value as a guide.

if max_results == kw['count']:
    page_num = max_pages # Prevent loop entry

while page_num < max_pages and len(tweets) > 0 and len(results) < max_results:

    # Necessary for traversing the timeline in Twitter's v1.1 API:
    # get the next query's max-id parameter to pass in.
    # See http://bit.ly/2L0jwJw.
    kw['max_id'] = min([ tweet['id'] for tweet in tweets]) - 1

    tweets = make_twitter_request(twitter_api.statuses.user_timeline, **kw)
    results += tweets

    print('Fetched {0} tweets'.format(len(tweets)),file=sys.stderr)

    page_num += 1

print('Done fetching tweets', file=sys.stderr)

return results[:max_results]

# Sample usage

twitter_api = oauth_login()
tweets = harvest_user_timeline(twitter_api, screen_name="SocialWebMining",
                                max_results=200)

# Save to MongoDB with save_to_mongo or a local file with save_json
```

9.22 Crawling a Friendship Graph

9.22.1 Problem

You'd like to harvest the IDs of a user's followers, followers of those followers, follow-ers of followers of those followers, and so on, as part of a network analysis—essen-tially crawling a friendship graph of the "following" relationships on Twitter.

9.22.2 Solution

Use a breadth-first search to systematically harvest friendship information that can rather easily be interpreted as a graph for network analysis.

9.22.3 Discussion

A breadth-first search is a common technique for exploring a graph and is one of the standard ways that you would start at a point and build up multiple layers of context defined by relationships. Given a starting point and a depth, a breadth-first traversal systematically explores the space such that it is guaranteed to eventually return all nodes in the graph up to the said depth, and the search explores the space such that each depth completes before the next depth is begun (see Example 9-23).

Keep in mind that it is quite possible that in exploring Twitter friendship graphs, you may encounter *supernodes*—nodes with very high degrees of outgoing edges—which can very easily consume computing resources and API requests that count toward your rate limit. It is advisable that you provide a meaningful cap on the maximum number of followers you'd like to fetch for each user in the graph, at least during preliminary analysis, so that you know what you're up against and can determine whether the supernodes are worth the time and trouble for solving your particular problem. Exploring an unknown graph is a complex (and exciting) problem to work on, and various other tools, such as sampling techniques, could be intelligently incorporated to further enhance the efficacy of the search.

Example 9-23. Crawling a friendship graph

```
def crawl_followers(twitter_api, screen_name, limit=1000000, depth=2,
                    **mongo_conn_kw):

    # Resolve the ID for screen_name and start working with IDs for consistency
    # in storage

    seed_id = str(twitter_api.users.show(screen_name=screen_name)['id'])

    _, next_queue = get_friends_followers_ids(twitter_api, user_id=seed_id,
                                              friends_limit=0, followers_limit=limit)

    # Store a seed_id => _follower_ids mapping in MongoDB

    save_to_mongo({'followers' : [ _id for _id in next_queue ]}, 'followers_crawl',
                  '{0}-follower_ids'.format(seed_id), **mongo_conn_kw)

    d = 1
    while d < depth:
        d += 1
        (queue, next_queue) = (next_queue, [])
        for fid in queue:
            _, follower_ids = get_friends_followers_ids(twitter_api, user_id=fid,
                                                        friends_limit=0,
                                                        followers_limit=limit)

            # Store a fid => follower_ids mapping in MongoDB
```

```
        save_to_mongo({'followers' : [ _id for _id in follower_ids ]},
                        'followers_crawl', '{0}-follower_ids'.format(fid))

        next_queue += follower_ids

# Sample usage

screen_name = "timoreilly"

twitter_api = oauth_login()

crawl_followers(twitter_api, screen_name, depth=1, limit=10)
```

9.23 Analyzing Tweet Content

9.23.1 Problem

Given a collection of tweets, you'd like to do some cursory analysis of the content in each to get a better idea of the nature of the discussion and ideas being conveyed in the tweets themselves.

9.23.2 Solution

Use simple statistics, such as lexical diversity and average number of words per tweet, to gain elementary insight into what is being talked about as a first step in sizing up the nature of the language being used.

9.23.3 Discussion

In addition to analyzing the content for tweet entities and conducting simple frequency analysis of commonly occurring words, you can also examine the *lexical diversity* of the tweets and calculate other simple statistics, such as the average number of words per tweet, to better size up the data (see Example 9-24). Lexical diversity is a simple statistic that is defined as the number of unique words divided by the number of total words in a corpus; by definition, a lexical diversity of 1.0 would mean that all words in a corpus were unique, while a lexical diversity that approaches 0.0 implies more duplicate words.

Depending on the context, lexical diversity can be interpreted slightly differently. For example, in contexts such as literature, comparing the lexical diversity of two authors might be used to measure the richness or expressiveness of their language relative to each other. Although not usually the end goal in and of itself, examining lexical diversity often provides valuable preliminary insight (usually in conjunction with frequency analysis) that can be used to better inform possible follow-up steps.

In the Twittersphere, lexical diversity might be interpreted in a similar fashion if comparing two Twitter users, but it might also suggest a lot about the relative diversity of overall content being discussed, as might be the case with someone who talks only about technology versus someone who talks about a much wider range of topics. In a context such as a collection of tweets by multiple authors about the same topic (as would be the case in examining a collection of tweets returned by the Search API or the Streaming API), a much lower than expected lexical diversity *might* also imply that there is a lot of "group think" going on. Another possibility is a lot of retweeting, in which the same information is more or less being regurgitated. As with any other analysis, no statistic should be interpreted devoid of supporting context.

Example 9-24. Analyzing tweet content

```
def analyze_tweet_content(statuses):

    if len(statuses) == 0:
        print("No statuses to analyze")
        return

    # A nested helper function for computing lexical diversity
    def lexical_diversity(tokens):
        return 1.0*len(set(tokens))/len(tokens)

    # A nested helper function for computing the average number of words per tweet
    def average_words(statuses):
        total_words = sum([ len(s.split()) for s in statuses ])
        return 1.0*total_words/len(statuses)

    status_texts = [ status['text'] for status in statuses ]
    screen_names, hashtags, urls, media, _ = extract_tweet_entities(statuses)

    # Compute a collection of all words from all tweets
    words = [ w
              for t in status_texts
                  for w in t.split() ]

    print("Lexical diversity (words):", lexical_diversity(words))
    print("Lexical diversity (screen names):", lexical_diversity(screen_names))
    print("Lexical diversity (hashtags):", lexical_diversity(hashtags))
    print("Averge words per tweet:", average_words(status_texts))


# Sample usage

q = 'CrossFit'
twitter_api = oauth_login()
search_results = twitter_search(twitter_api, q)

analyze_tweet_content(search_results)
```

9.24 Summarizing Link Targets

9.24.1 Problem

You'd like to have a cursory understanding of what is being talked about in a link target, such as a URL that is extracted as a tweet entity, to gain insight into the nature of a tweet or the interests of a Twitter user.

9.24.2 Solution

Summarize the content in the URL to just a few sentences that can easily be skimmed (or more tersely analyzed in some other way) as opposed to reading the entire web page.

9.24.3 Discussion

Your imagination is the only limitation when it comes to trying to understand the human language data in web pages. Example 9-25 is an attempt to provide a template for processing and distilling that content into a terse form that could be quickly skimmed or analyzed by alternative techniques. In short, it demonstrates how to fetch a web page, isolate the meaningful content in the web page (as opposed to the prolific amounts of boilerplate text in the headers, footers, sidebars, etc.), remove the HTML markup that may be remaining in that content, and use a simple summarization technique to isolate the most important sentences in the content.

The summarization technique basically rests on the premise that the most important sentences are a good summary of the content if presented in chronological order, and that you can discover the most important sentences by identifying frequently occurring words that interact with one another in close proximity. Although a bit crude, this form of summarization works surprisingly well on reasonably well-written web content.

Example 9-25. Summarizing link targets

```
import sys
import json
import nltk
import numpy
import requests
from boilerpipe.extract import Extractor

def summarize(url=None, html=None, n=100, cluster_threshold=5, top_sentences=5):

    # Adapted from "The Automatic Creation of Literature Abstracts" by H.P. Luhn
    #
    # Parameters:
```

```
# * n  - Number of words to consider
# * cluster_threshold - Distance between words to consider
# * top_sentences - Number of sentences to return for a "top n" summary

# Begin - nested helper function
def score_sentences(sentences, important_words):
    scores = []
    sentence_idx = -1

    for s in [nltk.tokenize.word_tokenize(s) for s in sentences]:

        sentence_idx += 1
        word_idx = []

        # For each word in the word list...
        for w in important_words:
            try:
                # Compute an index for important words in each sentence

                word_idx.append(s.index(w))
            except ValueError as e: # w not in this particular sentence
                pass

        word_idx.sort()

        # It is possible that some sentences may not contain any important words
        if len(word_idx)== 0: continue

        # Using the word index, compute clusters with a max distance threshold
        # for any two consecutive words

        clusters = []
        cluster = [word_idx[0]]
        i = 1
        while i < len(word_idx):
            if word_idx[i] - word_idx[i - 1] < cluster_threshold:
                cluster.append(word_idx[i])
            else:
                clusters.append(cluster[:])
                cluster = [word_idx[i]]
            i += 1
        clusters.append(cluster)

        # Score each cluster. The max score for any given cluster is the score
        # for the sentence.

        max_cluster_score = 0
        for c in clusters:
            significant_words_in_cluster = len(c)
            total_words_in_cluster = c[-1] - c[0] + 1
            score = 1.0 * significant_words_in_cluster \
                * significant_words_in_cluster / total_words_in_cluster
```

```
            if score > max_cluster_score:
                max_cluster_score = score

        scores.append((sentence_idx, score))

    return scores

# End - nested helper function

extractor = Extractor(extractor='ArticleExtractor', url=url, html=html)

# It's entirely possible that this "clean page" will be a big mess. YMMV.
# The good news is that the summarize algorithm inherently accounts for handling
# a lot of this noise.

txt = extractor.getText()

sentences = [s for s in nltk.tokenize.sent_tokenize(txt)]
normalized_sentences = [s.lower() for s in sentences]

words = [w.lower() for sentence in normalized_sentences for w in
            nltk.tokenize.word_tokenize(sentence)]

fdist = nltk.FreqDist(words)

top_n_words = [w[0] for w in fdist.items()
            if w[0] not in nltk.corpus.stopwords.words('english')][:n]

scored_sentences = score_sentences(normalized_sentences, top_n_words)

# Summarization Approach 1:
# Filter out nonsignificant sentences by using the average score plus a
# fraction of the std dev as a filter

avg = numpy.mean([s[1] for s in scored_sentences])
std = numpy.std([s[1] for s in scored_sentences])
mean_scored = [(sent_idx, score) for (sent_idx, score) in scored_sentences
                if score > avg + 0.5 * std]

# Summarization Approach 2:
# Return only the top N ranked sentences

top_n_scored = sorted(scored_sentences, key=lambda s: s[1])[-top_sentences:]
top_n_scored = sorted(top_n_scored, key=lambda s: s[0])

# Decorate the post object with summaries

return dict(top_n_summary=[sentences[idx] for (idx, score) in top_n_scored],
            mean_scored_summary=[sentences[idx] for (idx, score) in mean_scored])

# Sample usage
```

```
sample_url = 'http://radar.oreilly.com/2013/06/phishing-in-facebooks-pond.html'
summary = summarize(url=sample_url)

# Alternatively, you can pass in HTML if you have it. Sometimes this approach may be
# necessary if you encounter mysterious urllib2.BadStatusLine errors. Here's how
# that would work:

# sample_html = requests.get(sample_url).text
# summary = summarize(html=sample_html)

print("-------------------------------------------------")
print("              'Top N Summary'")
print("-------------------------------------------------")
print(" ".join(summary['top_n_summary']))
print()
print()
print("-------------------------------------------------")
print("              'Mean Scored' Summary")
print("-------------------------------------------------")
print(" ".join(summary['mean_scored_summary']))
```

9.25 Analyzing a User's Favorite Tweets

9.25.1 Problem

You'd like to learn more about what a person cares about by examining the tweets that person has marked as favorites.

9.25.2 Solution

Use the GET favorites/list API endpoint to fetch a user's favorite tweets and then apply techniques to detect, extract, and count tweet entities to characterize the content.

9.25.3 Discussion

Not all Twitter users take advantage of the bookmarking feature to identify favorites, so you can't consider it a completely dependable technique for zeroing in on content and topics of interest; however, if you are fortunate enough to encounter a Twitter user who tends to bookmark favorites as a habit, you'll often find a treasure trove of curated content. Although Example 9-26 shows an analysis that builds upon previous recipes to construct a table of tweet entities, you could apply more advanced techniques to the tweets themselves. A couple of ideas might include separating the content into different topics, analyzing how a person's favorites have changed or evolved over time, or plotting out the regularity of when and how often a person marks tweets as favorites.

Keep in mind that in addition to favorites, any tweets that a user has retweeted are also promising candidates for analysis, and even analyzing patterns of behavior such as whether or not a user tends to retweet (and how often), bookmark (and how often), or both is an enlightening survey in its own right.

Example 9-26. Analyzing a user's favorite tweets

```
def analyze_favorites(twitter_api, screen_name, entity_threshold=2):

    # Could fetch more than 200 by walking the cursor as shown in other
    # recipes, but 200 is a good sample to work with
    favs = twitter_api.favorites.list(screen_name=screen_name, count=200)
    print("Number of favorites:", len(favs))

    # Figure out what some of the common entities are, if any, in the content

    common_entities = get_common_tweet_entities(favs,
                                                entity_threshold=entity_threshold)

    # Use PrettyTable to create a nice tabular display

    pt = PrettyTable(field_names=['Entity', 'Count'])
    [ pt.add_row(kv) for kv in common_entities ]
    pt.align['Entity'], pt.align['Count'] = 'l', 'r' # Set column alignment

    print()
    print("Common entities in favorites...")
    print(pt)


    # Print out some other stats
    print()
    print("Some statistics about the content of the favorities...")
    print()
    analyze_tweet_content(favs)

    # Could also start analyzing link content or summarized link content, and more

# Sample usage

twitter_api = oauth_login()
analyze_favorites(twitter_api, "ptwobrussell")
```

9.26 Closing Remarks

Although this cookbook is really just a modest collection when compared to the hundreds or even thousands of possible recipes for manipulating and mining Twitter data, hopefully it has provided you with a good springboard and a sampling of ideas that you'll be able to draw upon and adapt in many profitable ways. The possibilities for what you can do with Twitter data (and most other social data) are broad, powerful, and (perhaps most importantly) fun!

 Pull requests for additional recipes (as well as enhancements to these recipes) are welcome and highly encouraged, and will be liberally accepted. Please fork this book's source code from its GitHub repository (*http://bit.ly/Mining-the-Social-Web-3e*), commit a recipe to this chapter's Jupyter Notebook, and submit a pull request! The hope is that this collection of recipes will grow in scope, provide a valuable starting point for social data hackers, and accumulate a vibrant community of contributors around it.

9.27 Recommended Exercises

- Review the Twitter Platform API (*http://bit.ly/1a1kSKQ*) in depth. Are there APIs that you are surprised to find (or not find) there?

- Analyze all of the tweets that you have ever retweeted. Are you at all surprised about what you have retweeted or how your interests have evolved over time?

- Juxtapose the tweets that you author versus the ones that you retweet. Are they generally about the same topics?

- Write a recipe that loads friendship graph data from MongoDB into a true graphical representation with NetworkX and employ one of NetworkX's built-in algorithms, such as centrality measurement or clique analysis, to mine the graph. Chapter 8 provides an overview of NetworkX that you may find helpful to review before completing this exercise.

- Write a recipe that adapts visualizations from previous chapters for the purpose of visualizing Twitter data. For example, repurpose a graph visualization to display a friendship graph, adapt a plot or histogram in Jupyter Notebook to visualize tweeting patterns or trends for a particular user, or populate a tag cloud (such as Word Cloud Layout (*http://bit.ly/1a1n5pO*)) with content from tweets.

- Write a recipe to identify followers that you are not following back but perhaps should be based upon the content of their tweets. A few similarity measurements that may make suitable starting points were introduced in "Measuring Similarity" on page 141.

- Write a recipe to compute the similarity of two users based upon the content that they tweet about.

- Review Twitter's Lists API, looking in particular at the /lists/list (*http://bit.ly/2L0fSzd*) and /lists/memberships (*http://bit.ly/2rE3mwD*) API endpoints, which tell you the lists a user subscribes to and the lists that a member has been added to by other users, respectively. What can you learn about users from the lists they subscribe to and/or have been added to by other users?

- Try to apply techniques for processing human language to tweets. Carnegie Mellon has a Twitter NLP and part-of-speech tagging (*http://bit.ly/1a1n84Y*) project that provides a good starting point.

- If you follow many Twitter accounts, it is virtually impossible to keep up with all of the activity. Write an algorithm that ranks the tweets that appear in your home timeline by importance rather than chronology. Are you able to effectively filter out noise and gain more signal? Can you compute a meaningful digest of the top tweets for the day based on your own personal interests?

- Begin amassing a collection of recipes for other social websites like Facebook or LinkedIn

9.28 Online Resources

The following list of links from this chapter may be useful for review:

- BSON (*http://bit.ly/1a1pG34*)
- d3-cloud GitHub repository (*http://bit.ly/1a1n5pO*)
- Exponential decay (*http://bit.ly/1a1pHEe*)
- MongoDB data aggregation framework (*http://bit.ly/1a1pGjv*)
- OAuth 2.0 (*http://oauth.net/2/*)
- Twitter API Documentation (*http://bit.ly/1a1kSKQ*)
- Twitter API HTTP error codes (*http://bit.ly/2rFAjZw*)
- Twitter NLP and part-of-speech tagging project (*http://bit.ly/1a1n84Y*)
- Twitter Streaming API (*http://bit.ly/2rDU17W*)
- Where On Earth (WOE) ID lookup (*http://bit.ly/2jVIcXo*)

PART III

Appendixes

The appendixes of this book present some crosscutting material that undergirds much of the content that precedes it:

- Appendix A presents a brief overview of the technology that powers the virtual machine experience that accompanies this book, as well as a brief discussion on the scope and purpose of the virtual machine.

- Appendix B provides a short discussion of Open Authorization (OAuth), the industry protocol that undergirds accessing social data from just about any notable social website with an API.

- Appendix C is a very short primer on some common Python idioms that you'll encounter in the source code for this book; it highlights some subtleties about the Jupyter Notebook that you may benefit from knowing about.

Information About This Book's Virtual Machine Experience

Just as each chapter in this book has a corresponding Jupyter Notebook, each appendix also has a corresponding Jupyter Notebook. All notebooks, regardless of purpose, are maintained in the book's GitHub source code repository (*http://bit.ly/Mining-the-Social-Web-3E*). The particular appendix that you are reading here "in print" serves as a special cross-reference to the Jupyter Notebook that provides step-by-step instructions for how to install and configure the book's virtual machine, facilitated using Docker.

You are strongly encouraged to use the book's associated Docker image as a development environment instead of using any existing Python installation you may have on your computer. There are some nontrivial configuration management issues involved in installing the Jupyter Notebook and all of its dependencies for scientific computing. The various other third-party Python packages that are used throughout the book and the need to support users across multiple platforms only exacerbate the complexity that can be involved in getting a basic development environment up and running.

The GitHub repository (*http://bit.ly/Mining-the-Social-Web-3E*) contains the most up-to-date instructions for getting started, including how to install Docker and launch a "containerized" image of all the software used in this book. *Even if you are an expert in working with Python developer tools, you will still likely save some time by taking advantage of the book's virtual machine experience on your first pass through the text.* Give it a try. You'll be glad that you did.

The corresponding read-only Jupyter Notebook, Appendix A: Virtual Machine Experience (*http://bit.ly/2H0nbUu*), is maintained with the book's GitHub source code repository (*http://bit.ly/Mining-the-Social-Web-3E*) and contains step-by-step instructions for getting started.

OAuth Primer

Just as each chapter in this book has a corresponding Jupyter Notebook, each appendix also has a corresponding Jupyter Notebook. All notebooks, regardless of purpose, are maintained in the book's GitHub source code repository (*http://bit.ly/Mining-the-Social-Web-3E*). The particular appendix that you are reading here "in print" serves as a special cross-reference to the Jupyter Notebook that provides example code demonstrating interactive OAuth flows that involve explicit user authorization, which is needed if you implement a user-facing application.

The remainder of this appendix provides a terse discussion of OAuth as a basic orientation. The sample code for OAuth flows for popular websites such as Twitter, Facebook, and LinkedIn is in the corresponding Jupyter Notebook that is available with this book's source code.

 Like the other appendixes, this appendix has a corresponding Jupyter Notebook entitled Appendix B: OAuth Primer (*http://bit.ly/2xnKpUX*) that you can view online.

Overview

OAuth stands for "Open Authorization" and provides a means for users to *authorize* an application to access their account data through an API without the users needing to hand over sensitive credentials such as a username and password combination. Although OAuth is presented here in the context of the social web, keep in mind that it's a specification that has wide applicability in any context in which users would like to authorize an application to take certain actions on their behalf. In general, users can control the level of access for a third-party application (subject to the degree of

API granularity that the provider implements) and revoke it at any time. For example, consider the case of Facebook, in which extremely fine-grained permissions are implemented and enable users to allow third-party applications to access very specific pieces of sensitive account information.

Given the nearly ubiquitous popularity of platforms such as Twitter, Facebook, LinkedIn, and Instagram, and the vast utility of third-party applications that are developed on these social web platforms, it's no surprise that they've adopted OAuth as a common means of opening up their platforms. However, as with any other specification or protocol, OAuth implementations across social web properties currently vary with regard to the version of the specification that's implemented, and there are sometimes a few idiosyncrasies that come up in particular implementations. The remainder of this section provides a brief overview of OAuth 1.0a, as defined by RFC 5849 (*http://bit.ly/1a1pWio*), and OAuth 2.0, as defined by RFC 6749 (*http://bit.ly/1a1pWiz*), that you'll encounter as you mine the social web and engage in other programming endeavors involving platform APIs.

OAuth 1.0a

OAuth 1.0[1] defines a protocol that enables a web client to access a resource owner's protected resource on a server and is described in great detail in the OAuth 1.0 Guide (*http://bit.ly/1a1pYHe*). As you already know, the reason for its existence is to avoid the problem of users (resource owners) sharing passwords with web applications, and although it is fairly narrowly defined in its scope, it does do very well the one thing it claims to do. As it turns out, one of the primary developer complaints about OAuth 1.0 that initially hindered adoption was that it was very tedious to implement because of the various encryption details involved (such as HMAC signature generation (*http://bit.ly/1a1pZe1*)), given that OAuth 1.0 does not assume that credentials are exchanged over a secure SSL connection using an HTTPS protocol. In other words, OAuth 1.0 uses cryptography as part of its flow to guarantee security during transmissions over the wire.

Although we'll be fairly informal in this discussion, you might care to know that in OAuth parlance, the application that is requesting access is often known as the *client* (sometimes called the *consumer*), the social website or service that houses the *protected resources* is the *server* (sometimes called the *service provider*), and the user who is granting access is the *resource owner*. Since there are three parties involved in the process, the series of redirects among them is often referred to as a *three-legged flow*, or more colloquially, the "OAuth dance." Although the implementation and security details are a bit messy, there are essentially just a few fundamental steps involved in

---

1 Throughout this discussion, use of the term "OAuth 1.0" is technically intended to mean "OAuth 1.0a," given that OAuth 1.0 revision A obsoleted OAuth 1.0 and is the widely implemented standard.

the OAuth dance that ultimately enable a client application to access protected resources on the resource owner's behalf from the service provider:

1. The client obtains an unauthorized request token from the service provider.
2. The resource owner authorizes the request token.
3. The client exchanges the request token for an access token.
4. The client uses the access token to access protected resources on behalf of the resource owner.

In terms of particular credentials, a client starts with a *consumer key* and *consumer secret* and by the end of the OAuth dance winds up with an *access token* and *access token secret* that can be used to access protected resources. All things considered, OAuth 1.0 sets out to enable client applications to securely obtain authorization from resource owners to access account resources from service providers, and despite some arguably tedious implementation details, it provides a broadly accepted protocol that makes good on this intention. It is likely that OAuth 1.0 will be around for a while.

Rob Sober's "Introduction to OAuth (in Plain English)" (*http://bit.ly/1a1pXD7*) illustrates how an end user (as a resource owner) could authorize a link-shortening service such as bit.ly (as a client) to automatically post links to Twitter (as a service provider). It is worth reviewing and drives home the abstract concepts presented in this section.

OAuth 2.0

Whereas OAuth 1.0 enables a useful, albeit somewhat narrow, authorization flow for web applications, OAuth 2.0 was originally intended to significantly simplify implementation details for web application developers by relying completely on SSL for security aspects, and to satisfy a much broader array of use cases. Such use cases ranged from support for mobile devices to the needs of the enterprise, and even somewhat futuristically considered the needs of the "Internet of Things," such as devices that might appear in your home.

Facebook was an early adopter, with migration plans dating back to early drafts of OAuth 2.0 in 2011 (*http://bit.ly/1a1pYa9*) and a platform that quickly relied exclusively on a portion of the OAuth 2.0 specification. Although Twitter's standard user-based authentication is still based squarely on OAuth 1.0a, it implemented application-based authentication (*http://bit.ly/2GZEa9a*) in early 2013 that's modeled on the Client Credentials Grant (*http://bit.ly/1a1q3KT*) flow of the OAuth 2.0 spec. As you can see, the reaction was somewhat mixed in that not every social website immediately scrambled to implement OAuth 2.0 as soon as it was announced.

Still, it's a bit unclear whether or not OAuth 2.0 as originally envisioned will ever become the new industry standard. One popular blog post, entitled "OAuth 2.0 and the Road to Hell" (*http://bit.ly/2Jege7m*) (and its corresponding Hacker News discussion (*http://bit.ly/1a1q2Xg*)) is worth reviewing and summarizes a lot of the issues. The post was written by Eran Hammer, who resigned his role as lead author and editor of the OAuth 2.0 specification as of mid-2012 after working on it for several years. It appears as though "design by committee" around large open-ended enterprise problems suffocated some of the enthusiasm and progress of the working group, and although the specification was published in late 2012, it is unclear as to whether it provides an actual specification or a blueprint for one. Fortunately, over the previous years, lots of terrific OAuth frameworks have emerged to allay most of the OAuth 1.0 development pains associated with accessing APIs, and developers have continued innovating despite the initial stumbling blocks with OAuth 1.0. As a case in point, in working with Python packages in earlier chapters of this book, you haven't had to know or care about any of the complex details involved with OAuth 1.0a implementations; you've just had to understand the gist of how it works. What does seem clear despite some of the analysis paralysis and "good intentions" associated with OAuth 2.0, however, is that several of its flows seem well-defined enough that large social web providers are moving forward with them.

As you now know, unlike OAuth 1.0 implementations, which consist of a fairly rigid set of steps, OAuth 2.0 implementations can vary somewhat depending on the particular use case. A typical OAuth 2.0 flow, however, does take advantage of SSL and essentially just consists of a few redirects that, at a high enough level, don't look all that different from the previously mentioned set of steps involving an OAuth 1.0 flow. For example, Twitter's application-only authentication (*http://bit.ly/2GZEa9a*) involves little more than an application exchanging its consumer key and consumer secret for an access token over a secure SSL connection. Again, implementations will vary based on the particular use case, and although it's not exactly light reading, Section 4 of the OAuth 2.0 spec (*http://bit.ly/1a1q3uv*) is fairly digestible content if you're interested in some of the details. If you choose to review it, just keep in mind that some of the terminology differs between OAuth 1.0 and OAuth 2.0, so it may be easier to focus on understanding one specification at a time as opposed to learning them both simultaneously.

 Chapter 9 of Jonathan LeBlanc's *Programming Social Applications* (*http://oreil.ly/18I8YTc*) (O'Reilly) provides a nice discussion of OAuth 1.0 and OAuth 2.0 in the context of building social web applications.

The idiosyncrasies of OAuth and the underlying implementations of OAuth 1.0 and OAuth 2.0 are generally not going to be all that important to you as a social web miner. This discussion was tailored to provide some surrounding context so that you have a basic understanding of the key concepts involved and to provide some starting points for further study and research should you like to do so. As you may have already gathered, the devil really is in the details. Fortunately, nice third-party libraries largely obsolete the need to know much about those details on a day-to-day basis, although they can sometimes come in handy. The online code for this appendix features both OAuth 1.0 and OAuth 2.0 flows, and you can dig into as much detail with them as you'd like.

Python and Jupyter Notebook Tips and Tricks

Just as each chapter in this book has a corresponding Jupyter Notebook, each appendix also has a corresponding Jupyter Notebook. Like Appendix A, this "in print" appendix serves as a special cross-reference to a Jupyter Notebook that's maintained in the book's GitHub source code repository (*http://bit.ly/Mining-the-Social-Web-3E*) and includes a collection of Python idioms as well as some helpful tips for using the Jupyter Notebook.

 The corresponding Jupyter Notebook for this appendix, Appendix C: Python and the Jupyter Notebook Tips & Tricks (*http://bit.ly/ 2IUWWVm*), contains additional examples of common Python idioms that you may find of particular relevance as you work through this book. It also contains some helpful tips about working with the Jupyter Notebook that may save you some time.

Even though it's not that uncommon to hear Python referred to as "executable pseudocode," a brief review of Python as a general-purpose programming language may be worthwhile for readers new to Python. Please consider following along with Sections 1 through 8 of the Python Tutorial (*http://bit.ly/2LHjGph*) as a means of basic familiarization if you feel that you could benefit from a general-purpose introduction to Python as a programming language. It's a worthwhile investment and will maximize your enjoyment of this book.

Index

degree graph metric, 300
degree of nodes in graphs, 294
dendograms, 151
density of graphs, 294
depth-first searches, 206
dereferencing, 131
Dice's coefficient, 195
digraphs (directed graphs), 292-295
dimensionality reduction, 128
dir Python function, 291
directed graphs (digraphs), 292-295
distributed version control systems, 283
    (see also Git version control system, Git-
       Hub)
Docker, iii, 381
Dockerfiles, iii
document-oriented databases (see MongoDB)
Dorling Cartogram, 138-140
double list comprehension, 28
dynamic programming, 150

E

edit distance, 141
ego (social networks), 49, 297
ego graphs, 49, 297-300
email Python package, 257
end-of-sentence (EOS) detection, 213, 216-220
Enron corpus
    about, 248
    analyzing sender/recipient patterns, 266-269
    getting Enron data, 254-256
    online resources, 280
    query by date/time range, 262-265
entities
    interactions between, 235-239
    property graphs representing, 292-295
entities field (tweets), 27, 348
entity extraction, 214, 231
entity resolution (entity disambiguation), 66
entity-centric analysis, 230-239
EOS (end-of-sentence) detection, 213, 216-220
ethical issues, xviii
extracting tweet entities, 28-30, 347
extraction (NLP), 214, 231

F

Facebook, 45
    (see also analyzing Facebook data, Graph-
       API)

analyzing graph connections, 59-83
Instagram and, 87
interest graphs and, 45, 296
OAuth 2.0 and, 385
online resources, 85
recommended exercises, 84
Facebook accounts, 46, 47
Facebook pages, analyzing, 63-83
Facebook Platform Policy document, 47
Facebook Query Language (FQL), 48
facebook-sdk Python package, 59
facial recognition systems, 112-114
false negatives, 241
false positives, 241
favorite_count field (tweets), 27, 349
feedparser Python package, 204, 216
field expansion feature (Graph API), 51
fields
    Facebook Graph API, 49
    LinkedIn API, 125
    Twitter API, 26, 348
folksonomies, 8
Followers API (GitHub), 304
following model
    GitHub, 303-315
    interest graphs and, 296
    Twitter, 7, 10, 45, 361, 364, 367
forked projects, 285
FQL (Facebook Query Language), 48
frequency analysis
    LinkedIn data, 130-131
    TF-IDF, 166-173
    Twitter data, 30-32, 37-41, 352
    Zipf's law, 176
friendship graphs, 367
friendship model
    Facebook, 49
    Twitter, 7, 361, 364, 367
Friendster, 324
functools.partial function, 339, 357
fuzzy matching (see clustering LinkedIn data)

G

General Data Protection Regulation (GDPR),
    xviii
GeoJSON, 160
geopy Python package, 136
Gephi open source project, 321
GET search/tweets resource, 20

About the Authors

Matthew Russell (*@ptwobrussell*) is a technology leader based out of middle Tennessee. At work, he tries to be a leader, help others grow into leaders, and build high performing teams to solve hard problems. Outside of work, he contemplates ultimately reality, practices rugged individualism, and trains for the possibilities of a zombie or robot apocalypse.

Mikhail Klassen (*@MikhailKlassen*) is Chief Data Scientist at Paladin AI (*https://paladin.ai*), a startup creating adaptive training technologies. He has a PhD in computational astrophysics from McMaster University and a BS in applied physics from Columbia University. Mikhail is passionate about artificial intelligence and how the tools of data science can be used for good. When not working at a startup, he's usually reading or traveling.

Colophon

The animal on the cover of *Mining the Social Web* is a groundhog (*Marmota monax*), also known as a woodchuck (a name derived from the Algonquin name *wuchak*). Groundhogs are famously associated with the US/Canadian holiday Groundhog Day, held every February 2nd. Folklore holds that if the groundhog emerges from its burrow that day and sees its shadow, winter will continue for six more weeks. Proponents say that the rodents forecast accurately 75 to 90 percent of the time. Many cities host famous groundhog weather prognosticators, including Punxsutawney Phil (of Punxsutawney, Pennsylvania, and the 1993 Bill Murray film *Groundhog Day*).

This legend perhaps originates from the fact that the groundhog is one of the few species that enters true hibernation during the winter. Primarily herbivorous, groundhogs will fatten up in the summer on vegetation, berries, nuts, insects, and the crops in human gardens, causing many people to consider them pests. They then dig a winter burrow, and remain there from October to March (although they may emerge earlier in temperate areas, or, presumably, if they will be the center of attention on their eponymous holiday).

The groundhog is the largest member of the squirrel family, around 16–26 inches long and weighing 4–9 pounds. It is equipped with curved, thick claws ideal for digging, and two coats of fur: a dense grey undercoat and a lighter-colored topcoat of longer hairs, which provides protection against the elements.

Groundhogs range throughout most of Canada and northern regions of the United States, in places where open space and woodlands meet. They are capable of climbing trees and swimming but are usually found on the ground, not far from the burrows they dig for sleeping, rearing their young, and seeking protection from predators. These burrows typically have 2 to 5 entrances, and up to 46 feet of tunnels.